Dylan Thomas

THE POET AND HIS CRITICS

Dylan Thomas

THE POET AND HIS CRITICS

R. B. KERSHNER, JR.

AMERICAN
LIBRARY
ASSOCIATION
CHICAGO
1976

THE POET AND HIS CRITICS

A series of volumes on the meaning of the
critical writings on selected modern British
and American poets.

Edited by CHARLES SANDERS, University of Illinois, Urbana

Robert Frost by Donald J. Greiner
William Carlos Williams by Paul L. Mariani

LIBRARY OF CONGRESS CATALOGING IN PUBLICATION DATA
Kershner, R   B   1944-
  Dylan Thomas.
  Bibliography: p.
  Includes index.
  1. Thomas, Dylan, 1914-1953—Criticism and
interpretation—History.
PR6039.H52Z733   821'.9'12   76-44511
ISBN 0-8389-0226-X

Copyright © 1976 by the American Library Association

Printed in the United States of America

For
Jane and Jesse

Contents

PREFACE   *ix*

CHAPTER 1: *The World of the Poetry and Prose*   *1*

CHAPTER 2: *Dylan Thomas: The Legend*   *24*

CHAPTER 3: *Thomas the Man: Biography and Psychology*   *36*

CHAPTER 4: *The Religious Poet*   *66*

CHAPTER 5: *The Twentieth-Century Context*   *106*

CHAPTER 6: *The English and Welsh Literary Contexts*   *157*

CHAPTER 7: *Poetics*   *192*

APPENDIX A: *Basic Sources for Thomas*   *235*

APPENDIX B: *Chronology*   *243*

APPENDIX C: *Index of Explications*   *245*

INDEX   *267*

Preface

This book is an attempt to explore the most important aspects of Dylan Thomas's work by means of the critical literature. The book should serve both as an introduction to the major areas of investigation for the reader whose interest in Thomas has no specific focus, and as a guide to more intensive studies for the reader who wishes to become acquainted with work already done upon a single aspect of the poet's writings. Thomas himself is a nearly legendary figure; his public image of the hard-drinking, womanizing, and iconoclastic Celtic bard does not obviously invite the academic sort of critical study. Thus many readers may be surprised at the sheer bulk of exegesis to which his work has given rise. As a matter of fact, he is probably the most thoroughly and frequently explicated modern poet. I think this state of affairs would cause him neither pleasure nor alarm: although he was far removed from the type of the poet-critic, such as Empson or Eliot, Thomas took his poetry very seriously indeed. He scorned both dry unemotional discussions which suggested the dissecting table and breathless poetry-society perorations smelling of gardenias and talcum. But he sought out specific criticism of each syllable of his poems by writers whose dedication and intelligence he respected and was not averse to exploring the principles of poetry with these people.

More than twenty years has passed since his death. Time, his old nemesis, has finally done him a favor: we are distant enough from both his fame and his notoriety to read his poems without preconceptions. The group of excellent studies published in the past five years bears witness to this fact. An entire generation has matured since his death and has discovered Thomas's work with the same shock of delight readers felt when he appeared so explosively in the mid-thirties. Now, however, the discovery sometimes occurs within the context of the classroom. Thomas usually survives this; his poems characteristically have a gnomic integrity that makes them remarkably resistant to dissection. Perhaps for that very reason they have engendered vast and sometimes violent critical dialogues. My aim throughout this book has been to reproduce the sense of an ongoing debate wherein each critic builds upon the work of his predecessors, forming his ideas and opinions in response to the comments of other readers as well as to the poetry itself. When the critics are of high caliber, as is often the case with Thomas, the result is a sort of dialectical advance, and we feel we are being brought progressively closer to the heart of the poetry.

The reader who is not completely familiar with Thomas's work should first consult the list of basic sources in Appendix A, which includes a discussion of bibliographical materials, Thomas's major works, and some essential critical apparatus. The list also indicates the abbreviations of Thomas's titles which I shall use throughout this book, for example, *D&E* for *Deaths and Entrances*. Chapter 1 should serve as a brief general introduction to the poet's work. Throughout this study my major emphasis is upon the poetry, but in the first chapter the prose and its criticism are discussed as well. Here I attempt to present the essentials of Thomas's poetic "world," the main assumptions, themes, and divisions of the poetry. The second and third chapters deal respectively with Thomas's "legend" and with his life and personality. Here again, the reader unacquainted with the outline of his career should consult the chronology in Appendix B. I make no attempt to summarize the poet's life within the body of the chapters. Instead, chapter 2 is concerned with the implications of Thomas's public persona, chapter 3 with interpretations of his life and psychology as they bear upon his work. Actually, this is a good starting place for any sort of critical study, since there is biographical evidence relevant to many facets of his work.

The fourth chapter presents the most significant and controversial thematic aspect of Thomas's poetry, the religious vision. Here, as elsewhere, I have tried to let the criticism organize itself. Critics range from those who deny that Thomas was importantly concerned with religion to those who feel his work illustrates one orthodoxy or another; the most valuable commentaries, though, in my opinion, are those which interpret his attitude and its reflection in the poetry as dynamic, either because it is in a state of constant change or because Thomas really holds several conflicting attitudes. The two chapters which follow are closely related, as I explain in chapter 5. Both deal with attempts to situate Thomas within relevant literary contexts. But where chapter 5 is concerned with Thomas as twentieth-century poet—the influence of writers, think-

ers, and major schools upon him and his place in modern literary
history—chapter 6 takes a broader view. Here, Thomas is compared
with the great romantic and metaphysical poets, both for signs of
influence and in order to arrive at an appreciation of the *kind* of
poetry he wrote. In this chapter his Welsh heritage is explored also,
as his work is considered in the context of the Welsh and Anglo-
Welsh literary traditions.

The final chapter, on poetics, is the most technical. It treats both
Thomas's ideas about his poetry and the classical questions of
rhyme, meter, form, rhetoric, imagery, and metaphor. I give considerable attention to the problem of "narrative" in his verse, while
much of the discussion—again reflecting the approach of most critics—turns about the problem of obscurity or ambiguity. Here, as
throughout this book, my emphasis is upon approaches which are
applicable to all the poems or to groups of poems; seldom is a single
poem discussed in detail. The exigencies of space and my general
conception of what the book ought to do make this impractical.
The reader who is primarily interested in a single poem should consult the "Index of Explications," Appendix C, containing references
to articles or sections of books which offer a substantial discussion
of each of the collected poems. Individual poems appear in the general index as well, but when they are noted in the following chapters the reference is an illustration of a larger idea.

At the end of each chapter is a list of the references used therein,
arranged alphabetically by author and chronologically when several
works by a single author are cited. Alternate editions of a book are
cited on first mention and not thereafter. Following this list, for
most of the chapters I have included a second group of relevant
readings to which no direct reference is made in the body of the
chapter. Several of the books and articles treated are in foreign languages, as indicated by their titles. Quotations from them in the
text are in my translations.

For the reader who wishes to examine Thomas's art in detail,
there are many general introductions to the poetry. The best brief
discussion is probably G. S. Fraser's thirty-five-page pamphlet,
Dylan Thomas (1957), in the British Writers and Their Work
series. T. H. Jones's somewhat larger book by the same title, published in America in 1966, is a roughly chronological discussion of
Thomas's life and work, and is particularly strong on his Welsh
background. Jones takes a commonsensical tone and makes refreshingly scathing remarks about critics of whom he disapproves. Derek
Stanford's 1964 revision of the 1954 edition, *Dylan Thomas: A
Literary Study*, treats the books of poetry in chronological order

and is generally reliable, although it lacks focus and is seldom exciting. On the other hand, Jacob Korg's volume, *Dylan Thomas* (1965), for the Twayne's English Authors series, is often illuminating, but constantly reflects his personal approach to Thomas.

Henry Treece's pioneering book, *Dylan Thomas: "Dog Among the Fairies"* (1949), should probably be avoided by the uninitiated: he gives no coherent picture of the poetry as a whole, and while he claims to be generally positive in his approach, the reader often feels that with friends like Treece, Thomas needs no enemies. Similarly idiosyncratic in places, Elder Olson's *The Poetry of Dylan Thomas* (1954) devotes some sixty pages to an extremely methodical analysis of the poet's techniques and themes, followed by a lengthy and controversial exegesis of his sonnet sequence. William York Tindall's *A Reader's Guide to Dylan Thomas* (1962) has an excellent short introductory section, while Ralph N. Maud's *Entrances to Dylan Thomas' Poetry* (1963) is probably the best introduction to the workings of his poetic mind. The latter is very unusual in organization, however, and should probably be read after a more conventional study. Similarly, William T. Moynihan's *The Craft and Art of Dylan Thomas* (1966) is the best single book on Thomas's technique but would be a rather confusing introduction to the poet. Clark Emery's *The World of Dylan Thomas* (1962) explicates the collected poems, arranged in thematic groups rather than in their conventional order.

Inevitably in presenting the ideas of a wide spectrum of writers I have encountered the problem of objectivity. In the first place, I have necessarily been selective in deciding which of the thousands of articles relating to Thomas should be represented in the text, which should be given among the additional references at a chapter's end, and which might be ignored entirely. Although I have tried to avoid the possibility, I am sure that some essays worth anyone's attention are not mentioned in this volume, through oversight, ignorance, or difficulty of access, and for this I apologize to the author and the reader. In the second place, although my aim has been to represent the thought of each critic fairly and adequately, as a rule I have also indicated my estimation of its importance and quality. I have tried, within limits, to avoid both a blanket dismissal of serious critics whom I think flatly wrong and an enthusiastic hypostatizing of those I think brilliantly perceptive. I have hoped to keep in mind Cromwell's words to the Church of Scotland: "I beseech you, in the bowels of Christ, think it possible you may be mistaken." I am aware, however, that I have not fully represented the negative criticism of Thomas, for several reasons: much of the

early reaction against his work is frankly uninformed, unimagina-
tive, and vituperative, while later, more reasoned adverse evaluations
often admit of little discussion, resting on assumptions about poetry
which automatically disqualify Thomas from consideration.

I am happy to acknowledge help from numerous sources. First,
from Professor Charles Sanders of the University of Illinois, whose
constant encouragement and enthusiasm—however little merited—
gave me the will and energy to complete this study. Several of my
students have volunteered help with parts of the book's apparatus:
I particularly want to thank Jerry Jowers, George Lee, and
Audrey Bach Burns. The Interlibrary Loan Department of the University of Florida Libraries under Mr. S. L. Butler has been unfail-
ingly helpful, courteous, and efficient despite my inordinate demands upon them. Mrs. Elizabeth Killebrew of the university's
Center for Studies in the Humanities typed the final manuscript
with speed and accuracy, and voluntarily spent hours of overtime
on the project. Like all recent writers on Thomas, I am indebted
to Professor Ralph N. Maud's painstaking scholarship and critical
acumen. Finally, to my wife, Jane, I owe more gratitude than I can
express. Despite the demands of her own career, her help has taken
many substantial forms, including typing, research, and editing—
and also that spiritual form without which I would have had no
desire to write.

CHAPTER 1

The World of the Poetry and Prose

The Poetry

> The force that through the green fuse drives the flower
> Drives my green age; that blasts the roots of trees
> Is my destroyer . . .

Here, in one of his first published poems, Dylan Thomas at the age of nineteen had already articulated the vision which he was to elaborate in the remainder of his work. Some of the early poems appeared insurmountably obscure to their first readers, but even when the particular poem's subject or statement was doubtful, the assumptions underlying the poem somehow were communicated with all the force of an explicit theme: Thomas and the world around him are inextricably intertwined, swept by forces of creation and destruction which are identical in their very opposition. Like most mystical truths, Thomas's truth is paradoxical. The poet is at once mankind, Christ, newborn infant, and cadaver, a microcosm of the spinning globe and universe in more than a metaphorical sense. "Glory, jest, and riddle of the world," he views his own contradictions, his doom and apotheosis, not with amused Augustan detachment, but with intense, bitter despair and passionate exultation. As poet he is continually stymied, "dumb to tell the crooked rose" or the lovers who are his audience the truth of their condition. Many of the poems are assertions of the impossibility of what the poem attempts: in memory of his aunt Ann Jones, Thomas can only make "a monstrous image blindly/ Magnified out of praise;" for the child dead in a London air-raid he can only attempt a "Refusal to Mourn;" and he admits that the lovers for whom he writes "pay no praise or wages/ Nor heed my craft or art." But again, paradoxically, the finest poems succeed in what they say is impossible. We feel the force through the green fuse, remember Ann Jones, and mourn the child. Lovers do heed his art and are changed by it, though his craft, as always, remains the province of the critic.

*   *   *

"The first and most striking unit of poetry larger than the individual poem," Northrop Frye has written, "is the total work of the man who wrote that poem." In Thomas's case this is a remarkably coherent, almost homogeneous unit. Unlike Yeats, whose "Celtic Twilight" lyrics might almost have been written by a different poet from the man who wrote the "Crazy Jane" sequence, Thomas shows no radical change from the first to the last poems. He is, as he admitted shortly before his death, "still after the same things" (John Malcolm Brinnin, *A Casebook on Dylan Thomas*, 1960, p. 287). Indeed, the prose and the poetry spring from the same sources and share a single vision of existence. In the essay on Thomas in his book *Poets of Reality* (1965), J. Hillis Miller describes the peculiar quality of Thomas's poetic consciousness in fundamental, phenomenological terms. Thomas is one of a group of twentieth-century poets who, Miller claims, in different ways transcend the Cartesian dualism of subject and object which has ruled Western thought for centuries (p. 190):

From the very first moment of its existence, even in the womb, even when the 'seed [is] at-zero,' the self, for Dylan Thomas, includes all the cosmos, lives its life and is lived by its life. . . . That identification is given with existence itself and can never be withdrawn. There is no initial separation between subject and object . . . Even when his poems are dialogues they are not the confrontation of two separate existences, but of two opposing parts of a single existence.

The poet's body is his "name," and its experience is a series of sharp, distinct events; its past also is available, immediately and without effort. "Inner" and "outer" are never separate worlds in the poetry, so that an "occurrence in the outside world is not the symbol of an occurrence in the mind or in the private world of the body. They are identical . . ." (pp. 193-94). Mind, body, and world overlap, allowing the domain of any one to be described in terms appropriate to any other. For Thomas, word and object are not distinct—in fact, "without words, mind and world would be split apart. Language is the place of their interpenetration."

The world, a totality, is "the anonymous subject of all possible activities or things" (p. 197), an "it" which Thomas invokes in the line from "Fern Hill," "All the sun long it was running, it was lovely . . ." Things of the world *are* what they *do*, in a perpetual process of becoming; further, they all interpenetrate, in a process symbolized as "love." The poetry's running participles, flowing diction, and syntax of continual opposition all demonstrate to Miller the transmutation of things into one another. This process occurs through time, which for Thomas is both a perpetual falling into an annihilation indistinguishable from the flowering of birth, and an "ever-experienced discontinuity," like still photographs of intense moments:

> The ball I threw while playing in the park
> Has not yet reached the ground.

Whatever was or will be, is, so in a sense all moments of destruction and creation are the same (pp. 201–2).

Where do things spring from and return to? God, which for Thomas is "an anonymous totality of being" (p. 203). Things cannot maintain themselves in existence, and perpetually return to the neutral "ground" of God to be reborn. Men may do this as well, often through the intermediary of a loved woman who is in contact with the "fountains of origin." But this respite is only momentary. For Thomas, Miller claims, the essential problem is the relationship and attitude to time; he considers yielding to it and denying it, but in the end the only solution possible is to accept it and then find himself poised within it in a "momentary stay" against the flux of existence (p. 212). This, in fact, is what the poem does for him. Through the poetic act Thomas transforms earthly things into images, in the interior of the poem. He does not deny the death of all things, including himself, but in anticipating this necessary destruction within the poem, by participating in it, Thomas can "save" the world (pp. 213–14):

To see it as if it were already dead is to know for the first time all we, the living, 'know and do not know.' Miraculously, the sensible vividness of the world is given back. Only by seeing things from the perspective of their death, only by willing their death, can they be recaptured in their vitality, and, paradoxically, saved from death . . .

By saving the world of his experience, Thomas is also his own salvation, since he is never separate from it. "Self, world, and deity dwell together in the ark of the poem."

This analysis by Miller reduces Thomas's poetic world to its essential structure and movements, but at such a level of philosophical abstraction that the casual reader may feel little closer to individual poems. An earlier essay by David Aivaz (Ernest Tedlock, *Dylan Thomas: The Legend and the Poet*, 1960, pp. 186–210) presents a similar poetic universe, but does so by way of Thomas's comments about his poetic method and an interpretation of specific early poems. The poet's method, a "dialectical" means of breeding images through opposition to a central "germ," yields a poetry of "process" (p. 195):

Process is unity in nature; its direction is the cyclical return; the force that drives it is the generative energy in natural things. Like the 'motivating centre' of a Thomas poem, it is 'destructive and constructive at the same time;' so that not only do life and death imply each other . . . but they are, in Thomas's mind, in essence the same.

The only absolute is flux, and Thomas's attitude is suitably reverential before it; he invokes the absolute through devotional images. The most common areas of connotation in Thomas's work, the religious and the sexual, both refer to the same process. In the end, the poet's attitude can only be one of acceptance, although in many of the early poems the sexuality seems almost pathological and the religion undermined or mocked. Time, which presides over process, often appears as a ghastly hunter. Even art sometimes seems to Thomas little more than illusion. But finally (p. 200),

It is the 'vision' . . . of process that transforms the early imagery of denial ('carved bird', moon, dark, disease, and the sexual images) to the later imagery of affirmation (sun, Son, the Biblical and devotional images) . . . It sees the absolute-in-flux, and not an absolute of illusion; process, and not the individual life or death.

Yet the poet is not merely a bystander who observes and needlessly celebrates, argues Aivaz: "The consciousness of man shapes the natural world by its awareness of it . . . Process, the subject of vision, needs man to 'happen' to it to give it life" (pp. 206-7).

Miller and Aivaz employ very different methodologies and assumptions. Aivaz, for example, only abandons the Cartesian subject-object dualism toward the end of his essay, but the two men arrive at similar conceptions of the poetic universe. As Elder Olson (1954, p. 12) implies, it is not so much that Thomas's world is difficult or obscure in its structure as that he expresses it strangely, from unusual perspectives:

We should see flowers on a grave; he sees the dead "who periscope through flowers to the sky." We should see the towering flames after a fire raid; he sees "the fire-dwarfed street" . . . He looks into what we should find opaque, looks down at something we are wont to look up at, looks up where we should look down, peers in where we should peer out, and out where we should look in.

Olson, throughout his chapter on "The Universe of the Early Poems," captures the atmosphere the poet creates. Men are described in animal, vegetable, or even mineral terms, while the world has a slow, ghostly, undersea quality. The poet's body makes its appearance almost clinically: blood, bone, hair, skin, and viscera are swept up in the world's flux. Sometimes the body is a mirror of natural processes, sometimes a geography to be explored. A gothic catalogue of ghosts, rent bodies, coffins, racks, and gallows populates the poetic world, while aged fetuses and walking corpses lend an air of the macabre and grotesque even to poems whose thrust is celebratory and affirmative. Nature is present in rather generalized fashion; a romantic sprinkling of flowers, birds, trees, seas, and winds tends to counteract the grotesquerie.

I find it difficult to isolate particular themes in the poems, since Thomas has a single major vision of life expressed by most of his works in one way or another. He seldom stops to analyze a single implication of his poetic world, but rather seems to restate its totality in each poem, in what G. S. Fraser (1957, p. 29) calls "the baffling simplicity of Thomas's unitary response." Nevertheless, there are groups of poems which emphasize certain aspects of the vision. For instance, Ralph Maud (1963, pp. 72–80), elaborating upon Aivaz's argument, isolates a group of "dream poems" like "Our eunuch dreams," "When once the twilight," and "I fellowed sleep." This subgroup of the "process poems" relates dream to waste (sexual and otherwise) and to onanism, which the poet finds a perversion of nature. Dreams are also related to the deceptive world of appearances, and thus are linked to images involving the movies and other "social" forms of illusion. From another group of poems, William York Tindall (1962, pp. 15–16) isolates the theme of poetic creation itself:

Creation, which includes world, child, and poem, may be cosmic, sexual, or aesthetic. The creator may be poet or God or both together with their common tool, the word—or any man, for whose tool Thomas found many words . . . When horror won life's duel, womb and tomb, indistinguishably one, seem a hole Thomas was trying to crawl back into. More cheerful than poems on this, his many poems on poems and his many portraits of the artist show the better side of creation and creator although these portraits are not without intimation of mortality and . . . not without self-criticism.

Where Tindall finds divinity to be Thomas's metaphor for the creating poet, other critics find religion and the nature of God to be Thomas's central theme; this idea has been explored by so many critics that I have devoted an entire chapter to it. Certainly the early sequence of sonnets explicated in Olson's book and the late sequence of poems entitled "Vision and Prayer" do seem to be talking about God in more than a metaphorical way. And other minor themes crop up frequently, always as a part of the total vision—love, the sterility of society, estrangement, politics (perhaps), Wales, war, and of course all the allotropes of sexuality. Thomas has been accused of having a limited poetic range, and to an extent this is true. He has little variety in tone, writes "cosmic" rather than occasional poems, and is perpetually concerned with life, death, sexuality, and God; but then those are, after all, the proper concerns of the lyric poet. And there is more richness in the elaborations of his vision than his detractors admit.

Although the poetry does form a remarkably coherent whole, there are divisions within it, both in differing "kinds" of poems and in differing emphases as the poet developed. Henry Treece (1949, pp. 85–94) was the first critic to point out at some length what had been obvious to most readers, the fact that a sizeable group of Thomas's poems is strikingly less obscure than the remainder. These include many of the last poems, published after the time Treece was writing, and also poems from *25P (Twenty-five Poems)*, *Map (The Map of Love)*, and *D&E (Deaths and Entrances)*: "This bread I break," "Ears in the turrets hear," "The hand that signed the paper," "I have longed to move away," "Twenty-four years," "The tombstone told when she died," "The Hunchback in the Park," and "In my Craft or Sullen Art." Difficulty, of course, is relative; others might want to add to or subtract from this list, but the fact remains that Thomas as "straight poet" was quite capable of a powerful lucidity. How he came to write those poems and how they relate to the remainder of his work are questions best left to later chapters.

Probably a more significant division distinguishes among three distinct "periods" in Thomas's work. Tindall (1953, p. 488) claims that he and Thomas, talking in a bar on West Twenty-third Street in New York, agreed that his early work, up to World War II, is generally based upon the "womb and tomb" motif; a second period, during the war, shows a greater involvement with others, as in the poem "Ceremony After a Fire Raid;" the final period, characterized by longer, narrative poems like "Fern Hill" or "Poem on his birthday," is one of acceptance of humanity and the human condition. Critics are not unanimous in their assent to these stages, but most detect some such movement. Where *18P (18 Poems)* shows very little interest in religion or in individuals, a religious note is struck in *25P* which never dies out; in *D&E* the London air raids appear, admittedly apocalyptically, but so do the child who dies in one, a couple who are killed on their anniversary, and another victim one hundred years old; the poet's aunt Ann Jones was one of the first such "individuals" to appear in the work, in *Map*. In addition, *D&E* includes "human interest" poems like "The Hunchback in the Park" and new poems on a large scale, "Vision and Prayer," "Ballad of the Long-legged Bait," and "A Winter's Tale." Many critics, like T. H. Jones (1966, p. 58), find this volume to be the core of Thomas's achievement. The language is more supple than in the earlier books, the imagery less compressed, the vision less obsessed.

The last poems continue the relaxing of syntax and image, and are less obscure than the earlier ones. There is an unmistakable note of affirmation in them, tempered by the poet's unabated awareness of mortality. As Olson puts it (1954, p. 20):

If the poetry of the dark early period is concerned almost wholly with personal problems, the poetry of the middle phase is charged with powerful and poignant feeling for others—for his wife, his children, his aunt, and the victims of air raids—and the poems of the later volumes are, for the most part, exultant expressions of his faith and love. There are even touches of humor in "Once below a time," the "Author's Prologue," and particularly in "Lament."

The last poems include some of Thomas's most widely-read efforts, and have earned considerable acclaim from critics. Nevertheless, many see a slackening of his poetic impulse in them, along with a somewhat labored quality; some of these poems were literally years in the making. His friend John Malcolm Brinnin (1955, p. 175) feels that toward the end of his life Thomas recognized "that his creative powers were failing, that his great work was finished . . . the means by which Dylan might continue to grow were no longer in his possession." A large group of contemporary critics agree with Brinnin to the extent that they prefer the idiosyncratic density and convolution of the early work, with all its gaucheries, to the facility of the later poems. There is no doubt that Thomas found it increasingly difficult to write poetry. Thomas had planned a cycle of poems to be entitled *In Country Heaven* (*QEOM* [*Quite Early One Morning*], pp. 113–15), of which "In country sleep," "Over Sir John's hill," and "In the white giant's thigh" were to form part. His biographer, Constantine FitzGibbon (*The Life of Dylan Thomas*, 1965, p. 290), frankly doubts whether he would have been able to complete this undertaking as a unity, if at all. Thomas, he feels, lacked the architectonic sense which might have made him one of the great poets of the language rather than what he styled himself—"captain of the second eleven."

Many sensitive and influential critics demur, however. Tindall sees strengths in each period, but generally defends the late poems against Brinnin's attack. G. S. Fraser (1957, p. 33) argues that "he grew and changed and at his death was still developing in the direction of a wider and more genial human scope," while Jones (1966, p. 96) calls the last poems "the final flowering of Thomas's genius." And of course the fruitless question, what would Thomas have gone on to write had he not died at thirty-nine, is complicated by his increasing involvement with prose. Thomas had experienced considerable success with the lighter, more relaxed stories of *Portrait (Portrait of the Artist as a Young Dog)* and with the semifictional narratives for radio which were posthumously published in *QEOM*. More important, his work writing filmscripts during the war had fostered a dramatic impulse which culminated in the highly successful *Under Milk Wood (UMW)*. According to Brinnin (1955, p. 212), Thomas was planning a new play for voices which would tell the story of a man and woman in Wales who should be lovers but never meet, or only meet after it is too late for both of them. Several days before leaving on the trip to America which was to kill him. Thomas told Philip Burton (Tedlock, 1960, pp. 67–70) about this play and about an opera libretto he would write for Stravinsky, to be set in a world nearly destroyed by atomic warfare. "I've got another twenty, or perhaps twenty-five, years to live," he told Burton. "I've got to try new things. This play is the beginning."

The Prose

Whether or not Thomas would have gone on to produce more plays for voices or stories is debatable. He had as much difficulty completing *UMW* as he did with any of the poems—to be strictly accurate, he never did complete it to his satisfaction. Treece (1954, p. 20) argues fairly convincingly that Thomas could not have become a novelist or dramatist because he lacked the sense of dramatic structure; his impulse was strictly lyrical. But this begs the question: Thomas certainly would not have written fiction or drama of a conventional sort, but many critics (and most of the public) find *UMW* exciting and satisfying despite its lack of traditional dramatic qualities. What he might have done with the short story is another question entirely; the popular stories of *Portrait*

have earned the respect even of critics who dislike Thomas's poetry, although they have received surprisingly little critical scrutiny. There is no consensus as to what the structural demands upon
a modern short story ought to be, and to what degree Thomas's
stories fulfill them; in any event, it is reasonable to assume that the
poet could have written more in the same vein had he so desired.
He had, however, abandoned writing these stories some sixteen
years before his death, just as he suddenly stopped writing the so-
called difficult early stories three years before that. Thomas's approach to prose was constantly changing.

    Even a brief survey of the prose reveals much clearer demarca-
tions than can be found in the poetry. The chronology of the prose's
composition (Maud, 1963, pp. 121–43) shows Thomas working
on drafts of the early stories during the same period he was writing
his first poems, between 1932 and 1935. These stories, of which
"The Burning Baby," "The Dress," and "The Visitor" are typical,
were published in various journals from 1934 onward; some were
collected in *Map* and, in America, *The World I Breathe,* along with
a selection of poems. Others appeared in his posthumous British collection *A Prospect of the Sea (Prospect)* and the posthumous American edition of *Adventures in the Skin Trade (AST)*; still others
remained uncollected until Walford Davies's edition of *Dylan
Thomas: Early Prose Writings* (1971). Although publication of
some of the early stories was delayed for years, it is clear that in
1938, after a three-year hiatus in the composition of prose, Thomas
suddenly began writing in a totally different vein with "The
Peaches."

    Vernon Watkins, in his "Introduction" to *AST* (p. viii) points
out the similarity of the early prose and verse:

The early stories, though less permanent than the poems, display the
same sexual preoccupation, the same adolescent groping, through
tactile images, from darkness to light, the same pressing, through a
multitude of symbols and observations, both imagined and real,
toward a place and a condition as familiar and truthful as a field . . .
Many combine the theme of awakening love with an acute sense of
the proximity of death. There is also an element of distrust in the
act of creation.

There are clearly surreal elements in these stories, and the narrative
line is at times so obscure or fantastic as to throw into doubt the
whole idea of treating them the way we do ordinary fiction; at
times they seem closer to such prose-poems as Rimbaud's *Illuminations.* Even where the "events" of these stories are external rather

than internal, they are usually rather gothic. In "The Burning Baby" a mad parson falls in love with his own daughter, who bears him a baby. In the story's climax he burns the dead child upon a hill; the parson's older son, who carries a dead and bloody rabbit about with him, lends atmosphere. In "The Tree," an elderly gardener tells the story of the Crucifixion to a little boy who later finds an idiot sitting under the tree in his garden, binds him to it, and goes off to get some silver nails. Madmen, lovers, and folk figures reminiscent of witches and warlocks abound, frequently interacting with a poet-protagonist. Sexuality and religion intermingle with their perverse variants. Through it all a dark vision of "process" remains, as in this frequently cited passage from "The Visitor" (*AST*, pp. 75–76):

It was to Peter but a little time before the dead, picked to the symmetrical bone, were huddled in under the soil by the wind that blew louder and harder as the fat flies dropped onto the grass. Now the worm and the death-beetle undid the fibres of the animal bones, worked at them brightly and minutely, and the weeds through the sockets and the flowers on the vanished breasts sprouted up with the colours of the dead life fresh as their leaves. And the blood that had flowed flowed over the ground, strengthening the blades of grass . . .

Until recently Thomas's early prose received little attention. Watkins's intelligent introduction to *AST* concentrated upon relating the poetry and prose and introducing these symbolically dense works to a rather reluctant public. The American press reserved judgment when the pieces appeared, while Kingsley Amis (1955, p. 227) probably spoke for many British critics when he characterized the *Prospect* stories as constructed upon "characters and situations . . . which people in full possession of their faculties would not find interesting or important." The most important early critical response to the prose was Jacob Korg's article "The Short Stories of Dylan Thomas" (1948, pp. 184–91), which addressed *The World I Breathe*. Korg argues that although the stories appear chaotic, they are "actually entirely coherent narratives of great beauty and power;" the reader must realize that the main characters are usually obsessed or impassioned; their imaginings, dreams, and reveries are expressed directly as fact rather than as metaphor. Korg notes the importance of the surrealist influence, drawing a parallel between the obsessions of the characters and Dali's concept of "paranoic-critical activity" in literature. The article lays out the basic perceptions upon which later critics have expanded: the elements of Welsh folklore (p. 187), the idea of a dualistic Nature warring against itself (p. 188), and the recurring pattern of sexual initiation (p. 190).

Following Korg's article there is a long hiatus in criticism of the early prose. Most of the introductions to Thomas published between 1950 and 1970 treat the early prose briefly, generally as an adjunct to the poetry. Korg expands upon his 1948 article in chapter 8 of his volume on Thomas (1965), while Derek Stanford (1964, pp. 155–68) treats the early prose as a "poetic by-product." T. H. Jones (1966, pp. 23–47) devotes part of a chapter to the prose, mostly from *Map*, and appears to be trying to convince himself that, "odd as they often seem, they *are* stories, in the sense that they do have characters and plots or themes, however slight these may be or however difficult to find them in the luxuriant jungle of the prose." Jones mentions the themes of loss and sexual initiation, and the interplay of Christian and pagan elements in the heavy religious overtones of the stories; he stresses Thomas's compassion.

Other scattered material tackles individual stories: Burton S. Glick (1957, pp. 149–54) offers a rather obvious psychoanalytic interpretation of "The Followers," while C. C. Muecke (1959, pp. 69–76) points to the theme of lost love in much of the early prose. In general, critics seemed to regard the work as a "poet's prose," mainly valuable for the occasional insights it could give into the poetry.

Clearly the most interesting essay of the period was Annis Pratt's brief commentary on the prose in C. B. Cox's collection of essays on Thomas for the Twentieth Century Views series (1966, pp. 117–29). A version of parts of Pratt's 1965 Columbia University dissertation, the essay is still the best short introduction to the early prose. Pratt's much more thorough and ambitious book, *Dylan Thomas' Early Prose: A Study in Creative Mythology*, followed in 1970. As the subtitle suggests, Pratt relies upon Joseph Campbell's ideas in her psychological-cum-mythical approach to the stories; on a more mundane level, Pratt is indebted to Donald Tritschler's (1971) study of Thomas's "Red Prose Notebook" now owned by the Lockwood Library of The State University of New York in Buffalo. Pratt makes her position clear at the outset (pp. xi–xii). She considers the early prose to be an important contribution to literature and "part of the symbolic universe of both the early and later poetry," whereas she feels that the later prose, including the *Portrait* stories, the unfinished novel *Adventures in the Skin Trade*, and *UMW*, are essentially a "minor genre within his writing" which he might later have developed seriously. This is of course a highly controversial position. Admittedly most of the later prose was written quickly—Thomas himself called *Adventures in the Skin Trade* "the only really dashed-off piece of work I remember doing" (*AST*, p. xi). On the other hand, the early stories were composed as laboriously as the poems, written on large cardboard sheets and posted about the room so that Thomas could keep an eye on the story's development as a whole (Korg, 1965, p. 52). But stories, after all, are not poems, even if the young poet treated them as such, and even if Pratt is able to find considerable depth and richness in them. At times it is difficult for the critic to remember that works which allow one boundless opportunities for interpretation and exegesis are not necessarily literary successes because they do so.

In the introductory chapters (pp. 12, 45–48), Pratt discusses various influences upon Thomas during his adolescence, with particular attention to Arthur Machen's supernatural thrillers and the novels of Caradoc Evans and T. F. Powys. She finds the essential narrative structure of most of the early stories to be based upon "the progress of the hero from desire through quest to release and renewal." The plots are commonly divided into sections "which succeed each other with the rhythm of ritual movements;" the culmination of each tale is usually a sacrament or rite, an act of sexual release, or an archetypal vision (p. 35). In Thomas's world, these events are not really very different from one another. In the remainder of the book Pratt devotes a chapter each to myth (a generalized myth, à la Campbell and Robert Graves, but with Celtic emphasis); theology, specifically the bardo-druidic system of beliefs set out in William ab Ithel's *Y Barddas;* the occult, with an emphasis on William Blake's prophetic books; and surrealism, where Pratt argues that Thomas used surrealist techniques in the stories without abandoning his critical attitude toward the movement. Pratt discusses a different set of tales in each chapter, although each of the categories she has chosen has some bearing upon all of the tales. Her arguments are sometimes shaky in strict scholarly terms, but the overall impression the book leaves is that Pratt has isolated the important themes and techniques of the prose. Her asides on the poetry are particularly illuminating, and although she seldom stays with a given story long enough to explicate it thoroughly, her treatment of the stories as a related series is excellent. Whether or not this justifies her claim for their intrinsic value is another question.

During the summer of 1938 Thomas spent an extremely happy time with his wife Caitlin in Laugharne, which was later to become his home. Working, perhaps, on a suggestion by Richard Church (FitzGibbon, 1965, p. 176), he had begun to write the series of stories which were to be collected in *Portrait* in a new, lighter style. He was writing fiction reviews regularly for the *New English Weekly* (most of which are collected in Davies, 1971). Frustrated by the difficulties he had encountered in publishing some of the early prose and encouraged by the possibilities of commercial success, he rapidly turned out a series of stories based upon his childhood, beginning with "The Peaches." These were published quickly during 1938–40 in various magazines and appeared in book form in 1940, greeted by almost universally warm reviews.

Pratt dismisses these as a weaker brew (p. 151): they share with the early prose and themes of initiation into the mysteries of love, madness, and death; but now, she argues, Thomas has created a mask of boyhood through which the narrator can observe others in their struggles. The goals, which had been personal, sexual, or mystical, now are often merely social. Be this as it may, the *Portrait* stories are important to Thomas's reputation. Nearly every critic who likes "Fern Hill" also approves of these, and some—such as Kingsley Amis—respect Thomas's later stories more than any of his poetry. Nevertheless, no one has given them a full-scale critical examination. Among the widely scattered reviews a few attempt something more than pleasant generalities, but in most, as Robert Phelps (1955, p. 683) remarks, "his prose has been oddly taken for granted." The early stories, he feels, are "refreshingly written but emotionally affected, pseudo-arcane fantasies" (p. 685), whereas the style of the later prose, especially of the *Portrait* stories, is something more than expository (p. 684):

What they do *not* say is part of their success. So too is their apt instinct for imagery, alliteration, assonance, personification, and the sudden flaring shift from concrete realization to zany vision. But above all, it is their pace which makes them live . . .

A number of the stories have been analyzed briefly in various teaching anthologies of short fiction, and Harold F. Mosher has discussed "The Structure of Dylan Thomas's 'The Peaches' " (1969). Mosher demonstrates that the story is not so loosely organized as it appears at first: "the juxtaposition of characters, the structure of the images of light, dark, warmth, and cold along with the change of pace on the last day of the action develop the theme of a boy's half-conscious introduction into the adult world . . ." Richard Kelly (1969) discusses the theme of the lost lover in "One Warm Saturday," drawing parallels to Joyce's stories in *Dubliners* and to his *Portrait of the Artist as a Young Man*. In this observation he was anticipated by Warren French (1967), whose much more thorough essay compares these "two portraits of the artist." French analyzes most of the stories briefly, demonstrating that they share the theme of loss and also become increasingly serious as the protagonist grows older. Walford Davies (1968) also touches on the influence of Joyce in the stories, drawing further parallels to Dickens and to Ambrose Bierce.

Thomas rapidly abandoned this vein of prose, however successful it proved. He had been writing against a December, 1939, deadline, and when the war intervened he spent considerable time and effort agonizing over the role he was to play in it. As it turned out, he was declared physically unfit and spent most of the war years writing documentary film scripts like the sentimental *Our Country*, a part of which is available in the American edition of *QEOM*. During this period he also began reading for the British Broadcasting Corporation (BBC). Relatively few poems were completed; of those which were, the narrative "Ballad of the Long-legged Bait" and the "Vision and Prayer" sequence are notable. Thomas clearly was intrigued with the possibilities of narrative, whether because of the success of *Portrait*, his film work, or the broadcasts he had begun. Apparently he was still feeling his way toward a narrative form which suited him. He was alternately excited and depressed about *Adventures in the Skin Trade*, which he began in 1941; but Thomas soon found he could not sustain the effort at a picaresque, semiautobiographical novel. The fragment is generally agreed to be among the least successful examples of his late prose, although it has moments of great humor and beauty.

Much of Thomas's work on films, both documentary and commercial, has probably been lost forever: according to FitzGibbon (1965, pp. 248–50), he worked on parts of many which were abandoned at various stages. FitzGibbon appends (pp. 351–53) a list of those about which he was able to gather information. Thomas's "documentary" entitled *Is Your Ernie Really Necessary?* seems to have appalled the ministry of information with its surrealistic irreverence. Probably his best effort was *The Doctor and the Devils*, which he wrote in collaboration with Donald Taylor, and which was later published in book form. The New Directions edition (1966) includes the half-completed script for Maurice O'Sullivan's *Twenty Years A-Growing* as well as *A Dream of Winter* and *The Londoner*. James Agee (1953, p. 38) described the script as extremely good hackwork, and pointed out the brilliance of Thomas's "vividly, effortlessly evocative" camera directions. According to his friend Maclaren Ross (FitzGibbon, 1965,

p. 252), Thomas was in fact extremely interested in the film medium, and devised a number of ambitious projects which failed for
lack of backing. Of those he did finish, *The Beach of Falesa* (based
on the Robert Louis Stevenson story), *Rebecca's Daughters,* and
Me and My Bike have since been published separately.

Although Thomas continued to work on film scripts through
1948, a new interest had intervened. In 1943 he had written "Reminiscences of Childhood" for the Welsh service of the BBC. His
services as reader and discussant were demanded with increasing
frequency, until by 1946-48 he was appearing nearly fifty times
yearly. Although the majority of Thomas's appearances were readings of verse, he prepared a number of poetic reminiscences, the
majority of which were published posthumously in *QEOM,* a volume he had planned. His beloved *A Child's Christmas in Wales* is
one such sketch. To an even greater extent than the stories, these
semifictional narratives have been ignored by critics. The book's
reviews were generally quite positive, but perhaps because the essays fit no genre neatly, perhaps because they seem immediately
accessible, no effort has been made to examine them closely.

In fact, as Ralph Maud has demonstrated (1963, pp. 8–13), the
best of them repay a close textual reading. Maud examines the first
paragraph of "A Child's Christmas" and finds the poet's technique
and imagination engaged in the same manner they are in the poetry:
"Thomas's instinct to create an original vision from the everyday
event leads him to use clichés and common phrases, just altered to
the extent that we have to think them out afresh, but within the
aura of their familiarity." As Maud shows, the paragraph plays with
implications of the phrases "around the corner" and "out of sound,"
and uses the ambiguous epithet "the two-tongued sea" for remarkably complex purposes. The analysis traces the phrase through the
versions of the essay, which are more fully examined by W.
Eugene Davis (1973).

There is little difference in texture between the stories of *Portrait*
and the reminiscences of *QEOM;* in fact, Emlyn Williams combined parts of both books and of *AST* in his popular dramatic reci-
tation entitled *Boy Growing Up.* Thomas's readings were anything
but makeshift affairs; most of his producers at the BBC have testified
to the extreme care with which he prepared his broadcasts—except-
ing a few minor lapses due to drink—and to the power and delicacy
of his readings (e.g., Arlott, 1954; Roy Campbell, Louis MacNeice,
and John Lehmann in Tedlock, 1960). Certainly his use of a linear
medium such as the radio encouraged the trend toward clarity and
a firmer narrative line in his later verse. But its most significant

effect upon the poet was to inspire his best-known work, the "play for voices" *Under Milk Wood*.

In 1939 Thomas had remarked to Richard Hughes that the people of Laugharne needed "a play about themselves" (FitzGibbon, 1965, p. 237). Gradually he came to realize that his broadcast talk "Quite Early One Morning," with its description of the dreams and wakings of a Welsh seaside town (probably New Quay), was the proper starting point for such a play. Thomas toyed with a number of ideas for it, notably a version entitled "The Town Was Mad," wherein an entire Welsh town was to be declared insane and the inhabitants would speak for themselves at a mass trial, deciding at the end that they wished to be cordoned off from the "sane" world about them. This idea was abandoned, and between 1944, when he started to work on it seriously, and his death in 1953, the play passed through some eleven versions. Frank Manley (1964) discusses some of these briefly, while Douglas Cleverdon (*The Growth of Milk Wood*, 1969), who produced the play for the BBC, has published a book-length study of bibliographical interest. In his introduction, Cleverdon discusses Thomas's career in radio and its relationship to the development of *UMW;* he then describes in detail five major variants of the play and concludes with a complete analysis of textual variations, including the standard 1954 Dent and New Directions editions. Brinnin (*Dylan Thomas in America*, 1955) discusses the chaos surrounding Thomas's final changes in the play just before his death in New York.

The critics generally have been kind to *UMW*. Criticism of the play is made difficult by the paradox of its success: quite obviously it has little or no dramatic development, no characters with any depth, and of course no action for the audience to appreciate. Yet despite these handicaps, which ought to be crippling, it has been played successfully ever since its initial reading. Drama critic Walter Kerr (1963, pp. 80–81) argues that this fact chiefly demonstrates the poverty of the language of contemporary theater. *UMW*, devoid of drama, is "the best possible case that can be made for the value of verse in the theater," a point also made by Raymond Williams in his more ambitious discussion of the play (Cox, 1966, p. 90). Williams notes that the central problem for Thomas was deciding upon a means of narrating: Captain Cat, the original narrator, became too strong a character, and was supplanted by a "First Voice," a "Second Voice," and the "Voice of a Guide-Book." Williams finds the narration the play's weakest feature, particularly in the descriptive passages, while the dialogue is rich in rhythm and somehow very real, although not in the naturalistic sense. Thomas's "pattern of voices" (p. 95) provides a preferable alternative to the verse drama of Christopher Fry or T. S. Eliot with their single voices. Williams demonstrates the similarity between parts of the "Circe" section of Joyce's *Ulysses* and parts of *UMW*, but adds that *Faust* and *Lear* are also dramatic precedents in their use of language. Although his discussion centers on technique, Williams adds (p. 97) that the play is "not inconsiderable" in substance.

Most discussion of the play recalls the effusive but vague early reactions to Thomas's poetry. Writers stress its "spontaneity," "compassion," and "joyous sensuality." William Arrowsmith (1954, p. 294) more imaginatively calls it "vigorous and lusty, a kind of massive rutting masque for the listening ear." Arrowsmith's discussion opposes *UMW* to Eliot's verse drama, *The Confidential Clerk*, which he finds sterile and abstract by comparison; he traces the difference to the religious vision underlying each—Anglican and world-denying in Eliot's case, "Eleusinian" and "a fertility-variant of Christianity" in Thomas's (p. 295). Plotless, undramatic, and without developed characters, it is still "a minor masterpiece." Perhaps critics have been overly surprised at the lack of "round" characters in the play; after all, Dickens, one of Thomas's favorite authors, manages to convince and entertain readers with thoroughly "flat" ones. Thomas is not trying to be realistic, but to capture in comic and lyric form the spirit of a place and people. Richard Hughes comments (Jones, 1966, p. 92) that

for anyone who has lived in Laugharne the composite portrait of the place and its people is perfect—and *yet* not a single character in it, individually, is drawn from the life—except perhaps Polly Garter.

Despite the generally favorable reaction to *UMW*, even in Wales, there is still a kind of sensibility which immediately recoils in horror upon realizing that "Llareggub" is "buggerall" spelled backwards. Of course there is bawdy irreverence and sensuality in the poetry as well, but in a poem it is usually cloaked in ambiguities or filtered through lyricism; in the play it cannot be missed. This presents no problem for the liberally-minded reader. But it does suggest more serious issues, such as whether there is any sort of moral vision behind the play at all; it is quite possible that the general tendency to term *UMW* a "minor" work reflects the lack of a moral center in it. David Holbrook argues rather passionately (Cox, 1966) that the play is not merely trivial but actually pernicious. He begins by arguing that Thomas's "place of love" is infantile instead of realistic (p. 100), and continues with a running comparison be-

tween *UMW* and Joyce's *Ulysses*, both of which capture a day in
the life of a town. Holbrook is convincing as he demonstrates that
Thomas's prose style is derivative, although he finally proves only
that some passages in Thomas sound like some passages in Joyce; he
is less convincing when arguing that the characters too derive from
models in *Ulysses*. But the essential difference between the writers,
aside from Joyce's greater technical finesse, is that Holbrook sees
a moral stance which underlies and redeems Joyce's work, and only
an infantile, sniggering dirty-mindedness behind Thomas's. Thomas
invites us to laugh cruelly at the characters with their eccentricities
and asks us to laugh also at their cruel impulses toward one another.

I think there are some obvious problems with Holbrook's analysis. Even if we grant that he has shown Joyce to be the better
stylist by comparing similar passages, that does not mean that
Thomas is a *poor* writer. Passages which suggest "necrophilia" to
Holbrook (p. 110), merely suggest to me Thomas's metaphysical
association between sexuality and death. But Holbrook is certainly
accurate about the play's total lack of moral complexity: it is indeed a child's vision of life, if we grant the child a precocious sexuality. The real question is whether that fact removes *UMW* from
serious consideration as literature. Lawrence Lerner in an essay entitled "Sex in Arcadia" (Davies, 1972, p. 262) explores this problem. Lerner argues first that the play is best viewed as a pastoral,
despite its nominally urban setting (p. 268); Llareggub is a simple,
happy place set apart from the world and its complications. Like
many pastorals, Thomas's work deals with the problem of love; his
solution is to advocate free love, including the erotic, as in Tasso's
Aminta, rather than chaste love of the sort argued in Guarini's *Pastor Fido*. Lerner demonstrates that Thomas's association of free love
with childhood, with Eden, and with the country rather than the
city has numerous literary precursors. Holbrook is mistaken in demanding of Thomas the sort of moral vision we might expect from
a novelist; by these standards, involved as they are with a "realistic"
representation of society, all pastorals would fail.

Nevertheless, as Lerner admits, Holbrook touches a sore spot
when he relates the play's lack of verisimilitude to its lack of moral
stance. There are gestures toward realism in *UMW*, hints of complex human relationships, as there must be in any dramatic narrative. I think that the weakness which Holbrook finds in all Thomas's
writing does haunt the prose if not the poetry. In his poetry
Thomas creates a world very different from the world of our experience; this is something which we expect of all poetry, though
we seldom find transformations as radical as those in Thomas. In

prose narratives, on the other hand, we expect to find a world close to our own. Thomas's early prose disappoints us in this, as it is a faithful representation of the poetic vision. The later prose presents a world much closer to our own, with characters we can recognize as human; but the only depth Thomas can give them must reflect their participation in the life of his own mind. Both the charm and the grotesquerie of characters in *Portrait* result from their appearance in a world which is not theirs in any essential way, while the characters of *UMW*, more at home in their world, are removed from ours. Finally, Thomas's genius lay in the verbal embodiment of his fantasies. He also possessed a talent for acute observation, and in the prose was able at times to hold these disparate qualities in suspension. For all the wit and beauty of his prose, it is limited by this tension between subjective and objective vision. But the poetry, on the other hand, generates its own universe, where "unjudging love" is possible, and time rests. If we are swept into it by the power of Thomas's language, we return changed.

References

Agee, James
  1953. "A Dylan Thomas Screen Play," *New York Times Book Review* Dec. 6, p. 38.
Amis, Kingsley
  1955. "Thomas the Rhymer," *Spectator* Aug. 12, pp. 227–28.
Arlott, John
  1954. "Dylan Thomas and Radio," *Adelphi* First Quarter, pp. 121–24.
Arrowsmith, William
  1954. "Menander and Milk Wood," *Hudson Review* Summer, pp. 291–96.
Brinnin, John Malcolm
  1955. *Dylan Thomas In America: An Intimate Journal.* Boston: Little.
  1960. (editor) *A Casebook on Dylan Thomas.* New York: Crowell.
Cleverdon, Douglas
  1969. *The Growth of Milk Wood.* London: J. M. Dent.
Cox, C. B.
  1966. (editor) *Dylan Thomas: A Collection of Critical Essays.* Englewood Cliffs, N. J.: Prentice-Hall.
Davis, W. Eugene
  1973. "The Making of 'A Child's Christmas in Wales,'" *Arizona Quarterly* Winter, pp. 342–51.
Davies, Walford
  1968. "Imitation and Invention: The Use of Borrowed Material in Dylan Thomas's Prose," *Essays in Criticism* July, pp. 275–95.

1971. (editor) *Dylan Thomas: Early Prose Writings*. New York: New Directions.

1972. (editor) *Dylan Thomas: New Critical Essays*. London: J. M. Dent.

Emery, Clark

1962. *The World of Dylan Thomas*. Coral Gables, Fla.: Univ. of Miami Pr.

FitzGibbon, Constantine

1965. *The Life of Dylan Thomas*. Boston: Little.

Fraser, G. S.

1957. *Dylan Thomas*. London: Longmans (for the British Council); also *British Writers and Their Work*, no. 5. Lincoln: Univ. of Nebraska Pr., 1965.

French, Warren

1967. "Two Portraits of the Artist: James Joyce's *Young Man;* Dylan Thomas's *Young Dog*," *University Review of Kansas City* June, pp. 261–66.

Glick, Burton S.

1957. "A Brief Analysis of a Short Story by Dylan Thomas," *American Imago* Summer, pp. 149–54.

Jones, T. H.

1966. *Dylan Thomas* (Writers and Critics series). New York: Barnes & Noble; also Grove, 1963; also Edinburgh and London: Oliver & Boyd, 1963.

Kelly, Richard

1969. "The Lost Vision of Dylan Thomas' 'One Warm Saturday,' " *Studies in Short Fiction* Winter, pp. 205–9.

Kerr, Walter

1963. "Word Pictures." In *The Theater in Spite of Itself*, pp. 78–82. New York: Simon & Schuster.

Korg, Jacob

1948. "The Short Stories of Dylan Thomas," *Perspective* Spring, pp. 184–91.

1965. *Dylan Thomas*. New York: Twayne (Twayne's English Authors series no. 20).

Manley, Frank

1964. "The Text of Dylan Thomas' 'Under Milk Wood,' " *Emory University Quarterly* Summer, pp. 131–44.

Maud, Ralph N.

1963. *Entrances to Dylan Thomas' Poetry*. Pittsburgh: Univ. of Pittsburgh Pr. (Critical Essays in Modern Literature series); also Lowestoft, England: Scorpion Pr.

Miller, J. Hillis

1965. "Dylan Thomas." In *Poets of Reality: Six Twentieth-Century Writers*, pp. 190–216. Cambridge, Mass.: Harvard Univ. Pr.; also London: Oxford Univ. Pr. 1966.

Mosher, Harold F., Jr.

1969. "The Structure of Dylan Thomas's 'The Peaches,' " *Studies in Short Fiction* Fall, pp. 536–47.

Moynihan, William T.

1966. *The Craft and Art of Dylan Thomas*. Ithaca, N. Y.: Cornell Univ. Pr.; also London: Oxford Univ. Pr.

Muecke, C. C.
  1959. "Come Back! Come Back!—A Theme in Dylan Thomas's
  Prose," *Meanjin* April, pp. 67–76.
Olson, Elder
  1954. *The Poetry of Dylan Thomas*. Chicago: Univ. of Chicago Pr.
Phelps, Robert
  1955. "In Country Dylan," *Sewanee Review* Autumn, pp. 681–87.
Pratt, Annis
  1970. *Dylan Thomas' Early Prose: A Study in Creative Mythology*.
  Pittsburgh: Univ. of Pittsburgh Pr.
Stanford, Derek
  1964. *Dylan Thomas: A Literary Study*. Rev. ed. New York: Citadel.
Tedlock, Ernest Warnock
  1960. (editor) *Dylan Thomas: The Legend and the Poet*. London:
  Heinemann.
Tindall, William York
  1953. "Burning and Crested Song," *American Scholar* Autumn,
  pp. 486–90.
  1962. *A Reader's Guide to Dylan Thomas*. New York: Noonday.
Treece, Henry
  1949. *Dylan Thomas: "Dog Among the Fairies."* London: Lindsay
  Drummond. Rev. ed. London: Ernest Benn; New York: de Graff,
  1956.
  1954. "Chalk-Sketch for a Genius," *Dock Leaves* Spring, pp. 18–23.
Tritschler, Donald
  1971. "The Stories in Dylan Thomas' Red Notebook," *Journal of
  Modern Literature* Sept. pp. 33–56.

Selected Additional Readings

GENERAL AND INTRODUCTORY ESSAYS

Crewe, J. V.
  1972. "The Poetry of Dylan Thomas," *Theoria* pp. 65–83.
Hogler, Raymond L.
  1972. "Dylan Thomas: The Development of an Idiom," *Anglo-
  Welsh Review* Summer and Winter, pp. 113–23, 102–13.
Huddlestone, Linden
  1948. "An Approach to Dylan Thomas," *Penguin New Writing*
  no. 35, pp. 123–60.
Lander, Clara
  1957. "The Macabre in Dylan Thomas," *Canadian Forum* March,
  pp. 274–75, 278.
Moore, Nicholas
  1948–49. "The Poetry of Dylan Thomas," *Poetry Quarterly* Winter, pp. 229–36.
Sachs, Arieh
  1964. "Sexual Dialectic in the Early Poetry of Dylan Thomas,"
  Southern Review (Australia), pp. 43–47.
Werry, Richard R.
  1950. "Poetry of Dylan Thomas," *College English* Feb., pp. 250–56.

THE PROSE

Allen, Walter
1954. "Words in Spate" (review of *QEOM*), *New Statesman*
Nov. 6, p. 586.
Davies, Rhys
1940. (review of *Portrait*), *Life and Letters Today* March, pp.
336, 338.
Gilmore, Haydn
1971. "Dylan Thomas as Journalist," *Journalism Quarterly* pp.
554–58.
Hauser, Marianne
1940. "Sketches of Youth" (review of *Portrait*), *New York Times
Book Review* Dec. 29, pp. 4, 14.
Lougee, David
1955. "Worlds of Dylan Thomas," (reviews *QEOM* and *AST*),
Poetry Nov., pp. 114–15.
MacNeice, Louis
1954. (review of *QEOM*), *New York Times Book Review*
Dec. 19, p. 1.
West, Anthony
1940. (review of *Portrait*), *New Statesman* April 20, p. 542.
Woodcock, George
1955. (review of *QEOM*), *Arizona Quarterly* Spring, pp. 79–81.

FILM, RADIO, RECORDING

Brinnin, John Malcolm
1963. (review of *Beach of Falesa*), *New York Herald Tribune
Book Week Magazine* Nov. 3, pp. 5, 23.
Deren, Maya; Parker Tyler; Dylan Thomas; and Arthur Miller
1963. "Poetry and the Film: A Symposium," *Film Culture* No. 29,
Summer, pp. 55–63.
Dobree, Bonamy
1953. "Two Experiments" (review of *Doctor & Devils*), *The Spec-
tator* June 12, pp. 763–64.
Erdman, Irwin
1952. "The Spoken Word" (review of the Caedmon recordings),
Saturday Review Nov. 29, pp. 68–69.
Frankel, Haskel
1963. (review of *Beach of Falesa*), *Saturday Review* Aug. 3, p. 18.
Korg, Jacob
1953. (review of *Doctor & Devils*), *The Nation* Nov. 14, p. 413.
MacNeice, Louis
1954. (review of *Doctor & Devils, UMW*), *London Magazine*
April, pp. 74–77.
Maud, Ralph N.
1970. *Dylan Thomas in Print: A Bibliographical History*. Pitts-
burgh: Univ. of Pittsburgh Pr. Reprints reviews of six minor
Thomas films from *Documentary Newsletter*, pp. 135–40.
McWhinnie, Donald
1959. *The Art of Radio*. London: Faber.

Slocombe, Marie, and Patrick Saul
   1961. "Dylan Thomas Discography," *Recorded Sound* Summer,
   pp. 80–95.
Tyler, Parker
   1955. (review of *Doctor & Devils*), *Poetry* Nov., pp. 116–18.

UNDER MILK WOOD

Baro, Gene
   1955. "Orator of Llareggub," *Poetry* Nov., pp. 119–22.
Cleverdon, Douglas
   1968. *"Under Milk Wood,"* *Times Literary Supplement* July 18,
   p. 761.
Gassner, John
   1960. *Theater at the Crossroads.* New York: Holt.
Hawkes, Terence
   1965. "Some Sources of 'Under Milk Wood,'" *Notes and Queries*
   July, pp. 273–75.
Hewes, Henry
   1953. "Broadway Postscript: The Backward Town of Llareggub,"
   Saturday Review June 6, pp. 24–25.
Jarrell, Randall
   1955. (review of *UMW*), *Harper's Magazine* Oct., p. 96.
Jenkins, David Clay
   1964. "Dylan Thomas' 'Under Milk Wood:' The American Element," *Trace* Winter, pp. 325–38.
Rea, J.
   1964. "A Topographical Guide to 'Under Milk Wood,'" *College
   English* April, pp. 535–42.
Talbot, Norman
   1965. "Polly's Milk Wood and Abraham's Bosom," *Southern Re-
   view* (Australia) pp. 33–43.
Taylor, Geoffrey
   1954. "Studied Wood-Notes," *Time and Tide* April 24, p. 550.
Tynan, Kenneth
   1954. "Prose and the Playwright," *Atlantic* Dec., pp. 72, 74, 76.
Wells, Henry W.
   1954. "Voice and Verse in Dylan Thomas's Play," *College English*
   May, pp. 438–44.

(See also the introductions and prefaces to various editions of the prose,
filmscripts, and *UMW;* e.g., Ralph Maud, "The London Model for Dylan
Thomas' *Under Milk Wood,*" in *The Doctor and the Devils and Other
Scripts.* New York: New Directions, 1966.)

CHAPTER 2

Dylan Thomas: The Legend

No study of Dylan Thomas, or even of Thomas's poetry in particular, can afford to ignore the man's life, personality, and reputation. Perhaps a more "anonymous" modern poet, like Eliot, could be read without reference to his life; but even the most naive or "pure" reader of Thomas's poetry must in some small part be conscious of the poet's inescapable legend, and this consciousness will inevitably add to (or detract from) the poetry itself.

Indeed, the "Dylan legend" is a stumbling block in nearly every published essay on the poet. Commentators who feel they were friends of his continually attempt to separate the legend from the man himself. Critics, depending upon their theoretical orientation, either deny that his life has any importance for his writing or try to show how his life and work were a unity; and of the latter group, those who in general approve of Thomas show how his life and work highlight each other's better qualities, while those who disapprove argue that the life and legend illustrate the poetry's failings. In this chapter I shall try to explore some of the ramifications of Thomas's reputation and his situation as a public figure; in the next chapter I shall concentrate upon the writer's life and personality as they illuminate his writing.

Thomas was not only a literary figure who won considerable recognition in his own time; he was, thanks to the communications media, a kind of cultural phenomenon. Through his work as a reader for the BBC in England, and later through his public readings and his recordings in America, he was given a degree of public exposure few poets have ever received. "It is tolerably certain," said the BBC actor Frank Atkinson (Grindea, 1953, p. ii), "that, in this country at least, more people would know and remember Dylan Thomas as an actor rather than as the poet." His riotous personal life became common knowledge. Details of his and his wife Caitlin's drinking, fighting, and generally obstreperous behavior were eag-

erly seized on by the public of two countries. Nor was this notoriety irrelevant to the popularity of his poetry. When he died at
the age of thirty-nine he was, in Karl Shapiro's words (John Malcolm Brinnin, *A Casebook on Dylan Thomas*, 1960, p. 167) not
only the "darling of the press" but also "master of a public which he
himself had brought out of nothingness." *Time* and *Newsweek*
magazines characteristically paid homage to the public figure in their
respective obituaries, "The Legend of Dylan Thomas" (May 30,
1955, pp. 90–91) and "Out of Tragedy a Legend and Words with
Wings" (Oct. 28, 1957, p. 96). In England, the *News Chronicle*
headed its obituary "The Poet They Called a Dangerous Cherub,"
and the *Daily Mail* ran five articles on "The Most Fantastic Character of Our Time." Even the staid London *Times* ran an obituary
five times longer than its usual allotment to literary figures.

The popularity of Thomas's poetry is one of the paradoxes of
contemporary literary history. His first book, published when he
was virtually unknown, rapidly sold three thousand copies (Fitz-
Gibbon, *The Life of Dylan Thomas*, 1965, p. 195). Richard
Church (1954, p. 40), an adviser for Dent, Thomas's British pub-
lisher, notes that Thomas was the only poet in the group Dent published who consistently sold well, even after the war. David Leitch,
in a Sunday *Times* article entitled "Dylan Thomas is Big Business"
(1963, p. 7), points out that while in England Thomas is always
among the five best-selling poets (along with Eliot, Pound, Auden, and Betjeman), in America during the early 1960s, at least,
he was the most read modern poet. His recordings outsell all others
worldwide, with Robert Frost a poor second. By 1962, according
to Louise Murdy (*Sound and Sense in Dylan Thomas's Poetry*,
1966, p. 14), the U.S. public had bought 400,000 copies of Thomas's
recordings. And yet Thomas, particularly in his earlier poems, is
undeniably a difficult poet, even an obscure one. His writings have
nothing in common with the popular versifying of a Rod McKuen
and little in common even with the apparent simplicity of Frost's
verse. Despite the obvious untranslatable qualities of his poetry, its
reliance on all the subtlest resources of the English language,
Thomas has been translated into most European languages; some
poems have even been rendered in Norwegian and Serbo-Croatian
(Leitch, 1963, p. 7). Renato Poggioli (1953, pp. 85–86), after commenting upon the difficulty of appreciating Thomas's work in
Italian translation, goes on to wonder at how much of the magic
does come through. Poggioli then points to Thomas's "plebian origins" (*sic*) and expresses hope that his work might, from an avant-
garde artistic position, nonetheless repopularize poetry.

If we are to account for Thomas's amazing popularity, despite all
the difficulties of his poetry, we must return to the figure of the man
himself. Certainly his public readings, particularly in America,
were essential; according to Lawrence Lipton (1959, pp. 193–207)
they were instrumental in spurring the West Coast revival of poetry
readings in the fifties. And certainly his semiautobiographical writings, particularly those in *Portrait of the Artist as a Young Dog* and
Quite Early One Morning, contributed to his popularity. But the
most significant factor was Thomas's public personality. He was,
claims T. H. Jones (*Dylan Thomas*, 1966, p. 1), "with the possible
exception of Pound, . . . the most sensational poet of our time." At
the age of eighteen Thomas, a cub reporter for the *Herald of
Wales*, began a story on an eccentric local poet (Jan. 23, 1932):

No one can deny that the most attractive figures in literature are always those around whom a world of lies and legends has been woven,
those half mythical artists whose real characters become cloaked forever under . . . the bizarre.

This was to be his fate and charm. And, consciously or unconsciously, Thomas capitalized upon his own semimythical status. As
a young man he was frantic to escape the restrictions of a provincial
Welsh town and virtually ignored its cultural heritage, but later his
"Welshness" contributed to his aura. He became the wild man from
the West, the Celtic bard with the magical rant, a folk figure with
racial access to roots of experience which more civilized Londoners
lacked.

Though he joined no literary cliques or movements, Thomas
soon became the focus of a vague rebellion. Again, his public personality contributed. In an era when poets by and large tended to
appear quiet, scholarly, and self-effacing, Thomas lived the bardic
role to the hilt. The Victorians had made poetry respectable; the
group of modern writers whom Roy Campbell had christened
"Macspaunday" (MacNeice, Spender, Auden, and Day Lewis)
made poetry seem serious, erudite, limited, and somehow innocuous.
Thomas, on the other hand, made it bawdy, sensual, prophetically
intense, and unlimited in ambition. His verse struck readers as somehow wholly different from what had come before. "Surrealists,"
"Apocalyptics," and other nascent literary groups claimed him as
their progenitor and attempted to adopt him; eventually, he was
seen as the "green fuse" which ignited a vast and amorphous literary
trend known as "neo-romanticism." On the other side of the Atlantic, the perennial bohemian Kenneth Rexroth (1957, p. 29)

classed him with the jazz musician Charlie Parker ("two great dead juvenile delinquents") as an immediate ancestor of the "beat generation." He was, after all, antiintellectual in most senses, vastly preferring limericks in a pub to academic discussions. The "disaffiliated" took him to their hearts, causing Frank Butler (1960-61, p. 83) to observe that although Thomas, like "Bird," "makes an apt hero for anyone more concerned with the emotional life of the man than with the art of the artist," the "beatnik ignores the fact that his poetry is no less controlled than that of A. E. Housman." Butler is perfectly correct, yet the idea of craftsmanship, which Thomas himself always stressed, was so foreign to his public image that only recently has the complexity and sophistication of his poetic technique been fully realized.

By the time of his death Thomas embodied, in the minds of many, "The Poet." James Mitchie (1954, pp. 77–79) observed, "Dylan was a figure, a character, a bard, even a card; he looked and behaved more like a poet than anyone since Yeats." The public gloom felt at his death was "almost patriotic." Donald Davie (1954, pp. 74–75) felt compelled to reply rather snappishly that all of this was not, after all, the business of literature: what we want is not poets but poetry. Few were inclined to listen, even among literati. Literary periodicals ran special issues devoted to Thomas. It seemed that in his case ordinary decorum did not apply; in death, as in life, he was set apart from ordinary mortals. As A. G. Pryse-Jones wrote in a memorial issue of *Dock Leaves* magazine (1954, p. 20), "one got the impression that, rather mysteriously perhaps and by some special dispensation, he was always within a state of grace." Mario Luzi (Tedlock, *Dylan Thomas: The Legend and the Poet*, 1960, p. 49) claims that even "those who knew little or nothing of him recognized that destiny or a fatal play of natural forces was at work within him." Many observers agree that there was something about the poet larger than life. Derek Stanford (1964, p. 3) asserts that "the disappearance of his person from the uninspired scenes in which we move, was like the theft of a force of nature." John Malcolm Brinnin *(Dylan Thomas in America*, 1955, p. 40), who knew Thomas in his last years quite closely, echoes the sentiment: ". . . to know Dylan was to know a personality having the power of a natural force."

Clearly Thomas's uninhibited life-style struck a responsive chord in the public. G. S. Fraser *(Dylan Thomas*, 1957, p. 5) explains: "he corresponded, as most poets do not, to some popular ideal, vision, or fiction of what a poet, in real life, should be. He was the pattern of the poet as a bohemian, and this was in many ways a misfortune for him." The French critic Marc Alyn (*Dylan Thomas*, Bokanowski, 1963, p. 57) points out "the resemblance of Dylan to a certain romantic image of the poet which is widespread in the United States, a mixture of Chatterton and Rimbaud, of Hart Crane and Villon, with an added weakness for childhood which . . . is the Achilles' heel of New World civilization." Harvey Breit (1961, p. 338), the *New York Times* literary critic who interviewed Thomas several times, agrees that "in the American triumph the poems are almost beside the point." They are important only in that they "permitted the poet better to conform to an ideal public image—the Pure Genius, the Romantic Anarchist."

Perhaps the reaction to Thomas the public figure says more about modern culture, particularly in America, where the reaction was most intense, than it does about Thomas himself. The bohemian has always been an object of mingled admiration and scorn, because although he may offend by trespassing upon a culture's taboos, he may also win admiration for getting away with it. Elizabeth Hardwick (Brinnin, 1960, p. 155) explores this idea. "Thomas was acknowledged, unconsciously perhaps, to be beyond judgment," she argues. "He was a success and a failure in a way we find particularly appealing . . . He had everything and 'threw it all away.' . . . He was Hart Crane, Poe, F. Scott Fitzgerald . . . and also . . . a great actor." People had to be aware that there was a kind of seriousness, a committed intensity, even to his debauchery. Hardwick (pp. 153–54) cites Eliot speaking of Byron:

. . . after the theatricalism, the posing, the scandals, you had to come back to the fact that Byron was nevertheless genuinely disreputable. And so it was with Thomas. Behind his drinking, his bad behavior, his infidelities, his outrageousness, there was always his real doom. His condition was clearly critical.

But of course there was an ugly side to the adulation as well. Conor Cruise O'Brien, discussing the "Dylan Cult" (1965, p. 14), argues that "the bourgeois fascination with the Bohemian . . . is made up of envy, voyeurism, and a desire to debase." Caitlin Thomas certainly blames her husband's American admirers for his degeneration and early death; and there is plenty of testimony to the fact that during his tours reporters, hosts, and strangers would sometimes force liquor upon Thomas in the desire to see the poet drunk. Thomas's most prolific adverse critic, David Holbrook, in his book *Dylan Thomas and Poetic Dissociation* (1964, p. 9 and *passim*), sees Thomas's life and the admiration accorded it as a dangerous sign of our schizoid modern culture. Thomas, Holbrook feels, "found adult reality impossible to tolerate and accept," and thus sought refuge in drink and debauch. That the poet's "flight from life" became the object of a "cult" Holbrook finds equally disturbing. Thomas, like a naughty but charming child, was exempt from the rules and restrictions of an adult world. His admirers saw him as an incongruously bawdy Peter Pan, for whom maturity would mean destruction. Anne Fremantle (1953, p. 285) quotes from John Logan's obituary poem:

> magician
>   and child
> you are conjured
> today
>   you are grown up

Robert Graves (1955, p. 113), another adverse critic, finds the admiration heaped on Thomas during his lifetime simply in bad taste; "the living poet hero is a modernism," he feels, and treats Thomas (along with Eliot, Pound, Yeats, and Auden) rather scornfully. Graves further seems to imply that, poetic merits aside, it is unfortunate to make modern idols of men who are either Americans or noncombatants or both.

By and large it is Thomas's death with which commentators find it most difficult to come to terms. Although, according to Breit (1961, p. 335), when the Welsh poet first arrived in America he was virtually unknown except among literati, his death "set off a public outcry unmatched since the death of Tennyson" (Baker, 1957, p. 201). All the major newspapers and popular magazines in England and America printed obituaries—almost all, without exception, very laudatory ones. Certainly the Thomas legend contributed to the impact of his death. "Everyone looked upon Thomas as the last of the young poets," writes Karl Shapiro (Brinnin, 1960, p. 167). "When he died, it was as if there would never be any more youth in the world." Stephen Spender, writing soon after the poet's death (1954, p. 17), states that even his poetry "seems affected instantly by his death." Whereas the early, obscure poetry had seemed merely morbid to some in its obsession with death and decay, "every poem today reads like the poet's epitaph."

His early death set a seal of authenticity and import upon Thomas's career. Inasmuch as he embodied the figure of the romantic poet, it seemed to many observers somehow inevitable that he should die young in order to complete the pattern his life formed.

Many of the obituaries were in poor taste, simply because their writers reacted so emotionally to his demise; perhaps few noticed the cruelty implicit in the assumption that he was fated for early death. Richard Eberhart (Tedlock, 1960, p. 57), a poet and friend of Thomas, writes that "he had been a long-term suicide . . . a drive to destruction was inextricably bound up with his genius . . . he could no more escape his death than he could his genius." "He only died too soon," says his fellow "prodigy" George Barker (Tedlock, 1960, p. 72) "because a man like him would always die too soon." Thomas was the poet of youth, claims Kathleen Raine (1953, p. 593), and "he died at the extreme point beyond which none may carry such youth." Alfred Kazin (1957, p. 164) puts the point in a telling paradox: his "posthumous life began before he died." Thomas "had no hope," Kazin claims, since like those around him he was puritan enough to feel that his outrageous life cried out for divine retribution. Anyone watching one of Thomas's last readings could have guessed that the poet would soon be dead. Or, as Bokanowski (1963, p. 65) put it, "the moment always comes when the legend takes its revenge by crushing its human support." Sidney Michaels's popular play *Dylan* (1964) adopts the myth of inevitable death for the poet, reinforcing it with the play's central image of a shooting star, symbolizing Thomas's meteoric career.

Howard Moss puts the problem most succinctly in an excellent essay first published in Brinnin's *Casebook* (1960, p. 290): "The adulation and derogation he suffered were the symptoms of his being himself." There was, on one level, nothing very surprising about his death, although it was "hard for many of his followers to believe that a lifetime of drinking can result in death from alcohol." Yet most people reacted by looking for something upon which to cast the blame. It is "only of interest to those who actually knew him as a person whether he was a victim of himself, or of the world that victimizes everyone," Moss feels.

Most writers disagreed with this dismissal. The British press blamed America. Caitlin Thomas (*Leftover Life to Kill*, 1957, p. 58) blamed his adulators and drinking companions in general and America in particular: "For Dylan, more than anybody, this was a poisonous atmosphere; he needed opposition . . . Nobody needed encouragement less . . . " American critics, naturally, tend to disagree. T. P. McDonnell (1958, p. 285) calls the accusation an example of "British lowbrow journalism" operating in the highbrow press. Helen Vendler (1966, p. 440) insists that no one in America forced liquor upon Thomas; he was a writer already in sentimental decline and bent upon self-destruction. R. V. Cassill (1956, p. 241) thinks the question is more difficult: "Whether it was the world or America that seduced him is a moral point so elusive that all the evidence of his verse and all the testimony of those who knew him best and longest would be required to approach an answer." Harvey Breit (1961, p. 339) insists that his death "was nobody's fault . . . to say that it was our way of life, our capacity to adore and worship and fête and feed that killed Thomas is to insult him."

Others take a more sweeping view of Thomas's significance, arguing that his death was somehow a response to the world and its ills. E. W. Tedlock, in the introduction to his collection of essays on Thomas (1960, p. ix), claims that although people called the Welshman a "slow suicide" through drinking, "the hidden cause was a milieu increasingly unsympathetic to man as man . . . He had struck a blow for basic humanity and died of the fight." Frederick Grubb (1965, p. 186), writing from a neo-Bloomsburian perspective, asserts that Thomas was neither a suicide nor hounded to death by his admirers, but simply "a prodigious and sensitive man benighted in a madhouse." The poet George Barker (Tedlock, 1960, p. 71) agrees that Thomas died because "the world as it is has become an intolerable place for such a man;" the cause of death, though diagnosed as a brain ailment, was actually "the undisguised intervention of the powers of darkness in our affairs."

David Daiches (Tedlock, 1960, p. 58) admits that Thomas "had been killed with kindness" in New York, while Harrison Smith (1954, p. 24) asserts boldly, "Our society is guilty of this death, not the poet," though without specifying why. Kazin (1957, p. 167) quotes from (without endorsing) Kenneth Rexroth's violent poem, which specifically blames bourgeois America:

> Who killed the bright-headed bird?
> You did, you son of a bitch.
> You drowned him in your cocktail brain.
> He fell down and died in your synthetic heart.

And Winfield Townley Scott (Brinnin, 1960, pp. 273–74) with equal bitterness examines the peculiar note of satisfaction in the popular reaction to Thomas's demise. "Why do people *like* to have a poet die?" he asks, and answers that while a living poet serves Truth, and is thus a rebuke to people in general, a dead poet is controllable. There is a "heightened satisfaction . . . when as in Thomas's case the death seems wilful . . . This way, they can have a poet and eat him too."

So, from a multitude of observers, a few basic themes emerge. Thomas, through being intensely and exclusively himself, won a mixture of admiration, envy, and disapproval from the public, but certainly captured and held its interest. However shocked and dismayed by his death, most writers felt it was in a larger sense unsurprising. From a mythic perspective the legend of Thomas recalls that of Orpheus, destroyed by his adulators, while from a social perspective he is seen as an outsider, both tempting and threatening. As Alyn (Bokanowski, 1963, p. 144) puts it, "the saint, the actor, the criminal, and the poet have that in common [in the public's eyes] which merits the same mixture of admiration and hatred: they follow out to the end their own acts and themselves." The darker face of the romantic hero, the aspect we see most clearly in Poe, Nietzsche, Rimbaud, or Baudelaire, is that of the Artist as Madman. "Genius and Madness Akin in World of Art" was the heading for one of Thomas's early newspaper articles (*South Wales Evening Post,* Jan. 7, 1933). Romantic egotism, as it becomes absolute, leads through rebellion and madness toward death. But though he had real affinities with such figures, Thomas's humorous and charming self-deprecation tended to distance him from them. More pragmatically, British observers are inclined to see the poet's death as particularly the result of his American experience, while Americans—especially those who, like Brinnin, might otherwise feel some share of guilt through their involvement in his last years—are more inclined to argue that his death was the inevitable result of self-destructive urges within the poet himself. Oddly, among all the talk about "Dylan Thomas: Everybody's Adonais" (Hynes, 1954, p. 678), only Richard Hughes, a novelist and close neighbor of Thomas's in Laugharne, thought to mention that he did not really fit the pattern of the romantic myth. He was *not* a promising writer who died young, but (Hughes, 1954, p. 5) "that ten times rarer thing, a promising middle-aged man."

Thomas's popular appeal, which was greater than could be explained simply through his talents as a reader and actor, lay in his ability to communicate on a direct and powerful emotional level with a mass audience through his poetry, regardless of whether the poems themselves were understood. His poetry—like all poetry, to a degree—is essentially performance, and just as we can sometimes respond to the emotional intensity of a great performance even if it is given in a foreign tongue, so his audience could respond to Thomas. The poet's public image, of course, heightened his audience's perceptions: especially toward the end of his life, he was clearly a man driven by pride, guilt, fear, and joy, a sort of emotional acrobat who never used a net. As Shapiro puts it (Brinnin, 1960, pp. 177–78),

This audience sees Thomas as a male Edna St. Vincent Millay, or perhaps a Charlie Chaplin; they hear the extraordinary vibrato, a voice of elation and anguish singing over their heads like a wind that tears all the blossoms off the trees. They know this is poetry and they know it is for them.

References

Baker, A. T.
  1957. "The Roistering Legend of Dylan Thomas," *Esquire* Dec., pp. 201–9.
Bokanowski, Helène, and Marc Alyn
  1963. *Dylan Thomas*. Paris: Pierre Seghers.
Breit, Harvey
  1961. "The Haunting Drama of Dylan Thomas." In *A Contemporary Reader: Essays for Today and Tomorrow*, edited by H. W. Rudman and Irving Rosenthal, pp. 335–41. New York: Ronald.
Brinnin, John Malcolm
  1955. *Dylan Thomas in America: An Intimate Journal*. Boston: Little.
  1960. (editor) *A Casebook on Dylan Thomas*. New York: Crowell.
Butler, Frank A.
  1960–61. "On the Beat Nature of Beat," *American Scholar* Winter, pp. 79–92.
Cassill, R. V.
  1956. "The Trial of Two Poets," *Western Review* Spring, pp. 241–45.
Church, Richard
  1954. "The Poet in Contemporary Society," *Adelphi* Fourth Quarter, pp. 35–50.
Davie, Donald
  1954. [Letter] *The London Magazine* March, pp. 74–75.
Fraser, G. S.
  1957. *Dylan Thomas*. London: Longmans, Green (for the British Council).
FitzGibbon, Constantine
  1965. *The Life of Dylan Thomas*. Boston: Little.
Fremantle, Anne
  1953. "Death of a Poet," *Commonweal* Dec. 18, pp. 285–86.
Graves, Robert
  1955. "These Be Your Gods, O Israel." In *The Crowning Privilege*, pp. 112–35. London: Cassell.
Grindea, Miron
  1953. "Editorial," *Adam* no. 238, pp. ii–7.
Grubb, Frederick
  1965. "Worm's Eye: Dylan Thomas." In *A Vision of Reality: A Study of Liberalism in Twentieth-Century Verse*, pp. 179–90. London: Chatto and Windus.

Holbrook, David
  1964. *Dylan Thomas and Poetic Dissociation.* Carbondale: Southern Illinois Univ. Pr.
Hughes, Richard
  1954. (review of *UMW*) (Sunday) *Times* March 7, p. 5.
Hynes, Sam
  1954. "Dylan Thomas: Everybody's Adonais," *Commonweal* March 26, pp. 628–29.
Jones, T. H.
  1966. *Dylan Thomas.* New York: Barnes & Noble.
Kazin, Alfred
  1957. "Posthumous Life of Dylan Thomas," *Atlantic Monthly* Oct., pp. 164–68.
Leitch, David
  1963. "Dylan Thomas is Big Business," (Sunday) *Times* Nov. 10, p. 7.
Lipton, Lawrence
  1959. "The New Apocalypse." In *The Holy Barbarians*, pp. 193–207. New York: Messner.
McDonnell, T. P.
  1958. "Who Killed Dylan?" *Catholic World* July, pp. 285–89.
Michaels, Sidney
  1964. *Dylan* [play]. New York: Random.
Mitchie, James
  1954. [Letter] *The London Magazine* Feb., pp. 77–79.
Murdy, Louise B.
  1966. *Sound and Sense in Dylan Thomas's Poetry.* The Hague: Mouton.
O'Brien, Conor Cruise
  1965. "The Dylan Cult," *New York Review of Books* Dec. 9, pp. 12–14.
Poggioli, Renato
  1953. "In memoria di Dylan Thomas," *Letteratura* Dec., pp. 84–87.
Pryse-Jones, A. G.
  1954. "Death Shall Have No Dominion," *Dock Leaves* Spring, pp. 26–29.
Raine, Kathleen
  1953. "Dylan Thomas," *New Statesman* Nov. 14, p. 594.
Rexroth, Kenneth
  1957. "Disengagement: The Art of the Beat Generation," *New World Writing* no. 11, May, pp. 28–41.
Smith, Harrison
  1954. "Whose is the Guilt?" *Saturday Review* March 13, p. 24.
Spender, Stephen
  1954. "Dylan Thomas," *Britain Today* Jan., pp. 15–18.
Stanford, Derek
  1964. *Dylan Thomas: A Literary Study.* Rev. ed. New York: Citadel.
Tedlock, Ernest Warnock
  1960. (editor) *Dylan Thomas: The Legend and the Poet.* London: Heinemann.

Thomas, Caitlin
  1957. *Leftover Life to Kill.* Boston: Little.
Vendler, Helen Hennessy
  1966. (review of FitzGibbon) *Yale Review* Spring, pp. 439–42.

CHAPTER 3

Thomas The Man:
Biography and Psychology

We come now to discussions of "Thomas, the man" as opposed to "Thomas, the legend," and here the major
sources are easier to categorize. The basic reference is Constantine
FitzGibbon's *The Life of Dylan Thomas* (1965). In a letter to the
Dublin Magazine (1970, pp. 56–58), FitzGibbon explains some of
the reasons he finally accepted the Thomas trustees's request that
he write the authorized biography: due to the "flood of 'reminiscences' . . . written apparently by almost every scribbler who had
ever drunk a pint of bitter with him from Sussex to Vancouver, and
by some who hadn't," FitzGibbon found that "my dead friend was
becoming a figure that was unrecognizable to me." FitzGibbon
apparently knew Thomas most closely during the period 1936–46;
unsurprisingly, the biography is strongest in its evocation of Soho
during the late thirties. As an attempt at debunking the "myth" of
Thomas, the biography is successful: it presents a complex human
being very different from the "stage Dylan" of some of the reminiscences and also very different from the driven, self-destructive man
John Malcolm Brinnin portrayed in his *Dylan Thomas in America*
(1955). FitzGibbon admits that the legendary figure, "the rip-roar-
ing, drunken exhibitionist poet with the outsize death wish . . .
must have existed, since so many intelligent and observant people
have described it, but it was a side of Dylan unknown to me."

The points upon which FitzGibbon abandons objectivity are
few, and Jacob Korg, in a review article (1966, p. 282), summarizes
them neatly. First, he is convinced that Thomas was not an alcoholic, but merely a person who enjoyed occasional drinking. Second, FitzGibbon feels that there was nothing abnormal, or even
significantly interesting, in Thomas's relations with women. "Some
thought him a sex-maniac, others Freudianly thought that he was
impotent or maybe even homosexual at heart. In fact, he just liked
the girls, and he told them so" (FitzGibbon, 1965, p. 186). Lastly,
he defends the poet's wife against those who have tried to give her

a large share of the blame for his breakdown. Essentially, Fitz-Gibbon feels, her concern was that Thomas should get on with his real work, the writing of poetry, and her outbreaks of temper were directed against those who distracted him from it—or against Thomas, when he distracted himself.

Brinnin's book is certainly more sensational. Although undoubt-edly accurate in its details, its assumptions (or prejudices) are closer to the surface. As Thomas's "manager" during his American visits, Brinnin is more intimately involved with his subject, and there is inevitably an element of self-justification in his book. Although he does not pretend to discuss Thomas's life as a whole, only the last three years of it, we still see very little of the poet—or even the writer of *Under Milk Wood*—and a great deal of the public per-former. Thomas's rows, seductions, and binges are described in painful detail, yet the man still seems to remain at a distance. Fur-ther, G. S. Fraser's objection (Fraser, *Dylan Thomas*, 1957, p. 9; *cf.* Jones, *Dylan Thomas*, 1966, p. 83) is echoed by many critics: al-though Brinnin's book is "agonizingly accurate" about the poet's last years, it "should not be taken as giving a fair idea of the charac-ter or personality of Dylan Thomas as his English friends knew him."

Brinnin is convinced that Thomas was already on the downhill slope as a poet when he arrived in America (p. 175): "I knew as well as he that his unhappiness lay in the conviction that his creative powers were failing, that his great work was finished." Thus, he feels that Thomas's drinking was defensive and his riotousness was the result of feeling himself inadequate, a kind of imposter. Despite moments of wit and humor—his own and the Welshman's—Brinnin on the whole paints the portrait of an unhappy, driven, and doomed man who was past his prime and knew it. Brinnin clearly felt am-bivalent toward Thomas and more than a little overwhelmed by him. He seemed to the American (p. 110) "the most exhausting, ex-asperating and most completely endearing human being I had ever encountered." Some critics, most notably R. V. Cassill (1956, p. 244) feel that Brinnin's esthetic assumptions, including a refusal to face the real dimension of "artistic creation as a trafficking with the diabolic or as a Dionysian commitment," limit his perspective. As Clark Emery (1961, p. 18) puts it, "dissipation, in fact, was not a dissipating but a recouping of the time wasted whoring after the false gods of Mortimer Street." Cassill sees Brinnin as alternating between a "Prufrockian sympathy" (p. 242) and a repulsion for Thomas; too often Brinnin represents (p. 245) "the deathless Puri-tan among us."

Thomas's wife Caitlin, in two books, *Leftover Life to Kill* (1957) and *Not Quite Posthumous Letters to My Daughter* (1963), makes few direct references to the poet himself; the only substantial sections (from *Leftover Life*) are reprinted in Brinnin's *A Casebook on Dylan Thomas* (1960, pp. 241–53). Thomas P. Mc-Donnell, writing in *Catholic World* (1958, p. 287), thinks Caitlin's first book is in bad taste, and calls it "a dubiously touching variation of the death-wish theory compounding the cult of Dylan Thomas, [which] only serves to perpetuate the myth itself." T. H. Jones (*Dylan Thomas*, 1966, p. 33) agrees that her "unhappy and in some respects misguided book" is in fact "one of the accretions of the 'Dylan Legend.' " Many of the reviews echoed McDonnell; Caitlin's style, alternately pyrotechnic, turgid, and self-indulgent, put off many critics, while her faults—an extreme self-absorption, a conscious bohemianism, and a certain jealousy of her husband's fame—are undisguised in these prolonged confessions. But Alfred Kazin (1957, p. 168) sees *Leftover Life* as honest, attractive, and useful: it *does* help to explain Thomas because his wife's character and attitudes are so strikingly similar to Dylan's.

Bill Read's *The Days of Dylan Thomas* (1964) is for the most part superseded by FitzGibbon's biography, although it has the considerable advantage of many photographs by Rollie McKenna and others. Read knew Thomas in America and visited him in Laugharne and his book is balanced and informative. Less informative are the endless reminiscences of Thomas which are scattered throughout the periodical literature from about 1950 on. The most valuable of these are collected in E. W. Tedlock's *Dylan Thomas: The Legend and the Poet* (1960), of which some 95 pages are devoted to biographical essays, as against 187 pages of critical discussion.

Several literary periodicals published memorial issues devoted to Thomas, and the reminiscences in these are of higher-than-average quality: *Dock Leaves* (a Welsh national literary journal), no. 5, Spring, 1954; *Adam* ("An International Review" published in London), no. 238 (1953); and the *Yale Literary Magazine* for November, 1954. *Poetry* magazine ran a special Thomas issue in November, 1955. A collection of verse tributes to Thomas, of uneven quality, was edited by George J. Firmage and Oscar Williams and entitled *A Garland for Dylan Thomas* (1963). A. T. Baker's article, "The Roistering Legend of Dylan Thomas," *Esquire* (Dec. 1957, pp. 201–9), deserves special mention as a collection of "Thomas stories," some apocryphal but all entertaining. Perhaps it should be noted that John Ackerman's misleadingly entitled *Dylan Thomas:*

His Life and Work (1964) is almost exclusively a critical study
which involves itself in the poet's biography only in order to but-
tress Ackerman's view of Thomas as a particularly "Welsh" poet.

Of course, the *Selected Letters of Dylan Thomas* (FitzGibbon,
1967) should and do shed much light on the poet's personality and
life; the letters to his early sweetheart, the novelist Pamela Hansford
Johnson, are particularly revealing. But for a number of reasons no
clear picture of the poet emerges. FitzGibbon admits that he has
been quite selective in the letters and parts of letters which he has
chosen to print: his rationale is to select passages which bear importantly on Thomas's poetic activity and—naturally—to omit passages which might prove embarrassing to persons still living. A more
striking (and silent) omission, however, is the group of letters to his
wife, some of which Caitlin had given to *McCall's* (Feb., 1966,
pp. 73, 178).

Personality and Psyche

Perhaps no set of letters, however complete, and no biography,
however honest and catholic, could bring into focus the poet's personality. FitzGibbon (1965, p. 47) explains the difficulty in presenting a composite image of Thomas taken from several sources:
"Even allowing for subjective factors, the pictures painted, the
memories retained, the stories told belong not to one man but to six
or eight." This multiplicity of personality, FitzGibbon argues, was
one of the poet's "deliberate devices," in an attempt to avoid being
trapped and labelled. Theodore Roethke (Tedlock, 1960, p. 50)
points to the same problem:

He was so rich in what he was that each friend or acquaintance
seemed to carry a particular image of him: each had his special Dylan,
whom he cherished and preserved intact, or expanded into a figure
greater than life . . . I think Thomas often knew exactly what each
person thought him to be and, actor that he was, would live up to
expectations when it suited his mood.

There is general agreement that Thomas played (or lived) a
series of roles, adopted a series of masks, from that of the bohemian
bard to that of the casual, friendly, and polite companion. It is less
clear just what relationship this fact bears to his poetry. Suzanne
Roussillat (Tedlock, 1960, p. 3) neatly defines Thomas's work as "a
lyrical inquiry into the springs of his own being." William York

Tindall remarks that "no matter what the ostensible subject of his prose or verse, Thomas always wrote about himself," (*A Reader's Guide to Dylan Thomas*, 1962, p. 16); Francis Scarfe calls Thomas's poetry "entirely autobiographical" (Brinnin, 1960, p. 33). Certainly the Welsh poet's subject was nearly always himself, but himself universalized rather than individualized. G. S. Fraser (*Dylan Thomas*, 1957, p. 7) points out that Thomas "was not, like Byron or Yeats, for instance, the poet as actor; he did not dramatize his personal life in his poetry . . . He did these things in conversation . . . " The poems are "exceedingly individual, but they are also impersonal."

But the impersonality Fraser refers to in the poetry is in part a function of Thomas's bardic stance; he speaks from a great elevation in his poems, and it is hard to believe that this is unrelated to the fact that he was viewed as "the only poet of our time who lived up to his poetry" (Hynes, 1954, p. 629). In one way or another, the poet is undeniably present in his poems. As Frederick Grubb points out (*A Vision of Reality*, 1965, pp. 181–82), Thomas "stages the production of the hero myth: himself" within his verse. He plays a number of roles therein: the child, the "emotional Hercules," the "multi-faceted 'modern' personality," the "devil-may-care sensualist." Stephen Spender (1954, p. vi) has pointed out that, in contrast to the relatively impersonal "I" of Auden's verse, "Dylan Thomas's 'I' is so much 'Dylan' to his readers that the 'Thomas' almost seems added through pedantry." Further, the poet's personality is at least in some sense thematic in the poetry: "Throughout Thomas's poetry there is a sustained joke (a joke of the kind that breaks into the most tragic moments of tragedy), a joke of the poet's rumbustious personality." Approaching more philosophically the relationship between Thomas's own masks and evasions and the necessities of his verse, Richard Eberhart (Tedlock, 1960, p. 55) comments:

Is not Thomas's poetry a continuous artifice . . . , a series of masks each paradoxically revealing the truth, or part of the truth, and is not his conscious craftsmanship itself an ability of the self to fend off reality . . . so that the total depth of life will never be exhausted?

If some observers saw a multiplicity of personalities in the poet, nearly all saw him as a man divided. This "split" is variously described: the poet versus the man, the poet versus the journalist, the bohemian versus the family man, the public Dylan versus the private Dylan, the "town Dylan" versus the "country Dylan"—the list is endless. With any such figure we must keep in mind the distinction

Yeats made between the poet and "the bundle of accident and in-
coherence that sits down to breakfast," but with Thomas this distinction is more striking than usual. At its broadest, there is the
apparent discrepancy Evelyn Broy points to between the "man
who died of an overindulgence in material 'pleasures' and the poet,
in love with the beauty and pure adventure of the spirit" (1965-66,
p. 498). A lingering idealism in the public image of the poet still
argues that his life should be spiritual and unworldly, even ascetic,
for him to be taken seriously. Surely Thomas's roaring public image
alone discouraged many conservative lovers of poetry from taking
an interest in him, as T. H. Jones (1966, p. 1) implies: "fate, modern publicity, and Dylan Thomas himself, conspired to raise as
many barriers as possible between the sympathetic reader of poetry
and the actual poetry that Dylan Thomas wrote." But even those
who were attracted rather than repelled by his Dionysian alter-
ego—Thomas the pub-performer—felt that this split contributed to
his destruction. William Saroyan (1964, p. 36), who met Thomas
in 1944, remembers his barroom monologues with pleasure and
awe: "He had talked poetry, perhaps great poetry . . . " Yet the performance was a strain for the poet: he "didn't know how to . . . put
off his best and greatest self and just be his least self, comfortably,
and not as if he were in combat with an inferior . . . He died a perfectly natural death for a genius who also had to perform at being
a genius . . . "

Perhaps the division that writers see in Thomas sometimes mirrors
their own tastes more clearly than it does a facet of the poet. Anthony West (1955, p. 106) sees "a Singer and a Spectre" in him;
the singer is the true poet, who also wrote most of the first half of
Quite Early One Morning; the spectre, or hack, wrote most of the
second part. Kingsley Amis (1970, p. 54) distinguishes between
"ranting, canting Thomas the Rhymer"—who wrote practically all
the poems and many of the stories—and the "comparatively disci-
plined, responsible Thomas" of *Portrait of the Artist as a Young
Dog,* which Amis feels is the writer's best work.

Karl Shapiro (Brinnin, 1960, p. 174) in a seminal article claims
there are two minds operative in Thomas: a "joyous, naturally religious mind," and the "almost pathological mind of the cultural fugi-
tive or clown." The second mind informs his work with rage or
with buffoonery; the "split in temperament," Shapiro argues, is "his
strength as well as his weakness." Paul West (1967, pp. 925–27)
agrees with Shapiro's diagnosis of a double vision, and argues that
"the visionary learns from the clown" in his work. Thomas represents a "dynamic fusion" of "dynast and midget, druid and buffoon,

Lear and Falstaff, demiurge and urchin." Howard Moss (1967, p. 186) also sees Thomas the poet as radically different from all his other aspects. His "letters reveal [that] his refusal to allow the journalist, entertainer, and comedian a foothold in the poems was absolute." But Moss feels (p. 185) that "the gulf between Thomas the poet and Thomas everything else . . . , rather than being divisive, was one of the signs of his hold on life." Thomas's friend Vernon Watkins (1961, p. 124) sees the poet's split as destructive. "The quality he prized most was seriousness, and he was a born clown." Yet the clown was his mask, and "a writer's mask can be fatal to him."

D. J. Enright, who has ties to the anti-Thomist group of writers associated with F. R. Leavis's *Scrutiny* magazine, distinguishes between the poet "Thomas" and the cultural and social figure "Dylan" (1966, p. 42): the former is a serious but minor poet, while the latter was seen by friends and critics as "the Villonesque king of the vagabonds," "a sort of Roi d'Ys," "an explosive mixture of Rimbaud and Verlaine," "a Promethean keeper of fire and secrets," "no piner for Fanny Brawnes," "a Donne to Christopher Fry's Marlowe," and "a sort of Peter Pan and William rolled into one." The poet sold out, Enright argues (p. 46). He

fell among literary touts, publicity hounds, non-writing writers agog to bring a writer down, and 'acceptable compromises.' The compromises were simple: instead of writing he was to talk; instead of being a poet and a person he was to be a 'character' . . .

Strangely, even Thomas's enemies often express the opinion that he was at heart a decent man and a talented writer, deluded by his admirers into playing the fool and obscuring his poetry with fireworks and childish games. J. H. Martin (1964, p. 235) was a friend of the poet in Cornwall, but he argues along the same line, presenting what might be termed "the plain man's view of Thomas." Thomas's poetic modernism, claims Martin, was basically a ploy, and as foreign to his natural tastes and inclinations as the public Dylan was to the private Dylan. Like FitzGibbon, Edith Sitwell, Vernon Watkins, and many of the poet's oldest friends, Martin remembers a "true" Thomas who was quiet, polite, an attentive listener, and a generally reasonable person who drank "because they expect it of me" or, as Enright (1966, p. 45) suggests, because he was disgusted by his own insensitive admirers.

The obvious question is, when and how did Thomas begin to assume his various roles? FitzGibbon (1965, p. 600) claims that

the process began in Swansea, between 1931–34, while Thomas was
doing some acting and working as a journalist. Pamela Hansford
Johnson (Brinnin, 1960, p. 264) remembers that when nineteen-
year-old Thomas first visited her he arrived with a prepared, "cultural" remark about a Gauguin exhibition; he soon abandoned this
approach, however, and while staying with her parents his pre-
meditatedly unconventional behavior caused a stir in the middle-
class neighborhood. Geoffrey Grigson (Brinnin, 1960, p. 256), an
early friend of the poet who later broke with him, remembers that
Thomas arrived in London "uncertain of his part"—he looked like
Rimbaud and talked poetry: Rossetti, Francis Thompson, James
Thomson, and Spender. Later (p. 258) he abandoned the esthete
image for that of the "Toughish Boy," or "Boy with a Load of
Beer." Grigson cites nicknames his friends attached to Thomas during this period: "the snotty troll," the "disembodied gland,"
"Ditch," the "ugly suckling." "When he disappeared," says Grig-
son (p. 259) "it was a relief; when he reappeared, a pleasure."

John Davenport (Tedlock, 1960, p. 77) found Thomas serious
in Laugharne where he had been a clown in London: "I realized,
for the first time, the intense seriousness which lay beneath that
social exterior that was a mixture of Puck and Panurge, with more
than a touch of Falstaff." But even after his arrival in London,
Thomas would alternate between bohemian and bourgeois facades.
Lawrence Durrell (1956, p. 34) remembers meeting the poet at
Anna Wickham's in 1937: "He was then a slim and neat young man
with cropped hair, tidily dressed—unlike the sublunary golliwog I
met sometime later." Further, "he was so self-possessed and so very
much his own man that I carried away the impression of someone
not over-expansive." Bill Read (1964, p. 122) testifies to this more
formal aspect of Thomas, generally unknown to Americans. Even
after 1949 in London, while Thomas was involved with BBC work
and film scripting, he would alternately attend the Savage Club—
genteel, and a haunt of successful artists and writers—and the Man-
drake Club, a cheap Soho dive. Thomas could act perfectly at home
in either. Read claims—and Caitlin Thomas bears him out—that the
poet would vacillate between a yearning for the *bon bourgeois* condition and spates of bohemian indulgence.

Read cites the testimony of Donald Taylor, who hired Thomas
for film work. According to Taylor, he and the Welshman would
actually decide on what roles they were to play when they went out
for a drink. Though Thomas's favorite role was the Welsh country
gentleman, he also enjoyed the conservative image of a BBC actor
and verse reader, nattily dressed, and that of the drunken poet with

a fag in the corner of his mouth, garbed in a black polo sweater and dirty raincoat. The poet, it seems, was often concerned to "dress the part," whatever the part might be. Wyn Henderson, with whom he stayed in Cornwall during 1936 (Read, 1964, p. 82), thought him "touchingly clothes-conscious." John Davenport, in a *Listener* article (1962, p. 24) claims that Thomas "thoroughly enjoyed his own legend." Davenport feels there were at least four "Dylans"—the domestic man, "mild and even conventionally henpecked;" the public man, a "tipsy little buffoon;" the creative man, intensely serious, even possessed, in the act of writing; and the private man, whom Davenport found congenial, quiet, and funny, who enjoyed reading and talking about Hardy, and who had a child's innocent fascination with horrors. "Never at his best in London," Thomas was "essentially a simple man." Yet there was nothing simple, or even consistent, about the impression he gave publicly. If he could seem all things to all men, he struck A. G. Pryse-Jones (1954, p. 27) as containing multitudes: "in quick succession he could reveal the imp, the cherub, the poseur, the angel, the literary showman, the dedicated craftsman, all of whom lived within him in a state of perpetual civil war."

Perhaps at the fringes of opinion on Thomas are those who saw him in a single aspect. Augustus John (Tedlock, 1960, pp. 22–28, *passim*) in a sense never took the man seriously, but saw him as "possessed" entirely by "The Lord of Laughter, the Elemental Clown . . . " Edith Sitwell (Rolph, 1956, p. xiv) remembers his "warmth, charm, funniness," and his love for humanity. "I do not for a moment deny that he sometimes 'went wild,' " asserts Miss Sitwell, "but I, personally, never saw him behave in any way unbecoming a great poet . . . " Roy Campbell, the poet and rather right-wing British patriot, best shows Thomas's talent for appearing as all things to all men. Thomas earned Campbell's undying respect and gratitude by befriending him during the late thirties, when he was ostracized by the reigning group of leftist writers. Campbell (Tedlock, 1960, p. 45) remembers the poet as "a deeply religious and great-hearted man who put love and friendship before everything else." Elsewhere, writing of Thomas during the war years (Campbell, 1954, p. 27), he asserts that "the army lost a good soldier and a grand comrade when Dylan failed in his 'medical' "—an astounding statement, considering what is known of Thomas's attitudes toward the war and his frantic efforts to evade the draft.

Complicating the already complex picture of the poet as child, bohemian, joker, pub brawler, henpecked husband, and boon companion is Thomas's apparent tendency toward self-dramatization.

From early youth the writer's health had been uncertain although, paradoxically, he was also in a small way an athlete and treasured in his wallet a clipping about his victory, at the age of twelve, in a Swansea grammar school mile race. Certainly Thomas had a kind of pluck and an endurance that amazed Brinnin in 1951; nevertheless, he apparently was something of a hypochondriac as well. Fitz-Gibbon (1965, p. 21) says:

Dylan himself talked with hyperbolic gusto about his ill health, past and present. For him a cold in the head was pleurisy, flu pneumonia, and every hangover incipient DT's. He told me, for instance, and as early as 1937, that he had had cirrhosis of the liver as a child; and, in his early days, his tuberculosis, the occasional spitting of blood, and the belief that he had only a short time to live provided a favourite conversational theme.

Obviously, this sort of physical morbidity is translated into the characteristic dwelling upon decay and death in Thomas's early poetry. Ralph Maud (*Poet in the Making*, 1968, pp. 34–37) cites a letter to Miss Johnson in late 1933, in which Thomas claims that his doctor gives him four more years to live; during the same period his father was undergoing treatment for cancer of the throat. Maud has the impression that while Thomas's verse does take a morbid turn at this point, it is also quite consciously "literary." The fact that he probably believed in his own ill health certainly did not prevent him from exploiting it for his own purposes—to gain attention, awe, sympathy, and special treatment, and to reinforce the image of the hard-living, doomed romantic poet. Rayner Heppenstall (*Four Absentees*, 1960, p. 95) recalls a walk to a pub with Thomas during which the poet coughed and spat, exclaiming, "Blood, boy! That's the stuff!" Somewhat later Heppenstall (p. 96) remembers him sighing, with a sort of self-conscious world-weariness, "O God, I'm so tired of sleeping with women I don't even like." Read (1964, p. 79) quotes a friend of the poet: he was "a bit in love with the traditional idea of the Young Poet with V.D., or the Young Poet with T.B."

But beyond any posing, Thomas evidently had some degree of real anticipation of early death, balanced only by his strong and—up to the last—justifiable confidence that he would somehow muddle through each disaster. In 1935 (Stanford, *Dylan Thomas*, 1964, p. 7) Thomas told R. B. Marriott, "I shall be dead within two years." "More than once," says A. T. Davies (*Dylan: Druid of the Broken Body*, 1964, p. 64, n.3) "he mentioned to me his premonition of an early death." Writing after his death, the poet's wife Caitlin (1957, p. 6) berates herself: "Dylan and dying, Dylan and dying. They don't go together; or is it that they were bound to go together; he said so often enough, but I did not heed him." And this, claims Fitz-Gibbon (1965, p. 227), is sufficient proof of Thomas's sincere belief, ". . . for he was far too sensitive and sensible to play-act in front of Caitlin and to her, too, he said repeatedly that he would not live till forty."

Still, there was a further element in his psychological stance toward death: he enjoyed, in a childlike way, frightening himself with real or imagined horrors. David Daiches (Tedlock, 1960, p. 59) describes seeing him off at the airport as he boarded a plane headed for the Western portion of his U.S. trip. " 'Westward into the night,' he said. 'I feel frightened. I don't think I shall ever come back. Perhaps I shall die in Utah.' " Daiches remembers Thomas as "sleepy and lost, deliberately frightening himself with melodramatic pictures of the lonely terrors of the West."

So much for Thomas's role-playing. The question remains, what needs and mechanisms drove him to such behavior? FitzGibbon (1965, p. 18) suggests that the cultural isolation of Wales encouraged Thomas to indulge his striking personality: "In 1931 it was much easier to be quite unself-consciously idiosyncratic in the Uplands than in Bloomsbury." His tendency to become a "character" was naturally fostered by his grammar school experience with acting and his early passion for the movies. Derek Stanford (1964, p. 19), on the other hand, believes that Thomas's "dionysian *alter-ego*" only flowered after his arrival in London, and "that it was, in fact, something which strategy demanded—Thomas's designed reaction to his removal from Wales." In this contention he is supported by Thomas's famous humorous essay "How to Be a Poet" *(QEOM)*, where he describes "the Provincial Rush, or the Up-Rimbaud-and-At-Em approach." Further, Thomas undeniably reaped some material benefits from appearing to each friend to be the person that friend would wish him to be. This, and his ability to make friends with incredible rapidity—what Ruthven Todd called "instant Dylan"—might lead one to suspect a degree of calculation in the poet's personal relationships. John Davenport, one of Thomas's models for the "Toughish Boy" pose, argues (Tedlock, 1960, p. 74) that one of the poet's motivations for public dissimulation was not only mercenary, but racial: "he concealed his total contempt of his idiotic patrons with the centuries-old skill of the Celt faced with the Saxon."

But there are three main objections to explanations of the man's behavior which portray him as a Machiavellian exploiter of his friends and his situation. First, while he was indeed his own best publicist, he was also far too erratic, unreliable, and in fact self-destructive to take advantage of anyone or anything very efficiently; and this is assuming—what is apparent only in hindsight—that Thomas's chosen facade *would* be effective in the long run. Secondly, his role-playing seemed to stem from deep psychological needs and was in fact part of a complex of total behavior which, while it had its own sort of coherence, was certainly not particularly rational. And finally we have from Thomas's friends and acquaintances—even, occasionally, from his enemies—truly overwhelming testimony to the man's fundamental friendliness, honesty, shyness, and innocence. Glyn Jones (1968, p. 202) recalls:

that after years of a quite unusual amount of praise and petting he remained natural, approachable and unspoilt . . . He was without malice, greed or pettiness. I do not think he ever hated anyone or held anyone cheaply, or tried to do anyone down. I remember also his devotion to his parents, especially his steady sympathy and concern for his sick and frustrated father.

The main elements of the dark side of his personality are well enough known. He was perpetually in debt and perpetually "borrowing" money, lodgings, even shirts from friends and strangers alike. Yet, particularly toward the end of his life, he could spend enormous sums of money in an unbelievably short time and have nothing left to show for it. He drank heavily through most of his adult life—although not, it should be added, when he was working, and seldom as heavily as on his American tours. He was notoriously unreliable; when he did meet an obligation he was always late. Or not *always*: he was unreliable even in his unreliability. Derek Stanford (1957, p. 207) recalls that during an American visit Thomas surprised everyone by showing up on time at a suburban lady's home to give a small private reading; after a professional and charming delivery, he was suddenly violently sick on the hearth.

His behavior at parties was, at the least, unusual. Geoffrey Grigson claims (Brinnin, 1960, p. 261) that even early in his career Thomas was capable of spoiling a party, insulting people randomly, and telling the celebrants "dirty chestnuts they had all heard in their childhood." FitzGibbon (1965, p. 131) rebuts this, pointing out that Grigson was not in attendance at the party he discusses, and that the partygoers themselves remember no such behavior. Stanford (1964, pp. 12–13) cites, without contradiction, Rosalind Wade's memories of an early party Thomas attended:

whatever the reason, the sight of the placid guests, relaxed and be-
nign after a good dinner, roused in him emotions of intense hostility.
He attacked everything and everybody, interlarding his comments
with any and every swear word.

Yet, Wade adds, "if he had hoped to disrupt the atmosphere of the
party he was disappointed."

Evidently, evidences of direct rudeness, such as this, are more
characteristic of the poet's early Rimbaldian phase than of his "mature" personality, when he was more likely to offend through
boisterousness or erotic advances. This last behavior pattern, the
womanizing, was naturally most obvious in the American tours
when he was not accompanied by his wife. Although no one could
claim that Thomas remained always the most faithful husband,
most of his flirtations were apparently just that and as Brinnin asserts (1955, p. 76) were not supposed to be taken seriously. Tindall
(1962, p. 290) recalls:

When I first met him at a party, he looked like, and acted the part of,
an amorous Volkswagen, driven by Harpo Marx. Chasing the girls
round the room, he blew down their dickies. Everyone, wives and
husbands alike, took this in good part, except John Malcolm Brinnin,
who sat frowning in a corner . . . It was plain, moreover, that the
harmless poet, doing his best, was doing what he thought was expected of him or else was hiding shyness under what he thought was
its opposite.

The sort of armchair psychoanalyzing that Tindall does here
casually and inoffensively seems irresistible to Thomas commentators. Nearly everyone has observed that Thomas acted irresponsibly because he felt guilty, or boisterously because he was shy, or
amorously because he was afraid of women; and probably there is
some truth in such cheap pronouncements. Apart from the occasionally revealing insights into Thomas's personality which can be
found scattered throughout the main biographical sources, there are
two major attempts to explain the poet's psyche. The first of these,
a sympathetic treatment, is by a practicing psychoanalyst, Dr. B.
W. Murphy; the second, a negative assessment, is by the critic
David Holbrook.

Murphy, who is apparently an orthodox Freudian, discusses
Thomas's case in an article in the *British Journal of Medical Psychology* (1968) entitled "Creation and Destruction: Notes on Dylan Thomas." His diagnosis:

Nosologically he can best be considered as suffering from a character neurosis, with increasing depression, dangerous alcoholic acting
out, tormenting worry, progressive creative inhibitions, indicating a
state of neurotic helplessness. Powerless in the grip of the repetition
compulsion, he was unable to direct his affairs in adaptive effort . . .

"Few," Murphy observes, "have manifested neurosis in a fashion
more baroque than Dylan Thomas" (p. 152).

Murphy relies upon three main sources for his interpretation of
the man's neurosis: an insightful *New Yorker* article by the poet
Howard Moss (1967, p. 188), who observes that "something compulsive seems to have lurked behind his difficulties in handling
money, in meeting commitments, in living up to promises"; Colin
Edwards's taped interview with Thomas's mother, which Murphy
feels shows her misleading air of "confidence based on denial of
painful realities . . . her inability to know her complex son and failure
to recognize her own lack of understanding" (p. 150); and upon a
personal letter from Thomas's friend Sir Herbert Read, who writes,

Dylan was a frightened youth who found it difficult to accept his
great gifts and feel equal to his celebrated peers. A great deal of this
came from lack of formal education: he just never learned how to
handle intellectuals . . . They knew they were his inferiors but *he*
didn't (p. 154).

This last observation—not a particularly Freudian one—is seconded by numerous sources. Shapiro called him (Brinnin, 1960, p.
177) "a tremendous talent who stung himself into insensibility because he could not face the obligations of intellectual life, which he
mistakenly felt he must." Many have commented on the discom-
fort he seemed to experience discussing "literary" matters; Hans
Meyerhoff (1955, p. 17) evokes the poet's "ill-concealed disdain
and suppressed anger" as he read through his notes on other poets,
before his assumption of an air of ease and power when he began to
read the poetry itself. And his adverse critic Grigson (Brinnin,
1960, p. 261) sees Thomas's degeneration as the outward sign of
the poet's recognition that he "was being compelled to live beyond
his spiritual or intellectual income—or capital."

On the other hand, most writers agree that, given his early sense
of the poetic vocation, his lack of aptitude for conventional scholarship, and his anticipation of early death, Thomas had little choice.
He concentrated all of his attention and energy upon poetry, and as
his childhood friend Dan Jones remarks (Tedlock, 1960, p. 18),

he would have needed twice the time to accomplish all that he did accomplish had he not discerned clearly and from the beginning the things that were of no use to him, or if he had not steadily ignored them.

"A man who is about to be hanged next week," adds FitzGibbon (1965, p. 44), "will not start to learn Chinese."

But to return to Murphy's analysis: he sees Thomas as a man tormented by unconscious guilt and perpetually punishing himself through his own improvidence and irresponsibility, much as Dostoevski did. Thomas, he claims, suffered from a profound *oral fixation* and a severe *castration fear*. One of the concomitants of an oral fixation is the tendency to regard others as food or as purveyors of nurture. One recalls Eberhart's famous comment upon hosting Thomas (Tedlock, 1960, p. 56): "I had to (and was delighted to) get him up in the morning by plugging his mouth with a bottle of beer, this wonderful baby." (Eberhart has also recalled to me, in conversation, the incident of Thomas staring at a plunging neckline during a party and announcing, "I would rather suckle at those breasts than go back to my old wife in Wales.")

Murphy points out that, while Thomas was indeed capable of mature, successful achievement, his very success mobilized the anxiety and guilt which manifested in various forms his regression to oral fixation—drinking, smoking, and general greed. The poet's work is full of phrases like "butterfat goosegirls," "breasts full of honey," and of images of animals devouring one another, culminating in the all-devouring worm. These Murphy sees as instances of oral sadism (p. 157). Oral regression in the face of general anxiety can be seen clearly in *Adventures in the Skin Trade* or the story "One Warm Saturday." Even the poet's early intrauterine poems can be seen as a disguised breast fantasy, while his preoccupation with early death may represent a wish for the sleep which follows an infant's feeding.

Murphy sees Thomas's castration anxiety as surfacing throughout his work: he cites in particular the story "A Prospect of the Sea" and the poem "All all and all the dry worlds lever." He notes (p. 160) that according to Read a lover reported Thomas to be timid, furtive, and inhibited. The poet used as defenses against phallic conflicts "denial, regression, counter-phobic activity, and the assumption of castrated roles, e.g., the clown."

Thomas himself told Harvey Breit in 1950 (Brinnin, 1960, p. 195): "Success is bad for me. I should be what I was . . . twenty years ago. Then I was arrogant and lost. Now I am humble and found. I prefer that other." Murphy feels (p. 162) that the poet would alternate between a hedonistic identification with his indulgent mother and a guilty, self-destructive identification with his misanthropic father. The unresolved Oedipal conflict—with an assist from his puritanical Nonconformist religious background—led to a need to punish himself, particularly when faced with the sort of success he found in later life. The poet's "public roles of clown, buffoon, drunkard, raconteur, and lecher were compulsively assumed," states Murphy (p. 153), and though his poetry allowed him to "work out" some of his tensions, it could never be sufficiently curative: "Although alcohol was a major cause, Dylan Thomas died of his neurosis" (p. 165).

If one accepts a Freudian view of art, the interpretation is convincing enough, although it does not, of course, explain the poetry itself, nor does it explain the particular dynamics of Thomas's life, e.g., his outburst of creativity following the war. Less convincing, and less sympathetic, is David Holbrook's series of writings on the poet. His first book on Thomas was published in England in 1962 as *Llareggub Revisited: Dylan Thomas and the State of Modern Poetry* and in America in 1964 as *Dylan Thomas and Poetic Dissociation*. Holbrook's thesis is that Thomas is a "schizoid" poet, whose popularity reflects our schizoid modern culture. The poet, he feels, never made the Oedipal break, thus leading to "a poetry of dissociated phantasy" (1964, p. 9). His writing involves us in a "disarmed acceptance of a morbid obsession with 'bad' elements of reality, at the expense of the whole and wholesome" (p. 13). Karl Menninger is invoked on alcoholism: the alcoholic characteristically takes in a magical substance with his mouth, and may become aggressive. This is reflected in the "babble-quality" of the man's verse and its magical attitude toward reality. Again, like the typical alcoholic, Thomas's great show of heterosexuality masked a great fear of women and of heterosexuality in general (p. 15). We may gather that Thomas's epigrammatic pronouncements, such as "first, I am a Welshman. Second, I am a drunkard. Third, I am a heterosexual," or his claim that he had come to New York "to continue my lifelong pursuit of naked women in wet mackintoshes," are instances of protesting overmuch.

Holbrook points to the flaws of character which most observers found in the poet, and finds their reflection in the poetry. Thomas is obsessed with himself, and so Holbrook feels that—even in the famous tribute to Ann Jones or the "Refusal to Mourn"—the poet is unable to empathize with or to evoke convincingly anyone outside himself. The religious sequence of poems "Vision and Prayer" can only be addressed to "God the Thomas" (p. 50). Holbrook unerringly locates the soft underbelly of Thomas criticism when he points out that Elder Olson, a sympathetic critic, finds the poet

verbose, strained, obscure, sentimental, apt to excite himself unnecessarily, able to write better than he did, lacking in the outflow of sympathy toward others, and essentially self-centered. But he does not see these as serious objections to the poet's being considered as a significant poet (p. 60).

Many reviewers, like John Wain (1965, p. 15), characterized Holbrook's book as "bad-tempered and envious priggery." "Holbrook sounds," notes Paul West (1967, p. 936) "like a cosmic headmaster writing little Thomas's school report." But Conor Cruise O'Brien (1965, p. 14) is probably fairer when he calls it admittedly "priggish and uncouth" but also "honest and courageous." The more interesting question is why Holbrook, who feels Thomas's moral stance is dangerous and finds that his poetry unhealthily "erects barriers and fosters dissociation," should still be so obviously fascinated by the man and his work. Tindall's comment (1962, p. 11)—"Unable to follow the more formidable poems, one critic wrote a book to express his inability"—is not really illuminating.

Holbrook's second book on the subject, entitled *Dylan Thomas: The Code of Night* (1972), is a great improvement, at least in tone. Since reading Thomas's *Letters* and the *Notebooks* edited by Ralph Maud, Holbrook has altered his estimate of the seriousness of the poet's endeavor. Perhaps more important, he has abandoned the vaguely Freudian psychological terminology of the earlier book in order to embrace existential psychoanalysis in general, the work of Harry Guntrip, and that of theoreticians of "object relationships" such as D. W. Winnicott. Holbrook makes further gestures in the direction of Buber, Binswanger, and Merleau-Ponty, and makes considerable use of R. D. Laing's study of schizophrenia, *The Divided Self*.

In *The Code of Night*, Holbrook argues (p. 4) that "because he had not been sufficiently 'confirmed' in that first 'meeting' by the 'creative reflection' of the mother, [Thomas] forever after sought to enlist others in confirming his confused identity, by getting them to supply him with some kind of self." Here he is working from Winnicott's idea of a primary existential confrontation between mother and child, wherein the child originally takes his sense of *being* from her; later, the child is normally "disillusioned," and is forced to develop a sense of separate identity. For Thomas, the process was never completed: the mother, who (Holbrook postulates) identified him with an earlier child who had died in the womb, failed to "be for" Thomas, and could only "do for" him. Further, she never "disillusioned" him, so that he never developed a sense of true being. Thus Thomas's schizoid patterns of behavior.

Holbrook argued in an earlier article (1968, p. 39) that such a sense of nothingness leads to false "strong" posturings such as the poet often assumed, and also to self-destructive, even suicidal behavior. The schizoid subject seeks a kind of death in order that he may be reborn, this time "for real." Here he argues (p. 147) that the man's cruelty to his wife and his promiscuity can be seen as a rejection of what he saw as a weak, "female" element in himself. The obscurity of his poetry came about because, although (p. 6) Thomas "devised a 'code of night' to 'strip off the darkness' and 'make clean' the heart of being," he also "seems deliberately to have sought to create and preserve chaos in his work" because he feared the integration which coherent work might have brought him. His schizoid need was "to *preserve chaos in self-defense* against the dangers of integration."

Almost grotesquely, Holbrook asserts (p. 19) that the effort of critics—including himself—to explicate the poet's darkest passages arises from one's subliminal recognition that Thomas is crying out for someone—the reader—to "be for" him, thus making the explication a kind of transferred act of mothering, or for male critics a kind of *couvade*. Though he still sees Thomas as dangerous, he now sees the poetry as a heroic achievement of art out of anguish. Thomas, he now admits, was "sensitive, intelligent, and painstaking," (p. 66) and "it is very little credit to his [Holbrook's own] former study that he tried to deny this."

The book is weakest, Holbrook admits, when he offers (p. 40) "very extravagant conjecture" as to D. J.'s motivations in naming his son Dylan, for example, or when he states programmatically (p. 183) that "when [Thomas] seems to be identifying with Christ we can read the poem as if he were writing about himself and the 'other'—the dead sibling with whom his mother confused him." Holbrook's view of what poetry ought to be still seems overly matter-of-fact. When he quotes Laing (p. 209) to support his view that a particular poem is written from a "schizoid feeling about reality" ("The self can relate with immediacy to an object which is the object of its own imagination or memory"), one wonders whether his suppositions allow for any distinction at all between schizophrenia and the poetic process. He quotes (p. 220) Tindall's passage about the amorous Volkswagen and is appalled, muttering about the "American *avant-garde* . . . ethos of schizoid dissociation." An essential humorlessness betrays him when he gives an extended deadpan reading of "Lament," arguing that the poem displays a horrifying schizoid inversion of values ("all the *deadly virtues* plague my death"); he does the same thing for *Under Milk Wood* in a chapter entitled "Laughing Delightedly at Hate."

Personality and Experience

Although Murphy and Holbrook are the two major Thomas psychoanalysts, a number of valuable comments, springing from no particular analytic framework, are scattered throughout the main biographical sources and the numerous reminiscences in periodicals. Relatively little attention has been paid to the particular social, historical, and economic situation into which Thomas was born and in which he lived, if only because his work and his personality struck so many observers as anomalous, eccentric, and original. Unlike poets of the Pound-Eliot axis or the Spender-Auden group which succeeded them, he seems less a product of his age than a living commentary upon it, bringing out the essential sameness of many of the literary and philosophical attitudes which surrounded him. "Most writers today," he commented in a *Sunday Referee* interview (Dec. 30, 1934, p. 3), "move about in gangs. They haven't the strength to stand and fight as individuals."

Of course one aspect of Thomas's immediate situation—his Welsh environment and inheritance—*has* been discussed at some length, notably by John Ackerman (1964), but this topic will be explored in a later chapter. Like most such critics, Ackerman discusses the poet within the context of a broad, almost amorphous cultural inheritance. But Thomas Taig (1968, pp. 23–27) points more specifically to the atmosphere in which Thomas first discovered himself as artist. Swansea between the wars was "still sufficiently small and cohesive to form one community," a mixture of classes freely mingling with one another. Thomas, performing with the Swansea Little Theatre group or heatedly reading and discussing poetry with a group of friends at Bert Trick's house, first articulated his ideas about art and life within the context of this community. There was a sense of discovery shared among artists there at the time—in Taig's opinion, a discovery of the older values of the culture. The special quality of this intellectual atmosphere was "connected with the fusion of the present and past on the one hand and on the other a direct contact, a kind of short-circuit, between the sense-world and the spirit . . . " Writing from a more formal social perspective, Geoffrey Moore (Tedlock, 1960, p. 262) argues that the poet's class background *did* emerge in his poetry. Swansea during his youth underwent a period of industrial depression which necessarily left its mark on the minds of its less wealthy inhabitants. Thomas knew directly, as his immediate environment, the factories and the slums which Auden and Company felt ought to be a modern writer's subject. But Moore admits that "these things are casual but nevertheless vital references in a poetry which is devoted to another end."

Certainly there were enough social differences between Swansea and the London in which Thomas soon found himself to give the poet a sense of cultural vertigo. As Jones points out (1966, p. 8), "Thomas belonged to a community, not a class; and this in itself was enough to set him apart from the English 'public-school' poets of the 1930's." On the other hand, Thomas, knowing himself to be an outsider in Bloomsbury, was, according to Edouard Roditi (1960, p. 429) "deeply class-conscious, in a curiously British way." Tindall (1962, p. 5) agrees with this assessment, asserting with American insouciance that much of the opposition to Thomas—and his own frequent social and intellectual uneasiness—stemmed from the fact that Thomas came from the lower-middle class. Yet the Welsh too are snobbish, observes FitzGibbon (1965, p. 7), though in a different way from the British: "they judge a man for what he is, for what he himself has made of his life."

Naturally this Nonconformist success-ethic can also be devastating, and Thomas the bohemian must often have felt more at home in the subculture of Soho than in Swansea. "Land of my fathers," he once intoned (FitzGibbon, 1965, p. 11), "and my fathers can keep it." His wife Caitlin (1957, pp. 12–13) certainly blames much of their unhappiness on the "sly, keen, prodding-fingered, always counting-the-cost Welsh," whose abiding motive is fear: fear of the neighbor's opinion, of sickness, and of their own inner selves. Yet clearly Caitlin suffered more in Wales than did her husband, for (p. 35) "he was much better than me at contenting himself with the very simple, I might justly say moronic, life." Further, Thomas may naturally have had more in common with his neighbors than did Caitlin. Most visitors remarked his air of ease and confidence around his rural countrymen.

"No blue-blooded gentleman was a quarter as gentlemanly as Dylan's father," she remarks (pp. 56–57), and the poet was not so emancipated from his family's values as he liked to believe. "There was a very strong puritanical streak in him, that his friends never suspected; but of which I got the disapproving benefit." John Mal-

colm Brinnin (1955, p. 263) recalls Thomas's disgusted reaction to
a couple they observed necking in a bar, and his subsequent comment, "I *am* a Puritan!" Surely Thomas himself was ambivalent
about the values of his background. Much of his behavior could be
traced to a general sense of not-belonging. At a conference of Scottish writers, he claimed (P. West, 1967, p. 923) to be "regarded in
England as a Welshman . . . and in Wales as an Englishman."

Thomas was born at the commencement of the First World War
and lived through the harrowing bombing of London during the
second. Tindall (1962, p. 70) suggests that his wartime birth may
have contributed to the writer's characteristic coupling of birth and
death. And even if, as Jones observes (1963, p. 59), "his few war
poems were obstinately and magnificently civilian," World War II
nevertheless affected him immediately and personally. He wrote
very little between 1941 and 1945. His sister-in-law Nicolette Devas (*Two Flamboyant Fathers*, 1966, p. 239) often housed Thomas
and his wife during the bombings, and testifies to his intense agita-
tion. During the raids he would characteristically wrap himself in an
eiderdown quilt and lie moaning and cursing in a corner of the cel-
lar. "It did not seem funny at the time," Devas observes. The next
morning he invariably emerged smiling and joking. Perhaps this
explains Roy Campbell's assertion (1954, p. 26) that, despite the
bombings, Dylan and Caitlin "never lost their wonderful zest and
good humour."

Others take a more serious view of the man's experience of war.
Despite Thomas's extreme reluctance to join the war effort, Fitz-
Gibbon (1965, p. 258) describes his intense disorientation when he
was rejected by the army on physical grounds. Taig (1968, p. 29)
pictures his friend on the day war was declared as "distraught and
for once almost speechless at the news . . . I sensed that he was suffering acutely in advance . . . all the horrors of the coming slaugh-
ter." Walford Davies (*Dylan Thomas*, 1972, p. 52) says that
Thomas reacted to the war with the "profound moral shock" which
resonates through poems of that period such as "There was a Saviour," "Deaths and Entrances," or the "Refusal to Mourn." Rayner Heppenstall (1960, p. 151) found a distinct, major personality
change in the poet upon meeting him in 1939. He had grown suddenly fat and, "no longer taking a stand against the war, he yet
seemed prey to some large resentment. He was unable to write. He
was hard up . . ." Heppenstall feels (p. 186), perhaps unfairly, that
Thomas's later behavior and attitudes depended upon the fact that,
about the age of forty, he was "confronted *for the first time* by the
notion that anything really unpleasant could happen to him."

Another major external circumstance which affected Thomas—
comparable in subjective intensity, if not in absolute magnitude, to
World War II—was his marriage to Caitlin. Caitlin Thomas was an
overwhelming personality in her own right, a dedicated, unconventional taster of life who in the poet's last years flirted with madness.
It is as difficult to account for Thomas without his wife as to imagine
Scott Fitzgerald without Zelda. Like Zelda, Caitlin had artistic am-
bitions and so, as with the Fitzgeralds, there were professional as
well as personal tensions and jealousies between the Thomases.

Observers differ vastly in their estimate of the effect of his marriage upon the poet. Most of his close friends and most reliable biog-
raphers—notably FitzGibbon and (with reservations) Brinnin—are
agreed that, despite the violent quarrels and physical abuse that were
so evident in the fabric of their life together, Dylan was painfully
in love with his wife, as she was with him (see, e.g., Brinnin, 1955,
p. 77; Campbell in Tedlock, 1960, p. 45; FitzGibbon, 1965, p. 185).
Caitlin's sister explains (Devas, 1966, p. 197):

It was the very passion of their love for each other which provoked
the violence, when they literally beat each other up with considerable
damage on both sides . . . any suffering it might cause them was quite
ordinary, like bickering to other couples. In effect, their rows were
an urgent form of self-expression . . . [of] feelings stronger than the
average person's . . .

Devas, like FitzGibbon, asserts that Caitlin's fury was directed
against Thomas only when she felt he was being untrue to his real
self, the poet. When her husband actually *had* to meet a final deadline, she would physically lock him in his room until he had completed the assignment. Thomas apparently recognized the necessity
of this procedure and was unworried by it.

But at least one writer, Evelyn Broy (1965–66, p. 504), traces
many of Thomas's later problems to his wife. His sexual relationship
with Caitlin, Broy speculates, must have been unsatisfactory, particularly since the poet attached a transcendent value to the sex act.
Finding he could not achieve transcendence through her, in dis-
appointment he attached inverted associations of decay and gro-
tesqueness to sexuality. Broy claims Thomas was anguished over
his wife's real or imagined infidelities, and points to the poem "I
make this in a warring absence" as evidence. Even the poet's suicide,
Broy suggests (p. 507), was the result of his frustrated love for a
vicious woman: "it might be said that he cut off his life to spite his
love."

Jack Lindsay (1966, p. 54–55) takes a more complex view of Thomas's sexuality, and is more ambivalent in his attitude toward Caitlin. "Dylan's love of life had to struggle every moment of the day and night in order to keep ahead or even abreast of his pursuing fear of death." His numerous attempts at seduction were his way of seeking an affirmation of life through human contact, but at the same time the wombs in which he sought solace were to him demanding, devouring places which reaffirmed his essential despair. Central to his attraction to and fear of women was his love-hate relationship with Caitlin. Lindsay, like Broy, sees a fear of his wife's betraying him as an important motive in Thomas, and points to the poem "Ballad of the Long-legged Bait" as illustration.

Lindsay goes on to tackle another major problem of the man's behavior, his compulsive petty thefts from wealthier friends. Fitz-Gibbon (1965, p. 198) documents this accusation, but does little to explain it. Lindsay (p. 58) suggests that "through his thefts . . . he got rid of his sense of inferiority by a demonstration that he looked on a patron as a mere instrument for his own convenience." More philosophically, Jacob Korg (1966, p. 283) notes that the writer's perpetual "borrowings" reflect his poetic practice of borrowing attributes from the animate and attaching them to the inanimate—"gilled stones," for example. Both practices are means of showing "the participation of all things in one another's existence." Like a mystic or a child, Thomas was no more really capable of feeling the distinction between "mine" and "his" than he was of showing in his poetry any boundary between himself and the world about him.

Perhaps all of Dylan Thomas's character traits stand out in such sharp relief because no matter what he did, he refused to employ half-measures. This resolution extended equally to his life and to his work; as FitzGibbon (1965, p. 202) observes, he had to be the *poorest* man, the *last* in his class, the *drunkest* partygoer in the same way he had to be the best poet. Indeed, he had an uncanny knack of living "on the edge" by imposing his imagination upon reality, not only in the roles he assumed, but in his very surroundings. Lawrence Durrell (Tedlock, 1960, p. 39) recalls an almost surrealist evening of pub-crawling with his Welsh friend, who "seemed to attract to him everything that was fantastic and unreal in the air about him." People in general seemed to sense that, if Thomas lived by special rules, it was because he inhabited a special world, and the poet's secondary genius was in allowing his acquaintances to share that world for as long as they shared his company.

Since much of the foregoing discussion has focused upon the Welsh writer's weaknesses and less endearing qualities, this may be

an appropriate point at which to stress the abundance of fine qualities which were at his disposal. As Stanford reminds us (1964, p.
16), people tend to forget that the man behind the self-generated
myth was "as modest, simple, affectionate, and tolerant as his bardic
alter-ego was arrogant and incorrigible." Numerous stories testify
to his essential timidity and shyness, which he perpetually disguised
with false bravado. Behind the role-playing, Thomas radiated a sort
of authenticity, an uncompromising honesty. "Thomas was an actor," says Louis MacNeice (Tedlock, 1960, p. 87), "but he was
not an attitudiniser." Certainly he never attempted to sustain the
"literary" pose: as Fraser (1964, p. 185) wittily phrases it, "meeting
Dylan Thomas was less like meeting Verlaine or Dowson than like
meeting Mr. Tony Hancock or Mr. Danny Kaye."

Conversation is the most transient of art forms. We have no way
of sharing the experience of the circle around Lytton Strachey and
Virginia Woolf, say, or Oscar Wilde, much less that of Dr. Johnson. Something of the power of Thomas's readings remains in the
recordings, but his talk—the mimicry, the timing, the reporter's
striking accuracy of detail, and especially the "wild, wilful, beautiful, buffoonish verbal exaggeration" (Tedlock, 1960, p. 82)—are
gone. The man's talk was usually all that was necessary to make con-
verts of the most antipathetic audience. Kingsley Amis (1970(p.
58), incidentally, was a rare exception. On first meeting Thomas in
a pub, he heard him deliver what was doubtless a prepared epigram—"I've just come back from Persia, where I've been pouring
water on troubled oil"—and reacted with sullen distaste. He did,
however, find a place for the episode in his novel, *Lucky Jim*. Amis
was almost converted by Thomas's reading, later at the university,
but observes (p. 60): "Although obviously without all charlatanry,
he did here and there sound or behave like a charlatan." Yet Amis
ends the article by berating himself for not realizing that what he
had taken for sullenness or disinterest on Thomas's part was really
the result of his shyness and unease in a university community.

And this, perhaps, exemplifies the fundamental reason Thomas's
figure continues to haunt the modern imagination: even in those
he offended, Thomas brought out a desire to explain, rationalize, or
excuse his behavior. If he offended on a basic level, he also appealed
on a basic level. If meeting Dylan was a novel experience, as Jack
Lindsay testifies (1966, p. 48), "you left him with the conviction
that you had known him for years." Some reacted simply and positively to the encounter. FitzGibbon (1965, p. 340) quotes Stravinsky as saying, "As soon as I saw him I knew that the only thing to
do was to love him." Others reacted more ambivalently. Nelson

Algren (Maud, 1970, p. 194) realized, "I had been with a great man, the only great man I had ever known," but "I had also been with a babyishly self-indulgent fellow carrying too much weight for his size. He was like a child who has discovered that it can have its own way by threatening a tantrum."

Just as the metaphor of the child runs throughout Thomas's writing, it is the ground bass of writings about him. As almost everyone has observed, the poet's personal failings and his best qualities were closely related: if he could be childish, in the pejorative sense, he could also be childlike in the purest sense. Edith Sitwell's introduction to Rolph's bibliography (Rolph, 1956, p. xii) is entitled "The Young Dylan Thomas:" "And so he remained, to the last day when I saw him," she begins. His childhood friend Vernon Watkins (1957, p. 13) mentions his "first impression of a rooted obstinacy, which was really a rooted innocence . . ." Thomas's personality embraced all the allotropes of youth. Even his public sexuality often seemed merely a pose to disguise a certain spiritual virginity—and in fact FitzGibbon hypothesizes (1965, p. 85) that "if he was not a virgin when he left Swansea for London, he was the next best thing."

Certainly Thomas's taste for sensationalism, his self-dramatization, was related to the mythos of the perpetual child. "An element of adolescent excitement-worship had its place in Thomas," says Stanford (1964, p. 15), and adds that he was (pp. 28–29) "always—in the end—lovable . . . Beneath his saloon panache there lurked a childlike innocence." T. H. Jones claims that the poet's social extravagances have the same explanation (1966, p. 56):

Thomas was never, as some people thought, a *naif* as far as poetry was concerned; but in many respects, as far as society, especially metropolitan society, was concerned, he remained a *naif* all his life . . .

Certainly Thomas capitalized upon the special, "exempt" social status of the child or adolescent in order to encourage others to take care of him, even when he was perfectly capable of fending for himself. "Like almost everyone else who came close to Dylan," observes Brinnin (1955, p. 40), "I assumed that he was far more helpless than actually he was." Again, his status as pseudo-child allowed him to criticize, with childlike bluntness, the faults which he saw in those around him. His friend Norman Cameron wrote a poem which FitzGibbon quotes (1965, p. 166) about this aspect of the poet. Cameron begins by asking, "Who invited him in? What was he doing here, that insolent little ruffian . . . ," goes on to describe the way in which the "dirty little accuser" would by his own actions parody his hosts' failings, describes throwing him out of the house, and concludes:

> Yet there's this check on our righteous jubilation:
> Now that the little accuser is gone, of course,
> we shall never be able to answer his accusation.

Finally, of course, there is the aspect of Dylan Thomas as a child from which his later poetry sprung and which must have contributed to his doom. Cid Corman (Maud, 1970, p. 202) has perhaps expressed this most beautifully:

He was, I think, that perpetual child with an ear for ditties and as though completely victimized by that moment when childhood fatefully recognizes, if it refuses to realize, that the world will not hold age back.

Critics disagree over whether Thomas's death resulted from his own recognition that "the term of the roaring boy was over" (Brinnin, 1955, p. 176) and that he had no resources with which to face artistic and personal maturity, or whether on the other hand he was just entering into what would have been his finest work. In any case it is undeniable that the poet's recognition of age, working against his yearning for childhood and his ability to evoke it magically, produced the creative tension of much of his greatest work. But, child or adult, Thomas reserved his stances and poses for those who could see through them, or for those whom he could not respect. A pub-keeper who knew him could only describe him as "a very *humble* man" (Tedlock, 1960, p. 81). The most common word people found to sum up the poet after his death, according to Howard Moss (Brinnin, 1960, p. 290), was "human." The word crystallizes both his distinction and our plight.

It seems unlikely that a man so intensely human, wracked with frustrations, neuroses, flaws and failings, could achieve the impressive body of work Thomas undeniably did achieve; it seems incredible that he could have transformed himself, time and again, into the Poet, speaking with the voice of angels, before the eyes of an audience who had seen him weak, fumbling, and bewildered. But, man and poet, self-transforming, he continually did exactly that. Marjorie Adix (Brinnin, 1960, pp. 288–89) has most poignantly described the phenomenon. Thomas visited a class of students at the

University of Utah in 1952; the beginning of the class, during which
Thomas attempted to respond to students' questions, showed him
as evasive and cryptic, apologetic or flippant. But at last he was asked
to read. He began by talking about his father,

And all at once the little poet began to read, and his voice raged and
surged with power and anger and a terrible desolation. He read "Do
Not Go Gentle into that Good Night." It was slow and rhythmic and
deep. His eyes were bent down on the book, but he was not reading,
for they would remain fixed for a long time and then wander over
both pages for a moment and then freeze again. I can't express how
startling the change was in him, from the shy, humble, apologetic,
patiently eager man, to this tidal wave of humanity. I was uneasy at
first because I felt that in either one position or the other he was only
acting, but I could find no trace of insincerity ever. I suppose he
knows best. He is lots of people.

References

Ackerman, John
   1964. *Dylan Thomas: His Life and Work*. London and New York:
   Oxford Univ. Pr.
Adam
   1953. No. 238, "Dylan Thomas Memorial Number."
Amis, Kingsley
   1970. "Thomas the Rhymer" and "An Evening with Dylan
   Thomas." In *What Became of Jane Austen? And Other Questions*,
   pp. 54–57, 57–62. New York: Harcourt.
Baker, A. T.
   1957. "The Roistering Legend of Dylan Thomas," *Esquire* Dec.,
   pp. 201–9.
Brinnin, John Malcolm
   1955. *Dylan Thomas in America: An Intimate Journal*. Boston:
   Little.
   1960. *A Casebook on Dylan Thomas*. New York: Crowell.
Broy, Evelyn J.
   1965–66. "The Enigma of Dylan Thomas," *Dalhousie Review* Winter, pp. 498–508.
Campbell, Roy
   1954. "Dylan Thomas—The War Years," *Shenandoah* Spring, pp.
   26–27.
Cassill, R. V.
   1956. "The Trial of Two Poets," *Western Review* Spring, pp.
   241–45.
Cox, C. B.
   1966. (editor) *Dylan Thomas: A Collection of Critical Essays*.
   Englewood Cliffs, N.J.: Prentice-Hall.
Davenport, John
   1962. "Patterns of Friendship," *Listener* Jan. 4, pp. 26–27.

Davies, Aneirin Talfan
  1964. *Dylan: Druid of the Broken Body*. London: J. M. Dent.
Davies, Walford
  1972. *Dylan Thomas*. n.p.: Univ. of Wales Pr. (Writers of Wales series).
Devas, Nicolette
  1966. *Two Flamboyant Fathers*. New York: Morrow, 1967.
Dock Leaves
  1954. No. 5, Dylan Thomas Number.
Durrell, Lawrence
  1956. [Letter] *Poetry* March–April, pp. 34–36.
Emery, Clark
  1961. "Two-Gunned Gabriel in London," *Carrell* June, pp. 16–22.
Enright, D. J.
  1966. "Once Below a Time." In *Conspirators and Poets*, pp. 42–47. London: Chatto & Windus.
Firmage, George J., and Oscar Williams
  1963. (editors) *A Garland for Dylan Thomas*. New York: Clarke & Way.
FitzGibbon, Constantine
  1965. *The Life of Dylan Thomas*. Boston: Little.
  1966. (editor) *Selected Letters of Dylan Thomas*. London: J. M. Dent.
  1970. "Dylan Thomas: A Letter," *Dublin Magazine* Vol. 8, No. 3, pp. 56–58.
Fraser, G. S.
  1957. *Dylan Thomas*. London: Longmans, Green (for the British Council).
  1964. "The Legend and the Puzzle," *Times Literary Supplement* March 5, pp. 185–86.
Grubb, Frederick
  1965. *A Vision of Reality: A Study of Liberalism in Twentieth Century Verse*. London: Chatto & Windus.
Heppenstall, Rayner
  1960. *Four Absentees*. London: Barrie & Rockcliff.
Holbrook, David
  1964. *Dylan Thomas and Poetic Dissociation*. Carbondale: Southern Illinois Univ. Pr.
  1968. "R. D. Laing and the Death Circuit," *Encounter* Aug., pp. 34–45.
  1972. *Dylan Thomas: The Code of Night*. London: Athlone Pr.
Hynes, Sam
  1954. "Dylan Thomas: Everybody's Adonais," *Commonweal* March 26, pp. 628–29.
Jones, Glyn
  1968. *The Dragon Has Two Tongues*. London: J. M. Dent.
Jones, T. H.
  1966. *Dylan Thomas*. New York: Barnes & Noble.
Kazin, Alfred
  1957. "Posthumous Life of Dylan Thomas," *Atlantic Monthly* Oct., pp. 164–68.

64 DYLAN THOMAS

Korg, Jacob
1966. "Receptions of Dylan Thomas," *Antioch Review* Summer, pp. 281–88.
Lindsay, Jack
1966. "Memories of Dylan Thomas," *Meanjin* Autumn, pp. 48–75.
Martin, J. H.
1964. [Letter] *Times Literary Supplement* March 19, p. 235.
Maud, Ralph N.
1968. (editor) *Poet in the Making: The Notebooks of Dylan Thomas.* London: J. M. Dent; New York: New Directions, 1967, as *The Notebooks of Dylan Thomas.*
1970. *Dylan Thomas in Print: A Bibliographical History.* Pittsburgh: Univ. of Pittsburgh Pr.
McDonnell, Thomas P.
1958. "Who Killed Dylan?" *Catholic World* July, pp. 285–89.
Meyerhoff, Hans
1955. "The Violence of Dylan Thomas," *New Republic* July 11, pp. 17–19.
Moss, Howard
1967. "A Thin, Curly Little Person," *New Yorker* Oct. 7, pp. 185–89.
Murphy, B. W.
1968. "Creation and Destruction—Notes on Dylan Thomas," *British Journal of Medical Psychology* vol. 41, pp. 149–67.
O'Brien, Conor Cruise
1965. "The Dylan Cult," *New York Review of Books* Dec. 9, pp. 12–14.
Poetry
1955. (Special issue), November.
Pryse-Jones, A. G.
1954. "Death Shall Have No Dominion," *Dock Leaves* Spring, pp. 26–29.
Read, Bill
1964. *The Days of Dylan Thomas* (with photographs by Rollie McKenna and others). New York: McGraw-Hill.
Roditi, Edouard
1960. "London Reunion," *Literary Review* Spring, pp. 425–29.
Rolph, J. Alexander
1956. *Dylan Thomas, A Bibliography* (foreword by Dame Edith Sitwell). London: J. M. Dent.
Saroyan, William
1964. "The Wild Boy," *Saturday Evening Post* Jan. 25, pp. 32–36.
Spender, Stephen
1954. "Greatness of Aim," *Times Literary Supplement* Aug. 6, p. vi.
Stanford, Derek
1957. "Dylan Thomas' Animal Faith," *Southwest Review* Summer, pp. 205–12.
1964. *Dylan Thomas.* Rev. ed. New York: Citadel.
Taig, Thomas
1968. "Swansea Between the Wars," *Anglo-Welsh Review* Summer, pp. 23–32.

Tedlock, Ernest Warnock
   1960. (editor) *Dylan Thomas: The Legend and the Poet*. London: Heinemann.
Thomas, Caitlin
   1957. *Leftover Life to Kill*. Boston: Little.
   1963. *Not Quite Posthumous Letters to My Daughter*. Boston: Little.
Thomas, Dylan
   1966. "Love Letters from a Poet to His Wife," *McCall's* Feb., pp. 73–178.
Tindall, William York
   1962. *A Reader's Guide to Dylan Thomas*. New York: Noonday.
Wain, John
   1965. [Review of Ackerman, Read, and Holbrook], *New York Review of Books* Feb. 25, pp. 12, 14–15.
Watkins, Vernon
   1957. (editor) *Dylan Thomas: Letters to Vernon Watkins*. New York: McGraw-Hill.
   1961. "Behind the Fabulous Curtain," *Poetry* May, pp. 124–25.
West, Anthony
   1955. "A Singer and a Spectre," *New Yorker* Jan. 22, pp. 106–8.
West, Paul
   1967. "Dylan Thomas: The Position in Calamity," *Southern Review* Autumn, pp. 422–43.
Yale Literary Magazine
   1954. (Special issue), November.

Selected Additional Readings

Burgess, Anthony
   1966. "The Writer as Drunk," *Spectator* Nov. 4, pp. 588 (on Thomas and Behan).
Porteus, Hugh Gordon
   1960. "Nights Out in the Thirties," *Spectator* Sept. 2, pp. 342–44.
Todd, Ruthen
   1971. "Dylan Thomas: A Personal Memoir," *Mediterranean Review* Spring, pp. 15–23.
Trick, Bert
   1960. "Dylan—The Eternal Swansea Boy," *Country Quest* Autumn, pp. 26–27.

CHAPTER 4

The Religious Poet

The view of Dylan Thomas as a religious poet has emerged only recently, claimed Thomas Saunders in 1965 (Saunders, 1965–66, p. 494). Perhaps that was true; critics probably were hesitant to commit themselves on such a question while Thomas was so evidently present and able to contradict them. Indeed, many took his bawdy, brawling, anything-but-saintly style of life as contradiction enough. But since his death the problem of religion in Thomas's poetry has emerged as the single most widely debated critical issue. The vast majority of critical discussions at least touch upon Thomas's religion, or lack of it, and two book-length studies centering on that problem were published in 1972.

From this debate little consensus has surfaced. A primary problem is that the word "religious" has acquired nearly the breadth of meaning which the term "mythic" has gathered in critical parlance; two critics may agree that Thomas is indeed a religious poet, but may mean divergent or even contradictory things by that statement. His poetry has been linked with Catholic and with Protestant systems of belief, with Gnosticism and Manichaeism, with a vaguely defined Christianity and with several varieties of pantheism. He has been called a pagan, a mystic, and a humanistic agnostic; his God has been identified with Nature, Sex, Love, Process, the Life Force, and with Thomas himself.

Poetry, Etienne Gilson has written, arises from the same depths as the need to pray. If we approach Thomas from this level of generality it seems clear that there is necessarily something religious about his work. His tone often has the elevation of praise or invocation; he appears to be talking about issues which, if not specifically theological, are at least eschatological. And he does so with an obvious multitude of references to the Christian tradition. The question is not whether religion, or Christianity, is involved in his poetry, because it clearly is; the question is the nature and extent of that involvement. What does it mean to call his poetry "sacramental" and his approach "vatic?" Does Thomas's writing assume a coherent system of religious belief which informs the work, does it show a religious doubt which the work somehow resolves, or does it merely use religious allusions metaphorically or ornamentally? Unfortunately, few commentators address such questions directly.

This problem is complicated by the apparent change or development in the poet's religious attitude as it is manifested in the poems. The "world" of the early poems in many ways differs from that of the later poems, and this change in the poet's orientation may well be reflected in a change in the quality or degree of religious belief characteristic of each stage. Thomas's earlier work alludes to Christianity relatively infrequently; in his "middle period" Christian references abound, within a rather violent context which gives us a feeling of doubt, struggle, and ambiguous resolution; the late poems are much quieter and, while often less explicitly Christian in subject matter, generally have an unmistakable tone of affirmation and celebration. Yet even here it is not clear precisely what is being affirmed or celebrated. Thomas recognized this ambiguity in his work at an early stage. In a quatrain from his notebooks (Maud, *Poet in the Making*, 1968, p. 29) he formulates the problem without resolving it:

> If God is praised in poem one
> Show no surprise when in the next
> I worship wood or Sun or none:
> I'm hundred-heavened and countless sexed.

Most discussions of Thomas invoke one or more of a series of statements he made about his belief. He told John Malcolm Brinnin (*Dylan Thomas in America*, 1955, p. 128) that his aim was to produce "poems in praise of God's world by a man who doesn't believe in God." Brinnin (p. 43) further recounts how, at a dinner party, "he made indiscreet and foolish attacks on the church which," according to Brinnin, "had little basis in his thinking." William York Tindall (*A Reader's Guide to Dylan Thomas*, 1962, p. 8) similarly remembers that his own wife was frequently rebuked and teased by Thomas on account of her Catholicism. And there is certainly no lack of evidence as to Thomas's frequent blasphemousness, however seriously one chooses to take that evidence. The poet in his public role refused to announce himself as essentially a Christian. Whereas Eliot has conveniently labelled himself a Royalist, Classicist, and Anglo-Catholic, Thomas preferred the more picturesque designations of Welshman, drunkard, and heterosexual.

Like Joyce with his Irish Catholic upbringing, Thomas was in perpetual revolt against his Welsh Nonconformist heritage, yet unable ever to escape it. Perhaps for this reason his direct pronouncements have a characteristic ambiguity: the same quotations are cited by different critics as evidence of diametrically opposed attitudes. Thus his famous Note to the *Collected Poems*:

I read somewhere of a shepherd who, when asked why he made, from within fairy rings, ritual observances to the moon to protect his flocks, replied: 'I'd be a damn' fool if I didn't!' These poems, with all their crudities, doubts, and confusions, are written for the love of Man and in praise of God, and I'd be a damn' fool if they weren't.

It is moot here whether the ringing affirmation of the last sentence is undercut by the ironic innuendo of superstition. Similarly, the poet's plan for a long "poem in preparation," of which "In country sleep," "Over Sir John's hill," and "In the white giant's thigh" were to form parts, has frequently been cited as evidence of a strongly religious vision toward the end of Thomas's life. The entire projected poem, which Thomas discusses in his posthumous volume *Quite Early One Morning*, would have as dramatic setting the lamentation of God for an Earth which has destroyed itself; but of course Thomas does not nakedly refer to "God," but rather

The godhead, the author, the milky-way farmer, the first cause, architect, lamp-lighter, quintessence, the beginning Word, the anthropomorphic bawler-out and blackballer, the stuff of all men, scapegoat, martyr, woe-bearer . . .

The focus of the poem—if indeed Thomas could ever have completed it—would be upon Earth; is his vague and multifarous God anything more than a dramatic device here?

The testimony of Thomas's friends, again, varies. His close friend Vernon Watkins mentions casually in his collection of Thomas's letters (*Dylan Thomas: Letters to Vernon Watkins*, 1957, p. 17) that, even early in their mutual critical relationship, "we were both religious poets," and clearly indicates that he felt his friend to be a Christian. Aneirin Talfan Davies (*Dylan: Druid of the Broken Body*, 1964, pp. 21–22) recalls that Thomas used to visit a neighboring vicar in Laugharne during the war and often accompanied him to the early morning celebration of the Eucharist. The vicar lent Thomas a number of books on theology. Davies uses this incident to support his contention that Thomas was moving toward Catholicism throughout his maturity. FitzGibbon (*The Life of Dylan*

Thomas, 1965, pp. 229–30) mentions the poet's close friendship with the Reverend Leon Atkin, a Nonconformist minister in Swansea who was also a socialist. According to Atkin, Thomas was a religious man but not a Christian. FitzGibbon cites William Empson, who called Thomas a "pessimistic pantheist," and then attempts to find a consensus among the poet's friends:

on one point, at least, all can agree: Dylan was not an atheist, though in some of his early poems there are echoes of his father's post-Nietzschean, almost Manichean, concept of an essentially malevolent divinity . . . as an artist he could not accept the view that it is all fortuitous chaos on the one hand . . . nor that it is all a mechanical, behaviorist and therefore ultimately predictable construction on the other . . .

FitzGibbon (1965, p. 231) says of Davies's contention of a movement toward Roman Catholicism, "neither in his writing, nor in his life, nor in his letters, nor in what his friends have told me can I see any sign of any such progress whatsoever," and adds that Thomas remained essentially an agnostic: "it requires much wrenching of language, both his and ours, to speak of him as a believer, in any meaningful sense." In a note to this page, FitzGibbon quotes a letter from Watkins as a kind of rebuttal:

If he was, as I believe, religious and Christian, he doesn't need my advocacy . . . I would call Dylan a Blakean Christian but even that would be only an approximation.

Perhaps the interpretation Thomas's friends put upon his faith reveals more about their own predilections and susceptibilities than it does about the poet himself; remember, Thomas had the gift of appearing all things to all men in his personal intercourse, and had a desire to please others that was as deeply rooted as his desire to entertain and to shock. Thomas's childhood friend Bert Trick (1966, p. 48) felt the young man "was deeply religious—not in any sectarian way," while Jack Lindsay (1966, p. 73), a man of Marxist sympathies who knew Thomas during the war, implies that the religious dimension of his poetry is irrelevant: "the use of 'God,' " he claims, "is the one blatant sentimentality in Dylan." But perhaps more striking than these impressions is Augustus John's story of spending the night with the young Dylan and Caitlin in a pub in Laugharne before the two were married: "Next morning Caitlin told me that during the night, on hearing strange sounds in the guest-chamber, she had entered it, to find the visitor kneeling stark naked on the floor and in an attitude of prayer" (Brinnin, *A Casebook on Dylan Thomas,* 1960, p. 277).

Since Thomas's prose pronouncements are equivocal and the testimony of his biography is ambiguous, the critic must turn his attention to where it belonged in the first place, the poems. Apparently, though, for many critics evaluating the religious element in Thomas's poetry is a subliminal process. The critic often simply pronounces the poet a Christian (for instance) and then either drops the issue or proceeds to interpret crucial, highly ambiguous poems in that light, without any obvious recognition that alternative interpretations are possible. Nevertheless, there does seem to be at least one critically "responsible" spokesman for each of the shades of opinion on Thomas's religion. The easiest way to tackle this diversity of approaches is thematically, so I shall briefly survey in this chapter first those writers who feel Thomas is either not essentially religious in any way we conventionally use the term, or not fruitfully approached from this angle; then a group of critics who explore his religious symbolism without clearly committing themselves as to the degree or kind of his belief; next, critics who claim that he is essentially a religious poet, and is best read as such; and lastly, those who feel that Thomas's religious attitude is ambivalent, incoherent, or a perpetual conflict, and who attempt to analyze this aspect of his writing.

Most critics, whatever their position, tend to discuss one or more of a small number of poems which seem to bear importantly on the question of the poet's religion, so I will frequently use a given critic's interpretation of one of these as a touchstone for his approach. Because my thematic approach to the problem of religion in Thomas necessarily scatters my discussions of the most important initial works, I shall list them here:

Elder Olson, *The Poetry of Dylan Thomas* (1954)
William York Tindall, *A Reader's Guide to Dylan Thomas* (1962)
H. H. Kleinman, *The Religious Sonnets of Dylan Thomas* (1963)
John Ackerman, *Dylan Thomas: His Life and Work* (1964)
Rushworth M. Kidder, *Dylan Thomas: The Country of the Spirit* (1973)

Non-Christian Interpretations

One of the first book-length studies, Derek Stanford's *Dylan Thomas: A Literary Study* (1964), plays down the religious element, dismissing it as (p. 196) "a limited pantheism—an intense and terrible vision of the world as subject to the law of diminishing returns." Far from viewing Thomas as a mystic, Stanford gleans from him "a kind of physical determinism." The most eloquent critic who assumes a stance like that of Stanford is William York Tindall. In an early article introducing Thomas to the American public, Tindall (1948, p. 435) explained that the poetry generally works simultaneously on three levels—the sexual, the literary, and the religious—but asserted that the religious elements, generally Biblical allusions, should be taken as mythic, symbolic in the way elements in a dream are symbolic. In the later poems, he goes on (p. 439), "the machinery of worship is Catholic now, or Anglo-Catholic." This is Tindall's approach in embryo. Although a critic like Reddington, who devotes an entire book to demonstrating that Thomas is a kind of Christian, claims Tindall as one of the majority of critics who view Thomas as religious (Reddington, *Dylan Thomas: A Journey from Darkness to Light*, 1968, p. 11), this is missing the point. Throughout his *Reader's Guide to Dylan Thomas* Tindall recognizes that "God and Christ are always around in Thomas's poetry" (1962, p. 8), but he stresses that they are "not in their proper capacities, . . . but as metaphors for nature, poet, and their creative powers." Tindall asserts (p. 7) that his being a religious poet is one of the seven "widely held notions" about Thomas that are not really true, and tends to interpret the effects of his religious heritage upon the poet in psychological rather than philosophical terms. Like Lawrence, he "remained essentially Protestant without being Christian;" "both remained Puritans" (p. 8).

Instead, Tindall sees Thomas's religion as that of the Poet (linking him to other twentieth-century heirs of romanticism and aestheticism) or, alternately, sees him as a heroic and martyred figure struggling in a Manichaean universe. Tindall's interpretations of the individual poems seldom neglect the Christian level of reference, but the thrust of his interpretations subordinates that level to others. Thus, in his discussion of the "Altarwise by owl-light" sequence in *The Literary Symbol* (1955, pp. 184–85), he admits that "Jesus is so evident in the sequence that some readers have mistaken parallel for theme." For Tindall, Genesis usually translates to Thomas's (or Everyman's) birth, the Crucifixion to the poetic agony, and Resurrection to a restoration of poetic and sexual potency. Thus the theme of the sonnet sequence, "like that of most of his early poems, appears to be Thomas's own development from conception to adolescence or maturity." Unsurprisingly, in the *Reader's Guide* (1962, pp. 116–17), Tindall sees "the hissing of the spent lie" in "I have longed to move away" as equally "the conventional morality and piety of the chapel," "the conventions of society," and "his own poetic past," but puts his main interpretive emphasis upon the

problem of the poet's personal and artistic development. The poem
sequence "Vision and Prayer," which to most critics appears explicitly religious in theme, hardly gives Tindall pause. Although
(p. 239) "we ask if this poem celebrates the poet's religious conver-
sion or if, as earlier poems suggest, religion serves again as metaphor for something else," our answer is immediate and pat:

The making of a poem, parallel to the birth of the child, seems a way
to the poet's remaking. Jesus seems the light to which child, poet, and
poem ascend. These seemings amount at last, like circumstantial evidence, to all but certainty. Here is another poem about the poet coming in from original darkness to the holy light of nature. All the rest
is metaphor . . . Thomas never went back to the chapel.

   Although Tindall is the most eloquent spokesman for this point
of view, numerous other critics sense that the poet's often "reverent"
tone and wealth of Christian imagery are merely metaphorical
means to some secular end. Karl Shapiro's brilliant essay on Thomas
traces the "piercing sacrificial note" in his poetry (Brinnin, 1960,
p. 168) to a personal pain; part of his pain is that he has (p. 169)
"nothing of philosophical or religious substance to fall back upon."
Shapiro finds a fatal pessimism in most of the poems, offset by a few
bursts of joy; Thomas's main positive symbol is masculine love,
while (p. 171) somewhere "in the background is God." Like Tindall, he detects a "puritanism" that "runs through his whole work,"
but ends by a contrast: while God is the chief process in Hopkins's
work, sex is the chief process in Thomas's.
   Of the essayists in C. B. Cox's collection (*Dylan Thomas: A Collection of Critical Essays,* 1966), Ralph Maud and Robert M.
Adams most explicitly question Thomas's religiousness. Maud sees
the poet's universe as post-Christian, postatomic, and absurd in an
existential sense (p. 80):

Thomas's God . . . is not a religious entity at all in the normal sense of
a presiding Being whose presence controls or at least justifies our
existence. Thomas's God does nothing to alleviate the absurdity of the
position of rational man in an irrational universe . . . He simply weeps,
offering none of the usual consolations.

Adams, who is mostly concerned with a discussion of both Thomas
and Crashaw as extreme examples of "metaphysical"—or perhaps
baroque—poets, does not make it clear whether he feels the "Altarwise by owl-light" sequence to be more a failure of tone or of
theme. "The point of view," he claims (p. 136) "is that at which

Crashaw only hinted—that Incarnation represents a vicious joke played by a malicious God on Christ, Mary, and mankind."

Like Shapiro, Alfred Kazin (1957, p. 165) finds "no philosophy or belief" in Thomas suitable to the poetry he hoped to write, and feels that Thomas's consciousness of this helped to destroy him. John Wain, one of the antiromantic British "Angry Young Men," and Frederick Grubb, a rather pragmatic neo-Bloomsburian, both attack with equal scorn attempts to, as Grubb puts it (1965, p. 170), "Baptize the Pagan." Like Rilke, Grubb argues (p. 182), Thomas was limited by his "deification of instinct." Wain, in a review of the *Collected Poems* reprinted in Brinnin's *Casebook* (1960 p. 69), identifies only three subjects in the poet's work—childhood, the viscera, and religion—and says that the "third subject, religion, seems to me Thomas's worst pitch: he never succeeds in making me feel that he is doing more than thumbing a lift from it." This appeal to the reader's experience does, of course, still leave open the question of Thomas's sincerity.

Two other critics argue against a religious interpretation of the Welsh poet from a more positive standpoint. Jean Garrigue (1959, pp. 111–12) claims that Thomas is postromantic: "whereas the romantic poet subscribes to a religion, and a heroic religion of the self in all its phases . . . Thomas broke with all that . . . turning to the anatomy not of the self but of its animal other, the body . . . As other poets wrote of gods, he wrote of God." Sex, however, is his essential subject. Similarly, Georges-Albert Astre, in an enthusiastic article entitled "Victoire de la Poésie" in the *Adam* memorial issue (1953, p. 41), grandly sums up,

Dylan Thomas thus exorcized his own shadows without real recourse to God or submitting to the temptations of surrealism: by doing this he would have lost this triumph of consciousness . . . which is its own justification.

Can a man be a "mystic" without being "religious"? Are there theological implications to the term "pagan"? Clearly, here we are involved in a jungle that is as much semantic as philosophical. Numerous critics who recognize that Thomas is no barefaced materialist, and who feel that he has a true "vision" of some sort, are nevertheless reluctant to take Thomas's Christian imagery as indicative of a Christian outlook. The parallel case of D. H. Lawrence comes to mind. Francis Scarfe (Tedlock, *Dylan Thomas: The Legend and the Poet*, p. 106) insists that "it would be ridiculous to claim Thomas for any Church," and suggests that the early poems, where "the

Bible appears as a cruel and crazy legend," reflect childhood memories of the Welsh Bethel. "The Biblical element is further confused by a primitive metaphysics, related in the last analysis to a sexual interpretation of the universe." The sonnet sequence shows "a double pattern of Biblical and sexual imagery" (p. 102) and its characters have secular equivalents:

Satan (identified with death and sin), sex (i.e., life, represented by Adam and even Gabriel), Mary (the justification of sex through child-bearing and suffering, but none the less a worldly symbol), and Christ (victim and blood-offering rather than hero).

Thomas, Scarfe claims, is nearer to Blake than to Eliot, but also "perilously near" the early, atheistic Rimbaud (p. 106).

Two important essays in Brinnin's *Casebook* (1960) tread the same uneasy line. W. S. Merwin adopts an almost anthropological stance in approaching Thomas "The Religious Poet." "A religious artist," Merwin promptly qualifies, "is primarily a celebrator. A celebrator in the ritual sense: a maker and performer of a rite" (p. 59).

That which he celebrates is Creation, and more particularly the human condition. For he will see himself, man, as a metaphor or analogy of the world. The human imagination will be for him the image of the divine imagination; the work of art and the artist will be analogous with the world and its Creator. In both man and the world he will perceive a face of love or creation which is more divine than either man or the world, and a force of death or destruction which is more terrible than man or the world.

Merwin traces numerous movements and developments in Thomas's poetry: compassion changes to hope and then to joy in the early poems, but retreats to despair in "When, like a running grave." Thomas gathers strength as he discovers his universal metaphors of microcosm and macrocosm, and in the late poems the exultation is (p. 64) the "exuberance of a man drunk with the holiness and wonder of creation, with the reality and terror and ubiquity of death, but with love as God, as more powerful than death." Interestingly, Merwin feels Thomas would have moved increasingly toward the dramatic, as the act of celebration became more "real" for him. Merwin seems to feel that Thomas tapped a strain of faith that predates Christianity; he finds in "A Winter's Tale" (p. 65) "most of the essential elements of a mid-winter ceremony of the re-birth of the year."

Perhaps it is the lack of moral structure to accompany Thomas's gestures of affirmation or despair which causes critics to qualify the poet's religious vision so heavily. Stuart Holroyd, in an essay entitled "Dylan Thomas and the Religion of the Instinctive Life" (Brinnin, 1960), says that Thomas's God is not moral, particularly not Christian, since he is attained *through* the senses rather than through denial. "Whereas the pantheist normally sees God in all things, Thomas saw sex in all things. In fact sex, together with the processes analogous to it in the natural world, was Dylan Thomas's god" (p. 144). Holroyd sees Thomas as believing in some vague, immanent Force or Power, and feels that his vision, however authentic, was limited. His poetry is unmetaphysical, and admits no despair or doubt. Eventually, Holroyd feels (p. 149), Thomas moved even further from the Christianity he feared to abandon totally, toward a pantheism in which the Fall was simply a cosmic accident. Stanley Moss (1967, p. 20) refers to the poet's "subjective half-pagan pantheism," and William Arrowsmith feels the presence of the same pre-Christian element (Brinnin, 1960, p. 100): "Christ, for instance, is in Thomas no Christian Christ, but amoral and pre-Christian: all Adonis."

Three essays in Tedlock's collection (1960) emerge from similar assumptions. David Aivaz's brilliant short study seems to identify Thomas's God as Process, as Aivaz defines it (p. 195): "Process is unity in nature; its direction is the cyclical return; the force that drives it is the generative energy in natural things . . . it is 'destructive and constructive at the same time.'" Thus, in the sonnet sequence, there is a "frequent identification of . . . Christian imagery with the imagery of process" (p. 198):

In these poems Satan never tempts, Adam never fails, stern gods never lay down laws; redemption is generation, the Judgment is the day of death, of re-immersion in process.

Thomas's mystical vision is not static, though, for in the later poems Thomas discovers that it is man's consciousness which shapes the world through his awareness; "Process, the subject of vision, needs man to 'happen' to it to give it life" (p. 207).

Although E. Glyn Lewis begins his essay on Thomas by asserting that he is "undoubtedly a religious poet" (Tedlock, 1960, p. 168), it soon becomes clear that we are to take this in a particular way. Thomas's world "has no law, no theology," and he shows an "amoral acceptance of all experience." As much as anything, Lewis is concerned to show "the poet's concern with fundamental problems of existence" (p. 172). Thomas has a vision, but he is neither a devotional poet like Donne, a mystical poet like Crashaw, nor a metaphysical poet like Eliot in the *Four Quartets*; instead, "Thomas's is a religion of profane existence; it is imbued with an intense . . . feeling of the unity of all forms of existence, without at the same time a realization that the unity of existence has its reason in the nature of God and in the person of Christ . . ." Unlike Christian mystics Thomas accepts the sequence of time, yet he identifies beginnings with endings; unlike them, he does not try to justify his invocations of womb-regression through any metaphysics. Quoting Berdyaev's *Freedom and Slavery* (p. 173), Lewis finds in Thomas the "thirst to return to primitive life, to cosmic life," "a pagan cosmo-centricity" which "sets itself up in the place of Christian anthropocentricity."

Without explicitly committing himself on the question of Thomas's kind or degree of belief, Marshall W. Stearns (Tedlock, 1960, p. 119) argues that "the major theme of man in Thomas's poetry is accompanied by the minor themes of religion and sex, which are sometimes fused at a high temperature." Although the poet subscribes to no formal religion, his verse reveals the constant influence of a strong religious background in which the evangelical preaching of the Welsh Bethel plays a large part. The critic feels that Thomas's "emotions are deeply involved in religious matters, although his references to this subject are likely to be characterized more by rebellion than conformity." Stearns proceeds to an imaginative and convincing explication of the last sonnet in Thomas's sequence, arguing that through Mary, "sex rises to eternal and asexual glory," at the moment of Crucifixion (p. 123).

By now it should be clear that for some critics, characterizing Thomas as a religious poet affirms his essential seriousness of intent and depth of vision, while for others the problem is approached thematically: if Thomas treats religious themes, then he is a religious poet. By the same token a critic like Tindall obviously feels that Thomas is serious without being particularly religious, while Wain implies that the poet is not *successful* as a religious poet, either through a failure of execution or through one of feeling. Indeed, for some critics, the argument that Thomas is a "serious" poet seems to lead inevitably to the conclusion that his work is in some sense religious. Thus Amos Wilder, in an essay on Thomas in his book *Modern Poetry and the Christian Tradition* (1952, p. 101), states that the "continual exploration of man at an existential level" which we find in his work "can only be called theological in its implications." The implication here is developed equally forthrightly by Edward A. and Lillian D. Bloom (1960, p. 139):

A religious poet in essence, . . . Thomas was engrossed in metaphysical speculations on man's origins and destiny . . . His poetry reflects many of the tenets of existentialism; like some of the 'official' existentialists, he devoted himself to a repudiation of traditionally acknowledged religious beliefs while continuing to search for a spiritual meaning.

The Blooms go on to find parallels to numerous existentialist trademarks in Thomas: the value of the individual, the fulfillment of personal being within a human community, the "nausea" before blank reality, an essential suffering. But many of their points seem more descriptive of Sartre and Camus than of Kierkegaard, leading us to wonder just how we are to take the term "religious." Edward Bloom, in an article in the *Western Humanities Review* (1960, p. 391), attacks this question rather confusedly. Thomas is not really a mystic, though we are tempted to call him one, and there is in his work a "constant acknowledgment of supernal authority." There is a "pantheistic reverence" in him; "whether the roots are sacramental or natural, his view of the universe is often theistic." Further complicating matters, Bloom finds in him "a profound religious impulse that is inseparable from the esthetic."

Ambiguous Symbolic Interpretations

One of the most influential discussions of the poet is Elder Olson's *The Poetry of Dylan Thomas* (1954). Olson brilliantly discusses Thomas's private "universe," his character and concerns, and scrupulously analyzes his various poetic techniques. But the most provocative section of his book is an extensive analysis of the sonnet sequence (pp. 63–89), wherein he detects six distinct levels of symbolism operating:

(1) a level based on the analogy of human life to the span of a year, which permits the use of phenomena of the seasons to represent events of human life, and vice versa;
(2) a level based on an analogy between the sun and man, permitting the attributes of each to stand for those of the other;
(3) a level of Thomas's 'private' symbolism;
(4) a level based on ancient myth, principally Greek, representing the fortunes of the sun in terms of the adventures of the sun-hero Hercules;
(5) a level based on relations of the *constellation* Hercules to other constellations and astronomical phenomena; and
(6) a level derived from the Christian interpretation of levels 4 and 5.

Clearly the most controversial aspect of this interpretation involves the fourth, fifth, and sixth "levels" of symbolism, and it is upon those that Olson concentrates in his reading of the poems. If, as he feels, Olson has discovered an arcane sort of "key" to the meaning of the poems, then that fact must be important.

Working from a realization that the pagan world saw in the constellations reflections of its mythology, and that Christian writers later adopted these original symbols within a Christian framework, Olson argues that Thomas is aware of and plays upon these various interpretations of the heavens (p. 66): "While he uses both the pagan and the Christian interpretations, he is committed to the Christian view from the first." Yet even this is not really descriptive of Thomas's method, as Olson sees it. Olson furnishes a chart listing the major constellations, the pagan interpretation of them, and Thomas's own interpretations. Sometimes these coincide with the Christian interpretation; thus Cygnus, known to the pagans as the swan of Hercules, is seen by Thomas as the Northern Cross, a symbol of Christ. This is orthodox Christian interpretation. But Olson identifies Scorpius, the scorpion, with Thomas's "furies" in the sequence. Although the association is possible enough, it is difficult to understand Olson's rationale. Further, there is nothing particularly Christian in the symbolism. Thomas's symbolism sometimes adopts pagan meanings, sometimes Christian ones, and sometimes he seems arbitrarily to assign his own meaning to a constellation.

Despite the complexity of Olson's mechanism, his general reading of the poem is reasonable and clear and not terribly at variance with Tindall's, for example: unlike Stearns, who sees the sonnets as a loosely connected sequence and who finds the eighth sonnet the climax, Olson considers them an interconnected whole. "The hero of the poem," he asserts (p. 83), "is a man who, aware of his sinfulness and mortality, faces the prospect of death." In Sonnet I, the man sees the changing seasons reflected in the changing stars, and decides that the sun and heavens themselves are mortal. In Sonnet II he finds everything a metaphor for death, even a child's growth, the birth of the planet, and the passage of the sun through the Milky Way. Sonnet III reveals the man imagining the sun's course from winter through the next autumn, and realizing the shortness of the year. In Sonnet IV he remembers a time when, having faith in God, he had gone through a period of questioning; Sonnet V is a nightmare interruption showing everything, including the stars, to be a dream of death. In the next sonnet he sees man as time's prey, like the sun; but in Sonnet VII he spurns time and, seeing the Cross in the heavens, asserts his faith in it. Yet in the next poem the Cross

sets, a symbolic Crucifixion which the hero accepts. Sonnet IX discusses Egyptian embalming (the preservation of a corpse) and writing (the preservation of the spirit), both of which are rejected; but
in the terminal sonnet the Cross reappears, symbolizing the coming
Resurrection and a renewed faith.

The images tell, step by step, a painful story, in which the Heaven he
had once hoped for spells out nothing but his doom, until the message
is complete, and he realizes that sin . . . is to a merciful God nothing
but the necessary condition of mercy (p. 87).

It is difficult to tell just what Olson's attitude is toward Thomas's
religious faith. He sees the early poems as transpiring in a universe of nearly unmitigated nightmare, and the sonnets as a turning point. Thomas called his poetry the record of his individual
struggle from darkness toward some measure of light; in the sonnets, according to Olson (p. 26) "there is undoubtedly a development from doubt and fear to faith and hope, and the moving cause
is love; he comes to love God by learning to love man and the world
of nature." Clearly, there is a conflict between this and the previous
quotation. Are we to read the sonnets positively or negatively? Further, what sort of God Thomas comes to is left ambiguous by Olson's concentration upon symbolism. Is he using Christian mythology in the same way he uses pagan, as an arbitrary but effective
means to express some other personal faith? C. Paul Verghese
(1968, p. 36) thinks Olson stresses the complexity of Thomas's symbolism without in any way suggesting that the sequence is fraught
with religious import. Verghese then goes on to call Thomas a sort
of pantheist whose God is the "cosmic energy" of destruction and
creation. Other critics, however, take Olson as assurance of a Christian interpretation of the poet. Tindall (1962, p. 127) seems to feel
Olson's stress is misleading: "Although cheerfully allowing the
presence of Jesus, Hercules, the stars, the zodiac, and a generally
neglected voyage, I think them analogies, not to be confused with
theme." Taking as authority Thomas's comment about the sonnets
as "only the writings of a boily boy in love with shapes and shadows in his pillow," Tindall feels the theme is "Thomas himself."
    Aside from its ambiguities with respect to a *thematic* reading,
Olson's methodology raises some general questions. An anonymous
Times Literary Supplement reviewer (Jan. 7, 1955, p. 10), who
apparently accepts Olson's methods and conclusions, calls the book
"in many ways a triumph of structural analysis," then proceeds to
criticize *Thomas* for his "arbitrary Gongoristic riddling tech-

nique." This exemplifies one problem. If Thomas found it necessary to use such a complex and arcane symbolic system, and the
poems cannot be fruitfully read without it, we would tend to think
less of him for that. But the basic problem is the feeling of many
critics that the mechanistic symbolic system Olson describes simply
doesn't sound like the way Thomas's poetic mind works. Mechanistic complexity is apparent in his poetic technique, but his symbolism seems fluid, loosely associative, and personal. As Jacob Korg
(*Dylan Thomas*, 1965, p. 131) puts it,

> Thomas was capable of making allusions to bodies of legend and to
> recondite lore, and even of working out sustained images involving
> them; but he would not be expected to weave his verse over the lat-
> tice of a prepared framework of information as Olson supposes him
> to be doing here.

Monroe C. Beardsley and Sam Hynes attack Olson's method in
an article entitled "Misunderstanding Poetry: Notes on Some
Readings of Dylan Thomas" (1960). Their discussion, in fact, is
relevant to the entire issue of Thomas's religious faith. They detect
four discrete "errors" in critical method among critics who have
approached the sonnet sequence. The first error, "Anti-explication"
or the "Literal Approach," is that of assuming that the poems *need*
little or no interpretation. Some critics—they cite John Bayley
(1957, pp. 186–227) as a relatively sophisticated example—working
from Thomas's insistence that his poetry should be read "literally,"
argue that the sonnets make sense directly. In his famous exchange
with Edith Sitwell on the interpretation of "Altarwise by owl-
light," (cited, e.g., by Olson [1954, p. 3], who explores this difficulty) Thomas claimed that her interpretation of the poem as a
comment on "this horrible, crazy, speed-life" was vague, and that
she neglected the "literal meaning: that a world-devouring ghost
creature bit out the horror of tomorrow from a gentleman's loins."
Beardsley and Hynes demonstrate what should be apparent: that
Thomas's "reading" of his poem is in fact anything but literal, and
is itself susceptible to interpretation.

The second error they cite is that of "Piecemeal Plucking, or the
Random Method of Explication" (p. 317). Many critics, particularly in explications, tend to give an ostensible "translation" of a
difficult Thomas poem which may seem to work on a line-by-line
basis, but which assumes and justifies no real context of interpretation. Their particular target is Bernard Kneiger's discussion of Sonnet I in the *Explicator* (1956), but the same charge could be levelled

at Clark Emery *(The World of Dylan Thomas,* 1962) or even
Tindall (1962). Kneiger, they claim, interprets the sonnet in Christian terms, but without showing why we should accept the symbolism at given points as Christian, when other interpretations are
equally likely. (Kneiger replies in *College English* [1962, pp.
623–28].)

The third error, that of "Hasty Levelling, or The Bulldozer
Method of Explication" (p. 319) is one that might be charged
against the majority of critics who argue that Thomas is a Christian
poet, and point to a few Christian references in a poem as evidence. In fact, the more sophisticated error of giving a poem's meaning "on the Christian level" is similar:

It is a prime error of explication to jump to the conclusion that because a poem contains certain related images it has a 'level,' in the
sense of an implicit commitment to a familiar doctrine.

Tone, for example, must be taken into account, as must the surrounding context of the poet's work.

Olson is their chief example of the "Error of the Imposed System, or the Runic Method of Explication" (p. 320). Olson's "plan
works out with remarkable consistency and completeness; the only
question is whether there is any evidence that these poems have anything at all to do with the constellation Hercules." Beardsley and
Hynes feel that this error is common among critics with a "hobby-
horse," whether it be Freud, Jung, or the constellations; as a sort
of counter-example they provide an explication of "Mary had a
little lamb" in constellational terms. Any system can, with enough
ingenuity, be applied to any literary work with apparent success,
as Frederick Crews's *The Pooh Perplex* (1963) wittily demonstrated. Ralph Maud (1955), working along similar lines, provides
a careful critique of Olson's methodology and conclusions. His
criticism gains force from his demonstrations that Olson's reasoning is at times inconsistent in its own terms (cf. Maud, 1968, pp.
167–69).

If Olson's reading is ambiguously Christian through omission,
J. Hillis Miller's view of Thomas's poetic universe (1965, pp. 190–
216) is ambiguously religious, though in quite explicit terms.
Miller's phenomenological sort of criticism is difficult to examine
thematically, but he does describe the "God" of Thomas's poetry
(p. 203):

God is an anonymous totality of being. He is 'the god of beginning in
the intricate seawhirl' (*CP* [*Collected Poems*], 44). He is the source

and end of all things, a dark fluid background against which they surge into being, and which they negate by being specific objects rather than the inclusive *I am*. Man always remains 'this side of the truth' (*CP*, 116), this side of a deity who combines contradictions and to whom moral terms do not apply. To God distinctions of good and bad, innocent and guilty, are nothing, since he sees all created things in terms of their inevitable return into 'the winding dark' where 'each truth, each lie' will 'die in unjudging love' (*CP*, 116, 117).

Elsewhere (p. 194) Miller identifies "God's all-creating Word" with "the coming to consciousness of the poet," but here he seems to be speaking from a closer identification with Thomas: the implied solipsism is more a function of his critical method than an "objective" commentary. For Miller, Thomas's world in general seems closer to that of the pre-Socratic philosophers than to that of any more readily labelled theology, though of course this similarity reflects the structure of the poet's consciousness rather than any literary debt. Miller's interpretation of Thomas is illuminating and —in his own terms—lucid, but difficult to appraise within the context of more conventional criticism.

A host of critics—certainly the majority—are willing to call Thomas's poetry "religious," but are less than explicit about how or why this is so. T. H. Jones (*Dylan Thomas*, 1966, p. 66) feels that the volume *Deaths and Entrances* made it clear "that Thomas was essentially a religious poet," but he does not elaborate. David Daiches (Cox, 1966, p. 17) finds in him a "celebration of unity in all life and all time" and (p. 23) a "sacramentalizing of nature." Gilbert Highet (1960, p. 182) finds his poetry, like the Welsh people, "deeply religious;" John Sweeney (1946, p. xi) admits his "temper was devout but his religion was hard to identify." Stephen Spender (1955, pp. 38–39) speaks of him as "a religious poet—a poet with a religion of life," and emphasizes Thomas's success in bringing the mystery of transubstantiation to life in a poem like "This bread I break." On the other hand, Ralph J. Mills (1965, p. 51), who examines Thomas's poetry at length, seems to be trying to get at his religious dimension through a series of qualifications. Although the poet's intentions "derive first from the biological side of life," in *Twenty-five Poems* he (p. 57) "examines more directly aspects of existence which will ultimately make of him an essentially religious, which is not to say orthodox . . . poet." In fact he has been a religious poet from the start. In his later poetry, the "ritual pattern of life . . . supplies a religious resonance" (p. 58), and we see a "developing mythic vision" (p. 59) and a "religious exaltation" (p. 67).

Ricaredo Demetillo (1962, p. 71) claims that "Thomas is one of the great religious poets of all time," and proceeds to point to various poems as evidence, while Edith Sitwell confidently asserts that in the poems (Treece, *Dylan Thomas: 'Dog Among the Fairies,'* 1949, p. 145) "all things are identified with God." Richard Austin (1954, p. 47) suggests a reason why Dame Edith was so attracted to the young Welsh poet, superficially so different from her, when he affirms that "Dylan Thomas, like his two great contemporaries T. S. Eliot and Edith Sitwell, was above all a religious poet." Although Austin avoids calling Thomas a Christian poet, he compares him to Rimbaud in Claudel's description—"a mystic in a wild state"—and remarks that his view of life, paradoxically, was "Catholic in spirit" rather than Protestant (p. 49). In another short discussion of Thomas as religious poet, Frederic Vanson (1958, pp. 22–23) argues—somewhat like Bloom—that the poet was religious because "the main themes of his poetry are all of an order we normally consider religious," and "his preoccupation with them amounted almost to an obsession." Like Daiches, he stresses that in the poems "all natural things are in some sense sacramental;" Vanson recognizes that Thomas experienced doubt and conflict, and believes that toward the end of his life he was moving "much nearer to a Christian view of life." Thomas Saunders (1965–66, p. 494) takes a similar stance, articulated in more sophisticated form; like Davies he feels Thomas was essentially religious, at least in his middle and late poetry, but not really Christian. He also notes that it is the sacramental side of Christianity which appealed to him—a concern already evident in *25P*—but finishes with the admission (p. 497) that "whether . . . he eventually became a Christian poet is a concern that lies beyond the scope of this article."

William T. Moynihan in *The Craft and Art of Dylan Thomas* (1966) takes a position akin to that of this group of critics. In the preface to his study (p. x) he denies that Thomas is either Christian or pagan; he is certainly "religious," but only "if we don't mind including a lot of polytheism and a good deal of magic under the idea of 'religious poet.'" As for the depth of his belief, Moynihan says that a poet needs only a vague "reverence for life" to give his work a religious tone. "Thomas was taking no chances; he'd be sure to have a place reserved for the unknown God. And it is Man whom he loves, not God; God is something to be praised." Moynihan finds (pp. 30–33) that the young Thomas rejected the Chapel in substance while retaining its structure, particularly its oppositions. But the "power of chromosomes was to Thomas a god; the madness that accompanies sterile attempts at writing he felt to be the devil."

Nietzsche and Blake loom large in the young poet's vision. Thomas was certainly not a materialist, but (p. 35) neither was he a pantheist: "pantheism seemed to Thomas an involvement with life at a lesser stage of being, at a lesser stage of intensity." In some of the early letters he stresses Man as the world's maker and driving force. This antipagan mysticism Thomas sometimes articulated as a belief in "the state of Christhood," which for him had communal and creative implications. "He cared nothing for Christ in a theological sense, he said, but cared very much for Christ as a symbol" (p. 38).

Moynihan's access to the poet's notebooks and to his unpublished letters, as well as his extensive conversations with friends of Thomas, allows him to document his assertions about the poet's religious beliefs at this stage much more fully than earlier commentators. His discussion of the later poems, on the other hand, seems to rely mainly upon internal evidence. Moynihan finds Thomas's mature spiritual beliefs to be much simpler in outline than his earlier ones. "Faith" and "love" both are basic terms in the poet's thought, and there is a new emphasis upon nature's creative self-renewal—for Thomas, a sort of "magic." Whereas Moynihan (p. 205) believes "And death shall have no dominion" is "simply and absolutely a highly imaginative statement of the scientific fact that matter cannot be destroyed," without reference to any spiritual afterlife, he sees the later poems as a movement toward affirmation and a conditional consent to the presence of death in life:

His final consent is dialectical. It is a temporarily achieved synthesis but one which—theoretically, at least—can yield to a new thesis. Thomas rejected and outgrew his obsession with the horror of death and the evil of sex. He also rejected the traditional Christianity of his childhood, but he learned to see nature as holy, faith in life as essential, and love as the best immortality.

Perhaps more illuminating than these attempts to approach the poet's religion through theme is Moynihan's discussion, in a later chapter, of the symbolic structure Thomas develops in his wrestling with the universe. Here (pp. 226–27), Moynihan finds the young poet invoking three different Gods, or perhaps three aspects of God: Jehovah the creator; a "God of attrition," often identified with Time and with Evil; and a God of love which is mostly an infused spirit in things. The figure of Christ is linked both with the God of Genesis and with half-evil humanity, and dominates the poetry of the middle period; Thomas's emphasis, as his work matures, moves from the first toward the last aspect of this triple God. Throughout, Moynihan astutely analyzes the poet's adaptation of

Biblical figures in his private symbology, but he makes it clear that Thomas employs these references for their "mythic" content rather than as signs of any theological commitment.

Jacob Korg (1965), in his book on Thomas for the Twayne series, devotes an early chapter to what he terms "The Rhetoric of Mysticism" (p. 27):

> The substance of Thomas's vision consists of a number of convictions about time, immortality, personal identity, the unity of existence, and similar matters which are the familiar principles of intuitive religion. The obscurities of the poems occupied with this vision are partly attributable to the limitations shared by all literature of mysticism . . . The spirit has no language of its own . . .

Thus, Korg argues, Thomas's idiosyncratic language in his early poems is the reflection both of a joy in playing with words and of a necessity to express the ineffable unity of the universe. This vision, which Korg describes (p. 29) as a "mythic consciousness" and "a rediscovery of the reality found in primitive religion," involves conflict within an overriding unity, and implies the same sort of driving forces and interchangeable processes all critics have found in the early poetry. Korg's particular contribution, however, is the hypothesis that, around Thomas's middle period, a greater concern with the specifics of external reality displaced the primary vision, "so that in the later poems ultimate realities are approached through nature and daily life instead of visionary imagery."

Korg recognizes that the poet's vision seems, in some poems, to coincide with Christian mysticism, but in his three major emphases—the unity of spiritual life, of matter, and of time—Thomas "goes beyond the Christian framework . . . and toward a more general mysticism" (p. 31) which corresponds closely with Cassirer's description of the symbolic structures which characterize primitive religious thought. The poet soon moves away from that world, however, and in the poem "Twenty-four years," in *18 Poems*, bids the vision farewell. The succeeding poems are more personal and less cosmic; like Wordsworth, the poet turns to the *memory* of mystical experience for the ability to imaginatively transform the reality of his current experience. As late as the "Poem in October" and "Fern Hill," Thomas is still affirming parts of his original vision, but without the signs of struggle and search for a spiritual rationale which vitalized his earlier work. "Poem in October," which Korg compares to "Tintern Abbey," is (p. 120) "a leap of the heart, not of the spirit," while in "Fern Hill," the "acceptance of death would be more convincing as a spiritual triumph if it were preceded by

evidence of resistance; but the transition from joy in life to resignation to death is smooth and untroubled . . ." More poetically, but in
essential agreement, Renato Poggioli (1953, p. 86) speaks of
Thomas as "a soul naturally pagan, in a barbaric rather than a classical sense, and then more pre-Christian than anti-Christian."

Almost as if he had taken Poggioli's comment literally, Robert K.
Burdette in *The Saga of Prayer: The Poetry of Dylan Thomas*
(1972) argues that Thomas's spiritual vision directly parallels that
of Gnosticism. Gnosticism, a religious movement of late antiquity,
has ties with early Jewish mysticism. Around the second century it
influenced, and was in turn influenced by, Christianity. Gnostics
hold that the material world is evil and illusory, a creation of a lower
form of the true Godhead, who is an absolute beyond predicates.
The unconscious soul of man strives for transcendent union with
the One, and can come to that state through the call of Jesus. This
call typically is heard in a visionary experience, rather than by way
of the Gospels or the sacraments. Gnostics deny the validity of
atonement and the humanity of Christ; they stress a doctrine of mystical election and deny that the physical universe is God's handi-
work or otherwise reflective of Him. As a general mystical system
of belief, strongly influenced by Platonism, Gnosticism relates to
many other forms of mystical doctrine up through twentieth-century theosophy; as a Christian heresy it is most clearly opposed to
the various Protestant sects and is most closely approached by Origen and Clement of Alexandria. Modern forms of Gnosticism tend
to be monistic, and have influenced idealists such as Hegel and
Goethe, while the ancient religion is dualistic.

Burdette's concern is to demonstrate parallels rather than to find
sources (p. 9): "Thomas's religious beliefs are in a long tradition
of religious experience that is closely allied to the 'occult tradition,'
represented here by Gnosticism," but this "does *not* mean that
Thomas can be called 'a Gnostic.' " Indeed, he flatly admits (p. 26)
that there is no evidence for the poet's having read Gnostic writings,
or even discussions of them. Nonetheless, many of the parallels he
discusses do seem to illuminate the poet's work, if only obliquely.
Burdette relies almost exclusively upon Hans Jonas's *The Gnostic
Religion* (1958), and quotes extensively from it. Early in the book,
he lays out the essential Gnostic cosmology which, although he
fails to develop the idea very fully, has clear correspondences to the
triple God which Moynihan identifies (Burdette, 1972, p. 15):

There are, then, two aspects of creation—the thought-cosmos (the
archetype) and its 'copy,' the sense-cosmos—which have a common

source, the Mind. God the Father is Mind, who produces Thought, or the Logos, the Son. The Son then 'makes' the sense-cosmos . . . Similarly, Mind, the Father, is thought of as impregnating Matter, the Mother, to produce the thought-cosmos, the Son. Father, Mother, and Son are aspects of God rather than separate deities.

God in this formulation is both transcendent and immanent, and comes to be known through mystical knowledge of the Self. This Self is multiple, a series of "envelopes"—Body, Spirit, and Soul—enclosing the deepest self, or Mind. Thus Gnostic imagery identifies "highest" and "innermost;" "heaven" is in "earth," and all essential phenomena are perceived internally.

Burdette's study focuses upon a group of images important to both Thomas and the Gnostics: "Light and Darkness," "The Celestial Sea," "House and Garments," "Sleep and Awakening," and "The Maiden Soul." Light, for Thomas, he argues, represents mystical revelation, found always within the darkness of the phenomenal world; black may also symbolize a soul in ignorance. More interesting is his discussion of the Celestial Sea, a common Gnostic image for the middle-ground between the original light and mundane existence: the spirit-soul, in its fall toward creation, is "clothed," made material, by this sea, which continues to surround us. Thus life on earth is frequently imaged as "undersea," bound by time and *becoming*. Ascending again toward the Source, the Gnostic soul "swims" upward, shedding its envelopes of mortal "clothing."

An alternate set of images describes life in this world as a sleep, and mystic revelation as awakening. Men enjoy their slumber, and are only with difficulty awakened by a messenger—the Prince of Light or Son of God, who also has appeared as Osiris, Adonis, Horus, and Hermes. Frequently this annunciation is dramatized, the soul being imaged as a bride and the revelation as a marriage or conception. Thus (p. 65) "when the 'light' and 'dark' aspects of man enter each other, meet each other, the savior has found the sleeper, the bridegroom has married the virgin, the man has found himself."

The remainder of Burdette's book consists of a reading of four of the longer poems within this context. The results are fairly predictable: most of Thomas's work appears as a discussion of the mystical experience, and his characteristic imagery is easily assimilated by the Gnostic framework. Oddly, Burdette does not capitalize on two aspects of Gnosticism which would seem to have special relevance to Thomas: the doctrine whereby the human body is seen as micro-

cosm, and the Manichaean emphasis in some Gnostic sects. Neither
does he attempt to assimilate Olson's astrological arguments. The
book as a whole is depressingly general and one feels that individual
poems, quoted out of context, are wilfully warped toward a single
subject. If we are to believe Burdette, Thomas's poetry is both
repetitive and relatively homogeneous, showing little real conflict
or development. But perhaps the strongest objection to Burdette's
reading is his implicit portrayal of Thomas as a world-denying
ascetic. To say that Thomas—at least in his later poems—dismissed
the natural world as evil and illusory, seems a gross misreading.

A somewhat more successful interpretation, though it shares
the shaky theoretical grounds of Burdette's study, is that of Annis
Pratt in *Dylan Thomas's Early Prose* (1970, pp. 85–103). In chapter 3 of her study Pratt suggests that the early prose and much of
the poetry shows correspondences to aspects of Welsh bardic religion. Pratt's main source for the system of "bardo-druidic beliefs"
is William ab Ithel's *Y Barddas*, compiled in 1862, a book which
modern scholarship regards as a sensitive and informative hoax,
much like MacPherson's Ossian. Further, Pratt admits that there is
no evidence Thomas had any knowledge of the book. From these
inauspicious foundations, though, Pratt does raise an imposing edifice of speculation, and one which seems to do less violence to
Thomas than does Burdette's parallel study. She emphasizes three
aspects of bardic religion: the use of Christ as a pagan solar deity,
the stress upon the original Logos or all-creating word and the
poet's religious search for it, and the assumption of an immanent
rather than a transcendent divinity, which brought the bards
close to the Pelagian heresy. As it turns out, these emphases do fit
Thomas's mystical symbology remarkably well, especially in the
early prose and the later narrative poems. The bardic mixture of
Christian and pagan elements coupled with a metaphysical and
theological concern with language seems the perfect recipe for the
poet's vision. What conclusions we should draw from this, though,
it is difficult to say.

Christian Interpretations

Apart from attempts to define Thomas's religiosity in intuitive
or ambiguous terms (mystic, sacramental, etc.), the majority of
criticism deals with Thomas's relationship to Christianity. Clark
Emery (1962, p. 15) defines the dispute:

Because he affirms a crucified Christ and is witness to the test, the fall, the judgment, the agony, and the redemption *in himself,* he may be said to be a kind of Christian. But in his sectlessness and his sexfulness, he is a Christian with a difference, one who may be said by more orthodox Christians not to be one at all.

Nevertheless, some critics take Thomas's Christianity as a given. T. P. McDonnell (1954, p. 501), immediately after the poet's death, pointed to the "deeply religious and Christian" later poems, while Howard Sergeant (1962, p. 59) claims that, "unlike those who became Christians by deliberate choice, he was never at pains to declare it . . . God, for him, was an established fact." Whatever ambiguities exist in the poetry's religious statements might be explained rather by Thomas's compositional process of conflicting images than by any religious uncertainty. Sister M. Roberta Jones (1966, p. 79) sees "A Winter's Tale" as the realization that "a man's search for love must seek beyond its fulfillment in sexual union," but otherwise she shows little sense of any ambiguity, conflict, or development in Thomas's Christianity. Bernard Kneiger's Christian interpretation of Thomas (1962) expands upon the *Explicator* article mentioned earlier and upon his later ones in that periodical (1959, 1960). D. S. Savage (Tedlock, 1960, p. 143) sees more ambivalence in the poet: although he makes central use of Christian myth and history, and resembles Christian mystics like Vaughan and Traherne in many ways, he is distinguished from them by "moral or spiritual passivity," an acceptance of inexorable nature. Savage sees a movement in the poetry from "speculative statement" to "bewilderment and questioning" to a final "positive, exulting note of acceptance and praise" (p. 145). Babette Deutsch (1963, p. 376), like Savage, sees an evocation of Traherne in the poet's later writing: "the beclouded pantheism of his early work gives place to a more orthodox religiosity, but expressed in the same intensely personal terms. Theologically, Deutsch contrasts Thomas with members of the "Apocalypse" group—Fraser, Hendry, and Treece—with whom he was often associated. Like them, Thomas starts with a private sort of religiosity, but unlike them does not move toward "a 'Personalism' that might be described as a kind of ethical anarchism" (p. 369). Just what Thomas *does* move to instead is less clear, but Deutsch sees most of the middle and later poems as an attempt "to see the wisdom and power of God" exhibited in a world of pain and banality.

H. J. Hammerton (1966, p. 73) makes a similar point, within a tacit assumption of the poet's Christianity. He sees Christian love as a central concept in Thomas's poetry, particularly in its implication of willing sacrifice: "In 'Over Sir John's hill' he leaves us with the suggestion that in nature's predatory system there is an element of self-offering." In the "Refusal to Mourn," we see human sacrifice and suffering transfigured by love and acceptance, and even Thomas's poetic discipline (p. 76) "was a sacrifice he willingly made to the highest good he knew." John Nist's "Reading of the Later Poems" (1962, p. 3) emphasizes that, rather than assuming the "pantheistic pantheism" with which William Empson taxed him, Thomas came gradually to embrace the Christian myth for a "structure of faith;" his personal anguish during the war years forced him toward this, away from his early narcissism, and the transformation can be seen in the "Ballad of the Long-legged Bait," where Nist interprets the bait as Christ's heart.

But, with the exception of Kneiger's analyses, none of the foregoing articles both approaches Thomas's religion systematically and justifies the approach through close reading of the poems. Probably the first such study, limited as it was, was Aneirin Talfan Davies's *Dylan: Druid of the Broken Body* (1964). Davies's twin themes are his subject's religious development and his debt to his Welsh culture; perhaps a subliminal sort of theme is the continuous —and rather paradoxical—parallel he establishes between Thomas's spiritual evolution and the life of a Christian saint. Davies admits that there are both agnostic and Nonconformist elements in the early work, but argues that Thomas moved toward a vision whose implications are not only Christian, but Catholic. Even the early poem, "This bread I break," Davies finds (p. 21) "a poetic restatement of the reality of the Sacrament of Body and Blood":

To what extent this poem signifies the poet's *belief* it is difficult to judge; but it is obvious that he finds the sacramental approach increasingly congenial, and as he developed, we see him take over, more and more, a Catholic imagery and symbolism.

Davies finds that the only way in which the poems can be taken seriously is to assume (p. 23) that Thomas had an actual experience of religious illumination. Davies's rather radical approach leads him to some unusual interpretations: thus he states (p. 9) that "I have longed to move away," rather than attacking religious orthodoxy, deals with "the question of integrity in relation to the poet's responsibility toward his craft as a poet and towards words." Similarly, (p. 24) "Before I knocked" is displayed as an example of Thomas's "wrestling with the challenge of orthodox Christianity." "In Memory of Ann Jones," Davies admits (p. 35), puts the poet in the po-

sition of a Welsh Nonconformist preacher—suggesting, beyond
that, the image of the druid—but he insists that this poem is "his
last Nonconformist utterance." Perhaps Davies's most convincing
example is his reading of "The Conversation of Prayer," where he
quotes the earlier insight of G. S. Fraser (Brinnin, 1960, p. 53): the
poem, if read literally, seems to advance the totally non-Protestant
concept of "the reversibility of grace,"

The idea that all prayers and all good acts cooperate for the benefit
of all men, and that God . . . can give the innocent the privilege of
suffering some of the tribulations which have been incurred by re-
deemable sinners.

As might be expected, Davies sees "Vision and Prayer" as the narration of a typical experience of Christian illumination.

One of the most sophisticated, scholarly, and intelligent books involving the question of Thomas's religion is H. H. Kleinman's *The
Religious Sonnets of Dylan Thomas: A Study in Imagery and
Meaning* (1963), in the Perspectives in Criticism series. Kleinman,
a former student of Tindall, unlike his mentor takes the religious
dimension of the sequence as central (p. 10):

I believe the sonnets are a deeply moving statement of religious per-
plexity concluding in spiritual certainty . . . There is a revelation in
the sonnets of a fearful struggle of the poet with his God . . . The
poem begins with a sonnet mocking the descent of the Word; it concludes in a spiraling ascent of faith.

Kleinman seldom grows more specific about Thomas's particular
breed of Christianity, assuming an inconsistent theology for the
poet (p. 45): "he might be a Sabellian, an Adoptionist, an Arian."
The book begins with brief characterizations of the sonnets' major
interpreters: Scarfe (Brinnin, 1960, pp. 21–33); Stearns (Tedlock,
1960, pp. 113–131); Daiches (Cox, 1966, pp. 14–24); Olson
(1954); and Tindall (1962). He then proceeds to a thoroughly
detailed sonnet-by-sonnet explication.

Kleinman's strengths are obvious: he brings to the study a broad
and deep reading, particularly in the Bible—Old and New Testa-
ment and Apocrypha—and in seventeenth-century mystical poetry. Although he argues that Thomas's acquaintance with such
arcane sources as the *Egyptian Book of the Dead* was greater than
has been supposed, he is careful to point out that the bulk of his own
discussion concerns echoes and parallels, rather than specific allu-

sions. When he does encounter a specific allusive image, such as the
pelican's feeding her young with her own blood, he is careful to
give an exhaustive background in the image's antecedents.

Like Tindall, Kleinman often gives a number of possible interpretations of a difficult image, though he is less inclined than Tindall to allow his readings to decay into total ambiguity. His reading
of the difficult Sonnet IV is undoubtedly the most illuminating one
available, although he manages to add surprising shadings even to
such thoroughly discussed sonnets as I and X. But despite the fact
that Kleinman's emphases are quite different from Olson's—represent, in fact, a more balanced approach to the poems—it does not
appear that Kleinman's interpretation greatly changes the broad
outline of meaning which Olson established. Indeed, although
Kleinman's perceptions and allusions are interesting in their own
right, one occasionally feels that an enormous scholarly apparatus
is being directed at the poetry without truly establishing much more
than a parallel between Thomas's mind and that of numerous Christian mystical poets. G. S. Fraser (1964, p. 186) adopts the "plain
man's" viewpoint when he complains, "the more scholars like Professor Kleinman explain to us what Dylan Thomas 'really means,'
the more the ordinary reader . . . begins to worry and wonder in a
depressed way whether he has ever understood a word of Thomas."

If Davies (1964) stresses Catholic or "sacramental" elements in
Thomas while Burdette (1972) stresses the Gnostic mystical vision
and Kleinman concentrates upon more conventional elements of
Christian mysticism, John Ackerman in *Dylan Thomas: His Life
and Work* (1964) gives the most detailed and intelligent account
of the influence of Welsh Nonconformism upon the poetry. Ackerman's primary theme is the presence of the Welsh heritage, in all
its forms, in the poet's work, but the religious motif is strongly
argued. Unlike many less perceptive commentators, Ackerman
shows a thorough awareness of the contradictions and ambiguities
of Thomas's religious thought.

Two earlier critics upon whom Ackerman relies are Karl Shapiro
and Vernon Watkins (1957). Shapiro's insights about Thomas's
religion (Tedlock, 1960, p. 276)—"direct and natural . . . simply
part of life"—and the "puritanism" (p. 283) which "sets up the tension in his poetry . . . the basic sexual tension, the basic theological
tension"—are both traced to the Welsh heritage. Ackerman argues,
rather generally, that Thomas soaked up through the social milieu
and through racial inheritance those elements of Welsh life and culture which he did not consciously adopt. Thus, despite his ignorance of "old Welsh poetry," he nevertheless (p. 6) displays its

awareness of the dual nature of reality, of unity in disunity, of the simultaneity of life and death, of time as an eternal moment rather than as something with a separate past and future.

Added to this basic existential stance are particular elements from Welsh Nonconformity, most importantly the Bible, which pervades Thomas's writing as it does that of most other Anglo-Welsh writers; but hardly less important is the Nonconformist ethic (p. 9) with its "concern with the individual conscience, sin and salvation." Ackerman sees in Thomas's poetry a reflection of the emotional, revivalist fervor of the chapel, particularly (p. 11) the "singing or chanting eloquence known as *hwyl*" practiced by Welsh preachers.

Less directly, through Anglo-Welsh poetry, come common elements which betray the "religious attitude to experience" (p. 16):

The celebration by the poet of all natural life, animal and vegetal, a celebration expressed usually in sensuous terms . . . the basis of this attitude is a sense of the unity of all creation, and this identity of all created forms is religious in character. The poet is aware of a sacramental universe in which the common things of life serve to illustrate profound mysteries.

In addition, Ackerman detects "a Hebraic element in the Welsh character . . . from which stems the belief that everything in the world is, for its own sake, holy." It should be noted that this is quite unlike the modern Christian tradition with its Platonic infusion.

Like Kleinman, Ackerman explores the influence of seventeenth-century Welsh religious poetry (p. 19): the interest in childhood as a state of grace and innocence; the alternating senses of separation from God and of mystical vision; and the attraction to wit and paradox, bordering on blasphemy. Like Donne, Thomas plays with the idea of divine versus sexual love; like Traherne, Vaughan, and Herbert, Thomas's introspective consciousness reveals a deep sense of sin and separation from God—a sense *not* shared by the English romantics, for example.

According to Ackerman, Thomas's close friend and poetic comrade Vernon Watkins fostered the Puritanism which was present even in the early poetry. He cites V. S. Pritchett on this general topic (p. 42), underlining his observation that Puritans tend to see life as a "drama of power and guilt" and are by nature almost morbidly introspective. Ackerman's book, after its introductory chapters, examines the books of poetry and prose in chronological order, focusing on the major poems and stories in some detail and

characterizing the stages of Thomas's poetic and spiritual development. He finds no real acceptance of a liberal Christian theology
to balance the Puritan strain in the early poems; in *25P* (p. 62)
Thomas is still interpreting Biblical narrative in terms of a personal
mythology, as in "Incarnate devil." Here, as elsewhere, Ackerman
realizes that Thomas shows a (p. 63) "dual attitude towards religious myth and symbol," one of reverence counterbalanced by
blasphemy; the poet's jokes and puns throughout the sonnet sequence are especially evident. This attitude Ackerman traces (pp.
64–65) to a "racial strain," the Welsh "ability to think of God and
Christ in easy, colloquial terms" which Stanford (1965, p. 24) has
already pointed out.

Ackerman (p. 67) interprets the poem "I have longed to move
away" as an example of Thomas's vacillation on the subject of
Christianity, and in particular his ambivalent feelings about the
chapel; as late as the poem "Lament," Ackerman realizes, the poet
is capable of a broad satire of Welsh Nonconformity. Nonetheless,
with the volume *D&E* he (p. 115) "attains his full stature as a religious poet." He assumes a "typically Welsh blend of Christian
and pagan thought and feeling: both attitudes are, however, religious in character." As one might expect, Ackerman sees the "Refusal to Mourn" as the fullest and richest exposition of Thomas's
new stance. But set against this bardic invocation is the celebrated
"Fern Hill" which Ackerman approaches (p. 122) as a mystical,
visionary attempt to recreate the childhood state of innocence and
grace—a vision Thomas shares with Vaughan and Traherne.

In the later poems, Ackerman thinks (p. 158) "that Thomas, in
his movement towards a more philosophic acceptance of Christian
faith and teaching, was deeply influenced by Vernon Watkins,
who has himself told me that Thomas tested every argument by
reference to the Christian faith." Though Thomas's belief was never
orthodox, by the time of "Poem on his birthday"

The poet has learned to accept even the terror of his own inner conflict; he has learned 'to praise in spite of.' The ideas of original sin,
salvation, and damnation, are the natural outcome of the attempt to
face the world, and in Thomas's final poems there is no retreat into
childhood. Not only does the poet claim an increasing faith as he approaches death, but the world, too, seems to sing its Creator's praises
more joyously.

Ackerman's book, though anticipated in some of its ideas by
Clara Lander's rather impressionistic article "With Welsh and Reverent Rook" (1958), is novel in the scholarly dedication it brings

to as vague an approach as the cultural-*cum*-racial. Ackerman is most convincing in his explications of specific poems, and makes good use of the poet's notebooks, personal interviews, and other then-unpublished material. It could of course be argued that what is "Welsh" about Thomas's poetry and religion is not its most important facet, or that, despite numerous parallels to other Welsh writers, nothing has been "proved" as to a Welsh inheritance; but that would be to do an injustice to Ackerman's goal and to his method. The problem of placing Thomas in a Welsh context is discussed further in chapter 6 below.

A much weaker, more recent book by Alphonsus M. Reddington, O.F.M. Conv., entitled *Dylan Thomas: A Journey from Darkness to Light* (1968) comes to conclusions about the poet's religion much like Ackerman's through a thematic methodology. Reddington (p. 6) thinks Thomas's poetry revolves about three central tensions, and moves toward a resolution in each case: from Death to Life (philosophical); from Sin to Innocence (moral); and from Doubt to Faith (theological). This rather arbitrary schema, which organizes Reddington's book, nevertheless does reflect the poet's tendency toward dualistic or even dialectical thinking. Thomas's personal religion he describes as (p. 12) "a blending of Christianity (treated mainly as myth or fable in his early poems) and other forms of belief which he borrowed from Welsh druidism and the occult." Reddington accepts—and translates in Christian terms—the three-stage division of Thomas's poetic career suggested by Tindall (1953) and since generally agreed upon. He claims (p. 30) that "these periods are not merely distinct, but also represent progressive stages of development." In the first period,

Thomas presents a sardonic appraisal of his situation, which combined a growing fear of death with an occasional burst of defiance of it; in his second period, he attempts to shake off his morbid preoccupation with death by giving up his isolation and feeling compassion for other men; in his third period, Thomas reveals not only a joyful celebration of life but also a peaceful resignation to his own impending death.

Reddington elaborates upon this pattern in the "Death to Life" chapter, interpreting specific poems in its light: thus the "dream poems" of the middle period, which Ralph Maud (1963, p. 79) sees as discussions of sexual waste, Reddington (p. 38) reads as concerning *spiritual* waste; "Ears in the turrets hear" he views as the poet revealing his fears of giving up his earlier isolation. Not until "Over Sir John's hill" does Thomas totally accept the idea of death, though his changing attitude is evident in the three birthday poems ("Twenty-four years," "Poem in October," and "Poem on his birthday"). Reddington stresses the effect of World War II upon the poet who, like Wilfred Owen before him, was forced by warfare to face the reality of death and his own community with mankind.

Reddington's discussion of the movement "from Sin to Innocence" relies greatly upon Olson's argument that Thomas is essentially concerned with moral questions (Olson, 1954, pp. 36–41, 50–52). Reddington claims that Aivaz's picture of the poet's world as "process"—pantheistic, mechanistic, and deterministic—applies only to the early work, and even there is modified by an overriding Manichaean vision. The early, Puritan Thomas (p. 57) sees sex as evil, and the sex-sin-death dilemma is not resolved until the "Ballad of the Long-legged Bait." Here Reddington, echoing Olson, sees Thomas's central theme as mortification of the flesh and fleshly desires—symbolized by the girl—in order to win salvation. Similarly, the movement "From Doubt to Faith" is accomplished (p. 76) through Thomas's change in emphasis from human to divine love, shown in "Love in the Asylum" and "A Winter's Tale." Although the poet implies a mystical mission of universal oneness in his last poems, Reddington insists (p. 78) that he "sought more than a general cosmic unity; he aspired to a personal union with the creator of all things." Elsewhere, Reddington speaks of (p. 69) "his 'spiral ascension' to Christ, 'the sudden sun.' " The acceptance of a personal God is marked in "Vision and Prayer."

Reddington's book is not positively misleading, but unlike Ackerman's or Kleinman's—or even Olson's—it shows no real appreciation for the contradictions and ambiguities of Thomas's work and vision. His method, quoting individual phrases or groups of lines out of context, allows him to advance his argument in spite of the poetry as well as through it; few individual poems are clarified by his rather simplistic approach, and many difficulties are glossed over. Reddington has read the basic critical sources (with the surprising exception of Ackerman), but shows no real scholarship even in his examination of Christian elements in the poetry.

Dynamic Interpretations

If critics like Reddington too often seem unaware of the conflicting Christian and anti-Christian elements in Thomas's work, his dynamic love-hate relationship with a coherent religion, there is a small group of critics who wish to examine the nature of the conflict itself rather than attempting a resolution which the poet himself may never have found nor felt. Derek Stanford, whose book on Thomas in its original edition (1954) showed considerable uncertainty about the nature and extent of the poet's religion, three years later attempted to come to terms with the problem in a *Southwest Review* article entitled "Dylan Thomas's Animal Faith" (1957, p. 205). Stanford uses George Santayana as his touchstone: the poet's faith in a work like "Poem on his birthday" suggests the famous *mot* on Santayana's thought, "there is no God, and Mary is his mother." Stanford (p. 211) invokes the philosopher's distinction between "moral" and "animal" faith: moral faith occurs when one man believes in another man's thoughts and feelings, whereas animal faith can be described as "a sort of expectation or openmouthedness." Thomas's religious enterprise is like the one Santayana describes in *Animal Skepticism and Faith* (1923): "I lay siege to truth only as animal exploration and fancy may do so, first from one quarter and then from another . . . My system is no system of the universe." Thomas's ambiguities—like the phrase "fabulous, dear God"—characteristically fuse doubt and belief in an intellectually chaotic but emotionally coherent way.

Other critics have shared this perception, and articulated it in alternative forms. The poet Louise Bogan (1955, p. 375), in a short review of *In Country Sleep and Other Poems,* noted that the book "contrasts a world of fairy tale and pagan folklore with a world of Christian ritual and belief." Interpreting the title poem very differently from Reddington, Bogan believes Thomas "contrived a connection between the two realms because he is aware of the buried instinctive life they share." Evelyn Broy (1965–66, p. 506) sees the essential conflict as a war between sexuality and a Puritan Christianity, a war in which neither side could win: "if he accepted the Christian way of life . . . he had also to accept the fact that sexuality, quite as important to him as religion, was ugly and reprehensible. This he was not prepared to do." Broy demonstrates the interconnection of the religious and sexual motives by pointing to the story "Peaches" in *Portrait of the Artist as a Young Dog* where Gwilym revises his love poems, changing all the girls' names to God.

Robert L. Peters approaches the "Uneasy Faith of Dylan Thomas" (1958) through unique and perceptive readings of "Over Sir John's hill" and "Poem on his birthday." He views Thomas (p. 25) as "a writer of unresolved conflict, a curious writer who, caught up in the sweep of his own rhetoric and imagination, was able to convince himself within the confines of a single poem of the soundness of contrary views." Much of the difficulty, Peters implies, springs from the problem of attitude: Thomas recognizes vast, unifying forces of life and of death in the universe, but is perpetually unsure whether the essential meaning of things is to be read positively or negatively. In "Over Sir John's hill" the poet, faced with the death of the innocent birds, "resolves finally to construct his own apotheosis" for them: "If no god exists to right such violence, and if there is no conventional immortality, man must be a substitute."

Similarly, Thomas tries to come to terms with his own impending death in "Poem on his birthday." "Heaven," he says behind his tangle of words, "exists only in the mind of man and is a fiction;" but he nevertheless tries to convince himself that Heaven is "true," and he, for one, is going to accept it. But toward the end of the poem he imagines that Heaven vividly as a blackberry woods, and God as an eternal berry-picker: dark now becomes "a long way," and as he moves closer to death the pagan life around him becomes increasingly meaningful (p. 29):

At this point, Thomas seems to have rejected fully a belief in the conventional Heaven, God, and Ghost of the earlier stanzas in favor of a temporal, though sobering, knowledge that he, like all men, is merely one of Nature's many properties and can expect to find no other immortality.

I quote Peters at such length only because it seems that in dealing with poems whose conflicts and ambiguities other critics have too hurriedly glossed over, he comes nearer to identifying their sources of energy. In general, even among those critics who view Thomas as a poet of spiritual struggle, all too few proceed to trace that struggle through the rhetoric of individual poems, or to recognize the "willed" or "forced" nature of Thomas's religious affirmation. Another critic who does adopt Peter's approach is Naomi Christensen (1963, p. 49):

when Christ promised eternal life . . . Thomas longed to accept this promise as fact. He wanted, as he put it in 'Vision and Prayer,' to be 'lost in the blinding/One.' His poems—particularly his later poems—are recurrently concerned with this struggle for faith. And in some of them he resolves the conflict in positive terms. But this resolution is artistic—i.e., existential—not essential, and it does not extend beyond the particular poem.

Christensen then proceeds to an explication of the sonnet sequence which, while relying in part upon Olson, shows more clearly in thematic terms the unresolved nature of the poet's spiritual vision.

But undoubtedly the most important critic to deal at length with specifically defining the problem of Thomas's faith is Rushworth M. Kidder in his book *Dylan Thomas: The Country of the Spirit* (1973). The distinguishing characteristic of Kidder's study is that he deals head-on with the problems of definition and terminology I have raised several times during this chapter; in fact part 1 of his book is devoted to a definition of "religious poetry." His main points are that (p. 6) "*Religion*, adequately defined, includes not only passive belief but also active *participation;*" that (p. 7) although Thomas was aware of other religions, specifically *Biblical* religion is the central religious influence on his work; and that (p. 9) the religious poet must feel a binding *obligation* to his work.

Kidder distinguishes (p. 13) between *praise* and *prayer*, and concludes that the former is the essence of his poetry. Perceptively, he identifies in Thomas (pp. 15–16) "the complementary notion that such a concept, too fragile for direct communication, must be packaged in a protective ambiguity that takes either the form of irony . . . or the form of verbal opacity . . ." Kidder then discusses four epithets which are often attached to Thomas's poetry: "mystic," "sacramental," "pantheistic," and "pagan." He concludes (p. 18) that, "too committed to the evidence of the senses to ignore materiality, . . . his poetry can be considered mystic (and then only occasionally) only in the broadest sense . . . ," rather than as an avowal or example of the traditional Mystic Way. Similarly, "sacramental" defines only an aspect of his poetry, though the word is particularly appropriate in those instances where he treats the act of poetry as celebration or ceremony; though sacrament involves ritual, Thomas is often unreligiously ritualistic as well. Pantheism and paganism are insufficient concepts to define his poetry. Pantheism involves an immanent, wholly knowable God, while in Thomas's work there is always a sense of separation. As noted by Moynihan (1966, p. 35), it is also too passive: "Pantheism seemed to Thomas an involvement with life at a lesser stage of being, at a lesser stage of intensity." In fact (Kidder, 1973, p. 22), the same objections hold for paganism, an essentially passive system of belief. Rather than accepting natural cycles like the seasons, the poet is always striving to rise above them.

In the remainder of part 1, Kidder explores the concepts of poetic ambiguity and poetic obscurity, and relates Thomas's avowed poetic aims and techniques to his practice. Quoting extensively from the poet's early correspondence, from his prose works, and from his critical essays, Kidder firmly establishes religion as a conscious concern of the poetry. Part 2 of the book takes the next logical step, an attempt to analyze the religious "density," as it were, of individual poems. Kidder's central realization is that the mere presence of Biblical or liturgical imagery does not necessarily constitute a religious commitment for the poet, or even a "religious" dimension for the poem. In the simplest kind, *referential* imagery (p. 67), "Thomas treats the Bible not as a basis for religion but as a body of mythology." *Allusive* imagery is more complex; the reference is in some way disguised and made ambivalent. It may point indirectly to a Biblical event or character, or may (p. 80) "attain a functional complexity" by "blending the Biblical with the sexual, the obstetrical, the anatomical, and even the comical."

But allusive imagery, though more poetically sophisticated a device than referential, still does not necessarily imply a religious statement within the poem. Kidder's last category, *thematic* imagery, does. It is (p. 91) "propositional: its theme can be stated in sentence form as a proposition." Because of the multifoliate, expansive meanings of a thematic image, the particular proposition cannot be identified simply by examining the image, or even the image within the context of the poem, but must be inferred from the whole body of similar images in Thomas's work. Kidder gives at the outset (p. 47) an example of each of these kinds of imagery from the poem "Holy Spring," a poem about a springtime fire raid during World War II. In the lines "the Spring time is all/Gabriel and radiant shrubbery," Thomas makes reference to Gabriel's two Biblical functions: telling Mary of her divine maternity and warning Daniel of impending war. Thus, (p. 48) "Gabriel comes to tell of a Saviour, amid the 'radiant shrubbery' of burgeoning spring; as a prophet of destruction he comes to foretell desolation, amid the 'radiant shrubbery' of a burning landscape."

However ingenious, the "referential" image is neither truly complex nor disguised. On the other hand, the lines "My arising prodigal/Sun the father his quiver full of infants of fire" contains imagery which is both. The rising sun, seen by the poet arising from bed after a night bombing, is both spendthrift and a returned wanderer; "sun the father" implies a pagan deity, and simultaneously the Christian doctrine of incarnation; the remainder of the "allusive" image establishes this arising sun as the poet's penis, ready to produce children like arrows (see Psalm 127:4-5). But a greater depth of meaning still is evident in the phrase "the cureless body," a "thematic" image. Here "cureless" means both mortal—and thus mortally ill—and without a priest for the "cure of souls." But "counted," as we can appreciate only after examining the image in numerous other poems by Thomas, had for him specifically Christian overtones—"accounted" or "judged," but also "numbered" or "marked," as God numbers and judges all things. Thus (pp. 50–51) the "faith expressed in the phrase 'cureless counted body,' then, is that the body, although priestless and subject to process, is under divine care."

It should be stressed that what Kidder has identified are not merely different poetic techniques, to be used arbitrarily in a given poem, but processes involving different sorts of spiritual commitment, almost different *languages*, in Cassirer's sense. Not surprisingly, the greater part of the religious imagery in the early volumes is referential or allusive, while the bulk of the thematic imagery occurs in the last volumes. As Kidder admits, the use of a thematic image does not prove explicitly the poet's adherence to a religious faith at any given point; but because of its very nature, thematic imagery is imbedded deeply within the poetic consciousness. Its occurrence strongly suggests that the proposition behind it is held by the poet as "true" for him. As can perhaps be seen from the examples above, identifying "allusive" and "thematic" imagery often depends on recognizing Biblical associations, and Kidder is unparalleled in the associations he can unearth; occasionally they seem arbitrary, obscure, or unlikely, but it is well to remember that Thomas admitted to having been saturated with the Bible in his youth. Clearly, Kidder's three types of imagery interpenetrate, and it is sometimes difficult to see why a given image belongs to one category rather than another, or indeed why it should be taken as religious at all. But these are quibbles. Kidder's methodology is at the least an excellent vehicle for his explications of individual poems. Equally importantly, it allows for the variations and conflicts within Thomas's changing faith and its poetic expression, and this I think must be the *sine qua non* of future Thomas criticism.

References

Ackerman, John
1964. *Dylan Thomas: His Life and Work*. New York: Oxford Univ. Pr.
Astre, Georges-Albert
1953. "Victoire de la Poésie," *Adam*, no. 238, pp. 40–42.
Austin, Richard
1954. "Dylan Thomas: A Religious Poet," *The Bell* (Dublin), April, pp. 47–50.
Bayley, John
1957. "Dylan Thomas." In *The Romantic Survival: A Study in Poetic Evolution*, pp. 186–227. London: Constable & Co., reprinted

in *Dylan Thomas: A Collection of Critical Essays*, edited by C. B. Cox. Englewood Cliffs, N.J.: Prentice-Hall, 1966.

Beardsley, Monroe C., and Sam Hynes
1960. "Misunderstanding Poetry: Notes on Some Readings of Dylan Thomas," *College English* March, pp. 315–22.

Bloom, Edward A.
1960. "Dylan Thomas' 'Naked Vision,' " *Western Humanities Review* Autumn, pp. 389–400.

Bloom, Edward A., and Lillian D.
1960. "Dylan Thomas: His Intimations of Mortality," *Boston University Studies in English* Autumn, pp. 138–51.

Bogan, Louise
1955. "The Later Dylan Thomas." In *Selected Criticism*, pp. 374–76. New York: Noonday.

Brinnin, John Malcolm
1955. *Dylan Thomas in America: An Intimate Journal*. Boston: Little.
1960. (editor) *A Casebook on Dylan Thomas*. New York: Crowell.

Broy, Evelyn J.
1965–66. "The Enigma of Dylan Thomas," *Dalhousie Review* Winter, pp. 498–508.

Burdette, Robert K.
1972. *The Saga of Prayer: The Poetry of Dylan Thomas*. Paris: Mouton.

Christensen, Naomi
1963. "Dylan Thomas and the Doublecross of Death," *Ball State Teacher's College Forum* Autumn, pp. 49–53.

Cox, C. B.
1966. (editor) *Dylan Thomas: A Collection of Critical Essays*. Englewood Cliffs, N.J.: Prentice-Hall.

Davies, Aneirin Talfan
1964. *Dylan: Druid of the Broken Body*. London: J. M. Dent.

Demetillo, Ricaredo
1962. "The Poetry of Dylan Thomas." In *The Authentic Voice of Poetry*, pp. 68–74. Univ. of the Philippines, Office of Research Coordination.

Deutsch, Babette
1963. "Alchemists of the Word." In *Poetry in Our Time*, pp. 349–88. Rev. ed. New York: Doubleday.

Emery, Clark
1962. *The World of Dylan Thomas*. Coral Gables, Fla.: Univ. of Miami Pr.

FitzGibbon, Constantine
1965. *The Life of Dylan Thomas*. Boston: Little.

Fraser, G. S.
1964. "The Legend and the Puzzle," *Times Literary Supplement* March 5, pp. 185–86.

Garrigue, Jean
1959. "Dark is a Way and Light is a Place," *Poetry* May, pp. 111–14.

Gingerich, Martin
1973. "Dylan Thomas: Curse-Bless," *Anglo-Welsh Review* Spring, pp. 178–82.
Grubb, Frederick
1965. "Worm's Eye: Dylan Thomas." In *A Vision of Reality: A Study of Liberalism in Twentieth-Century Verse*, pp. 179–90. London: Chatto & Windus.
Hammerton, H. J.
1966. "Christian Love in Dylan Thomas," *Theology* (London) Feb., pp. 72–77.
Highet, Gilbert
1960. "Thomas: The Wild Welshman." In *Powers of Poetry*, pp. 151–57. New York: Oxford Univ. Pr.
Jones, Sister M. Roberta
1966. "The Wellspring of Dylan," *English Journal* Jan., pp. 78–82.
Jones, T. H.
1966. *Dylan Thomas*. New York: Barnes & Noble.
Kazin, Alfred
1957. "Posthumous Life of Dylan Thomas," *Atlantic Monthly* Oct., pp. 164–68.
Kidder, Rushworth M.
1973. *Dylan Thomas: The Country of the Spirit*. Princeton: Princeton Univ. Pr.
Kleinman, H. H.
1963. *The Religious Sonnets of Dylan Thomas: A Study in Imagery and Meaning*. Berkeley: Univ. of California Pr.; also New York: Cambridge Univ. Pr.
Kneiger, Bernard
1956. [Sonnet I], *Explicator* Dec., #18.
1959. [Sonnet II], *Explicator* Nov., #14.
1960. [Sonnet III], *Explicator* Jan., #25.
1962. "Dylan Thomas: The Christianity of the 'Altar-Wise by Owl Light' Sequence," *College English* May, pp. 623–28.
Korg, Jacob
1965. *Dylan Thomas*. New York: Twayne.
Lander, Clara
1958. "With Welsh and Reverent Rook," *Queen's Quarterly* Autumn, pp. 437–47.
Lindsay, Jack
1966. "Memories of Dylan Thomas," *Meanjin* Autumn, pp. 48–75.
Maud, Ralph N.
1955. "Dylan Thomas Astro-navigated," *Essays in Criticism* April, pp. 164–68.
1963. *Entrances to Dylan Thomas's Poetry*. Pittsburgh: Univ. of Pittsburgh Pr.
1968. (editor) *Poet in the Making: The Notebooks of Dylan Thomas*. London: J. M. Dent.
McDonnell, T. P.
1954. "The Emergence of Dylan Thomas," *America* Aug. 21, pp. 500–2.

Miller, J. Hillis
  1965. "Dylan Thomas." In *Poets of Reality: Six Twentieth-Century Writers*, pp. 190–216. Cambridge, Mass.: Harvard Univ. Pr.
Mills, Ralph J.
  1965. "Dylan Thomas: Poetry and Process." In *Four Ways of Modern Poetry*, edited by Nathan A. Scott, pp. 51–69. Richmond, Va.: John Knox.
Moss, Stanley
  1967. "Fallen Angel," *New Republic* June 10, pp. 19–20.
Moynihan, William T.
  1966. *The Craft and Art of Dylan Thomas*. Ithaca, N.Y.: Cornell Univ. Pr.; also London: Oxford Univ. Pr.
Nist, John
  1962. "No Reason for Mourning: A Reading of the Later Poems of Dylan Thomas," *Approach* Winter, pp. 3–7.
Olson, Elder
  1954. *The Poetry of Dylan Thomas*. Chicago: Univ. of Chicago Pr.
Pratt, Annis
  1970. *Dylan Thomas's Early Prose: A Study in Creative Mythology*. Pittsburgh: Univ. of Pittsburgh Pr.
Peters, Robert L.
  1958. "The Uneasy Faith of Dylan Thomas: A Study of the Last Poems," *Fresco* (Univ. of Detroit), pp. 25–29.
Poggioli, Renato
  1953. "In Memoria di Dylan Thomas," *Letteratura* dicèmbre, pp. 84–87.
Reddington, Alphonsus M.
  1968. *Dylan Thomas: A Journey from Darkness to Light*. New York: Paulist Pr.
Saunders, Thomas
  1965–66. "Religious Elements in the Poetry of Dylan Thomas," *Dalhousie Review* Winter, pp. 492–97.
Sergeant, Howard
  1962. "The Religious Development of Dylan Thomas," *Review of English Literature* April, pp. 59–67.
Spender, Stephen
  1955. "Greatness of Aim." In *The Making of a Poem*. London: Hamish Hamilton, pp. 35–44.
Stanford, Derek
  1957. "Dylan Thomas's Animal Faith," *Southwest Review* Summer, pp. 205–12.
  1964. *Dylan Thomas: A Literary Study*. Rev. ed. New York: Citadel.
Sweeney, John L.
  1946. "Introduction" to *Selected Writings of Dylan Thomas*, pp. vii–xxiii. New York: New Directions.
Tedlock, E. W.
  1960. (editor) *Dylan Thomas: The Legend and the Poet*. London: Heinemann.
Tindall, William York
  1948. "The Poetry of Dylan Thomas," *American Scholar* Autumn, pp. 431–39.

1953. "Burning and Crested Song," *American Scholar* Autumn, pp. 486–90.

1955. *The Literary Symbol.* New York: Columbia Univ. Pr.

1962. *A Reader's Guide to Dylan Thomas.* New York: Noonday.

Treece, Henry

1949. *Dylan Thomas: 'Dog Among the Fairies'.* London: Lindsay Drummond.

Trick, Bert

1966. "The Young Dylan Thomas," *Texas Quarterly* Summer, pp. 36–49.

Vanson, Frederic

1958. "The Parables of Sunlight: Dylan Thomas as a Religious Poet," *Methodist Magazine* Jan., pp. 22–24.

Verghese, C. Paul

1968. "Religion in Dylan Thomas's Poetry," *Literary Criterion* (Mysore) Winter, pp. 35–41.

Watkins, Vernon

1957. (editor) *Dylan Thomas: Letters to Vernon Watkins.* New York: New Directions.

West, Paul

1970. *Doubt and Dylan Thomas.* Toronto: Univ. of Toronto Pr.

Wilder, Amos N.

1952. "Man and Nature in Dylan Thomas." In *Modern Poetry and the Christian Tradition,* pp. 100–2. New York: Scribner.

CHAPTER 5

The Twentieth-Century Context

Placing Thomas in a literary or cultural context seems to be an ineluctably attractive undertaking for critics. This kind of activity, if it is attempted with enough imagination and discrimination, can transcend mere pedigree-hunting; Thomas's work both illuminates and is illuminated by the poetry of his predecessors. As Borges neatly puts it, "every writer *creates* his own precursors. His work modifies our conception of the past, as it will modify the future." Yet the problem of placing Thomas is made more difficult and in a sense unrewarding by the strong impression of pure originality his work gives. Particularly on its first appearance his poetry seemed utterly unprepared for and unparalleled. Thomas's early defenders and publicists, such as Edith Sitwell and Herbert Read, were inclined to statements like Read's famous, "these poems cannot be reviewed: they can only be acclaimed"—a "review" which, as John Wain points out (Brinnin, *A Casebook on Dylan Thomas*, 1960, p. 68), "drew such furious abuse and raillery that nowadays no one dare be so outspoken." Still, when Read called Thomas an "absolute" poet—as opposed, presumably, to a "contingent" one—he did seem to be making a real point. Louis MacNeice perhaps best summed up the dilemma when he pointed out (Tedlock, *Dylan Thomas: The Legend and the Poet*, 1960, p. 85)

two distinct and opposite dangers—the danger of trying to equip him too exactly with a literary pedigree and the danger of isolating him as a sport, . . . a wild man who threw up works of genius without knowing what he was doing.

To a degree both these dangers have receded with time. Thomas's most vociferous enemies have been shouted down, and with the publication of his notebooks, worksheets, and letters it has become clear that he was witty, intelligent, rather well-read, and a thor-

oughly conscious craftsman rather than the drunken Celtic bar-
barian some had originally mistaken him for. Further, succeeding
generations of poets have assimilated and indeed rebelled against
his influence, so that Thomas at last seems ready to take his place in
the literary continuum, in meaningful relationship to other writers.
His originality is no longer in question but, in the perspective of
some twenty years since Thomas's death, neither is the fact of his
situation in the poetic pantheon.

This chapter and the following will attempt to cover a number
of areas which are often approached by different sorts of critics,
operating from different sorts of assumptions. In this chapter I shall
first discuss the more or less biographical evidence for Thomas's
readings and the influences upon him—favorite authors, on the one
hand, and writers or groups with whom he associated (or who associated themselves with him) on the other. Then, I shall move to a
broader consideration of Thomas as a twentieth-century author: his
relationship to "modernism" and to particular modernist authors; his
situation within the changing poetic fashions of the century; his relationship to dominant intellectual trends of the period, such as
Freudianism or Marxism; and his situation with regard to various
modern "schools" or "movements." All of the foregoing considerations involve what structuralists would call a "diachronic," or his-
torically oriented, approach.

The kind of approach I shall use in the next chapter, the "synchronic," views Thomas as a particular *kind* of poet—a romantic,
for example—without particular regard to his situation in literary
history or the evolution of poetry. In part, this sort of approach is
indebted to Eliot's idea of tradition: all major poets are ideally contemporaries, engaged in a vast dialogue whose terms continually
change as the pantheon expands. The advantage of this approach
to a poet is that "extrinsic" considerations such as the poet's life,
associations, and even his reading, are beside the point; the only critical evidence is provided by the poetry itself, and if Thomas's work
shows more similarities to that of Whitman or Donne or traditional
Welsh poetry than it does to that of his contemporaries, then so be
it. In practice, however, I shall be much less programmatic in my
approach than the division into diachronic and synchronic will suggest, and hardly concerned at all about the kinds of evidence critics
marshall in an attempt to "place" Thomas. In any such complex
undertaking the critic needs whatever tools and materials he finds at
hand.

A few critics have attempted to list briefly the major literary influences upon Thomas. Henry Treece (*Dylan Thomas: "Dog*

Among the Fairies," 1949, p. x), who can never make up his mind
just how original Thomas's poetry really is, at one point suggests
that the "early poems might have been expressed by a formula
(where H=Hopkins, S=Swinburne, J=Joyce, etc.)" and at another lists the major influences upon Thomas as Hopkins, Hart
Crane, Swinburne, Rimbaud, and Francis Thompson, in that order.
Thirteen years later, Tindall's more exhaustive list (*A Reader's
Guide to Dylan Thomas,* 1962, pp. 12–15) includes some of the
poet's favorite writers: Yeats and Joyce, as well as Hopkins, Eliot,
Auden, Owen, Hardy, de la Mare, and Empson. Hart Crane and
Whitman were Americans whose work he praised; Dickens, Melville, Tennyson, Beddoes, Wordsworth, and Blake extend the list,
with the seventeenth-century poets Donne, Marvell, Vaughan,
Herbert, and Traherne. Finally, of course, the King James Bible,
particularly Genesis, the Gospels, Epistles, and the Apocalypse, was
an endless source of imagery and rhythms, with his father's passion,
Shakespeare, brooding over all. At various times he stressed others.
According to Geoffrey Grigson (Brinnin, 1960, p. 256), on his
arrival in London Thomas talked enthusiastically about D. G.
Rossetti, Francis Thompson, James Thomson, and Stephen Spender. Obviously it would be difficult to extract patterns from this
chaos; yet to place his work in a literary context, this must be done.

But first, one continuing problem does perhaps deserve discussion, the question of literary influence. As Harold Bloom points out,
we know virtually nothing of the real mechanism by which one
literary artist's work affects that of another. We tend almost unconsciously to adopt psychological "models" for the process, such
as the father-son relationship: thus Thomas may be said to have
come under T. S. Eliot's influence as an adolescent, consciously imi-
tating the latter's verse, and later may have "rebelled" against it—
which itself constitutes a sort of negative influence. And as we may
claim to see traces of the father in the rebellious son, so we may
claim that early literary influences are never "written out" of the
mature verse, no matter how strongly the poet may "repress" them.
Nor is this necessarily a bad thing. André Gide's epigram, "influence creates nothing; it awakens something," indicates the limitations of a romantic view of artistic integrity: poets can learn from
one another not only an abstract "craft," but a way of becoming
more deeply themselves. Thus Pound helped both Yeats and Eliot
to develop the mature styles which seem so perfectly to define
them as poets. It seems likely that a writer who descends to slavish
imitation has not really been "seduced" by influence, but is merely
demonstrating his own essential lack of a personal poetic voice.

Of course, in a writer as idiosyncratic as Thomas, this is not a major consideration. The primary question is not whom he sounds like—since, despite Treece, he usually sounds like no other writer—but how we are to detect an influence in the first place. The publication of Thomas's notebooks, written between 1930 and 1934, has only made it more apparent that by the age of eighteen or nineteen the poet had somehow developed a unique and characteristic poetic voice which was to persist, virtually unchanged, at least until the publication of *Deaths and Entrances* in 1946. The first question, then, is what influences in Thomas's childhood and adolescence helped give form to the outpouring of verse between 1931 and 1934 which was to provide the bulk of his first two books.

Biographical Evidence

Thomas's father, who had spoken Welsh as a child, was in love with the English language. He taught English at Swansea grammar school, and regularly read Shakespeare to his son, while young Thomas was teaching himself to read with the popular British comic books—*Punch, Rainbow,* and *Tiger Tim* (FitzGibbon, *The Life of Dylan Thomas,* 1965, p. 33). Both classical and popular tastes apparently stuck with him: at a conference at the University of Utah during one of his American tours Thomas was still, unoriginally, asserting that Shakespeare was the greatest English poet (Tedlock, 1960, p. 63), while to the end of his life he read and enjoyed mysteries and gothic adventures. In fact (Read, *The Days of Dylan Thomas,* 1964, p. 96), as a *Morning Post* reviewer, he wrote extensively on Rex Stout, John Dickson Carr, Ngaio Marsh, Agatha Christie, and others; Ralph Wishart, a bookseller and friend of the poet's, remembers (Tedlock, 1960, pp. 31–33) his fascination with cowboy films, women's magazines, and books for boys. According to Tindall (1962, p. 12), *Dracula* remained one of his favorite books, while Devas (*Two Flamboyant Fathers,* 1966, p. 202) recalls that during the war years he read comics to relax. On the other hand, D. J. Thomas's influence was not, of course, limited to Shakespeare; his library included the great English poets since Chaucer. Dylan, often a sickly child, absorbed most of this before adolescence.

Thomas's early passion for poetry soon pushed him beyond his father's range of interests. FitzGibbon (1965, pp. 50–53) quotes an article the poet wrote at the age of fourteen or fifteen which intelligently discusses the Georgian poets, "transitional" figures like

Hopkins, Bridges, de la Mare, and the "moderns"—Eliot, Joyce, and Yeats. He mentions specifically W. H. Davies, John Gould Fletcher, Richard Aldington, the Sitwells, Sassoon, Brooke, Owen, Graves, Lawrence, Blunden, and Pound. How many of these figures he had read in any depth by 1929 is of course difficult to say, but it is likely that most of them had at least a passing attraction for him; Maud (*Poet in the Making*, 1968, pp. 13–17) discusses some of these early influences. Years later, he claimed,

I wrote imitations of whatever I happened, moon-and-print struck, to be goggling at and gorging at the time: Sir Thomas Browne, Robert W. Service, de Quincey, Henry Newbolt, Blake, Baroness Orczy, Marlowe, Chums, the Imagists, the Bible, the Magnet, Poe, Grimm, Keats, Lawrence, Austin Dobson and Dostoievski, Anon and Shakespeare. (FitzGibbon, 1965, p. 40)

In early adolescence he was enthusiastic about Thomas Lovell Beddoes as well. Clearly, his tastes were eclectic; with the years they grew less so, or else Thomas was generously broadening his remembered interests, for Caitlin (Thomas, *Leftover Life to Kill*, 1957, p. 55) later recalled her husband reading interminable Dickens novels, but refusing to look at Proust, Austen, Tolstoy, or Dostoevsky.

Around the beginning of his adolescence, Thomas was making friends who both broadened his literary exposure and gave it focus. Dan Jones, a poet and musician who was his contemporary, recalls (Tedlock, 1960, p. 17) that Dylan's early influences were Yeats, Aldington, Sacheverell Sitwell, Lawrence, and Hopkins, "in that order." Jones introduced him to the Imagists and the Symbolists, and probably to the English "metaphysicals" and Rimbaud as well—the latter in translation, of course (FitzGibbon, 1965, p. 72). Perhaps equally important, the two writers collaborated on poems which often were little more than word games, opportunities for a kind of musical exercise; Jones comments (Tedlock, 1960, p. 18), "In those early years, words occupied Dylan's mind to the exclusion even of the things with which they have some connection."

Thomas's other early friends—the painter Alfred Janes, the moribund poet Trevor Hughes, the socialist grocer and intellectual Bert Trick—undoubtedly helped to fill out his idea of the cultural and intellectual world beyond Swansea. Trick in particular was most responsible for awakening the poet's social conscience, resulting in a long, relatively fruitless flirtation with the idea of communism. But more important as a poetic influence than any of these was the poet Vernon Watkins, whom he met near the end of his Swansea period. The voluminous correspondence between the two poets, of which the surviving portion is printed in *Letters to Vernon Watkins* (1957), reveals that the interchange was basically technical, given over to poetics and to esthetic considerations; but Thomas must have been affected by Watkins's profound religiousness and rather etherial sensibility. Watkins, like Jones, was extremely well-read; but there is no telling what, if anything, this meant to Thomas. According to Watkins (p. 17) his friend thought Yeats the "greatest living poet," but personally preferred Hardy; he was ambivalent about Auden, admiring his versatility and wit, but uninterested in his themes. Like most of Thomas's friends, he feels the poet most admired Joyce among prose writers (cf. Treece, 1949, p. 51; Tindall, 1962, p. 13). Since Thomas was officially a member of no literary "school," his literary associations in London tell us less about him than would be the case with, say, Auden. After an unsuccessful meeting with T. S. Eliot, Thomas fell in with the group around the mystic and esthete Victor Neuburg, editor of the "Poet's Corner" section of the *Sunday Referee*, where most of Thomas's earliest poems were published. Neuburg, who was attempting to form a coterie of "Zooists," or "Creative Life" worshippers, appears to have had little effect on Thomas, but through his publication Thomas did meet the poet and novelist Pamela Hansford Johnson, with whom he soon fell in love; his correspondence with her is available in *Selected Letters of Dylan Thomas*.

On moving to London in 1934, Thomas took up bohemian residence in Chelsea, rapidly making a variety of literary contacts. According to Read (1964, pp. 78, 81), among his closest friends were Ruthven Todd, Bernard Spencer, Norman Cameron (book editor of the *Morning Post*), and Geoffrey Grigson (editor of *New Verse*). The relationship with Grigson decayed after several years, however: *New Verse* (1933-39), which was one of the major outlets for poets who needed an alternative to the periodicals of the thirties, encouraged Thomas by publishing him frequently at first. As Thomas's fame grew, however, Grigson in particular vehemently (and sometimes irresponsibly) attacked the poet. Along with David Holbrook, the group around F. R. Leavis's *Scrutiny*, and the iconoclastic Robert Graves, he is one of the major negative voices in Thomas criticism.

Grigson (Brinnin, 1960, p. 287) claims that what distinguished the group of Thomas's friends of this period, like Norman Cameron, was that they were literary lights (of whatever luster) independent of "modernism's higher command"—Eliot, Auden, etc.— and the higher command definitely "was not impressed" with

Thomas. Nevertheless, he admits that Stephen Spender was "one of the first unlooney persons to remark on" the poems Thomas had published in "Poet's Corner." Though Spender at one time accused him of poetic irresponsibility, he later emerged as a staunch defender. Indeed, from a contemporary perspective, there certainly does not seem to have been any conspiracy of silence on the part of the literary leaders of Thomas's time—the reverse, if anything, is the case. If T. S. Eliot did not leap at the chance to have Faber publish his first book, Edith Sitwell and Herbert Read, two very powerful voices, were vociferous in his praise and defense.

But the fact remains that Thomas throughout his career stayed generally aloof from literary cliques, groups, and movements, and so in a sense was denied the specious security such membership affords. His friends in general defended him through personal loyalty or real literary enthusiasm rather than as part of a program or in hopes of mutual back-patting in small magazines. Roy Campbell, for one, valued Thomas's friendship especially because he felt himself ostracized from the predominantly leftist literary circles of the thirties for political reasons. Though Thomas might have disagreed with Campbell's characterization of London's literary lights as "tough old suffragettes and aging nancies" (Heppenstall, *Four Absentees*, 1960, p. 169), he regarded them with the suitable irreverence of youth. Grigson's story (Brinnin, 1960, p. 262) of an afternoon with Thomas spent dubbing rocks with the names of famous literary figures and then smashing them sounds in character for the "Rimbaud of Cwmdonkin Drive." But in addition, Thomas had an honest sympathy for the underdog and a real disagreement over literary aims and methods to separate him from the reigning writers. Eliot, whom he called "The Pope," had turned to unsensual and religious poetry, while the Auden-Spender axis, he felt, often substituted political enthusiasm for craftsmanship. Heppenstall (1960, p. 179) recalls Thomas reading a poem by Spender "apparently addressed to a young German airman coming down by parachute, riddled with bullets," and laughing uproariously at the line, "You were a better target for the kiss." However, since the poem to which Heppenstall refers seems to be Spender's well-known "Ultima Ratio Regnum," a poem about the Spanish Civil War involving neither Germans nor parachutists, either Thomas's memory or Heppenstall's is playing us tricks.

Thomas was probably thought to be most closely associated with a number of young writers in the thirties whom we would today call "neo-romantic" or (to some extent) "surrealist." David Archer's Parton Street bookstore, which provided the funding for

Thomas's first book, was popular with leftist literary intellectuals, but also published a volume of poems by David Gascoyne, a surrealist poet then sixteen years old, and one by George Barker, who was twenty (FitzGibbon, 1965, p. 137). Although Thomas was—and is—often linked with these two figures, he positively disliked the work of Gascoyne; according to Heppenstall (1960, p. 179) he often read aloud passages from Barker which he found ludicrous and in fact parodied his rival in one part of his satirical essay "How To Be a Poet" in *Quite Early One Morning*. Somewhat later, when Henry Treece attempted to draft Thomas into his "Apocalyptic" literary movement, Thomas refused even to contribute to an anthology. His standards were quite high, though difficult to determine and at times idiosyncratic (*viz.* his passion for Beddoes). Theodore Roethke, whom he wanted very much to meet on his arrival in New York (Brinnin, *Dylan Thomas in America*, 1955, p. 8), claims that "the list of contemporaries he valued was a great deal shorter than might be generally supposed" (Tedlock, 1960, p. 52). Thomas was by no means above the enjoyment most young writers feel in spotting weaknesses in the work of their better-known contemporaries. In 1940 he and John Davenport collaborated on a satirical fantasy called *The Death of the King's Canary* which pillories many of the prominent poets of the time. Parts of it are available in Davies's *Dylan Thomas: Early Prose Writings* (1971); others are still too libelous for publication. In addition, of course, the poet's Rimbaldian, iconoclastic persona was more effective if he could present himself without context or connections, a poet *sui generis*.

Although Thomas himself on numerous occasions explicitly denied that he was in any way a surrealist (see, e.g., his letter to Richard Church, *SL*, pp. 160–62), biographical evidence alone shows that his statement, while perhaps true, is misleading. Certainly around 1936, when he was working intently on a series of obscure, evocative, and highly symbolic stories, he was at least flirting with surrealism. He published three of these stories in Roger Roughton's surrealist magazine *Contemporary Poetry and Prose* (1936-37), and participated informally in the "International Surrealist Exhibition" held in the New Burlington Galleries that year and attended by Salvador Dali. He knew Gascoyne and was close friends with Ruthven Todd, then an avowed British surrealist. Through his friend Norman Cameron, who was at the time translating Rimbaud, he must have gathered a substantial amount of insight into recent French poetry. An acquaintance of his named J. H. Martin (1964, p. 235), in a letter to the *Times Literary Supplement*, claims that

Thomas told him that he would draft the general scheme of a stanza and then take out his "dictionary"—a notebook of ordinary words he kept with him—and try several on for size; if nothing seemed to fit, he might try several from the top lines of various books, often Djuna Barnes's *Nightwood*. This procedure, if not explicitly surrealist, does argue for a smaller degree of conscious control over the poem than Thomas generally claimed. FitzGibbon (1964, p. 273), in a reply to Martin, admits that in 1936 Thomas was, "I think for the only time in his life, prepared to write poems the meaning of which he did not understand." Indeed, Vernon Watkins (*LVW*, p. 15) recalls his friend saying of one of the poems of this period that "so far as he knew it had no meaning at all."

Thomas's experience with London surrealism brought him as close as he would come to the set of expatriate writers of the twenties and thirties. Lawrence Durrell (Tedlock, 1960, p. 51), who met him about this time, tells of his great admiration for Henry Miller and extreme shyness at the prospect of actually meeting him. Durrell found him enthusiastic over Dickens and also over Lawrence (an enthusiasm which is sharply tempered by criticism in many of the early letters). He was "not, I thought, very widely read," and though he had heard of Freud and Jung he claimed to have read neither. Thomas, as it happens, was then staying in Cornwall at the house of Anna Wickham, herself a devout Freudian. Other expatriates such as Djuna Barnes and Joyce—both of whom had an important influence on his prose—Thomas merely admired from afar.

Meanwhile his circle of London friends was growing. Soon after Edith Sitwell's very laudatory review of his first book Thomas grew to know her and her circle. But he was never really an intimate part of it, setting aside the mutual affection and respect between himself and Dame Edith. Perhaps the aristocratic social tone of her gatherings was too much for an apprentice Soho bohemian. A more natural group of friends for him were the avowed Marxists and Communists with whom he had considerable sympathy on the grounds of his political ideals. Although Thomas himself undoubtedly was never a member of the Communist party, many of his friends were, or nearly were (Read, 1964, p. 134), among them Jack Lindsay, Edgell Rickword, John Sommerfield, and Randall Swingler. And, aside from the leading "groups" and "circles," Thomas had a number of uncategorizable—and often unexpected—friends such as William Empson, Hugh Porteous (an admirer of Wyndham Lewis), Oswell Blakeston, and the historian A. J. P. Taylor and his wife.

During the war Thomas's work with the BBC brought him into contact with another group of literary figures who worked there, particularly Patric Dickinson, Aneirin Talfan Davies, Roy Campbell, and Louis MacNeice (Read, 1964, p. 116). Of these, perhaps he was closest to MacNeice; Heppenstall (1960, p. 167) mentions that the "predominantly Irish . . . clique or claque" which patronized the Stag's Head Tavern in London would alternately devote themselves to Thomas and to MacNeice. But a more direct and important clue to his literary tastes at the time is provided by his broadcast readings of other poets' works. One such list (Maud, *Entrances to Dylan Thomas' Poetry*, 1963, p. 157, n. 7) includes, besides MacNeice, Yeats, Norman Cameron, Herbert Read, John Betjeman, Robert Graves, Alun Lewis, L. A. G. Strong, Edward Thomas, Walter de la Mare, Vernon Watkins, W. H. Auden, W. S. Graham, George Barker, Bernard Spencer, Norman Nicholson, Ruth Pitter, Hardy, Blake, Herbert, Smart, Peele, Hopkins, Lawrence, Browning, William Barnes, John Clare, and Vaughan. Theodore Roethke asserts that Thomas "had a wide, detailed and active knowledge of the whole range of English literature, and a long memory" (Tedlock, 1960, p. 51). As late as 1950, Thomas would handcopy favorite poems by Edward Thomas, Hardy, Ransom, Housman, W. R. Rodgers, and W. H. Davies, claiming that that was the only way he could come to know a poem intimately enough.

In general, it seems clear that Thomas's knowledge of contemporary letters was greater than people were inclined to give him credit for. He disliked talking analytically about literature, particularly the work of his contemporaries, but when he did so he usually did it very well. In the mid-thirties a series of reviews he wrote for the *New English Weekly* (1932-49) included Beckett, Williams, Kay Boyle, Wells, DosPassos, Kafka, Flann O'Brien, Erskine Caldwell, Frederic Prokosch, and Dorothy Parker; these reviews, available in the *Early Prose Writings* (Davies, 1971), are an interesting addition to the essays on Welsh poets, Wilfred Owen, de la Mare, and others available in *QEOM*.

It is likely, though, that the collected body of Thomas's criticism would yield no very coherent views of literary excellence. John Malcolm Brinnin, organizing the poet's American tours, was careful to note his social and literary tastes (Brinnin, 1955, p. 87): his deep regard for Faulkner, Lowell, Hart Crane, and Roethke, his "amused curiosity" about Capote, his dislike for Stevens. "More than once I heard him say that he preferred to judge poetry by the character of the poet," comments Brinnin (p. 71). "While this was most likely a facetious evasion, it was evident that Dylan was never quite sure of just what poetry he could say he liked." Probably Brinnin overstates the case here: while the letters, for example, usually show strong literary likes and dislikes, they seldom show these feelings in a context of thought response to the whole of poetry, as would be the case with Empson or Eliot. Thomas's taste was generally good—he even had a rare ability to assess accurately the work of close friends and associates—but it was a response more intuitive than intellectual, part of the poet's "obsessive antipathy to poetry as a public forum–activity" (Brinnin, 1955, p. 71).

Tindall (1962, p. 13), who discussed literature with Thomas intently and at length, illustrates the problem and its explanation:

Finnegans Wake . . . he proclaimed the greatest book of our times and his favorite above all others . . . Certainly Joyce's verbal play and his vision of cyclical process had an effect on Thomas, yet when I spent an hour or so with him over a copy of *Finnegan*, everything we came across seemed news to him . . . Nobody has found better use for fewer pages of *Finnegan* than he.

Thomas read sufficiently widely that it is unsafe to state firmly that he could not have been influenced by a particular source, whether it be Swift (Longcore, 1963) or the seventh-century Indian poet Bhartrihari (McCord, 1961). According to Pratt (*Dylan Thomas's Early Prose*, 1970, p. 11), he read the *Mabinogion*, the *Rig Veda*, and the *Egyptian Book of the Dead*. On the other hand, his reading was seldom exhaustive and analytical; like Joyce—surprisingly—he would tend to value a work as much for the way it stated something as for what it said. Thus his work undeniably abounds in verbal echoes, but the significance of their sources for a given poem remains moot. Further complicating the picture, he had a genius for intuiting the possibilities of form and theme opened up by a writer like Joyce without necessarily reading at all deeply in him. From adolescence on, Thomas could unerringly pick what he needed from the expanse of English literature, while such was the intensity of his absorption in himself and his art that he may never have lifted his head to look about him, categorize what he saw, or locate himself within the landscape.

The Twentieth-Century Situation

If Thomas was uninterested in "placing" himself as a poet—apart from his childhood aim to be a greater writer even than Keats

—critics, and sometimes other poets as well, have frequently attempted to put his work in perspective. The most direct way to
confront the question is the "literary-historical" approach: assuming that the twentieth century has produced a literature which in
some way reflects the life of that period, what strands, forces, or
movements can be seen within it? What relationships exist between
one group of twentieth-century writings and another? In essence,
this procedure is both analysis, in that it breaks down a larger mass
of writing into smaller bodies, and synthesis, in that it necessarily
groups together the works of individual writers to make up those
bodies. Thomas's writing, unfortunately, resists such synthesis.

Nearly always intertwined with the process of analyzing and
synthesizing is the very loosely related process of evaluating, placing
individual writers—or even groups—in some sort of hierarchy of
quality. It would be possible but, I think, finally unrewarding to
trace instances of this last procedure—Thomas's "critical reception"
—since 1935. Most evaluations of his work have come embedded in
a historical or esthetic argument which both betrays and attempts
to defend the writer's critical bias. So, rather than attempting to display individuals' rankings of Thomas as a poet, I shall instead discuss
a representative selection of "guides," "histories," and "keys" to
modern poetry in the light of their placement and evaluation of
Thomas, and then attempt some generalizations about his varying
stature.

Most histories of modern poetry are agreed upon its bare outlines. At some time after 1880 poetry entered a time of "crisis," a
response to the apparent exhaustion of the poetic forms and to the
growing questioning of assumptions about both art and life which
the Victorians had seemed to hold quite comfortably. "Transitional" figures like Hardy and Gerard Manley Hopkins in England
or Emily Dickinson in America heralded a coming change; meanwhile, in France, the Symbolist poets, notably Baudelaire, Rimbaud, and Mallarmé, had been eating away at intellectual and
esthetic conventions there since the middle of the nineteenth century. Yeats, who began writing as a sort of belated romantic, and
"decadents" such as Wilde and Ernest Dowson, attempted to capture the tone of these recently discovered French writers. But the
storm broke with the arrival of what we now call "modernism,"
which in poetry centered upon the work of Pound and Eliot shortly
before World War I.

Although "modernism" seemed a coherent, largely negative response to whatever had gone before in literature, it soon became
clear that it was a terribly amorphous movement pointing simul-

taneously in several directions. The tendency of Pound to concentrate upon a spare, hard image led to "Imagism," a movement benignly presided over by T. E. Hulme; while Eliot's techniques of juxtaposition and ellipsis and his characteristic tone of cynical exhaustion led, in *The Waste Land* and "The Hollow Men," to a perfect expression of postwar disillusionment.

Modern poetry in general was freer of form and much more obviously subjective, in its concentration upon the poetic persona's own feelings, perceptions, and ideas, than what had preceded it, although modern poets paradoxically felt they had captured a new objectivity in their scrupulous removal of sentimentality and oration from the poetic field. The "bardic tone" was abandoned. And indeed, in the work of poets like Empson and his followers, a spare, hard, intellectual verse emerged which seemed the inverse of romantic. Characteristically, the modern poet turned his back upon society and social themes, instead taking Art as its own end and subject. By the 1930s a reaction had set in, spearheaded by the writing of W. H. Auden, C. Day Lewis, and Stephen Spender in *New Signatures* (1932) and *New Country* (1933), a group later joined by Louis MacNeice. The writing of these poets turned explicitly to social themes, from an avowedly leftist standpoint. "Verse will be worn longer this year, and rather Red," wrote Hugh Porteous in 1933 (quoted in Symons, *The Thirties: A Dream Revolved*, 1960, p. 9). The mystique of Art and the Artist faded, with Auden's line "Poetry makes nothing happen" and MacNeice's concept of the artist as a sophisticated sort of entertainer. Wit, irony, and social conscience were the watchwords, the latter particularly evident in John Lehmann's collections in the *Penguin New Writing*.

Clearly, this thumbnail sketch of literary history is a vast oversimplification, but at least it is a generally accepted one. What happens during and after the 1930s is less clear and more hotly debated. John Wain (1957, pp. 356–58) in an essay entitled "English Poetry: The Immediate Situation," argues that Auden's influence had been paramount during the thirties, so that "the change, when it came, was one of the most sudden and complete that literary history has to show. Overnight, the Auden convention was dissolved." Two obvious reasons for the change were the arrival of World War II, which fostered an apocalyptic spirit among poets, and Auden's departure for America which, Wain claims, knocked the bottom out of everything. "An entire generation of the English intelligentsia were up the creek. But not, fortunately, without a paddle. The paddle was Dylan Thomas." Although Thomas had been writing since 1933, he suddenly found that the main current of literature had shifted so as to flow through his work and personality. Dozens of rather poor imitations of Thomas were published in magazines like *Poetry Quarterly* during the forties.

By the fifties a revolt against Thomas's sort of poetry occurred, with the writing of the "Movement" poets, collected in D. J. Enright's *Poets of the 1950's* (1955) and Robert Conquest's *New Lines* (1956) anthologies. These poets—writers such as Philip Larkin, Kingsley Amis, Conquest, Donald Davie, and Wain himself—set a new, commonsensical tone opposed to what they considered the barbaric, bombastic rant of the previous decade. Intelligibility and wit were again at a premium, and the postwar indulgence in subjectivity, myth, and obscure personal symbolism was scorned. By 1957, Wain claims, a certain balance had been restored. Poets whose stock had fallen unjustifiably, like Empson and Graves, were restored to their rightful stature, while the great contribution of Thomas could also be appreciated without ignoring his moments of fruitless obscurity or the incompetence of most of his followers.

Wain's outline of contemporary literary history (which he extends in an essay in Walford Davies, *Dylan Thomas: New Critical Essays*, 1972, pp. 1–6) is as easy to grasp as our earlier sketch, and perhaps even more misleading. John Lehmann soon retaliated (1958, pp. 582–84) with an article in the same journal, entitled "The Wain-Larkin Myth." Lehmann starts with a criticism of Wain's characterization of the thirties, pointing out what can be easily seen by perusing the work of Spender or Auden during that period —that poetry was by no means restricted to political or even social topics. Further, Lehmann claims that Auden's departure made no particular impression on writers. Most writers either left for America when war broke out or attempted (like Thomas) to find government posts. Thomas was in fact quite popular throughout most of the "political" thirties, while Auden remained popular long after his departure. Nor was Thomas alone in the earlier decade, with George Barker first published in 1933 and Gascoyne still going strong after abandoning surrealism. During the forties, poets who do not satisfy Wain's characterization as "ranters"—Roy Fuller, Alun Lewis, Laurie Lee, Norman Nicholson, and Herbert Read—were producing some of the decade's best work, while Stephen Spender, officially a thirties poet, was writing his most successful poetry.

A third perspective, different from that of Wain and of Lehmann, is offered by Karl Shapiro (Tedlock, 1960, pp. 270–83), who sees Thomas as a turning point in modern poetry. Eliot and Auden he lumps together as "classicists" and "impersonal" poets, whereas

Thomas introduced the idea of "personal" poetry into the modern literary situation. Thomas is to modern literature what Hopkins is to Victorian, claims Shapiro, a kind of antidote; he is an "antithesis to Auden, as to Eliot." Stephen Spender (1952, pp. 780–81) similarly groups Eliot and Auden together as classicists, since the poetry of both men is an "intensely imagined portrayal of ideas." Thomas, by contrast, works from emotion and the "feel" of words. He embodies a revolt against modern classicism, against Oxbridge intellectualism, and against the "King's English" of London which was the dominant poetic diction of the time. Robin Mayhead in 1952 (p. 142) observed disapprovingly that it had become conventional practice among critics to call Eliot, Auden, and Spender "classical" and Thomas "romantic." From this perspective a different outline of literary history emerges, with major turning points around 1910 and 1940.

There is something to be said on all sides of this controversy. Clearly there is such a thing as changing poetic taste and fashion, so that the work of a given decade may well have a different "texture" or "feel" from that of another. In addition, we need not go along with Virginia Woolf's radical observation that somewhere around the year 1910 human nature changed, to admit that literature as a whole does respond to external events; the tone of disillusionment following the First World War is an example. Each new writer or group tends to minimize its debt to those who immediately preceded it, so that it is only from the perspective of many years that we can look back upon the broad outlines of literary evolution. But writers of importance notoriously refuse to be pigeonholed. Sometimes, in fact, we label our pigeonholes wrongly. We may be misled to characterize an era by its most radical and outspoken group of artists, who may indeed be the vanguard of a coming cultural change—as were Pound and Eliot—or who may be merely an eddy out of the literary mainstream, like the British surrealists.

Each new "movement" attempts to assume legitimacy by caricaturing its predecessor. Thus Conquest wrote in his introduction to the *New Lines* collection (quoted in Cox, *Dylan Thomas: A Collection of Critical Essays*, 1966, p. 1) that in the forties "poets were encouraged to regard their task simply as one of making an arrangement of images of sex and violence tapped straight from the unconscious." To this stick figure Conquest opposes the "Movement" poet, with his restraint, sensitivity, intelligence, and responsibility. Conquest is not being irresponsible here; perhaps his description does characterize most of the poets of that decade, though not the best of them. In Derek Stanford's happy phrase (1964, p. 406), he is merely "Bashing the Forties." The perspective from the beginning of the forties was quite different, however. Elizabeth Drew and John Sweeney in *Directions in Modern Poetry* (1940, p. 112) point to Thomas as a successful illustration of the fact that the poet "must do more than reflect the situation of the sensitive, intelligent individual in an uncongenial environment. He must seek to ally himself with forces which are timeless and universal." For Sweeney and Drew, Thomas represents the mystical, intuitive, and subjective side of poetry, and is allied with Eliot in his Christian mysticism, Lawrence in his cult of blood-knowledge, and Yeats in his occult systematization. Empson and Auden join most Victorians on the opposite side of the coin, as would Conquest and Wain, had they been writing in 1940.

Perspectives vary. David Daiches (1943, pp. 150–59) was one of the first relatively disinterested parties to announce the death of " 'thirties poetry," pointing to Lehmann's anthology *Poems for Spain* (1939) as a kind of anticlimax of the political movement in poetry. MacNeice's *Autumn Journal* (1939) heralds a return to self-revelation and a reversal of Hulme's canons of objectivity and impersonality, which had been dominant in poetry since 1913. Daiches points to Tambimuttu's magazine *Poetry (London)*, founded in 1939, as a representative periodical of the new avant-garde—undoctrinaire, less puritan than its predecessor, and focused upon Man rather than Society. Understandably, Thomas was published frequently here. The new sort of verse is romantic in a subdued way, "personal and limpid and often elegaic;" its practitioners, among whom Thomas is a dominant figure set somewhat apart from the rest, tend to resent the intellectual gymnastics of modern criticism and the *ex cathedra* tone of Eliot and Hulme. Daiches points to Tambimuttu's collection *Poetry in Wartime* (1942) and Cyril Connolly's magazine *Horizon* (founded in 1940) for examples of the new poetry.

Daiches's cultured and reasonable tone and assumption of an inevitable evolution in poetry, give no clue to the virulence of the esthetic disputes of the time. It is almost as if the violence of political feelings of the thirties, frustrated, turned personal in the forties. Geoffrey Grigson was notorious for his insults of writers like Barker, Swingler, and Heppenstall in his magazine *New Verse*, sometimes after those writers had received encouraging reviews there. The work of Thomas, who soon came to be seen as the leading figure of a poetic avant-garde, was attacked by the Left. Spender called it "just poetic stuff with no beginning nor end, or intelligent or intelligible control," while MacNeice characterized it as ". . . a series of nonsense images, the cumulative effect of which is usually vital and sometimes even seems to have a message" (quoted in Tedlock, 1960, p. 248). But both these writers, as well as Auden, later found much to praise in Thomas. The most violent and unrelenting attacks on the poet were in fact carried out by Grigson in *Polemic* (1945-47) and by numerous critics writing in F. R. Leavis's *Scrutiny* (1932-54), rather than by Auden's followers. John Wain (Brinnin, 1960, p. 69), who is well aware of Thomas's failings, refers to his treatment in *Scrutiny* as "disgraceful." An idea of the level of discourse can be obtained by examining the letters section of *Poetry (London)* (June-July 1948, pp. 46-47) wherein Grigson calls the editor's comments "muddled and liquescent" and his magazine "the most foolish . . . periodical of its time;" Tambimuttu replies that Grigson's arguments are "not criticism at all but a form of braggadocio based on half-understood facts and specious argument." Thomas had good reason to remain aloof from the battle.

Writing in the same year as Daiches, Edith Sitwell (1943, pp. 71-97) sees not a succession of decades, each with its own poetic assumptions, but a general growth and liberation of poetry during the modern era which was unaccountably interrupted by the "political piety" and "new form of intolerance" of the thirties. Sitwell excepts Auden and Spender from her condemnation of the period, which otherwise produced a "great number of bad and dull poets." Around 1918, she claims, there had been a few good poets writing —notably de la Mare, W. H. Davies, Blunden, and Yeats—within a generally insipid expanse of Georgian poetry. The introduction of "organic form" by Eliot, H. D., and Sacheverell Sitwell constituted a revolution.

Sitwell sees "modern" verse as stressing technical experiment, a concern for the "texture" of the poem, and an extreme concentration. Sitwell's rather idiosyncratic list of ground-breakers reflects the fact that she and her brother Sacheverell were guiding spirits behind the periodical *Wheels* (1917-21), conceived as an alternative to the staid collections of *Georgian Poetry* (1911-22). Today few would rank Sacheverell Sitwell even with poets like MacNeice, let alone Eliot, although Maud (1968, pp. 13-14) makes a case for his influence upon Thomas's adolescent verse. But Dame Edith herself, whose poetry undeniably has historical importance in the development of modernism, and whose reputation has suffered many vicissitudes, is certainly a figure to be reckoned with, both as poet and critic. Her relationship with Thomas alone deserves more attention than it has received (see Botterill, 1946, and Julian, 1957). She, at least, saw Thomas and George Barker as continuing the real tradition of poetic modernism. Sitwell's experiments in sound, the rapid succession of images, the elements of "nonsense" in her verse, her subjectivism, and her religious sense of the bardic vocation all show similarities with the work of Thomas; but whether her work constitutes a true influence upon his is another question.

An intelligent and complex essay on "Writing in the Thirties" by Julian Symons (1945, pp. 90–109) attempts to define the decade in broader terms than does Wain or Sitwell. The great figures of the twenties, he claims, are no longer living influences; literature is now seen as existing within a social context. The role of the artist is now less individual and dramatic, and art itself is less of an icon—witness Grigson's dismissal of "that nauseating concern for poetry." A rediscovery of Skelton, Anglo-Saxon poetry, Hopkins, and poetic ballads, along with the influence of Kafka and Rilke, has changed the form and tenor of verse. Symons sees Lehmann's proletariat *New Writing* and Grigson's *New Verse* (founded in 1933) as representing the Left and Right wings of the same movement.

The writing of the thirties was born of the depression in 1931 and in reaction to the rise of Fascism in Germany; it waned with the collapse of the Popular Front in France, the defeat of the Republican cause in Spain, and the disillusionment with Russian Communism following the Moscow trials. Symons is not optimistic about the new verse. Surrealism, he points out, was merely a phase most young writers of the thirties went through, not a fruitful literary impulse; Grigson's dropping of Gascoyne and adoption of Frederic Prokosch and Kenneth Allott with their wit and elegant sense of doom marks a change, but not a hopeful one: Allott he describes as "sired by MacNeice out of Constipation." Thomas alone represents a real hope. With the publication of *18 Poems* "Auden's simplicity semed sometimes tepid, Spender's bareness partly lack of appreciation of rich potentialities in the word and the world." But his followers, the "Apocalyptics," stressed his "least happy and least imitable sides," the "Blarney and personal imagery," producing "verse which was Thomas and water." Apparently, Symons felt considerable ambivalence about Thomas's poems, which he elsewhere describes as "Jokes, rhetorical intellectual fakes of the highest class" (1940, p. 67). Symons more fully elaborates his view of the decade in *The Thirties: A Dream Revolved* (1960).

Spender himself, attempting to characterize the poetry of the Second World War immediately afterward (1946) fails to detect a body of "war poetry" as such. The best work, he feels (p. 10), was produced by older unmobilized writers of the thirties; while Sitwell developed, the finest single work was probably Eliot's *Four Quartets*. He points to the disillusionment of his generation and their ambivalent feelings about the war, citing (p. 34) Day Lewis's lines:

> It is the logic of our times,
> No subject for immortal verse—
> That we who lived by honest dreams
> Defend the bad against the worse.

Spender notes (p. 44) the post-Auden reaction "toward the involuntary, the mysterious, the word-intoxicated, the romantic and Celtic." Thomas, who produced his finest work after 1943, he identifies as Auden's only rival as a poetic influence among young writers; but he dismisses the work of Barker and most of the self-styled Apocalyptics, singling out for praise only Vernon Watkins and G. S. Fraser.

George Woodcock (1950, *British Poetry Today*, pp. 1–12) agrees with Spender that there was no true group of war writers, and cites the reappearance of Eliot and Herbert Read after 1939. Like Symons he sees the trend of *New Signatures* continued in *New Verse* and in Symon's own *Twentieth Century Verse* (1937–39) with poets like Charles Madge, Kathleen Raine, Allott, and Roy Fuller. Thomas he sees as "one of the most significant of contemporary English poets" but, like most critics, warns that he is dangerous to imitate; his most salubrious effect has been fostering a return to more concrete imagery and a "more catholic appeal to wider feelings and more personal problems." Among important new poets he cites Alex Comfort, Durrell, Watkins, Fraser, Nicholas Moore, and D. S. Savage—the latter four all connected in some way with the Apocalyptic movement.

By 1947 it had become clear to most that the trend of poetry had in some way shifted; defining the shift was more difficult. In March, 1947, *Poetry* (Chicago) devoted an issue to introducing what it termed "Post-War Romanticism in England." Henry Treece and the Apocalyptics are discussed, as are Barker and Thomas, who were seen as decisive influences on the new trend. Daiches (1958, p. 57), writing a decade later in *The Present Age in British Literature*, notes that "the perspective has changed, but we can still recognize that both Hulme's " 'hard dry' image and the tight cerebration which Eliot brought into English poetry had not . . . the prestige they once had." The main movement in the late 1940s, he notes, "seemed to be toward the visionary, with Blake rather than Donne the presiding genius." But this contrast, which Durrell (1952, p. 196) discusses as a choice between Thomas's "sensuality and incantation" and Empson's intellectual compression—the prophetic versus the mystical—no longer seems as strong as it once did. Rexroth's line, "Thomas discovered poetry on his hand like blood, and screamed aloud," perhaps indicates a liberating impulse leading to the American "beats." But we now recognize (Daiches, 1958, p. 58) that "Thomas was neither a whirling romantic nor a metaphysical imagist, but a poet who used pattern and metaphor in a complex craftsmanship in order to create a ritual of celebration." Daiches (p. 65) denies that poetry of the forties, such as that of Barker and Thomas, was part of an esthetic movement aimed at overthrowing the school of Eliot; "the Eliot revolution has proved permanent," as witnessed by the attempt of critics like Elder Olson to treat his work as a variety of the modern metaphysical. Such attempts, Daiches warns, are only partly justified.

Perhaps it is the ambiguous nature of Thomas's poetry which has led to his varied reception in America, until the sixties under the sway of the New Criticism. John Crowe Ransom (1951, pp. 452–53) once categorized the poets of 1900–50 as "major" (Hardy, Yeats, Robinson, Frost, and Eliot), "minor" (Bridges, Williams, Pound, Cummings, Tate, etc.) and "intermediate" (Housman, Stevens, Auden, and Thomas). Thomas's work appealed to American critics because of its energy, yet many seem unsure of how to approach it. Some, like William Carlos Williams (1954, pp. 338–39), feel that American poetry demands an American rhythm and idiom. While deploring the return to Pope's meters among young poets, he admits that "Dylan Thomas is thrashing around somewhere in the wings but he is Welsh and acknowledges no rule—he cannot be of much help to us." M. L. Rosenthal (1960, pp. 203–19) attempted to compare the work of Thomas and that of the American Hart Crane, a poet with whom he has many affinities (cf. Moynihan, *The Craft and Art of Dylan Thomas*, 1966, pp. 105–6); he finds Thomas superior to Crane in the exuberance and daring of his language, inferior to him in the courage to avoid unearned final assertions in poems: "sometimes Thomas was a little too much the slick professional." Like many American critics Rosenthal ignores the Apocalyptics, adopting a standard view of the thirties which puts Auden and Thomas on opposite sides of the fence. Rosenthal also tends to ignore the poetic movements of the fifties in Britain (Wain, Amis, Larkin, and others), taking John Betjeman as a representative figure: "except for Dylan Thomas, British poets, since the last war at least, have been dominated by the amateur spirit." On the other hand, Tindall (1962, pp. 5–7) asserts that Americans have been by and large immune to the anti-Thomas reaction following his death, spearheaded by the Movement poets. Geoffrey Moore (Tedlock, 1960, pp. 248–51) in a 1955 *Kenyon Review* article made an ambitious attempt to "place" Thomas "against the unfolding pattern of modern verse as a whole." Moore points out the numerous heartfelt tributes paid by the younger generation of poets during a memorial BBC program in 1953. Thomas was for young poets what Graham Sutherland was for painters or Henry Moore for sculptors during the thirties: "he seemed to be going somewhere in a way that they could feel in their bones was necessary." Moore identifies two groups for whom Thomas was *not* the only guiding spirit—the "neo-Thomist fringe" who were most in sympathy with the later, mystical Eliot, and another group of cerebral and craftsmanlike "Empson-sympathizers"—but neither of these, Moore feels, was as large or as representative as that for whom Thomas was the central poet and figure. Moore's tribute is clearly personal as well as esthetic, and comes closer to capturing the spirit of the generation most affected by Thomas than to literary-historical analysis; his most concrete assertion is that, though Thomas was neither dadaist nor surrealist, "his verse may be seen as the climax of a process of poetic development which includes these phenomena."

Although occasionally writers still may stress a poet like Barker over Thomas (Thwaite, 1961, p. 105) or even, like Vivian De Sola Pinto *(Crisis in English Poetry,* 1958, pp. 202–4) approach him as a watered-down Sitwell, contemporary critics in general accord him high status. Percy Marshall, whose *Masters of English Poetry* (1966, p. 214) devotes individual chapters to major figures, claims that Thomas is "the one poet born within the twentieth century in Britain who may, without fear of contradiction, be recognized to have possessed genius." (Note that Yeats, Pound, and Eliot are automatically disallowed from the competition.) It must be recognized, however, that although the "critical establishment" has by now overwhelmingly accepted Thomas, there is still a strong negative and conservative voice in Britain which dismisses him much as did Grigson. Noel Jones in the *British Annual of Literature* (1949, pp. 12–16) treated him as an incomprehensible "literary oddity" who was nevertheless dangerous—presumably he could corrupt young writers—while in the latest *Concise Cambridge History of English Literature* (Churchill, 1970, pp. 862–64), Thomas's "over-praise" is compared with Chatterton's. While his "comparatively few comprehensible poems," reveal a pleasing romantic gift, he compares poorly with, say, his countryman Edward Thomas.

Equally egregiously, David Holbrook, in a chapter of *The Modern Age*, volume 7 of the "Pelican Guide to English Literature" (1961, pp. 415–28), launches one of his characteristic attacks on Thomas's poetic responsibility and maturity, comparing him very unfavorably with T. F. Powys. This sort of thing is misleading, and not really representative of Thomas's reputation in England; responsible critics, from Daiches to Wain, and poets, from Spender to Kingsley Amis, all have considerable praise for his best work.

Having considered, in roughly chronological order, a spectrum of critics who attempt to place Thomas within modern literary history, I shall now turn to a group of writers who view him from a more restricted perspective—as part of an eccentric movement or as illustrative of a specific tendency. These articles, many of them written as reviews of a group of books, concentrate upon a particular theme. While they throw only oblique light on the poet, the intensity of that light sometimes reveals aspects of his literary background which vanish in a broader perspective. Theodore Maynard (1940, pp. 312–14), for example, writing on "The New Artificiality," surprisingly lumps Thomas together with Kenneth Patchen, Muriel Rukeyser, and Reuel Denney. Although his comments on Thomas's verse and prose are valuable only as entertainment—the former derives from "the assonance of Wilfred Owen and the analyzed rhyme of my old schoolfellow, Frank Kendon," the latter are "a cross between Mother Goose and Caradoc Evans"—it is useful to remember that many critics in 1940 would have agreed with Maynard's blanket condemnation of all the above poets.

He finds their work greatly unintelligible, although striking, and feels they are doomed by an obsession with novelty and pretentiousness. Certainly, compared with what most poets claimed and attempted in either the preceding or the succeeding decade, Thomas's poetry seems "pretentious" and obscure as well. He "played all his shots from the net," in Durrell's words. So did poets who imitated him, including most of the Americans Maynard reviewed. He meant each poem to involve the ultimates of experience; in an "unsophisticated" way, he expected no less of art, and of his reader, than did Joyce or Shelley. In less capable hands, or in his own less successful moments, pretentiousness is the inevitable result. For most critics today, his greatest poems justify this; for others, and for many of his contemporary judges, the price was too high.

Arthur Mizener launched a related criticism in the *Kenyon Review* (1944, pp. 123–26). He complains of the widespread adoption among younger poets of what he terms "the decorative baroque style," pointing to Thompson, Thomas, Barker, Karl Shapiro, and Robert Lowell in particular. Each of these poets, he feels, is mainly interested in the form of the expression rather than the thing expressed, producing "a poem in which a very simple structure of meaning supports a vast and intricate elaboration of cloudy details." Thomas's technique, for instance, is to put five adjectives in the place of one. As Robert Horan (Tedlock, 1960, pp. 132–33) points out in a rebuttal article, this hinges on where one looks for meaning in a poem; in Thomas "the subject *is* the detail." The subject is not a generalized proposition abstracted from the poem. Mizener's linking of Thomas and Lowell now seems surprising, but as John Berryman (1947, p. 80) later noted, both poets are similarly "packed" and in fact have similar diction in describing movement, though influence would be hard to prove.

Conrad Aiken (1944, p. 26), whose verse we now would tend to associate with Thomas's, if only by virtue of its lyricism, writes on "the New Euphuism." He points out that, if we restrict ourselves to an examination of poetic diction, Eliot determined it between 1916 and 1930; Auden succeeded Eliot during the thirties, as a corrective, and Thomas has functioned as a corrective to Auden. Aiken seems to regret the results—a concentration on words with English roots rather than Latin, and "a spate of poetic purple" capable of limited effects and little development. From a literary-historical perspective, Aiken is probably quite right: Thomas's poetry is itself a kind of endpoint in its own direction, like *Finnegans Wake*, rather than a stimulus to further exploration, like the early work of Eliot. Perhaps this is what Daiches (1958, p. 64) means when he says Thomas "had no lessons to teach others, as Pound and Eliot had."

Horace Gregory, in an article entitled "The Romantic Heritage of Dylan Thomas" originally published in the March 1947 issue of *Poetry* (Brinnin, 1960, pp. 131–38), was one of the first writers to discuss Thomas as a "neo-romantic." He finds the sources of this modern movement in Welsh literature, in Clare, Poe, Darley, and Beddoes, and in English devotional poetry. More modern exemplars are Yeats, Edith Sitwell, and de la Mare, while within Thomas's generation Barker, Henry Treece, and Vernon Watkins share in the tradition. Gregory is not explicit about the ways in which this differs from poetry which springs from sources in Wordsworth, Keats, Shelley, or Coleridge; he does seem to stress a dark "richness of expression" and a mystically religious orientation in the poets he includes. While admitting that the writers from Yeats on were influenced by French symbolism, he points out that, for Thomas, what "so closely resembles the technique of Symbolist poetry in his poems is of the same nature that guided W. B. Yeats in his re-creations of the Celtic myth that he drew from the lives of those around him and himself." Although he does not expand upon the idea, Gregory here is clearly hinting at a synchronic approach rather than one based on influence or tradition. This sort of criticism will be dealt with in the following chapter.

In an interesting review of Thomas, Williams, and Elizabeth Bishop, Robert Lowell (1947, pp. 493–97) ranks Thomas below Auden but above Empson and Graves—about on a par with Bishop (though Thomas has greater moments he is less consistent) and ri-valled by MacNeice. Lowell compares Thomas's negative critical reception with the early attacks on Ezra Pound, and parallels his poetry with that of Hart Crane: both are "subjective, mystical, ob-scure and Elizabethan" in rhetoric, while both poets treat the themes of childhood and sexuality through symbols. Lowell analyzes what he considers Thomas's weaknesses—repetition and redundancy, a symbolism sometimes unsupported by the context, and an omission of "numb" or supporting lines to help our reading—but admits that Wallace Stevens is Thomas's only rival among modern poets as a metrician.

If Lowell examines technique, George Every in *Poetry and Personal Responsibility* (1949, pp. 32–40) discusses theme and at-titude. Expanding upon an article of his in the Winter 1948 *Humanitas*, Every argues that

The younger poets who came to light in 1937–42, such voices as Dylan Thomas, David Gascoyne, Alex Comfort, and Sidney Keyes, have never suffered from any illusions about the future of our civili-zation. For them the urgent problem is the imminence of death, the need of some significance that can be attached to dying in a world where there is no common belief in immortality.

Every points to the renewed influence of Eliot and of Christians such as Graham Greene, but also to a different tone springing from the bawdry of Joyce and Powys, the cynicism of Yeats or Rex War-ner. The present age (1949), he claims, thus appears a "new age of Sidney Keyes," a sort of late medievalism. How Every means this is difficult to say; probably he is speaking of the more universal and more human focus of poetry replacing the social concerns of the thirties which, coupled with a baroque and bawdy texture of lan-guage and a visionary approach, could give the impression of a me-dieval art. How illuminating this comparison can be is questionable, considering that Every himself postulates the absence of faith as an axiom of the poetry he describes; yet Treece (1949, pp. 72–84) makes a similar one.

In contrast to Every's rather tortuous arguments, Melville Cane (1954, pp. 9, 41) gives an optimistic popular view of the state of the art in a *Saturday Review* article entitled "Are Poets Returning to Lyricism?" Cane characterizes early modern poetry as "intellectual," the result of poets thinking like critics. Dylan Thomas and Christopher Fry, however, offer signs of hope that this sterile intellectualism may be dying out. Cane's article serves as a reminder that, in the popular press at least, the myth of Thomas as word-drunk lyricist, devoid of intellectual concern, was still strong after his death. As Daiches points out (1958, p. 64), Thomas, unlike Eliot, was "by instinct a popular poet;" however baffling the details of a given poem of his might be, his public unerringly sensed this distinction, which intellectual critics often gloss over.

Modern Intellectual and Esthetic Influences

Narrowing our focus still further, we now come to the matter of particular influences which thinkers, other artists, or artistic movements may have had upon Thomas. Here too there are problems not merely of critical procedure but of epistemology. Obviously we have no way of knowing what a poet's work would have been like had he never read a given writer. Literary history abounds in instances of two writers chancing independently upon the same theme or technique, not in response to a mutual source or to knowledge of one another's work, but to some felt demand or possibility the times offered. Even when we know Thomas was acquainted with a body of work, as he was undeniably acquainted with Eliot or Hopkins, to demonstrate the effect of that acquaintance is often a slippery task. Thus Clark Emery (*The World of Dylan Thomas*, 1962, p. 249) spends a page listing verbal echoes of Eliot's work in the poem "We Lying by Seasand" in an attempt to show that the younger poet, who must have been reading deeply in Eliot at the time, shared some of his pessimistic vision; thus Henry Treece (1949, p. 71) appends to his chapter on Thomas's "Debt to Hopkins" a page of similar compound words from the two poets' works in an attempt to prove and specify the debt.

Probably it is only in the matter of actual verbal echoes that the critic can come close to establishing influence, and even there the proof is not conclusive. When it comes to theme or idea we are on shakier ground; there are few, if any, totally new ideas in poetry. Nevertheless, the poetry of each century does seem to bear the impress of a few great ideas. Probably the dominant ones in our own century spring from the intellectual systems of Freud and Marx. Existentialism and phenomenology, springing from roots in Nietzsche and in Hegel, are certainly important movements in philosophy, and from the forties onward exert increasing influence upon writers, but Thomas, the least "intellectual" of writers, was certainly not influenced by these ideas in any direct sense. Dorothy Goodfellow (1955, p. 80) finds the "nightmarish quality" of his poetic world "almost (in 1934) a foretaste of existentialism," while Edward and Lillian Bloom (1960, pp. 138–58) elaborate the same theme. More convincingly, Moynihan (1966, p. 32) suggests that Thomas's early writing shows clearly Nietzschean themes—the Ubermensch, the "Death of God," and recurrence. Since the poet's father was a reader of Nietzsche, further investigation here might well be fruitful. It is far less likely that Thomas's work reflects a fourth major intellectual stimulus of the century, the revolution in physics with the work of Einstein and Heisenberg. Except insofar as all modern writers are peripherally aware of the concepts of relativity and indeterminacy, Thomas was undoubtedly ignorant of these. His cyclic idea of time springs more directly from sources in mystical poets than from metaphysical thinkers.

Freud, Marx, and Modernism

On the other hand, the ideas of Freud and Marx undeniably had some sort of influence upon him. Early in his career he committed himself in his response to an "Enquiry" sponsored by Grigson's *New Verse* (Oct. 1934; reprinted in Brinnin, 1960, pp. 102–3, and FitzGibbon, 1965, pp. 142–43). Asked whether he took his stand with any political party or creed, he replied:

I take my stand with any revolutionary body that asserts it to be the right of all men to share, equally and impartially, every production of man . . . for only through such a revolutionary body can there be the possibility of communal art.

Asked whether he had been influenced by Freud, he replied:

Yes. Whatever is hidden should be made naked . . . Freud cast light on a little of the darkness he had exposed . . . poetry must drag further into the clean nakedness of light more even of the hidden causes than Freud could realize.

It is possible, as some modern critics hold, that a man's political views must be reflected in his writing; but that reflection certainly need not be direct. Although Thomas never abandoned the leftist views he shared with most artists and intellectuals of the thirties, his writing remained mainly apolitical. Even in the few poems which have a political dimension, like "The hand that signed the paper," the poet's stance appears to be a vague and politically disengaged humanism. It was not so much that Thomas did not *wish* to write politically "engaged" literature as that he realized his own genius, for better or for worse, lay elsewhere. "I, too, have had occasion to sleep under the blanket of the stars, in the country, among the dispossessed of a city," he wrote in a guarded review of Prokosch's *Night of the Poor* (Davies, 1971, p. 198), "and when prosperity returned, I would attempt . . . to write stories about the poor I had slept, talked, and shivered with. These stories were always false."

Most writers agree that Thomas's ideas about politics were derivative and naive; from time to time he did collaborate informally with friends in writing humorous verse or filmscripts, but it is hard to imagine him engaged in a serious work of "communal art" like the "Oxford Collective Poem." His poetry is idiosyncratic and, in a peculiar sense, private; it follows none of the accepted canons of socialist art in the thirties. There is nothing surprising in the fact that Samuel Sillen in the *New Masses* (1943, pp. 24–25) dismissed his work as bourgeois and decadent; it is more surprising that he was comparatively well received during the fifties in *Masses and Mainstream*.

Despite Augustus John's repeated assertions (Tedlock, 1960, p. 22; Brinnin, 1960, p. 277), Thomas in all likelihood was never a member of the Communist party, though some of his friends were. FitzGibbon (1965, p. 78) comes to this conclusion, as does Jack Lindsay (1966, p. 67), the brother of his close London friend and scriptwriting associate Philip. As he aged, his revolutionary ardor cooled somewhat; by 1938, according to Treece (1949, p. 41), Thomas felt that his "Enquiry" statement on politics no longer applied. Thomas was deeply affected by the Spanish Civil War and was a strong supporter of the Republican cause; like some other leftist artists he opposed the Second World War on pacifistic grounds, even going so far as to circulate an antiwar petition, but whether this feeling sprung mainly from political or from personal motivations it is difficult to say. Heppenstall (1960, p. 150) tells of receiving a pacifist letter from the poet pointing out with a wry logic that "the best poems about death were always written when the poets were alive."

Lindsay (1966, p. 68) feels that Thomas's work on documentary films during the war did politicize his thinking somewhat, pointing particularly to the script of *These are the Men*. Although this script does show a stronger if rather diffuse social conscience in the poet, as does the script *Our Country* in its vision of an essential unity in British laborers, much of this may result from the exigencies of the format. FitzGibbon (1965, p. 237) claims that Thomas, deeply affected by the revelations of the German concentration camps, first planned the work that was to become *Under Milk Wood* as a fable of a "mad" town which the rest of the world had shunned and surrounded by barbed wire; the point, of course, is that the rest of the world is the real concentration camp. Though he discarded this superstructure, some of the implications are present in the final version of the play.

The social dimension of the poetry is even more limited. Tindall (1962, pp. 7–8) is practically alone among major critics in spotting a socialist theme in poems like "Our eunuch dreams" and "All all and all," and even he admits that "Thomas's poetic method, surely not that of communal art, hid the pinkness of his heart." Although some critics have seen a reference to the postwar depression in the imagery of sterility and waste of early poems like "I see the boys of summer," it is only in the poems of *D&E* that the outside world really begins to intrude into the poetry. Notably, all four poems Thomas wrote about the war—"A Refusal to Mourn," "Deaths and Entrances," "Ceremony After a Fire Raid," and "Dawn Raid"— are about the only aspect of war Thomas experienced firsthand, the bombing of London. And even in these poems, the closest he seems to come to "social statement" is his underlying assertion of the brotherhood of all men, a conviction which, in its implications throughout the body of his poetry, seems more deeply rooted in the vision of Donne than in that of Marx. Thomas, says Stanford *(Dylan Thomas, A Literary Study*, 1964, p. 52), "was the least politically-minded of poets." This is not to say that Thomas learned nothing from the poets of the thirties. Undoubtedly Auden had much to teach him about lyricism and the adaptation of colloquial language. A great deal of absurd "nonsense" verse was written during the thirties and very probably influenced his comic writing. It is even possible that Auden, Day Lewis, and Spender's abandonment of titles for some poems in their early books, which was so shocking at the time, encouraged Thomas to do likewise. But between his poetry and theirs there remains a philosophical chasm.

Henry Treece (1949, pp. 15–27) begins his book on Thomas with an interesting essay entitled "The Poet and Mechanistic Ide-

ology." He argues that poetry of the thirties was dominated by
images of mechanism and a mechanistic sense of language; he traces
this "cult of the machine" among left-wing poets and critics to
Christopher Caudwell's influential socialistic approach to esthetics
Illusion and Reality (1937). Citing in support of his position comments by others of the new generation of poets, notably Roy Fuller
and Kenneth Allott, Treece opposes Thomas to Auden and others.
Thomas's writing is subjective rather than objective, organic rather
than mechanistic, concentrates upon fantasy rather than tangible
things; he creates his own individual myth rather than endorsing the
communal myth of Marxism. Basically, Treece is arguing not that
there is no room for Thomas's work in a Marxist esthetic, but that
his work differed vastly from the particular form of Marxist esthetic
which was most popular during his time. As Spender put it (1954, p.
16), "Thomas's poetry was a criticism of the assumption of Marxist
critics . . . that a poem is ultimately reducible to terms of social
ideas."

On the whole, as John Sweeney admitted in the introduction to
the *Selected Writings of Dylan Thomas* (1946, p. x), Thomas was
more Freudian than Marxian. "He was primarily concerned with
the spiritual regeneration of the individual. That individual was
himself." Sweeney's implication here is also suggested by Thomas's
response to the "Enquiry": that his poetry functioned as a sort of
therapy for him, bringing up repressed material from the subconscious and dealing with it in some sort of integrative fashion. Several
points should be noted about this observation. First, if one subscribes to a Freudian theory of art, this is simply the way any artist
functions, whether he has heard of Freud or not; Thomas's consciousness of the procedure would probably tend to make it less
effective from a psychological standpoint, not more. Ralph Maud
(1963, pp. 83–89) makes this point. When asked about Freud's
influence, in 1951 (FitzGibbon, 1965, pp. 326–27), Thomas admitted to having read *The Interpretation of Dreams* but denied
any specific "influence" other than an awareness of his pervasive
presence in twentieth-century literature. Further, the Freudian approach can easily be given the wrong stress, making of Thomas a
programmatic surrealist who simply brought up words through free
association or chance. Thomas himself strenuously denied this implication: however the source "material" of a poem arose, he scrupulously and quite consciously selected, arranged, revised, and revised again before regarding a poem as finished.

David Holbrook (*Dylan Thomas and Poetic Dissociation*, 1964;
Dylan Thomas: The Code of Night, 1972) furnishes an example of

the critic whose own interpretive method, based on Freudian analysis, makes a weakness of what other critics regard as a strength
(see chapter 3 herein). The wealth of sexual and pseudo-sexual material in the poetry convinces Holbrook that Thomas was a se-
verely disturbed personality attempting to come to terms with his
problems through writing; Holbrook then turns around and attacks the poetry as limited esthetically because of the poet's imma-
turity. But whatever the difficulties with Holbrook's methodology,
they are due more to the influence of Freud upon the critic than
upon the poet. Here our interest is in the ways in which the thought
of Freud through its various popularizations and adaptations—for
example, through D. H. Lawrence—affected the thought and art
of Thomas. For instance, Sweeney (1946, p. xv) called the poetry
"Freudian in its paradoxes and leaps; in its synthesis of unconscious
experience." Whether or not Sweeney realizes it, these are really
two different orders of interpretation, the first primarily regarding
form, the second content.

What do we mean when we say Thomas's poetry bears the impress of Freud's thought? I see three main areas of implication.
First, Thomas's poetry in its "argument" may assume or suggest
Freud's ideas about human life: the concept of a buried reservoir of
sexual energy basic to the human psyche which may find outlet
either directly or through the various "mechanisms" of projection,
sublimation, and so forth; the concept of basic dramatic "tableaus,"
such as the Oedipal relation; or, more generally, the idea that sexuality is an omnipresent and powerful factor in human life from
birth onward. Since Freud was the first great psychologist to stress
the role of human sexuality this strongly, we often term a writer
"Freudian" if he too does so, regardless of the source of his thinking. Thus, it would be difficult to separate Thomas's debt to Lawrence, who used Freud's ideas thematically, from his debt to the
psychological literature. And from the evidence of his letters and
published comments there is little doubt that Thomas did accept in
modified form many of Freud's ideas.

Another broad area of Freudian influence would be upon
Thomas's particular poetic symbolism. Thus we would expect to
find pencils, thumbs, needles, and worms representing the phallus
while lakes, caves, turtles, and such should represent the womb;
images of interpenetration ought to imply the sex act, and so forth.
And indeed, especially in the early poetry and prose, this seems to
be the case, as Tindall (1948, p. 432) was one of the first to point
out. We should realize, though, that this use of image and symbol
predates Freud. "We do not need Freud to tell us that scythe, thorn,

stem, tower, mast, paddle, and sun are male symbols, and fats, flower, and bud are female," observes Maud (1963, p. 90). Further, Thomas warns us, "I, in my intricate image, stride on two levels." His symbolism is very seldom unequivocal; as often as it is sexual, it may simultaneously be religious or mystical, Biblical or Blakean.

It should also be noted that Jung developed an equally complex system of symbols to interpret myth, dream, and art in terms which were not necessarily sexual at all, but usually reflected the mechanisms of self-confrontation. Thomas's work, particularly in the long narrative poems like "A Winter's Tale" or "Ballad of the Long-legged Bait," seems equally amenable to Jungian interpretation. Annis Pratt (1970) in her study of Thomas's early prose explores the poet's use of Jungian achetypes, arguing that the issues of *transition* magazine, which he read assiduously, would have given him a thorough acquaintance with the psychological aspects of myth. G. S. Fraser *(The Modern Writer and His World,* 1964, pp. 335–45) notes that a group of poets during the forties including Robert Graves, Kathleen Raine, John Heath-Stubbs, Edwin Muir, and sometimes Edith Sitwell quite consciously and deliberately employed archetypes like those of Jung in order to give their poetry a depth, resonance, and universality. But this is a sort of symbolism which—at least in the case of Graves—borders upon allegory, in that the poet alludes to a body of knowledge—such as that set forth in *The White Goddess*—which goes far to "explain" the poem. Aside from its invocation of archetypes, this sort of poetry is much more transparent in texture than that of Thomas. Fraser makes the important distinction that where Thomas's poems begin in a set of warring, essentially inexplicable images, which may have Freudian or Jungian overtones, those of poets like Graves begin from a clear abstraction. Olson *(The Poetry of Dylan Thomas,* 1954, pp. 5–7) establishes this point at some length, claiming that while Thomas does connect birth with emergence from water, in good Freudian form, he uses "fruit" as a child symbol, whereas in Freud its referent is the female breast, with no implication of offspring. "Whereas, for Freud, caves, churches, and chapels refer to the female genitalia, Thomas uses caves to signify the innermost recesses of the self, and churches and chapels—particularly sunken ones—to signify lost pristine faiths . . . the reader who has the Jungian archetypes in mind is likely to fare no better . . ." Even questioning some of Olson's specific readings, his point remains valid. There is certainly no single symbolic "key" to the work.

Finally, Freudian influence can be seen in the poet's poetic techniques. His frequent use of dreams, fantasies, and folktales as a narrative structure is in itself a gesture toward Freud's demonstration of their importance. "From Freud," says Tindall flatly, "Thomas learned about dreams" (1948, p. 431). Later, he asserts (1962, p. 9) that "the Biblical images of the early poems—water, towers, snakes, and ladders—must owe something to *The Interpretation of Dreams*." And the dream poems themselves "seem constructed according to Freud's dreamwork; by condensation, displacement, and symbolizing." Again, in discussing the poet's use of dreams we are speaking of a broad twentieth-century trend. Tindall in *Forces in Modern British Literature, 1885-1956*, (1956, pp. 239–40) places Thomas within a chapter on "The Unconscious" which also treats such differing writers as Robert Graves, May Sinclair, Lawrence, Joyce, the Auden group, and the surrealists.

Several of the mechanisms to which Freud pointed as significant emerge in Thomas's poetic technique; for instance the process of verbal association, puns, and wordplay. Joyce, whose own art owed much to Freud in this respect, is undoubtedly the major influence upon Thomas's verbal technique (as opposed to his poetics). E. P. Bollier (1954, pp. 394–97) discusses the problem of Freud's influence on symbol, theme, and technique. Francis Scarfe (Tedlock, 1960, pp. 96–112), in an important early essay on the poet's technique, asserts that the only important influences upon his work are from Joyce (linguistic), the Bible (mythological), and Freud (psychopathological). His "basic device," Scarfe argues, "is the invention of words," and proceeds to analyze Thomas's most prominent verbal inventions (see chapter 7). Of course Joyce's influence was not confined to verbal gymnastics; as Every (1949, pp. 32–40) points out, Joyce brought to light the unconscious mind; treated prose nonrepresentationally (an important influence on Thomas's "surreal" stories); and exploited the world of dreams in *Finnegans Wake*. Thomas was exposed to this and other instances of editor Eugène Jolas's "Revolution of the Word" through *transition*. Freud, Joyce, and other influences on the prose are discussed in chapter 1 above.

All Thomas's interpreters mention the psychosexual thematic element, but few discussions go beyond its relevance to particular poems. Clearly some of the poems in *18 Poems* and *Twenty-five Poems* deal with inversion, frustration, and other aspects of adolescence. The problem is that they do so in a depersonalized way, which makes conventional Freudian analysis strangely futile. We are not shown an individual psyche tormented and molded by sexual experience, as we are in Lawrence; instead we are given speakers who are universal—Christ, Everyman, and Poet combined—or who are fantastic personae, such as the speaking fetus in "If my head hurt a hair's foot." The poems present experience made generalized and mythological rather than individual. Frederick Hoffman (1957, pp. 286–88), discussing Thomas in *Freudianism and the Literary Mind*, makes an attempt at analysis which points up this problem. In the prose he finds evidence of Thomas's "progress toward his ultimate mythical awareness of the unconscious and the dream-life," which is also linked to a full realization of his sexuality. But notwithstanding his "Enquiry" reply, is this in fact Thomas's goal? Certainly by the time of the later poems his goal seems to be more closely linked to a spiritual, mystical, or religious awareness than to a confrontation with the self. Hoffman finds that while "death" is often used as a "symbol of detumescence," "life" is also linked to decay and frustration. Thomas invokes the womb so frequently because it is for him a "source of renewal when the initial helplessness is duplicated in later social or psychic distress." The "womb thus becomes animate," a "creative medium." Questions immediately arise. Would it not be equally valid to take images of detumescence as symbolizing death? Do we need the Freudian apparatus of womb-regression to justify using the womb poetically as a creative medium? Thomas links fertility and life, sterility and death, and both sets of symbols together in an endless round; to take sexual statement as fundamental seems arbitrary and an injustice to the scope of his vision.

The case for the particular influences of Joyce and of Lawrence is stronger than that for Freud, if only because we know he was directly acquainted with their work. Joyce, says Tindall (1962, p. 14), "rules Thomas' words as Lawrence his themes," pointing to the theme of rebirth and "the world of bird, beast, and flower" (a phrase from Lawrence's *Apocalypse* that Thomas echoes in "A Refusal to Mourn"). His attitude toward Lawrence, however, was more complex than this might imply. Moynihan (1966, pp. 35–41), who writes with a knowledge of the poet's notebooks and correspondence, discusses the question more thoroughly than earlier critics. Thomas had an early aversion to pantheism, in part because he felt it was a form of materialism, denying the spiritual, and in part because he felt Man, not Nature, to be central. In a review in the February 1935 *Adelphi* he attacks Lawrence for his "paganism." Paganism, which he defined as sex and sun, is materialistic and leaves no room for art; Lawrence, he felt, would have written nothing if illness had not kept him from a life of pure sensuality. Further, Thomas perceptively noted that Lawrence's world was based upon a totalitarian capitalism, which he opposed strongly on political grounds.

Moynihan notes, however, that few of these disputes seem at all evident in Thomas's poetry, especially in the later verse where nature comes to the fore. The two writers, he concludes, have a similar veneration for the "life force," but their attitude toward death distinguishes them. Where Lawrence sees death as a release, Thomas fears and fights it, attempting perpetually to make death somehow creative and affirmative. Though Moynihan is correct in making these distinctions, they are overshadowed by broad areas of agreement: the emphasis on sexuality, the denial of authority, the need for a personal mysticism, the philosophical bias toward the organic and abhorrence of the mechanistic, and so forth.

Joyce's influence on Thomas's use of words has already been discussed; clearly he had some effect on the poet's themes as well. Tindall (1962) throughout his *Reader's Guide* emphasizes Thomas's portrayals of the "artist as a young man." Clearly the two artists had similar notions of the writer as priest, as is evident in the transubstantiation Thomas attempts in "After the funeral." Thomas uses Biblical symbolism much as Joyce does, more or less independently of his degree of Christian belief. "He cared nothing for Christ in a theological sense," says Moynihan (1966, p. 38), "but he cared very much for Christ as a symbol." From Joyce as much as from Lawrence, Thomas could have learned the serious (and humorous) literary uses of sexuality. Finally, of course, Joyce provided him a model of narrative technique, from the comparatively realistic *Portrait of the Artist as a Young Dog* to the dream-visions of the *Map of Love* stories. Asked about Joyce's influence upon him (FitzGibbon, 1965, p. 326), Thomas registered his extreme admiration for the writer and replied rather confusedly, "I do not think that Joyce has had any hand at all in my writing; certainly his Ulysses has not. On the other hand, I cannot deny that the shaping of some of my Portrait stories might owe something to Joyce's stories in the volume, 'Dubliners.' " Here I think we can safely assume that Joyce's influence was more fundamental than Thomas realized. Walford Davies (1968, pp. 290–95) and Warren French (1967) both discuss the influence of Joyce's *Portrait* and *Dubliners* on individual stories by Thomas. As with Lawrence, the affinities between the two writers are too numerous to mention.

Many of Thomas's affinities with Joyce are in fact simply the handmarks of modernism, elements we might expect to find in Joyce, Eliot, or even Auden: complexity, allusiveness, irony; the struggle for the *mot juste* despite harsh and violent elements in the verse; the use of a mixture of public and private symbology; the conscious manipulation of ambiguity; an extremely dense verbal texture. Such a list could be expanded almost indefinitely. Thus when

Holbrook (1964, p. 13) attacks Thomas's grotesquerie, the "element of revulsion" in his poetry, and traces it to Pound, Eliot, Gautier, and Baudelaire, he is actually attacking a major element of modernism. He terms it a "degenerate aestheticism," while other critics feel it as an honest response to contemporary urban life, and find that the poets Holbrook mentions were attempting to broaden the scope of poetic discourse. The "maggot" in Thomas's "stool" clearly identifies him as a post-symbolist poet, while the occasional movies, telephones, and air raids mark him as twentieth-century. Unlike Auden, he chooses to present these artifacts indirectly—Leslie Fiedler (1947, p. 105) is probably technically correct when he says the poet excludes from his work "all manufactured things more recently invented than ships"—but this is a matter more of rhetoric than of substance. Thomas consciously attempted a style of poetic "elevation" which seldom allowed him to invoke the mundane. Nevertheless, to read him carefully is to realize that he is irrevocably of our time. The shared assumptions of modern poets make the problem of detecting specific influences of one upon another especially trying. Winifred Nowottny (1965, pp. 202–7) analyzes the difficulties involved in deciding whether we are justified in finding echoes of Eliot in "There was a Saviour." According to John Davenport (1954, p. 2), Thomas frequently acknowledged a debt to Pound; yet no critic, to my knowledge, has had the temerity to open his Pandora's box. Usually the most we can say for certain is that, like Eliot, Pound, and Joyce, Thomas is "modern."

Symbolism, Surrealism, and the Apocalypse

Certainly one of the main currents of modern poetry—perhaps "undercurrents" would be more descriptive—is the discovery of the subconscious and the irrational. In strictly literary terms the discovery antedates Freud and Jung, as indeed they were the first to point out. French surrealism, which flourished in the twenties, was the main literary focus of the doctrine of the "unconscious," but in many respects was indebted to symbolist doctrine as codified by Mallarmé around the turn of the century. British surrealism during the thirties, hardly a full-scale movement, led in turn to the New Apocalypse of the forties, and influenced numerous writers who were members of none of these groups. Somewhere in the middle is Thomas, whose work demands comparison with each of these in turn, though he belongs to none.

The three main figures of "le symbolisme," Baudelaire, Rimbaud, and Mallarmé, produced very different sorts of work and in fact their conscious poetic aims differed considerably. Baudelaire is the prototypical alienated artist; his sensibility is religious, but in an inverted way, so that he is drawn to the base and the demonic. The urban world about him he finds both beautiful and obscene. His doctrine of "correspondences," however, mystical synesthetic connections among sounds, odors, and colors, suggesting the possibility of discovering through poetry a reality beyond reality, influenced Rimbaud. But Rimbaud, a prodigy stifled by provincial life, cut himself off from society more completely than Baudelaire had dared. Declaring the artist a law unto himself, he submitted himself to a willed confusion of the senses through drugs, alcohol, perversion, and flirtation with madness. His interest was not so much in personal expression as in attaining an almost mystical state beyond the ordinarily human, whereby his trances and visions would show him a more intense and true world. His poetry, which runs the gamut from tightly constructed sonnets to prose poems, abounds in violent and colorful images. Rimbaud too saw hidden correspondences in nature, and assigned the poet a more active role in their discovery, if only in the violence of his quest to become passively receptive to the "I" who is "another." In his "Les Voyelles" he attempted to show hidden connections between words and things.

In contrast to his bohemian predecessors, Mallarmé, a mild school teacher, elaborated his theories at length, gathering about him a literary movement as he did so. Poetry, he insisted, was an autonomous domain which alone allowed the discovery of a higher reality. Poetry should evoke rather than state, and through the symbol it must attempt to capture this otherwise inexpressible reality. Unlike Rimbaud, Mallarmé stressed the struggle for the *mot juste*, the most precise shade of connotation that could be exacted from language within the context of a "pure" poem which aspired always after the condition of music. Poetry *becomes* the world, the only world worth having: turning inward, it seeks to describe itself. Such ideas were to mark permanently the edifice of modernism. Wallace Stevens and Paul Valéry were centrally influenced by Mallarmé, while Paul Claudel, despite his Catholicism, owed much to Rimbaud. First through the turn-of-the-century British "Decadents" or "Aesthetes," more importantly through T. S. Eliot's discovery of Jules Laforgue and Tristan Corbière, the French movement came to pervade English poetry.

Critics have paid surprisingly little attention to Thomas's relationship with French symbolism. Karl Shapiro in an influential essay (Tedlock, 1960, p. 274) insisted that Thomas was *not* a symbolist,

in that his procedure is the opposite of "purifying the language of
the tribe." In the sense that we now tend to associate symbolism with
the explicit attempt to achieve a poetically pure language à la Mallarmé, Shapiro is doubtless correct, although Thomas does explicitly
or implicitly echo many symbolist themes, as Tindall points out
throughout his *Reader's Guide* (1962). But we also associate some
aspects of symbolism with a "dark romantic" tradition, best embodied in Rimbaud. Of course Thomas, who read no languages
other than English, was not directly influenced by any of these
writers, but through the translations of Norman Cameron he must
have been aware of their work. At the very least, we might expect
some discussion of the ways Thomas and the symbolists responded
in poetically innovative ways to the broad currents of modern life
and ideas. Babette Deutsch (1963, pp. 349–88), in a chapter of
Poetry in Our Time entitled "Alchemists of the Word," points to a
vague tradition of writers who attempt some sort of romantic and
religious transcendence of ordinary language, a tradition which
harks back to Rimbaud, Whitman, and Poe, and which includes
Hopkins, Graves, Barker, Jean Garrigue, James Agee, the Apocalypse poets, and Thomas. Similarly, Stuart Holroyd (1957) devotes separate chapters to Thomas and Rimbaud in *Emergence
From Chaos* (1957), a study of modern poets who have searched
for a religious transcendence of the self, but he makes few explicit
comparisons.

Probably because of the rediscovery of Rimbaud's work following the twenties and Thomas's own comments about playing "the
Rimbaud of Cwmdonkin Drive," the comparison between the two
poetic prodigies was made relatively early. Treece (1949, pp. 51,
55) lists Rimbaud as the fourth major influence on Thomas's poetry,
following Hopkins, Crane, and Swinburne. Among the correspondences between their poetries he mentions the musical quality, the
systematic derangement of the senses, incantation, the use of colorful and exotic images, violence, the predominant themes of death
and corruption, and a characteristic use of the sea as a basic image. French critics, naturally enough, invariably recognize what
Georges-Albert Astre (1953, p. 41) calls the "génie de Rimbaud"
in Thomas. Bokanowsky and Alyn (*Dylan Thomas*, 1963, pp.
34–41), writing in the Thomas volume of the "poètes d'aujourd'hui"
series, cite the similarities between Rimbaud's "Voyelles" and the
Welsh poet's "Especially when the October wind," or between "Les
Premières Communions" and "On the Marriage of a Virgin." They
go so far as to assert a direct influence, probably through Cameron's
translations, and suggest that, through Vernon Watkins, Thomas

was made aware of the work of other European poets with whom he bears comparison—Francis Jammes, Laforgue, Hölderlin, and Rilke.

The only extended comparison between works of these two poets is Glauco Cambon's "Two Crazy Boats: Dylan Thomas and Rimbaud" (1956, pp. 251–59). Cambon's discussion of "Ballad of the Long-legged Bait" and "Le Bateau Ivre" concentrates upon structure, technique, and vision, and succeeds in enlightening both poems. Cambon admits that "the astonishing fact is that Thomas was avowedly unaware of his French forerunner's creation when he wrote his 'ballad,' which, I think, makes the affinity only the more interesting." On the other hand, T. H. Jones (*Dylan Thomas*, 1963, p. 79) strongly disagrees with such a comparison of the two poems. So does Maud (1963, p. 158, n. 8), who specifically attacks the comparisons made by Tindall (*The Literary Symbol*, 1955, p. 155), Stanford (1964, p. 119), and Treece (*How I See Apocalypse*, 1956, pp. 45–56) by asserting that Thomas's "Ballad" is *allegorical*, unlike "Bateau Ivre." Maud approvingly cites one of Thomas's numerous public denials of Rimbaud's influence, as do MacNeice, Davenport (Tedlock, 1960, p. 86), and many other critics. Maud's denial, it should be noted, occurs within a section of his book where he discusses and dismisses most of the suggested "influences" upon Thomas, from Hopkins and Welsh poetry through Rilke. His point, a valid one, is that the poet's work is better understood through an intense examination of his unique sort of expression than through a hunt for literary parallels. But in a more recent discussion, Martin Dodsworth (Davies, 1972, pp. 115–17) suggests Thomas may have read Edgell Rickword's *Rimbaud: The Boy and the Poet* (1924) and assimilated some of the French poet's ideas about poetry, the mind, and the senses, joining them to those he had gleaned from Blake. Dodsworth is apparently unaware that Rickword was a friend of Thomas's, which lends more strength to his hypothesis.

Several critics, among them George Steiner and Reed Whittemore, mention Thomas's symbolist inheritance in the context of a larger argument on the dangers of broken syntax and private meaning. Whittemore (1957, pp. 357–71), who is an American parallel to the British Movement poets of the fifties, attacks the "modern idiom" in poetry, which has roots in the symbolists and in the metaphysicals whom Eliot rediscovered. Thomas is included among an odd assortment of sinners—Brinnin, Wilbur (!), Lowell, Crane, and Howard Moss. Like Kingsley Amis, Whittemore cannot see why Thomas could not use the clear syntax and rhetoric of his later prose in his poetry. Steiner (1961, p. 207) suggests that in the hands of lesser followers of Rimbaud and Mallarmé, "the attempt to make language new is diminished to barrenness and obscurity." In Thomas, a case in point, "there is . . . less than meets the dazzled eye."

Apart from critically conservative reactions, the symbolists themselves have by now gained general acceptance. This cannot be said of the surrealists, a tightly-knit and vocal group of writers organized by André Breton in the early twenties. Breton and Phillippe Soupault had been experimenting with "automatic writing," an attempt to short-circuit the censorship of the conscious mind in an effort to discover direct verbal manifestations of the subconscious. Gathering about him other writers, notably the Marxist Louis Aragon and Paul Eluard, Breton attempted to codify the tenets of the group in the *First Surrealist Manifesto* (1924). Breton had survived the dadaist movement of Tristan Tzara, which had been a short-lived general attack upon all conventional notions of art and, with his knowledge of Freud, felt that a more systematic and solidly based movement should be possible. Partly because of his desire for an ideological merger with Marxism, Breton gradually revised his original definition of surrealism as "pure psychic automatism" and began to stress the possibility of encounter with "reality," a reality composed of both "inner" and "outer" worlds.

Clear predecessors to whom Breton acknowledged indebtedness were Lautréamont, Tristan Corbière, and of course Rimbaud. As they were joined by the painter Salvador Dali, certain characteristics not necessarily following directly from their theoretical precepts began to be evident from the group's work; the use of "shock tactics," inherited from dada; a preponderance of violent Gothic and sometimes sadistic imagery; an underlying sexuality; an emphasis upon "meaningful coincidence" bordering on the occult (later described by Breton as "objective chance"); wild humor and paradox; experimentation with words and even puns in an effort to discover their hidden logic; juxtaposition of surprising images, as in the celebrated umbrella and sewing machine which meet upon a dissection table. Irrationality and even madness were given new value in the surrealist attack upon what the bourgeois, mundane world seemed to accept as "reality."

Paul C. Ray in *The Surrealist Movement in England* (1971) traces the spread of the French movement across the Channel. From his discussion it emerges that while David Gascoyne may have been the only thoroughgoing surrealist—and that only for several years—the movement was embraced by several important literary figures, notable among them Herbert Read. It found sympathizers in the editor of *Contemporary Poetry and Prose*, Roger Roughton; the essayist Hugh Sykes Davies; Eugène Jolas, who edited *transition;* and the poet and novelist Ruthven Todd. The Surrealist Exhibition held in London in 1936 awakened a mostly amused interest among the British, but at least established the movement in the public consciousness. Critical reaction to surrealist writing was in general strongly negative; critics, usually ill-informed about the theoretical bases of the movement, tended to dismiss it as a resurgent romanticism. In fact many British surrealists, including Read, stressed its continuity with earlier romantic movements, such as the Gothic novelists and the Pre-Raphaelites. The few examples of surrealist writing from the British thus tended to be coherent verbal descriptions of an incoherent Daliesque landscape or of a dream, both of which missed the point the continental writers were making about a surrealist attitude toward language itself. This is why Roland Mathias (1954, p. 36), for example, argues that Thomas is not surrealist because his poems develop from *words* rather than the image; his point holds good for British surrealism but not for French. Even fewer British seemed to appreciate the fact that surrealism was not meant to be looked upon as a "literary movement"—which was itself a bourgeois concept, like esthetics or morality—but as an entire way of life.

Many critics, particularly negative ones, who were writing in response to Thomas's work when it was still new, lumped him together with British surrealists. Thomas was at pains to point out what he saw as an essential distinction between his work and theirs, that he exercised conscious control over his poem, once the "given" images or phrases were on the page (see his "Poetic Manifesto," *Texas Quarterly* Winter 1961, p. 44; reprinted in FitzGibbon, 1965, pp. 323–28). Further, he insisted in a letter to Richard Church (*SL,* Dec. 9, 1935; quoted in FitzGibbon, 1965, pp. 174–75) that in his writing "every line *is* meant to be understood; the reader *is* meant to understand every poem by thinking and feeling about it, not by sucking it in through his pores, or whatever he is meant to do with surrealist writing." His intention, of course, begs the question—Thomas had a strange sense of the "literal" meaning of his poems and, as his letters to Vernon Watkins show, what he thought to be an easily accessible line could be obscure indeed. The fact remains that some of his poems and many of his stories from the mid-thirties *look* in some respects like what avowed surrealists were writing.

Treece (1949, pp. 28–38) devotes an entire chapter to his compatriot's "Relations to Surrealism." "Because of his complexity, his unusually startling and fertile flow of images, and his conceptions of other realities, Dylan Thomas has been connected . . . with the Surrealists . . ." Treece admits that Thomas and the surrealists both, with the impetus of Freud, aim at exploring the subconscious; in both, the *image* is the important factor in composition (here Treece is responding more to the ideas of British surrealists). But, echoing Thomas, Treece stresses the Welsh poet's craftsmanship and conscious control and selection of material; he too sees this distinction as all-important, and dismisses surrealism as diverting in theory but futile in practice.

The majority of critics are not even as analytical as Treece in their approach to the problem. Many use "surrealism" as a synonym for "automatic writing" (e.g. MacNeice, *Modern Poetry*, 1938, pp. 159–60; Wain in Brinnin, 1960, p. 70). Bogan (1955, pp. 374–75) refers to his earlier poetry as "surrealist" in a review of *In Country Sleep and Other Poems*, and suggests that his use of paradoxical epithet ("mustardseed sun") is a holdover from it. H. R. Hays, discussing the "Surrealist Influence in Contemporary English and American Poetry" (1939, pp. 202–9), refers to the "associative method" of composition adopted by Harold Rosenberg and Charles Henri Ford in America and by Thomas and Gascoyne in England. Thomas he describes as the least contemporary and the least surrealist; the objects in his verse and its texture suggest a "personal metaphysical poetry" recalling Rimbaud and Lautréamont. Hays seems to be using the British interpretation of surrealism here, as he evokes the sense of "magic" in all poetry, which he relates to Coleridge's term "fancy." Andrews Wanning (1941, pp. 792–810) in a massive review of recent poetry groups Lorca, Charles Ford, and Thomas as surrealist in a general way, in that they rely on "thought generated by metaphor" rather than elaborating statements through metaphors. Thomas, for whom he has much praise, is too conscious to be surrealist, but Wanning suggests that the form of his poetry is often musical rather than being dictated by the sequence of an argument. J. M. Cohen in *Poetry of this Age (1908–1965)* (1966, pp. 167–71) puts Thomas in an international perspective of poets influenced by surrealism, along with Sitwell, Crane, Jules Supervielle, and Vincente Aleixandre. He notes that Thomas was saved by his "fine formal sense" from Sitwell's disastrous fall into free verse.

Today, a majority of critics probably agree with Walford Davies (1972a, p. 33), who argues that "there has been a silly over-defense of Thomas against certain surrealist implications in his poetry." They are clearly there in the stories and poems of the mid and late thirties. When surrealist stock plummeted so completely in the Anglo-American literary world, his defenders were anxious to

point out that Thomas, by contrast, was writing *real* poetry. Ray
(1971, pp. 277–86), who has the fullest discussion of Thomas in
the surrealist context, claims that "of the major poets of our time,"
he was "the one most influenced by surrealism." Ray cites similarities
in both theory and use of the image between Breton and Thomas,
suggesting a number of particular instances where Thomas appears
indebted to surrealist writings; throughout, he cites Lita Hornick's
Columbia University Ph.D. dissertation (1958) entitled "The Intricate Image: A Study of Dylan Thomas." Ray discusses in detail
several of the stories from *Adventures in the Skin Trade and Other
Stories*. One of these, "The Lemon," "comes closest, of all English
writing influenced by surrealism, to breaking down the distinction
between dream and reality." Nonetheless, Ray also stresses that
Thomas arrives at surreal effects through conscious control of his
material. Bokanowski and Alyn (1963, pp. 84–86) admit that
Thomas's obscurity is of a different sort from that of the surrealists,
being eventually explicable, but find correspondences between his
use of sex and that of Aragon or Robert Desnos. They find an even
closer parallel with the work of Pierre Jean Jouve. Provocatively,
they suggest (p. 21) that Thomas's "goût du scandale" may have
originated in his contact with the surrealists. Annis Pratt (1970) devotes an entire chapter to Thomas's relationships with "Surrealism
as a Literary method." She agrees with the majority of critics in seeing a clear distinction between Thomas's ideas and those of the surrealists. Pratt's main contribution, however, is the idea that at certain
points in the early stories Thomas inserts surrealistic passages in order
to show psychological breakdown or artistic sterility on the part of
the protagonist; the poet is *using* surrealism within a broader context, actually writing an extended criticism of it in his prose fiction.

Most historians of modern British poetry treat surrealism and the
New Apocalypse as aspects of the same movement. However inaccurate this may be with regard to the continental movement, it
makes sense in the British context. Bullough (*The Trend of Modern Poetry*, 1949, p. 206) argues that both were reactions against the
"intellectual privacy" of Empson's sort of verse. He implies that
where the influence of the metaphysicals, through Eliot, had been
to foster a progressive union of emotion with thought in the poem,
poets like Thomas worked organically in a "centrifugal" process,
relying less upon the intellectual content of words than upon their
associations. More often, critics view the Apocalyptics as a reaction
against the dry, witty political verse of the thirties. Leslie Fiedler
(1947, p. 103) argues that they and the looser group of "neo-romantics" who succeeded them represent an alternate line of devel-

148																																																																																																																																											DYLAN THOMAS

opment from Yeats and Eliot "toward a concern with the self
rather than the State, the myth rather than history, romantic love
rather than comradeship, the apocalyptic awareness of death rather
than the millenial hope of salvation."

Whatever its antecedents, in the late thirties and early forties a
group whose central members were J. F. Hendry, Henry Treece,
and G. S. Fraser appeared, complete with a poetic "Manifesto"
(1938) which damned the machine and Politics and embraced
Myth and Man. Thomas, who refused to sign the Manifesto, did
say that he "mostly" believed in it (*SL*, p. 220). The group had the
blessings of Herbert Read; it issued several anthologies, including
The New Apocalypse (1939), *The White Horseman* (1941), and
The Crown and the Sickle (1944). Looking back on the movement,
Fraser (1964, p. 324) regrets the title, which "lent itself all too easily to jokes about epileptic, apoplectic, elliptical, and apocryphal
writing." Barker and Thomas were rather reluctant forebears of the
Apocalypse, and significantly both Treece and Fraser later wrote
books on Thomas.

Fraser (1941, p. 3), writing a description of the movement's genesis in *The White Horseman*, claims that the New Apocalypse "derives from Surrealism" and "embodies what is positive in Surrealism," with the addition of the poet's conscious control over his
poem's final shape. It is easy to see why Tindall neatly characterized
the Apocalyptics as "midway between surrealism and sanity." Fraser
cites the observation of Hendry, the group's principal theoretician,
that poetry should include both the inner and outer worlds. Fraser
stresses the subjective element; "too much clearness and abstraction
sterilizes the image . . ." He calls Thomas an Apocalyptic poet in
that he "responds to a situation, not to a play of ideas." Where Auden and his followers were "classical," Thomas and the Apocalyptics are "romantic," and in their personalism (p. 29) are "more or
less resigned to losing touch with a great many of the superficial
interests of common life." The qualities of "gloom, loneliness, ex-
cess" and the obscurity which had been noted in the group's work
so far "are the results of disintegration, not in ourselves, but in society"—a rather surprising line of defense.

There seems to have been considerable confusion from the start
about aims and theories. Hendry tended to stress the psychoanalytic
function, while Treece (1940, p. 58) was particularly hard on
surrealism, dismissing it as "little more than an irresponsible party
game" at its worst, at best "a psychotherapeutic exercise in the Freudian manner"; but "it is never poetry." Fraser (1964, p. 324) comments that, like all literary movements, the Apocalyptic unity was

mostly illusory—he himself never met Hendry, and met Treece only long afterwards. He claims that he and other, peripheral members, like Vernon Watkins, Tom Scott, and Nicholas Moore "were already writing the sort of poetry we would write anyway, but were pleased to be anthologized and too naive, then, to realize the disadvantages of being given a label." Thomas, who refused to contribute, was never so naive.

Vague enough at the outset, the group's aims became vaguer still; it first dissolved into a movement called "personalism," and finally into an all-encompassing vagueness under the rubric of the "New Romanticism." Under its various names, the movement published during the 1940's a confusion of anthologies: the *New Road, Transformation, Orpheus, Voices,* and *Poetry Scotland* annuals; it filled the pages of Tambimuttu's *Poetry (London)* and of John Lehmann's various *New Writing* and *Daylight* periodicals, annuals, and anthologies. (Ray, 1971, pp. 290–91)

The transition from Apocalypse to neo-romanticism occurred smoothly enough, in the process engulfing the work of Thomas. By 1946, Treece (p. 173) was presenting a "Bird's Eye View of a Romantic Revival" in his book *How I See Apocalypse.* This revival included the Paris movement (Henry Miller, Anaïs Nin), personalism (Stefan Schimanski), a group of religiously oriented poets (Anne Ridler, Norman Nicholson), and various "isolated romantics" (Vernon Watkins, W. R. Rodgers) along with the Apocalyptics. Deutsch (1963, p. 369) implies that most of the Apocalyptics in fact turned toward a personalism "that might be described as a kind of ethical anarchism, in which a leonine Christianity lay down with a lamblike Freudianism," but the emphasis of her essay is upon a modern religious trend in poetry. The new romanticism had room for this, as for the anarchist-pacifist poems of Alex Comfort, or Nicholas Moore's attempt (Bullough, 1949, p. 225) to cross Auden's influence with Thomas's in *New Poetry* (founded in 1946). Like surrealism and the Apocalypse, the amorphous neo-romanticism was heralded by Herbert Read. Following the March 1947 issue of *Poetry* which introduced neo-romanticism to its readers and the article by Horace Gregory in the same issue placing Thomas in the context of the movement (reprinted in Brinnin, 1960, pp. 131–38), most historical criticism has tried to show Thomas's relationship to his "romantic" contemporaries and followers.

A host of books, spearheaded by Francis Scarfe's *Auden and*

150

DYLAN THOMAS

After: The Liberation of Poetry 1940–1941 (1942) and John Bayley's *The Romantic Survival* (1957), have dealt with modern romanticism. Miller, Slote, and Shapiro speak of a subdivision of this which they term "the New Paganism" in *Start With the Sun* (1960). Herbert Read in *The True Voice of Feeling* (1955) argues that there is a healthy romantic strain in modern poetry toward a more natural diction and a looser verse structure, a "cult of sincerity" with roots in Shakespeare, Coleridge ("organic form"), Wordsworth, Hopkins, Whitman, Lawrence, Pound, and Eliot. In reply, Geoffrey Moore (Tedlock, 1960, pp. 260–68) suggests a counterstrain of romanticism, a "cult of irrationality." This strain, which also begins in Shakespeare, passes through the Coleridge of "Kubla Khan," the symbolists and surrealists, and culminates in Thomas. Read's tradition, Moore finds, stresses visual imagery, whereas Donne, Blake, Hopkins, and Keats lay equal or stronger emphasis upon connotative power and verbal alchemy—"mind-music," as Moore terms it. Moore suggests that Read's incorporating the movement toward free verse into his romantic line of development ignores the fact that formally structured verse can also be "organic," as is Thomas's poetry. "What Hart Crane did in America and what George Barker, W. S. Graham, W. R. Rodgers and Christopher Fry are doing . . . in England . . . is indicative of a feeling for the music and magnificence of language." Geoffrey Grigson (Tedlock, 1960, pp. 155–58) predictably argues the obverse of the coin, deploring the new "Romance" in England, which he finds "a romance without reason: it is altogether self-indulgent and liquescent." Barker and Thomas are of course preeminent among these "decadent" and "anarchic" romantics; more surprisingly, he tars Spender with the same brush, which at least indicates how widespread the movement was thought to be.

With the new romanticism, in Fiedler's words (1947, p. 103), "Dylan Thomas comes to define focally not only his immediate followers but also his immediate predecessors, and is, in turn, defined by them." There, indeed, is the justification for a study of the poet's literary context. We find Thomas now less strange than he at first appeared, anticipated by symbolists, modernists, and surrealists, adopted by Apocalyptics and hailed by neo-romantics, of whom the contemporary "confessional" poets such as Sylvia Plath are only the most recent avatar. Belonging to no group or movement, Thomas has affinities with many. But the historical perspective, while valuable, is self-limiting; poetry either crosses temporal boundaries or else has no essential purpose. We turn now to Thomas's situation in a much wider perspective.

References

Aiken, Conrad
1944. "The New Euphuism," *New Republic* Jan. 3, pp. 26–27.
Astre, Georges-Albert
1953. "Victoire de la poésie," *Adam* pp. 40–42.
Bayley, John
1957. *The Romantic Survival: A Study in Poetic Evolution.* London: Constable; New York: Oxford Univ. Pr.
Berryman, John
1947. "Lowell, Thomas, etc." *Partisan Review* Jan.-Feb., pp. 73–85.
Bloom, Edward A., and Lillian D.
1960. "Dylan Thomas: His Intimations of Mortality," *Boston University Studies in English* Autumn, pp. 138–51.
Bogan, Louise
1955. "The Later Dylan Thomas." In *Selected Criticism*, pp. 374–76. New York: Noonday.
Bokanowski, Helène, and Marc Alyn
1963. *Dylan Thomas.* Paris: Pierre Seghers.
Bollier, E. P.
1954. "Love, Death and the Poet—Dylan Thomas," *Colorado Quarterly* Spring, pp. 386–407.
Botterill, D.
1946. "Among the Younger Poets," *Life and Letters Today* Nov., pp. 93–94.
Brinnin, John Malcolm
1955. *Dylan Thomas in America: An Intimate Journal.* Boston: Little.
1960. (editor) *A Casebook on Dylan Thomas.* New York: Crowell.
Bullough, Geoffrey
1949. *The Trend of Modern Poetry.* 3rd ed. London: Oliver & Boyd.
Cambon, Glauco
1956. "Two Crazy Boats: Dylan Thomas and Rimbaud," *English Miscellany* pp. 251–59.
Cane, Melville
1954. "Are Poets Returning to Lyricism?" *Saturday Review* Jan. 16, pp. 8–10, 40–41.
Churchill, R. C.
1970. "The Age of T. S. Eliot." In *The Concise Cambridge History of English Literature*, 3rd ed., edited by George Sampson, pp. 862–64. Cambridge: Cambridge Univ. Pr.
Cohen, J. M.
1966. *Poetry of This Age (1908-1965).* Rev. ed. New York: Harper & Row.
Cox, C. B.
1966. (editor) *Dylan Thomas: A Collection of Critical Essays.* Englewood Cliffs, N. J.: Prentice-Hall.
Daiches, David
1943. "Contemporary Poetry in Britain," *Poetry* June, pp. 150–64.

1958. *The Present Age in British Literature*. Bloomington: Indiana Univ. Pr.

Davenport, John
1954. [Letter], *Sunday Times* Feb. 21, p. 2.

Davies, Walford
1968. "Imitation and Invention: The Use of Borrowed Material in Dylan Thomas's Prose," *Essays in Criticism* July, pp. 275–95.
1971. (editor) *Dylan Thomas: Early Prose Writings*. New York: New Directions.
1972. (editor) *Dylan Thomas: New Critical Essays*. London: J. M. Dent.
1972a. *Dylan Thomas* (Writers of Wales). N.p.: Univ. of Wales Pr.

Deutsch, Babette
1963. "Alchemists of the Word." In *Poetry in Our Time*, pp. 349–88. Rev. ed. New York: Doubleday.

Devas, Nicolette
1966. *Two Flamboyant Fathers*. London: Collins; New York: Morrow, 1967.

Drew, Elizabeth, and John Sweeney
1940. *Directions in Modern Poetry*. New York: Norton.

Durrell, Lawrence
1952. "Poetry in the Thirties." In *A Key to Modern British Poetry*, pp. 196–208. Norman: Univ. of Oklahoma Pr.

Emery, Clark
1962. *The World of Dylan Thomas*. Coral Gables, Fla.: Univ. of Miami Pr.

Every, George
1949. *Poetry and Personal Responsibility*. London: SCM Press.

Fiedler, Leslie
1947. "The Latest Dylan Thomas," *Western Review* Winter, pp. 103–6.

FitzGibbon, Constantine
1964. [Letter], *Times Literary Supplement* April 2, p. 273.
1965. *The Life of Dylan Thomas*. Boston: Little.

Fraser, G. S.
1941. "Apocalypse in Poetry." In *The White Horseman: Prose and Verse of the New Apocalypse*, edited by J. F. Hendry and Henry Treece, pp. 3–31. London: Routledge.
1964. *The Modern Writer and His World*. Rev. ed. London: André Deutsch; New York: Penguin.

French, Warren
1967. "Two Portraits of the Artist: James Joyce's *Young Man*; Dylan Thomas's *Young Dog*," *University of Kansas City Review* June, pp. 261–66.

Goodfellow, Dorothy W.
1955. "Dylan Thomas: 'The Boy of Summer.'" In *Lectures on Some Modern Poets* (Carnegie Series in English), pp. 77–90. Pittsburgh: Carnegie Inst. of Tech.

Hays, H. R.
1939. "Surrealist Influence in Contemporary English and American Poetry," *Poetry* June, pp. 202–9.

Heppenstall, Rayner
1960. *Four Absentees*. London: Barrie & Rockcliff.
Hoffman, Frederick J.
1957. *Freudianism and the Literary Mind*. Rev. ed. Baton Rouge: Louisiana State Univ. Pr.
Holbrook, David
1961. "Metaphor and Maturity: T. F. Powys and Dylan Thomas." In *The Modern Age* (Pelican Guide to English Literature, Vol. 7), edited by Boris Ford, pp. 415–28. Baltimore: Penguin.
1964. *Dylan Thomas and Poetic Dissociation*. Carbondale: Southern Illinois Univ. Pr.
1972. *Dylan Thomas: The Code of Night*. London: Athlone Pr.
Holroyd, Stuart
1957. *Emergence from Chaos*. London: Gollanz; Boston: Houghton Mifflin.
Jones, Noel A.
1949. "Dylan Thomas as a Pattern." In *British Annual of Literature*, pp. 12–16. London: British Author's Press.
Jones, T. H.
1966. *Dylan Thomas*. New York: Barnes & Noble.
Julian, Sister Mary
1957. "Edith Sitwell and Dylan Thomas: Neo-Romantics," *Renascence* Spring, pp. 120–26, 131.
Lehmann, John
1958. "The Wain-Larkin Myth: A Reply to John Wain," *Sewanee Review* Autumn, pp. 578–87.
Lindsay, Jack
1966."Memories of Dylan Thomas," *Meanjin* Autumn, pp. 48–75.
Longcore, Chris
1963. "A Possible Echo of Jonathan Swift in Dylan Thomas," *Notes and Queries* April, p. 153.
Lowell, Robert
1947. "Thomas, Bishop, and Williams," *Sewanee Review* Summer, pp. 493–503.
MacNeice, Louis
1938. *Modern Poetry: A Personal Essay*. London: Oxford Univ. Pr.
Marshall, Percy
1966. *Masters of English Poetry*. London: Dennis Dobson.
Martin, J. H.
1964. [Letter], *Times Literary Supplement* March 19, p. 235.
Mathias, Roland
1954. "A Merry Manshape (or Dylan Thomas at a distance)," *Dock Leaves* Spring, pp. 30–39.
Maud, Ralph N.
1963. *Entrances to Dylan Thomas' Poetry*. Pittsburgh: Univ. of Pittsburgh Pr.
1968. (editor) *Poet in the Making: The Notebooks of Dylan Thomas*. London: J. M. Dent.
Mayhead, Robin
1952-53. "Dylan Thomas," *Scrutiny* Winter, pp. 142–47.

Maynard, Theodore
    1940. "The New Artificiality," *Virginia Quarterly Review* Spring, pp. 311–14.
McCord, Howard L.
    1961. "Dylan Thomas and Bhartrihari," *Notes and Queries* March, p. 110.
Miller, James E., Jr.; Karl Shapiro; Bernice Slote
    1960. *Start With the Sun.* Lincoln: Univ. of Nebraska Pr.
Mizener, Arthur
    1944. "Verse and Reality," *Kenyon Review* Winter, pp. 123–26.
Moynihan, William T.
    1966. *The Craft and Art of Dylan Thomas.* Ithaca, New York: Cornell Univ. Pr; London: Oxford Univ. Pr.
Olson, Elder
    1954. *The Poetry of Dylan Thomas.* Chicago: Univ. of Chicago Pr.
Pinto, Vivian De Sola
    1958. *Crisis in English Poetry.* London: Hutchinson's Universal Library.
Pratt, Annis
    1970. *Dylan Thomas's Early Prose: A Study in Creative Mythology.* Pittsburgh: Univ. of Pittsburgh Pr.
Ransom, John Crowe
    1951. "The Poetry of 1900–1950," *Kenyon Review* Summer, pp. 445–54.
Ray, Paul C.
    1971. *The Surrealist Movement in England.* Ithaca, N.Y. and London: Cornell Univ. Pr.
Read, Bill
    1964. *The Days of Dylan Thomas.* New York: McGraw-Hill.
Read, Herbert
    1953. *The True Voice of Feeling: Studies in English Romantic Poetry.* New York: Pantheon.
Rhys, Keidrych
    1955. [Letter], *Times Literary Supplement* March 19, p. 255.
Rosenthal, M. L.
    1960. "Exquisite Chaos: Thomas and Others." In *The Modern Poets,* pp. 203–25. New York: Oxford Univ. Pr.
Scarfe, Francis
    1942. *Auden and After: The Liberation of Poetry, 1940-1941.* London: George Routledge.
Sillen, Samuel
    1943. "Mr. Sillen Comments," *New Masses* Sept. 14, pp. 24–25.
Sitwell, Edith
    1943. "Lecture on Poetry Since 1920," *Life and Letters Today* Nov., pp. 70–97.
Spender, Stephen
    1946. "Dylan Thomas, George Barker, David Gascoyne." In *Poetry Since 1939,* pp. 44–50. London: Longman's, Green.
    1952. "A Romantic in Revolt," *Spectator* Dec. 5, pp. 780–81.
    1954. "Dylan Thomas," *Britain Today* Jan., pp. 15–18.
Stanford, Derek
    1964. *Dylan Thomas, A Literary Study.* Rev. ed. New York: Citadel.

Steiner, George
    1961. "The Retreat from Word," *Kenyon Review* Spring, pp. 187–216.
Sweeney, John L.
    1946. "Introduction" to *Selected Writings of Dylan Thomas*, pp. vii–xxiii. New York: New Directions.
Symons, Julian
    1940. "Obscurity and Dylan Thomas," *Kenyon Review* Winter, pp. 61–71.
    1945. "Of Crisis and Dismay: A Study of Writing in the Thirties." In *Focus One*, edited by B. Rajan and Andrew Pearse, pp. 90–111. London: Dennis Dobson.
    1960. *The Thirties: A Dream Revolved.* London: The Cresset Press.
Tedlock, Ernest Warnock
    1960. (editor) *Dylan Thomas: The Legend and the Poet.* London: Heinemann.
Thomas, Caitlin
    1957. *Leftover Life to Kill.* Boston: Little.
Thwaite, Anthony
    1961. "Dylan Thomas and George Barker." In *Contemporary English Poetry: An Introduction*, pp. 93–109. Philadelphia: Dufour Editions.
Tindall, William York
    1948. "The Poetry of Dylan Thomas," *American Scholar* Autumn, pp. 431–39.
    1955. *The Literary Symbol.* New York: Columbia Univ. Pr.
    1956. *Forces in Modern British Literature, 1885-1956.* Rev. ed. New York: Random.
    1962. *A Reader's Guide to Dylan Thomas.* New York: Noonday.
Treece, Henry
    [1940]. "An Apocalyptic Writer and the Surrealists." In *The New Apocalypse*, ed. J. F. Hendry, pp. 49–58. London: Fortune Pr.
    1946. *How I See Apocalypse.* London: Lindsay Drummond.
    1949. *Dylan Thomas: "Dog Among the Fairies."* London: Lindsay Drummond.
Wain, John
    1957. "English Poetry: The Immediate Situation," *Sewanee Review* Summer, pp. 353–74.
Wanning, Andrews
    1941. "Criticisms and Principles: Poetry of the Quarter," *Southern Review* Spring, pp. 792–810.
Whittemore, Reed
    1957. "The 'Modern Idiom of Poetry,' and All That," *Yale Review* Spring, pp. 357–71.
Williams, William Carlos
    1954. "On Measure—Statement for Cid Corman." In *Selected Essays*, pp. 338–40. New York: Random.
Woodcock, George
    1950. *British Poetry Today.* Vancouver: Univ. of British Columbia.

156

DYLAN THOMAS

Selected Additional Readings

Butler, Frank A.
1960-61. "On the Beat Nature of Beat," *American Scholar* Winter, pp. 79–92.

Bruns, Gerald L.
1973. "Daedalus, Orpheus, and Dylan Thomas's Portrait of the Artist," *Renascence* Spring, pp. 147–56.

Cullis, Michael F.
1937. "Mr. Thomas and Mr. Auden," *Purpose* April-June, pp. 101–4.

Frankenberg, Lloyd
1961. "Dylan Thomas." In *Pleasure Dome: On Reading Modern Poetry*, pp. 325–32. New York: Doubleday.

Grubb, Frederick
1965. "Worm's Eye: Dylan Thomas." In *A Vision of Reality: A Study of Liberalism in Twentieth-Century Verse*, pp. 179–90. London: Chatto & Windus.

Hicks, Granville
1955. "Dylan Thomas and George Orwell," *New Leader* Dec. 26, pp. 16–17.

Lipton, Laurence
1959. "The New Apocalypse." In *The Holy Barbarians*, pp. 193–207. New York: Julian Messner.

Mills, Clark
1940. "Aspects of Surrealism," *Voices* Spring, pp. 47–51.

Montague, Gene
1968. "Dylan Thomas and *Nightwood*," *Sewanee Review* Summer, pp. 420–34.

Neill, Michael
1970. "Dylan Thomas's 'Tailor Age,' " *Notes and Queries* Vol. 17, pp. 59–63.

Press, John
1965. *Rule and Energy: Trends in British Poetry Since the Second World War*. London: Oxford Univ. Pr.

"Questionnaire"
1950. [On Thomas's influence: respondents Horace Gregory, Marianne Moore, Robert Penn Warren, Wallace Stevens, Allen Tate, James Laughlin, William Carlos Williams.] *Focus Five* London: Dennis Dobson.

Rexroth, Kenneth
1957. "Disengagement: The Art of the Beat Generation," *New World Writing* No. 11, May, pp. 28–41.

Untermeyer, Louis
1955. "Dylan Thomas." In *Makers of the Modern World*, pp. 753–57. New York: Simon & Schuster.

Vendler, Helen Hennessy
1966. "Thomas and Lowell," *Yale Review* Spring, pp. 439–44.

CHAPTER 6

The English and Welsh Literary Contexts

The Romantic Tradition

Harold Bloom, in *Yeats* (New York: Oxford Univ. Pr., 1970), comments,

> Our studies of poetic influence, as a critical subject, are still so primitive in theory and pedantic in procedure that we really know very little about the relation of English Romantic poetry to its ancestors in the English Renaissance, or for that matter the relation between Romantic and modern poetry.

This is in fact the problem with which many contemporary critics of Thomas are wrestling. Earlier writers, realizing that to compare Thomas with the great romantics might seem to elevate him prematurely to their stature, generally approached the question hesitantly, strewing qualifications and apologies along their advance. More recent writers, such as the contributors to Walford Davies's collection *Dylan Thomas: New Critical Essays* (1972), are less shy about attempting to place him within the pantheon of English poets. As the preceding chapter should make clear, Thomas's work originally seemed anomalous in its own century, though it is now easier to see its links with the rest of twentieth-century verse. Because of this "timeless" quality of his writing we immediately seek parallels and antecedents for it in earlier centuries.

Recognition of the "neo-romantic" current in modern writing led naturally to revaluations of the romantic poets' continuing influence. Among the more notable of these is John Bayley's *The Romantic Survival: A Study in Poetic Evolution* (1957). The first part of his book is devoted to a discussion of romantic themes and attitudes with particular emphasis on the response of the romantic mind to the modern world. The second part of the book devotes separate chapters to Yeats, Thomas, and—surprisingly—Auden as examples of three different poetic "strategies" within a romantic revival. Yeats, he argues, shifts from a traditional romanticism to the "new" romanticism of his later style. Bayley calls Auden a romantic because of his idea of innocence and his nostalgia for the remote and mysterious, both embedded in irredeemably lyric lines. The self-confidence of Auden's narrative stance, his comfortable resort to rhetoric, implies the very bardic authority which he attempts consciously to deny; similarly, Auden is drawn to the same idea of poetry as magical utterance which he explicitly discredits. Psychologically, Bayley finds the same "adolescent attitude" of antiauthoritarianism, the same "childish delight" in description of the world's particulars in Auden which we find in Byron, for example.

Bayley's comments on Auden are important here because his comparison between the modern poets is mostly implicit. His discussion of Thomas centers upon one major idea: that the poet's use of language alternates between several different conceptions of poetic utterance. Analyzing a group of lines from the poetry, Bayley finds several examples of a "stock romantic usage" (p. 193) where a word is used for the sake of its "sound and exotic unfamiliarity" rather than its denotation—the sort of thing we might expect in Swinburne. (Bayley's example here, the word "petrol" in "Turning a petrol face blind to the enemy," seems a poor one, since Thomas probably intends the implication "inflammable"; but his point remains valid.) At other times, as in "a capsized field where a school sat still," the poet uses words with Donne's metaphysical wit: the field seems the size of a schoolboy's cap, time has overturned it, the memory spills on his table like ink, and so forth. When Thomas uses the words "Egyptian" or "Eastern" he usually refers to a private symbology where the reference is to Time. Thus frequently, reading Thomas, it is "as if the attitudes to language of Donne, Blake and Swinburne were all to be encountered in the same poem" (p. 194).

Bayley finds Thomas's attitude toward theme very much like Wordsworth's "inspired egotism." He is not retrospective like Wordsworth, however, but immediately involved in the experience as he writes: where Wordsworth stands outside the poem, Thomas seems to stand within it. This is responsible for the strange way in which his poems seem to narrate themselves. In Thomas, *seeing* and *being* are perceived as a language (p. 213): words immediately become things and vice versa. This, Bayley affirms, is an old romantic tradition of poetic perspective, but one in which Thomas indulges more radically than his predecessors. Bayley extends his remarks in an essay entitled "Chains and the Poet" in Davies (1972, pp. 56–

72). Here his stress is on Thomas's difference from Auden rather than their debt to a common tradition. Pound, Eliot, Yeats, and Auden all represent an "intellectualization of the poetic world," an implied view of poetry as social achievement. Thomas is part of an antithetical movement which includes Blake, Whitman, and the surrealists: like Whitman he "must make his poetry his own ego," like Blake his stance is bardic. Thomas is compelled (p. 62) "not to express but to embody the experience of being himself," which leads to a highly personal, sometimes obscure idiom. His refusal of conventional clarity is a measure of "his rejection of the civil poetry of his time." Bayley still finds the division in Thomas's work between "poem-as-man and poem as comment by the man who is standing outside it." Interestingly, he finds that the later poems such as "Fern Hill" and "Poem on his birthday" fall into the latter category of "metaphysical" poetry, and are correspondingly less successful.

Another such study of the romantic vision is John Press's *The Fire and the Fountain* (1955), which explores poetry's origins in "inspiration," madness, dreams, religious visions, and other manifestations of what modern writers call the unconscious mind. Press concentrates upon Thomas's use of imagery, which he feels (p. 169) set the poetic "fashion" for the next generation of poets. Imagery may be (a) visual and "painterly," (b) nonvisual, imaginative, and sensuous, as in Keats, or (c) descriptive and emotive, as in the metaphysical poets. He finds Thomas less successful when he distracts us with a series of visual images which will not cohere, more successful when (as in the end of Sonnet X) his imagery becomes symbolic and nonvisual. Press's discussion focuses on the sonnets, where he finds that the theme suggests that of Donne in "We think that Paradise" or Herbert in "The Sacrifice," but wherein the technique is closer to that of Blake.

The theme shared by Press and Bayley—the mixture in Thomas of metaphysical and romantic elements—is continued in Giorgio Melchiori's *The Tightrope Walkers* (1956, pp. 213-42). Melchiori argues that our own age displays a mannerist or Rococo style of art for which he coins the term "Funambulist." We are currently moving from a mannerist period ("metaphysical" in poetry) toward a new baroque style whose forms express greater stability. Thomas's poetry has baroque characteristics: a "predilection for curious though balanced patterns, the predominance of the decorative invention," and a pattern of organic growth like that of a Bach fugue, but it lacks a fundamental "sense of repose, of balance and completeness" (p. 215) which characterizes mature baroque art. Melchiori, like Press, finds that Thomas uses pictorial imagery sparsely, and when he does use color, for example, it is often emblematic. His inspiration instead is fundamentally verbal. Thomas's imagery differs from that of Hopkins in that it appeals "not to what we see, but to what we know." Like Donne, Thomas uses "intellectual" images and metaphors drawn from scientific inventions—the phonograph and the film, for example. The main difference is that in Donne a religious scheme is basic to the poetry, while in Thomas the religious symbolism is only metaphorical (p. 231). In his later poetry Thomas tends toward what Melchiori terms a "romantic Baroque" like Herbert and Crashaw. Finally Melchiori moves into an extended comparison with Blake, suggesting a tradition of visionary poetry which is physical, nonpictorial, and nonallegorical, running from *Revelations* through Webster, Donne, Blake, Hopkins, and Kafka.

Melchiori's argument is difficult to follow; he seems to use the terms baroque, mannerist, metaphysical, and romantic sometimes in a special sense, sometimes loosely, but his specific comments on the poetry are often worthwhile. There are great difficulties in transferring terminology from the graphic arts into a literary context (cf. Wylie Sypher's studies), especially when discussing imagery. Joseph Wittreich (1969, pp. 198–99) approaches Thomas's idea of the function of the image in strictly literary terms, quoting his famous passage on "warring images." Although numerous critics have made the comparison with Blake, Wittreich's article is one of the few which explore the implications of the comparison. Thomas, like Blake, sees the world in terms of oppositions, and in his work attempts "redeeming the contraries with secretive images" (*Selected Letters of Dylan Thomas*, p. 151), an idea Wittreich claims is adapted from Blake's *Milton*. Both poets believe in the necessity of form, but an organic form founded in the imagination rather than one "superimposed" by the poet. Ralph Maud (1968, pp. 22–33) in his edition of the *Notebooks* has pointed to the specific influence of Blake upon a number of Thomas's earliest poems. Some of these parallels have occurred to Harry Williams (1972, pp. 107–18) as well; he extends Wittreich's argument in terms of poetic theme. Thomas's religious vision was founded in Blake, he argues. Both poets see the prophetic imagination as redeeming the evils of abstract reasoning; both celebrate time, in that they see redemption as following apocalyptic annihilation. They share the sense of a past Golden Age which must be restored through a rebirth of the sensual; both see God as made in man's image and attack conventional religion. Blake and Thomas prophetically fuse past and future into a timeless mythical world, but for Thomas the Word itself takes the place of Blake's mythical identities in the drama of his vision. At first language is what divides heaven from hell in the original, unfallen world (as in "Incarnate devil,") but later the Word becomes redemptive.

Martin Dodsworth (Davies, 1972, pp. 112–17) discusses the Blake parallel in phenomenological and more conventional philosophic terms, relying especially upon the early letters. He is apparently unaware of Ruthven Todd's assertion that Thomas not only read Blake deeply but read S. Foster Damon's study of Blake's ideas and symbols as well (William Moynihan, *The Craft and Art of Dylan Thomas*, 1966, p. 33). Dodsworth sees Thomas's concept of the mind-body relationship as central to his poetry; searching for an alternative to the mechanistic Cartesian dualism, he argues, Thomas adopted Blake's view that the physical world is merely an aspect of the spiritual. Blake's idea that the five senses—as opposed to the sterile Reason, of course—are "the chief inlets of the Soul in this age" explains the mixture of sensuality and spiritual concern in Thomas's work and finds expression in a poem like "When all my five and country senses see." Thus Thomas's comment to Miss Johnson, "I am in the path of Blake" (*SL*, p. 20). Dodsworth relies in part on Winifred Nowottny's earlier, rhetorically oriented discussion of Blake and Thomas in *The Language Poets Use* (1962, pp. 187–217). Despite his stress on Thomas's Blakean mythologizing and philosophical ground, Dodsworth argues that the poet's language must be seen in a modern context as following Eliot's and Hulme's admonition to avoid mechanistic "counter language" in poetry: "Thomas's poetry should be seen at least as an extension of modernist practice in English as much as a revival of something called Romanticism" (p. 120).

Probably more critics have pointed to the correspondences with Blake than to any other romantic poet, whether they stress the religious vision, the nonpictorial, somewhat surrealist imagery, the self-centered mythologizing, or the vision of innocence. But in the "romantic egotism" of his work he has ties to many others. Shelley is generally too ethereal, but in the sensuousness of his verse Keats, Thomas's boyhood idol, offers a parallel. Spender (1952, p. 781) finds in Thomas's work something close to Keats's imagined "life of sensations." Davies (1972, pp. 150–52) suggests a kind of "negative capability" in the open sensibility that is a precondition of Thomas's work. In both he sees "pagan temper without its dogma." Ruth de Bedts (1957, pp. 51–54) traces the influence of "The Eve of St. Agnes" throughout Thomas's "A Winter's Tale," arguing persuasively that both works show the same progression of images at important junctures.

A greater number of critics have suggested the parallel to Wordsworth, particularly in the later, "pastoral" poems. John Sweeney (1952, pp. 22–23) points to the "Prelude" and "Intimations" as a source for "Fern Hill" and much of "Over Sir John's hill," while Korg (*Dylan Thomas*, 1965) makes continual references to Wordsworth throughout his book on Thomas. He sees the later Thomas as sharing Wordsworth's preoccupation with the loss of the imaginative powers of childhood, associated in both with primeval innocence. The theme surfaces in "In country sleep" and "Fern Hill," while "Poem in October" Korg finds to be essentially a recapitulation of "Tintern Abbey:" "Through an experience with a familiar landscape, the mature man secures a momentary access to the lost imaginative powers of childhood, and what he remembers infiltrates the present moment with a joyful though obscure sense of order" (p. 119). On the other hand, Myron Ochshorn (1954, pp. 53–56) makes a strong argument that whatever similarities there might be in theme, Thomas's approach is very different from the earlier writer's. Where Wordsworth philosophizes about lost spontaneity, Thomas recreates it in the poem. In their nature poetry Wordsworth remains the observer while Thomas's "attachment to nature is primitive . . . His is an inside perspective." C. J. Rawson (Davies, 1972, p. 81) makes this distinction in pejorative terms, asserting that in these late poems "the childhood vision is . . . sentimentalized in a quite unWordsworthian way." Nevertheless, Ochshorn finds romantic qualities in Thomas—if anything, his relationship with nature seems *more* romantic than Wordsworth's. He sounds a familiar refrain, calling Thomas "a Romantic who has absorbed into his swinging poetry all the niceties and intricacies of the metaphysical poets" (p. 46).

Whether we try to identify the distinctly unromantic note in the poetry as metaphysical, classical, or modern, it soon becomes clear that there is a split in Thomas's sensibility between qualities we call romantic—the exploration of the poet's own mind and body, the reverent approach to nature, the bardic tone—and qualities we know are not. Treece (1949, p. 72) suggests the term "Romantic realist.'" His friend Bert Trick in a very early local review (quoted in Maud, *Dylan Thomas in Print*, 1970, p. 51) insisted Thomas's "poetry is granite-hard, shed of all romantic illusions," and indeed to the extent that we think of romanticism as a vague, misty sentimentalizing of experience, Thomas seems unromantic. As many have remarked, his early poetry is much less about love than about sex, an attitude still present in the late poem "Lament." We begin to suspect a conscious stifling of romantic impulses except in the single direction of divinity, like Gwilym in his story "The Peaches" altering the names of girls in his love poems to God. Moynihan (1966, p. 24) says of Thomas's Grammar School poems:

The veiled presence of the Romantic poets is constantly evident. One wonders whether Thomas's later antagonism to Wordsworth, for example, may not have sprung from an earlier infatuation—that is demonstrably the case with Rupert Brooke, a poet Thomas several times berated in his correspondence, but whom he imitated (with subsequent regret) when only twelve . . .

Hints of Shelley and Poe haunt the earliest poems and indeed some of the notebook poems, until their influence is overridden by that of Eliot. Sweetness and light quickly give way to a darker, sometimes Gothic strain.

Indeed, if we are looking for a literary corrective to Thomas's early, immature romanticism, Eliot is one of the best places to look: he combines penetrating realism of observation with lyricism while retaining an almost decadent romantic note from the French symbolists. In one sense, Eliot shares the "romantic egotism" of Keats, Byron, and Yeats, as Olson (1954, p. 23) implies when he likens Thomas to this group of poets who create worlds in their own image, rather than Dante, Chaucer, Shakespeare, or Browning, who see through many men's eyes. Davies (1972, pp. 156–60) sees Eliot's influence most strongly in his treatment of the city, which offered a model for Thomas's self-consciously suburban adolescent verse. Eliot's realism and irony offered an antidote for romanticism, while the "magical sense of the macabre" Desmond Hawkins noted in both poets as early as 1933 (Maud, 1970, p. 100) kept Eliot within Thomas's sphere of appreciation. Thus we might see Eliot as strengthening some romantic tendencies in Thomas, while weakening others.

Yeats is in much the same position. Often called the "Last Romantic," Yeats was a towering figure during the thirties whose work was in some odd manner taken for granted. Maud (1968, p. 13) has noted an ambivalence in the young Thomas's attitude: he was writing both imitations and parodies of the older poet during the same period. Still, Thomas was probably more attracted to Yeats's work than poets of the previous decade had been. Shapiro, (Tedlock, *Dylan Thomas: The Legend and the Poet*, 1960, p. 270), who calls Thomas "the first modern romantic you could put your finger on," finds that the poet's generation, avoiding the example of Auden, were drawn to Yeats's rhetoric, his apocalypticism, and his later disillusioned tone. Thomas in particular was attracted to Yeats's theatricality, Shapiro feels, because he lacked a sound philosophical or religious structure to fall back upon; he might have added that the later Yeats shows an unsentimentalized sexuality which would have appealed to Thomas. It would also be easy to invoke Yeats's use of Celtic and personal myth, but here the problem of Blake's influence on both poets suggests a morass of speculation.

Thomas has affinities with two different streams of romanticism. One is the "dark" romanticism traced by Mario Praz in *Romantic Agony* (London: Oxford Univ. Pr., 1933), a visionary, often Gothic or decadent strain to which Thomas referred when he called Trevor Hughes "one of the dark-eyed company of Poe and Thompson, Nerval and Baudelaire, Rilke and Verlaine" (*SL*, p. 15). The other, a "bright" romanticism, is equally visionary, but constitutes an affirmative vision, a poetry of celebration. James E. Miller, Jr. in an article entitled "Four Cosmic Poets" (1957, pp. 312–14) links Thomas with Whitman, Crane, and Lawrence in this context. Each of the later poets, he claims, penetrated beneath the "democracy and science" of Whitman's surface to the cosmic scheme embodied in his work. Miller, Bernice Slote, and Karl Shapiro enlarge on this theme in their book *Start with the Sun* (1960), which ambitiously seeks to define a counter tradition in modern poetry which opposes the "New Puritanism" of Eliot, Pound, Lowell, and Stevens. They term this the "New Paganism" (pp. 3–4), a poetry of "pagan joy and wonder" which is "religious, physical, passionate, incantatory," and "affirmative in its constant sense of life." The tradition has roots in the romantics, especially Blake and Wordsworth, comes to a focus in Whitman, and is best embodied among the moderns by Thomas, Hart Crane, Lawrence, Vachel Lindsay, Carl Sandburg, W. C. Williams, and—a strange bedfellow —Joyce. Crane, another modern romantic, is of course similar to Thomas in many respects. His possible influence is discussed by Treece (1949, pp. 51–53), who quotes Thomas's denial of any knowledge of Crane's work before the early forties, and by Moynihan (1966, pp. 105–6), who stresses their differences. The approach through mutual influence is undoubtedly a more rewarding one.

Miller and Slote (pp. 169–90) undertake a detailed comparison of Thomas with Whitman not so much to show influence as to show their mutual participation in a tradition. Thomas in a letter to Vernon Watkins called himself a "middle-class, beardless Walt"; the authors point out that both poets equate body and soul in a "bardic invocation of chant and song." They embrace the

whole of experience with a positive attitude toward the physical
and the sexual. Each sees himself as microcosm and pagan priest.
There are differences in tone and emphasis: Thomas stresses generation, Whitman the erotic. Whitman is generally more sanguine.
But each identifies man with the elemental forces—tides, seasons,
wind, and fire; and most importantly, they share a vision of great
patterned cycles of generation and decay in the universe. They see
a union in oppositions, a personal integrity in the duality of soul and
body: Whitman states, "I am the poet of the Body and I am the
poet of the Soul," while Thomas asserts "I, in my intricate image,
stride on two levels." In the poetry of both light, usually the sun,
wins finally over darkness in an immortality envisioned in Thomas's
"Refusal to Mourn" or Whitman's "When Lilacs Last in the Dooryard Bloomed."

Miller (pp. 43–53) makes some additional, more technical comments about the two writers' poetics. Whitman's description of the
"breeding" method of composition is closely related to Thomas's,
and both generate an organic form. Both poets stress suggestiveness
and connotation rather than literal statement; among their favorite
images are grass, the sea, birds, and the sea voyage used to show the
cycle of death and rebirth. Dreams and phantasmagoria recur in
their work. Both, of course, rely heavily upon sexual, and particularly phallic imagery. Both play with diction, juxtaposing levels of
language or interjecting neologisms and hyphenated epithets. Admittedly Thomas might have thought Witman's "barbaric yawp"
too loosely structured for his taste, but, Miller argues, they both
really wrote the same sort of primarily oral poetry, a poetry of
"controlled abandon." Grace Yerbury (1964, pp. 67–70) in an unrelated article notes that an archetypal image of "the city beside the
river" is crucial in Whitman's "Crossing Brooklyn Ferry" and in
Thomas's prose-poem "Prologue to an Adventure" (*Adventures in
the Skin Trade and Other Stories*); the same image pervades Eliot's
Waste Land and Henry Miller's *Tropic of Cancer*.

Many writers, searching for a way to define Thomas's romantic
qualities, modify the age-old "classic" versus "romantic" distinction which, despite Lovejoy, still seems to correspond to our feeling
about the different kinds of poems we encounter. Edith Sitwell
(1960, p. 24) borrows Dante's distinction between "urban" and
"rustic" verse, and further subdivides the "urban" into "combed
and slippery" or "shaggy and rumpled." She finds Milton and Shelley "combed" while Thomas is "shaggy," but both are urban; Ben
Jonson and Donne on the other hand are rustic. Although it is always difficult to tell what Sitwell is getting at in her criticism, she

probably means (ironically?) to equate urban verse with a sort of learned and allusive romantic idealism, rustic verse with a forceful Renaissance version of classicism. Paul Rosenfeld (1940, pp. 399–400) opposes classic to "decadent" art, quoting Huysman's description of decadence: an art which "depreciates the importance of the whole for the benefit of its parts, and strives after the virtues of individualism." Here we seem close to Melchiori's sense of "mannerist" verse. Rosenfeld claims that Thomas subordinates intellectual and even intuitive meanings to "emotive" ones (a rather obscure distinction), and points to Thomas's "fastidiously fashioned verse" whose satisfactions are "almost exclusively for the eye and ear." The formal elegance of the poetry, he implies, lends it a sophistication which belies the lack of intellectual control and solidarity. Although much of his essay is negative in attitude, he admits that the poetry does at times achieve an "eighteenth-century vigor and stateliness."

This last parallel, to the antiromantic Augustan age, is predictably the one explored by the fewest critics, although—particularly in his prose—Thomas does have something in common with the eighteenth-century satirists. He was a keen parodist, as is appreciated even by critics like Amis who dismiss the bulk of his poetry as "rant." C. J. Rawson in an essay entitled "Randy Dandy in the Cave of Spleen: Wit and Fantasy in Thomas . . ." (Davies, 1972, pp. 73–106) argues that a characteristically Augustan wit pervades his prose and crops up in the poetry as well. Rawson describes a type of "inward-looking and mockingly self-exploratory Romanticism" which runs from Sterne through Byron, Browning, and Laforgue, and coexists with the more "expansive" Whitmanesque variety in Thomas. Unfortunately, the best examples of this sort of Shandean humor are to be found in the letters. More apparent in his poetry is the "pseudo-surreal" image, usually grotesque, which Rawson traces to sources in Pope and Fielding; equally apparent is the Swiftean note of "visceral, scatalogical and vermicular jokeyness." Rawson is critical of the poet's tendency to self-indulgence even in his apparent self-mockery. His "irony and his comedy are often so self-centered" because (p. 101)

they suffer from a constant compulsion to touch up his image of himself. But there are occasions when these limitations are transcended, or at least transfigured. Then Thomas achieves a Popeian poise, in a witty and unevasive self-distancing, most usually in contexts of stylized fantasy.

Rawson's comments certainly help illuminate Thomas's literary personality, although a reader unfamiliar with the poet's letters, where most of the substantiating quotation is to be found, might question how much of this is directly relevant to the poetry. Interestingly enough, Rawson seems to value the same quality of self-distancing in Thomas which Bayley, in his essay earlier in the book, finds to be Thomas's weakest suit. This is particularly curious since both critics value Thomas's earlier, more convoluted poems and denigrate those later ones in the genre of "Fern Hill."

The Metaphysicals

Among the numerous contradictions of Thomas's poetry a good many emerge when we consider it under the category of metaphysical verse; some of these contradictions stem from the category itself, some from the peculiar qualities of the poet's work. The "metaphysicals" were never a school; Johnson's term, which he applied disparagingly to Donne and Cowley, only later came to designate the verse of Herbert, Carew and Crashaw, Marvell and Vaughan as well, referring to their tendency to introduce "nice speculations of philosophy" and wit even into amorous or religious poems. Their contemporaries referred to their work as "strong-lined," however, to indicate its compression and intellectual difficulty. Johnson's term "philosophy" meant not only abstract speculation but the "new philosophy" of the natural sciences which around Donne's time was throwing doubt upon the Elizabethan world view; the metaphysicals' occasional scientific or technological allusions offended Augustan ideas of decorum.

Merely to call Thomas "metaphysical," then, immediately raises problems. Clearly his lines are compressed and difficult beyond Donne's most elliptical verses; he is freely allusive both in Biblical references and in less frequent references to science or technology, and the allusions often function as part of a complex poetic statement (see Kidder, *Dylan Thomas: The Country of the Spirit*, 1973). But there is considerable doubt whether the difficulty of Thomas's poetry is only—or even mainly—intellectual. He seldom seems to be engaged in a complex argument; we do not find the "linear" or narrative difficulty of Donne being legalistic about love, but rather a "vertical" complexity wherein a single statement may be elaborated associatively through several stanzas.

On the other hand, there is definitely some sort of correspondence between Thomas and some metaphysical verse. For example, metaphysical poems often are based on analogy, reflecting the Elizabethans' analogical view of the universe wherein the human world modelled the divine and a single man was microcosm. Clearly this is closely related to Thomas's poetic universe, where the poet himself contains the world about him or enacts the dramas of Christ and of Adam. Roland Mathias (1954, p. 33) argues that Thomas is metaphysical in the manner of Vaughan because both poets use a vocabulary dominated by a fixed group of symbols, or "key-words," which indicate a relationship between parallel worlds. Among Thomas's favorites are *weather, shape, father, muscle, worm, screws, oil, forks,* and *maggot.* Mathias does not specify the worlds thus connected, and admits that the "settled orders" of Vaughan's world do not apply to Thomas, but insists that the poetic method is similar nonetheless.

The most general discussion of this problem and its esthetics occurs in Robert M. Adams's *Strains of Discord: Studies in Literary Openness* (1958) which includes a chapter comparing Donne with Eliot, Herbert with Auden, and Crashaw with Thomas (pp. 128–45, adapted in Cox, *Dylan Thomas: A Collection of Critical Essays,* 1966). Adams discusses a problem of critical importance for our evaluation of Thomas: some types of literature do not exhibit the "unity" or the "closed" structure which, from Aristotle and the Augustans through the modern formalist critics and their contemporary successors, has been a major criterion of literary excellence. Donne's work, for example, sometimes fails to achieve a logical thematic resolution, as in the "Third Satire." Though there are clearly numerous aspects of a work which may lack closure or unity—a poem's formal requirements, a novel's plot resolution, the tone of either—Adams in the relevant chapter is mainly concerned with the characteristic strains and stresses of theme and tone which are defining characteristics of the metaphysicals.

One such stress comes from the farfetched comparison, such as Donne's famous comparison of two separated lovers to the points of a compass in "A Valediction: Forbidding Mourning." Thomas's conceits are clearly equally farfetched, when he speaks of "two-gunned Gabriel" or refers to God as "an old cock from nowheres"; in both we feel a great disparity in the contexts (love versus plane geometry, the angelic order versus cowboys), but in Donne the point of the comparison is in its logical working out, while in Thomas we are left with the bare metaphor, with a new context immediately following. The implications of both for the reader are complex. In Donne, we sometimes feel that such wit is in a sense its own end; it points to the mind able to make such a comparison, in a paradoxical variety of romantic egotism. In Thomas too we feel the subject to be the poet's own thoughts and feelings, but in a more

radical way; instead of pointing us away from the poet only to lead
us back to him, his poems never really leave the sphere of his sensibilities. Adams points out that Donne's directing us toward the dramatic speaking voice is a variety of the essential metaphysical
method, the juxtaposing of two or more spheres of existence or
points of view in dramatic contrast. Unresolved tension is part of
its esthetic. Certainly this too is relevant to Thomas, whose avowed
method was based on "warring images."

Adams confines his explicit discussion to the sonnets, in a comparison with Crashaw, and in the general context of a discussion of
the meaning of "good" and "bad" taste in the poetry of "devotional
athletes." He assumes that the theme of the sequence is the Incarnation as "a vicious joke played by a malicious God on Christ, Mary,
and mankind" (p. 140). Where questions of interpretation arise, he
tacitly assumes Olson's view. Adams does not argue the seriousness
of Thomas's devotional intent in the sonnets, a problem with implications for his entire esthetic discussion. The very fact that Thomas
treats religious matters in a huge variety of tones, in metaphorical
contexts which Donne, the Augustans, and many modern critics
would consider screamingly inappropriate, leads us to question
whether the poems are meant to convey religious affirmation, bitter despair, or both; we have no such problem with Crashaw, at
least on the immediate level of intent.

Donne, Adams argues, spoke of Crashaw's primary topic, the
yearning for a physical union with God, in consciously metaphorical terms. He realized he was indulging in hyperbole, almost a joke.
In Crashaw there is less self-display involved because of the apparent depth of feeling:

The poet loves God as a baby loves its mother's breast and as a martyr loves the final spear-thrust; he loves God as a gaping wound and a
voluptuous mouth, in sophisticated paradox and childish innocence
... The unity of opposites, of pain with pleasure, life with death, frui-
tion with denial, assertion with surrender, is his favorite theme (pp.
130–31).

Though it is beyond the terms of Adams's discussion, this offers a
clear parallel to Thomas's later poetry, whether we are speaking of
direct influence, indirect influence through the strikingly similar
poetry of Hopkins, or simply the necessities of one sort of mystical
vision. Though Thomas shares Donne's consciousness that he is close
to blasphemy or joking, and in fact seems to appreciate fully the
humorous possibilities of "two-gunned Gabriel," he is much closer
to Crashaw in overall poetic structure. Crashaw's poems often elabo-

rate a single theme, proceed emotionally rather than intellectually, and enclose their extravagances and grotesqueries within tight formal controls. The image of the Magdalen in "The Weeper" who follows Christ about the mountains with eyes that are "two faithfull fountaines;/Two walking baths . . . Portable, and compendious oceans" approaches Thomas in surrealism. Like Thomas, Crashaw gives "a chaotic mingling of many different sorts of anguish, a phantasmagoria of pain and grief."

Crashaw and Thomas apparently represent the lowest, or "mannerist" stage in a hierarchy of metaphysical poetry which leads upward through the "dramatic" and the "philosophical" (Donne) to the "visionary" (Herbert), with the greatest violence evident toward the bottom of the ladder. Surely, this scheme of Adams's both oversimplifies Thomas and bears its own esthetic. Thomas belongs to the "philosophical" group inasmuch as he constantly deals with the great metaphysical question of the relation between the spirit and the senses; yet he is hardly metaphysical at all in that his abundance of conceits seldom contributes to any argument or persuasion. In later poems like "Vision and Prayer," many critics have pointed out a correspondence in both theme and method to Herbert's "visionary" work. Nearly always he is "dramatic" within Adams's definition, embroiled in argument with himself. Thomas at times occupies each rung on the ladder, although many of his characteristics seem to preclude his being called metaphysical at all. At some times it is difficult to decide: if Olson's interpretation of the sonnets is right, Thomas is making continual reference to arcane lore, in the form of medieval theological interpretations of the constellations—a standard sort of metaphysical procedure. If other critics are right, Thomas seldom alludes to arcana in any substantial way. We must decide what Thomas is doing before categorizing him.

Confounded by such difficulties, most critics have pointed out a theme from Marvell, a technique like Herbert's, an echo of Donne, without broadening the discussion (Garlick, 1954, pp. 4–5). Many discuss the metaphysical influence as an aspect of the Welsh inheritance, since Donne, Vaughan, and Traherne all were in some sense Welsh. Others discuss their influence primarily as religious writers who have contributed to Thomas's spiritual and poetic vision, postulating a chain of influence running from the Bible through the metaphysicals and thence to the powerful influence of Francis Thompson (Treece, 1949, pp. 56–57). Tindall (1962, pp. 14–15) adopts a positive tone without letting us in on the evidence. Thomas, he states, "seems commonly to have confined his reading to Grierson's anthology of metaphysical lyrics; for all but two or three of the poems are there . . ." Tindall claims he knew the familiar poems of Donne, the best-known Devotions, and the last sermon, whose theme ("Wee have a winding sheete in our Mothers wombe") could précis his early poetry. Vaughan shares this and adds the glories of childhood recaptured.

He read Marvell on worms and graves, Herbert on Easter wings, and Milton on Christ's Nativity, all in Grierson. Though sometimes as extravagant as Crashaw or as juicy as Cleveland, with his "jelly in a glove," Thomas passed both by.

How do we know? Bayley (Davies, 1972, p. 66) rejects Adams's comparison with Crashaw because to him Thomas, far from a "devotional athlete," projects a sense of lolling helplessness before the Creator. Similarly Holbrook *(Dylan Thomas and Poetic Dissociation,* 1964, p. 50) denies the usual comparison between "Vision and Prayer" and Herbert's "shaped" poems because of Thomas's "cosmic egotism and sense of omnipotence." Such contradictory judgments test one's intuitive sense of the poet's general attitude.

Sometimes we can decide about a particular echo in a particular poem. Leitch (1972, p. 341) finds the "kissing poles" of "I see the boys of summer" prefigured in Herbert's "The Search," surrounded by similar images. His argument from parallel contexts is convincing. Sweeney (1946, p. xvi) finds an echo of Marvell's "The Gallery" in the sequence of images in "On the Marriage of a Virgin," but Maud *(Entrances to Dylan Thomas's Poetry,* 1963, p. 4) rejects this on the grounds that Thomas's drafts for the poem show totally different images. Thomas probably looks more metaphysical in the twentieth-century context, as compared to Auden, than he does when we use a wider perspective. D. S. Savage (Tedlock, 1960, pp. 141–42) says Thomas is metaphysical because he presents not ordinarily apprehended experience but "aspects of that experience . . . seen in extra-mundane relationship to their absolute . . . conditions." Whatever this means, it sounds equally applicable to Shelley. Clearly there is a need for a more rigorous investigation of Thomas's relationship to the metaphysicals, firmly based upon a sophisticated and lucid idea of poetic aims and strategies.

The Welsh Inheritance

Attitude and Setting. Considering Thomas's "Welshness" we are confronted with the same contradictions and ambiguities we

find when placing him in any other conventional context. *Is* he
Welsh in any significant way, or simply an English poet who was
born and lived much of his life in Wales? Since he spoke little or
no Welsh, does the powerful and well-defined body of literature in
the Welsh language bear meaningfully upon his work? Ignoring
literary questions for the moment, what effect did the surroundings
in which he spent much of his life have upon his work?

Thomas at times felt his writing was a response to this environment:

I gladly accept the fact that I first saw the light and screamed at it
in a loud lump of Wales . . . Of course my writing could not now be
what it is—always experimental and always completely unsuccessful—
if it had not been for the immortal fry of the town in which I sim-
mered up (quoted in Moynihan, 1966, pp. 12–13).

But notice the qualifications and evasions, which may simply attest
to his habitual self-mocking irony, or may show an ambivalence he
did not wish to stress in a public broadcast. Notoriously, he proclaimed himself first a Welshman, second a drunkard, third a heterosexual. Equally notoriously, he failed to keep his priorities in order,
at least in America. Never a "professional" Welshman, he had no
interest in the Welsh nationalist movement, entangled as it was with
the revival of the Welsh language. Moore reports (Tedlock, 1960,
p. 254) that Thomas had just three words to say on the subject,
and two of them were ". . . Welsh Nationalism." Occasionally he
extended his benediction to the whole country: "Land of my
fathers, and my fathers can keep it" (FitzGibbon, *The Life of
Dylan Thomas*, 1965, p. 11). His filmscript for *Three Weird Sisters*
(1948) describes the Welshman as having "a lie in his teeth and a
hymn on his lips," and was bitterly resented in Wales.

Yet he returned there again and again. His Swansea friends were
the closest to him. He was much more productive in Wales than in
London, usually confining his drinking to beer; at Laugharne he
mixed easily with the townspeople and seemed at home in this thoroughly bourgeois environment in a way that frustrated and baffled
his wife Caitlin. The Welsh themselves were never sure what to
make of him, glad to claim a literary figure of some stature but annoyed that he could write only in English, ignored the nationalist
cause, and chose to live for so long in London. During one of these
exiles he addressed the Scottish Society of Writers in Edinburgh
(quoted in Tedlock, 1960, pp. 7–8):

> I am a Welshman who does not live in his own country, mainly because he still wants to eat and drink, be rigged and roofed, and no Welsh writer can hunt his bread and butter in Wales unless he pulls his forelock to the *Western Mail*, Bethesdas on Sunday, and enters public-houses by the back door, and reads Caradoc Evans only when alone, and by candle light . . . Regarded in England as a Welshman (and a waterer of England's milk), and in Wales as an Englishman, I am too unnational to be here at all.

Yet a writer can be irredeemably Welsh regardless of his attitude to his country or its attitude toward him. Caradoc Evans, the great debunker of Welsh "hypocrisy," had Thomas's admiration and affection. He and Glyn Jones visited the older writer in 1934 and the three "made a tour of the pubs in the evening, drinking to the eternal damnation of the Almighty and the soon-to-be-hoped-for destruction of the Tin Bethels" (FitzGibbon, 1965, p. 141). Like Joyce exposing the moral corruption of Dublin, but with less deadly seriousness, Thomas realized that his character and his art were formed in reaction to the Nonconformist ethic and provincial standards he decried.

He began and ended his life in two Welsh seaside towns, Swansea and Laugharne. Swansea, an industrial town, was suffering a heavy postwar depression. Split between English and Welsh speakers, country and urban elements, it nonetheless exuded a peaceful sense of community. Nor was it a cultural and intellectual wasteland. Swansea boasted two theaters, an art gallery, a university, and frequent concerts. It produced during this period the painters Evan Walters, Ceri Richards, and Alfred Janes; the musician Daniel Jones; Wynford Vaughan Thomas in prose and radio; Vernon Watkins and Thomas himself in poetry (FitzGibbon, 1965, p. 19). His friend Thomas Taig (1968, pp. 23-32) argues that "Swansea Between the Wars" produced, partly as a result of the war, a revival of great energy. Writers as different as Saunders Lewis, Watkins, and Thomas show a characteristic humor (both common-sensical and surreal) and a manner of fusing past and present, sense and spirit, which reflect the quality of the movement as a whole. Swansea was not that far from London—just far enough that its young artists could cultivate their own stance and manner free of esthetic self-consciousness.

Elements of the Swansea setting are obviously present in the poetry and prose: the "capsized" field and hunchback's park, for instance, and especially the ever-present sea. Walford Davies (1972, pp. 137–45) traces the way in which Thomas in the notebook poems attempted to capture his suburban milieu with its pots of ferns and pianolas, aspiring after Eliot's realistic but evocative images. Much of this element was later written out of his poetry, though it survives in the stuffed fox of "After the funeral." Sometimes local references survive unrecognized in his more cosmic mature style: the "ghost with a hammer, air," of "If my head hurt a hair's foot" echoes local boxing hero Jimmy Wilde, nicknamed "the ghost with a hammer in his hand." Early drafts of poems like "I have longed to move away" retain more descriptive reference to the Swansea world, "half convention and half lie." Much later, Thomas returned to a pastoral version of his childhood setting in the poetry, a genial and rustic version in the stories of *Portrait of the Artist as a Young Dog*. In these, the significant detail charms and amuses but seldom cuts.

Critics have argued over the degree of Thomas's consciousness of the social conditions of Swansea between the wars. Those who, like Tindall, are convinced that there is more social content in his poetry than immediately strikes the eye generally find a reflection of the industrial depression in the sterility and bitterness of the early poems. But the poet's middle-class household was to an extent isolated from the worst effects of the depression. As T. H. Jones points out (*Dylan Thomas*, 1966, p. 9), Thomas showed his understanding of conditions among the miners of South Wales in a broadcast talk on Welsh poets in 1946; yet little of this emerges in the poetry or the prose. Walford Davies (1972, p. 20) finds attempts at socially conscious verse in lines from the early notebooks about "young men with fallen chests and old men's breath" and "the living dead left over from the war." Without exception these are unsuccessful in the poems, and rejected by Thomas. Whatever the reason, Thomas found he could not use Auden's themes.

Laugharne "fits" the later poetry more unambiguously than Swansea does the earlier. It is nonindustrial, quaint, and beautiful. Min Lewis in his coffee-table book on *Laugharne and Dylan Thomas* (1967, pp. 11–16) finds it relatively cosmopolitan, heir to a tradition of feistiness and idiosyncrasy, and less oppressively Nonconformist than Swansea. Located in the southwest area of the country often called the "Little England Beyond Wales," it nonetheless abounds in local legends, characters, and customs, some of which Thomas captured in *Under Milk Wood*. Terence Hawkes (1960, p. 346) shows that Thomas even managed to capture some of the town's Welsh dialect in his play. Richard Hughes, a Welsh novelist and friend of Thomas's who seldom wrote anything even faintly Welsh, wrote in the picturesque Castle House, while Thomas

and his family inhabited the famous Boat House, even more pic-
turesquely nestled against the sea-cliff below. Laugharne, claims
Gwyn Jones (1954, p. 114), is "easy and pretty."

There is no difficulty in recognizing the Laugharne topography
in Thomas's later poems. Sir John's Hill and its surroundings obviously were necessary and effective inspiration for them; pastoral
Wales is as intimately connected with Thomas as is the Lake Country with Wordsworth. Thomas, the avowed suburbanite, had come
to present a thoroughly rural face to the world. But such topographical observations do not really take us very far. If, as Moynihan claims (1966, p. 15), Wales "eventually provided a symbolic
resolution for the complexities that were slowly denying him life,"
much as the New England countryside did for Frost, it would be
interesting to know the psychological and spiritual processes by
which this came about. Anthony Conran (1960, pp. 12-14) attempts to define the young poet's psychological attitude toward his
country, claiming that "Dylan Thomas as a young man exemplifies
to perfection the world of Wales falling apart." Though he was
proud of being Welsh, "he never really appreciated either her greatness or her solidarity. He was an 'outsider,' a man shut in by his
own soul, lacking a community." The limitations of his poetry—his
difficulty in entering into a bond of imaginative sympathy with
other individuals (rather than with mankind in general)—reflects
a problem that is "partly sociological: conditions in Wales *do* drive
a great many young people . . . into the kind of metaphysical revolt he personifies." According to Conran, Thomas is unique not
in his kind of alienation, but in his ability to harness it to produce
personally therapeutic and generally important literature. Perhaps
the poet's deepest attitudes toward his country changed in his last
years; certainly the tenor of the poetry changes. But if this is so,
the study of that transformation has yet to be written.

Culture and Tradition. Rather than confine their remarks to the
demonstrable effects of Thomas's Welsh experience, many critics
prefer to discuss the ways in which his work reflects or embodies
the Welsh culture and literary tradition. Many of the earlier books
on Thomas stress the Welsh perspective, notably T. H. Jones
(1966) and A. T. Davies (*Dylan: Druid of the Broken Body*,
1964), while the earliest, Treece (*Dylan Thomas: 'Dog Among the
Fairies'*, 1949), devotes a section to Thomas's use of Welsh prosody
through the intermediary of Hopkins. But all of these are really
subsumed by John Ackerman's more thorough study, misleadingly
entitled, *Dylan Thomas: His Life and Work* (1964). Ackerman's

major aim, in his own words, is to offer "an interpretation of Dylan Thomas's life and work in relation to his Welsh background."

As is the case in Ireland, there are two separate but related kinds of national literature: Welsh literature proper and Anglo-Welsh literature, which is written in English. Ackerman divides the "Welsh influence" upon Thomas into three areas for discussion (cf. Woodcock's similar categorization, 1954, pp. 295–302): first, the influence of the particular community in which he lived—its social and religious forms, its traditions and conventions; next, the influence of Anglo-Welsh writers to whom he may have been exposed, and whose work might directly affect the form and theme of his own; and lastly the broader influence of the "culture existing in and through the Welsh language."

Since we have already discussed the geographical and social implications of Thomas's years in Swansea and Laugharne and will treat Anglo-Welsh writers somewhat later on, our main interest here is in Ackerman's last category, clearly the most tentative and ambiguous of the three. In a review of Ackerman, Korg (1966, p. 284) points out the weakness in his argument: although the critic may demonstrate many qualities which Thomas's poetry shares with classical Welsh literature, this is not enough to establish a relationship between the two. For what Ackerman says of Welsh literature could be said certainly of other Celtic literatures, like Irish or Scottish, and often could be said of unrelated genres like romantic poetry or mystical writing. Ackerman assumes, reasonably enough, that the character of a national language and literature will seep into the national consciousness, reflecting and finding reflection in the characteristic assumptions, expressions, and perceptions of Welshmen, whether or not they speak Welsh. In the nineteenth century this sort of argument often was phrased in terms of racial character or spirit; later, critics spoke of a racial unconscious. Matthew Arnold's famous *Study of Celtic Literature*, which Ackerman frequently cites, speaks of the "spirit" of the Celtic people, blandly moving from racial generalizations to specifics of literature or of society. The essay has been influential even among literary scholars, including Yeats, despite the fact that Arnold could read no Celtic languages. Ackerman of course is more sophisticated in his orientation, but occasionally flirts with the dangers of the *Volkgeist*.

Thomas was certainly aware of the Welsh bardic tradition. Welsh poetry began around the sixth century and reached a flowering around the fifteenth and sixteenth. In the Middle Ages the Celtic bard was a personage, even after the coming of Christianity stripped from him much of his priestly or "druidic" function. Supported by kings, he could give a sort of immortality to patrons or relegate enemies to public scorn. Worse, his satires were thought to have the power of causing sickness and death in their victims. Welsh verse, whose extremely complex rules of prosody were codified by bardic "schools" when poetry was still primarily an oral art, has retained its emphasis on auditory effects through modern times. During the nineteenth century, many ordinary Welsh citizens saw nothing strange in writing and publishing verse in the old language; one such, William Thomas, was the uncle of Thomas's father. His "bardic name," Gwilym Marles (or Marlais), descended to his grandnephew. Gwilym was a political radical and a preacher as well as a poet, and indeed the characteristic "hwyl," an incantatory, passionate alliterative style of elevated invocation from the pulpit, bears resemblances to accepted Welsh poetic styles—as it does to the style of Thomas's own readings.

D. J. Thomas, the poet's father, clearly wished to perpetuate his celebrated uncle's name in his son. His first name, "Dylan," came from the Fourth Branch of the *Mabinogion*, where it was bestowed by a magician-king upon the son of Arianrhod, the Welsh White Goddess (Jones, 1966, p. 4). In the story, "Dylan Eil Ton," "Sea Son of the Wave," immediately dashed off into the sea and became part of it. This was certainly a curious name for the liberal and progressive D. J. to have given his son; in 1914 it was little known even in Wales (FitzGibbon, 1965, p. 23), and his father made little effort afterward to imbue Thomas with elements of the Welsh language or culture. Perhaps he simply meant it to be decorative and unusual, a gesture toward a native culture in which he otherwise showed little interest; Ackerman and others see it as a talisman, the external signature of Thomas's essential Welshness.

For it cannot be denied that in many of the poetic qualities where Thomas is most unlike his immediate English predecessors, he is very like Welsh poets. His sense of the bardic vocation and its elevated status are Welsh. Ackerman (p. 5) points to the apparent paradox in bardic poetry, where the poet's exuberant personality is confined only by the "craftsmanlike devotion to composition." Formal care and elaboration to the point of the merely decorative have long been recognized as characteristic of Celtic arts. Reprising, with modification, Arnold's essay, Ackerman notes other relevant facets of Welsh poetry: an "awareness of the dual nature of reality, of unity in disunity, of the simultaneity of life and death"; the violent yoking together of discordant images; the odd structure, which displays a pattern of experience without conventional narrative design; the "concentric" rather than "linear" development of meaning; the

relation of parts to an imagined whole, which substitutes for a con-
secutive relationship; and an emphasis on technical rather than intellectual discipline. As Arnold noted, style itself is more evidently
important than in English poetry, so that technical skill in a sense
supplants intellectual skill. Sensual detail abounds, despite the pervasive feeling of "other-worldliness" and the emphasis upon the spiritual realm. What Arnold calls the "magic" of Celtic verse often
comes from the juxtaposition of unexpected, almost surreal elements
within a lyrical context.

Ackerman analyzes the devices of sound and meter found in
Welsh poetry, and in a long analysis of "Fern Hill" (chapter 9)
shows their echo in Thomas's work. As for theme, he points to the
mingled pagan and Christian elements of Welsh poetry (p. 114);
since his reading of Thomas is basically Christian, he finds many
parallels among the bards. The nostalgia and "deep-set pessimism"
(p. 70) to be encountered in the poet's work are like the "Titan-
ism" Arnold describes, while Thomas's compositional method (p.
53) reflects the "destructive-creative continuum" implied in Welsh
poetry, where opposites usually join in a nonanalytic, emotional, or
mystical unity. In contrast to Ackerman's careful analysis, other
critics usually are content to mention broad cultural characteristics:
Wain (1965, p. 14), for instance, mentions the "open emotional-
ism" and "large verbal gestures" of the Welsh. Moore (Tedlock,
1960, p. 254) describes them as a "lively, quick-tempered and
proud" people who sing spontaneously, exult in their religion, and
so forth; "and if this sounds like *How Green Was My Valley*,"
insists Moore, "it is none the less true." Clara Lander speaks of the
Welsh Nonconformist attitude to God, a mixture of familiarity and
fear. She notes, "the average Welshman is more familiar with visions
of Sodom and Gomorrah than with the sights of Swansea and Cardiff." Much of T. H. Jones's discussion is of the same order, although he does note (1966, p. 85) that Thomas, particularly in his
prose, uses a technique like that of the Welsh "dyfalu," a pell-mell
piling-up of words and puns in catalogue fashion.

Walford Davies (1972a) in his volume on Thomas for the Writers
of Wales series supplies an intelligent continuation of Ackerman's
thesis, although he is much more cynical about any direct influence
from Welsh prosody. Since Thomas did not speak Welsh, Davies
finds it unlikely that the Welsh language even distorted his syntax.
But he cites with approval (p. 8) FitzGibbon's observation that
"because the English words and syntax do not always and exactly fit
the ideas and images to be expressed, the recently Anglicized 'Celt'
will examine his language with a very close attention." As a Welsh-

man, he feels, Thomas has "a kind of collective sense of his responsibility towards form." The Welsh, like Thomas, want "a poem to look like a poem, and to sound like poetry." Davies (p. 23) sees little specific influence of Thomas's Swansea upbringing on his work, claiming that, aside from a few topical allusions, it is simply that of a bourgeois, puritan society upon a sensitive adolescent. Like most critics he finds the "Caitlin" poems—"I make this in a warring absence," "Into her Lying Down Head," "Not from this anger"— less successful than many of the others, commenting (p. 42) that the "Welsh element in Thomas . . . was not geared to the exploration of utterly individual emotion." "Poem in October" he finds particularly Welsh (p. 56) in "the way its structure is provided not by argumentative development but by the tonal unity of its geographical narrative."

It seems unfortunate that the critics have fallen into opposing camps, either affirming Thomas's continuity with the tradition of Welsh poetry because of the way his work sometimes resembles it in spirit, style, and phenomenology, or denying any relationship because of his admitted ignorance of the language. At least regarding the poet's language, his distinctive poetic idiom, some agreement should be possible. Although Thomas personally adopted a "cut glass" accent, a mildly lilting variant of BBC English, he was obviously well aware of several dialects of English spoken in Wales, and used an approximation of them for dialogue in stories. Frequently, as in Ireland, elements of Celtic syntax, vocabulary, and idiom carry over into the English speech even of nonnative speakers (Woodcock, 1954, p. 301). It would seem that the problem of the "Welsh element" in Thomas's language is one for a linguist. Lacking any careful analysis of Thomas's idiom, it is fruitless to argue over its Welshness.

Welsh and Anglo-Welsh. Of the two different literary traditions in Wales, the Welsh goes back well into Medieval times, while the Anglo-Welsh goes back perhaps three hundred years. That is a generous estimate; some critics fail to detect a genuine Anglo-Welsh literary tradition until the twentieth century. As with "Anglo-Irish" literature, the problem is which writers one chooses to include. Must they be Welsh by birth, or is it sufficient that they have spent considerable time in Wales? Must they write about Wales? Is it necessary that they consider themselves primarily Welsh writers, or may they regard themselves as part of the English literary tradition? There are no really satisfactory answers to these questions, a critic's response often depending upon his degree of nationalistic feeling and the stature of the literary candidate. Most scholars of Anglo-Welsh literature feel, like Gwyn Jones (*The First Forty Years*, 1957, p. 14), that it is ironic that such an ambivalently Welsh writer as Thomas should be the most famous exemplar of the tradition. But most agree that, for the world at large, he is the best-known Anglo-Welsh writer.

It should be realized that there has always been a strong anti-Thomas faction among enthusiasts of Welsh literature. American critics often are unaware of the extent of the debate because so many of the relevant articles have appeared in Welsh publications—*Yr Einion (The Welsh Anvil), Dock Leaves, Rann,* or *The Welsh Review*—which are specialized and difficult of access. The most conservative faction among the critics is probably represented by the Welsh language teacher Bobi Jones (1955, pp. 84–85), who attacks the "deadening perverse *furor poeticus* of Fry and Dylan Thomas." Seconding the *Scrutiny* attacks on Thomas, which he regards as overly generous, Jones deplores the imitation of Thomas among young Welsh writers in both languages. Thomas's decadent artificiality is a measure of the bankruptcy of the English literary tradition, "the inevitable development of a language and society that have lost their creative distinction." J. Gwyn Griffiths (Maud, 1970, p. 56), who is much more sympathetic to Thomas, nevertheless feels that his debt to the Welsh literary tradition is "nil."

Keidrych Rhys, the editor of *Wales* magazine, with which Thomas was associated for a time, is usually regarded as a defender of the "Welsh" tradition. In this he is opposed by Gwyn Jones, whose rival *Welsh Review* stresses the term "Anglo-Welsh" (R. G. Thomas, 1963, p. 140). Nevertheless, Rhys represents a much more liberal element in Welsh criticism than does Jones. Discussing the contributors to his volume of *Modern Welsh Poetry* (1944), which include Thomas, David Jones, Alun Lewis, Treece, and Watkins, among many more avowedly Welsh writers, he comments (Rhys, 1946, p. 19) that for a real Welshman, it "is hard to convince oneself that either Dylan Thomas or Alun Lewis ever felt or thought as a Welshman: they seem either unaware or unable to get inside." Nonetheless, Rhys connects Thomas with a modern Welsh renaissance, the "liberation of a long pent-up Celtic imagination," and suggests (p. 19) that Thomas's *Portrait* may be the best literary reflection of the Welsh way of life the country has to offer. George Woodcock (1954, p. 294) endorses the idea of a modern renaissance. He suggests that we see Thomas as part of a group of young poets including Glyn Jones, Keidrych Rhys, Alun Lewis, Vernon Watkins, and others, all of whom were in rebellion against the "colorless Georgianism" of Wyn Griffith and Huw Menai, distinguished poets of the older generation.

One of the reasons for the problem in placing Thomas within the context of modern Anglo-Welsh literature is that he actually appears very early among the twentieth-century writers, within a group who are often quite critical of Wales, its culture, and its people. Aside from much earlier, "peripherally Welsh" writers such as Henry Vaughan or John Donne, the immediate antecedents of the tradition (Rhys, 1946, p. 17) are the scholar Ernest Rhys, the Gothic writer Arthur Machen, the poets W. H. Davies and Edward Thomas, and the novelist T. F. Powys (whose Welshness is very questionable). But most critics feel that modern Anglo-Welsh writing begins with the bitter, satirical novels of Caradoc Evans, whose My People (1915) according to Gwyn Jones (1957, p. 7) smashed the genteel tradition of Welsh writers like Allen Raine and provoked violent reactions from the Welsh.

Glyn Jones (The Dragon Has Two Tongues, 1968, pp. 46–47), himself a Welsh speaker, traces a growing interest in Welsh nationalism in the generations since this patriotically inauspicious beginning, from the first generation of Evans, Thomas, Rhys, Davies, and Vernon Watkins through the second generation, associated with the early Wales magazine (Glyn Jones himself, Keidrych Rhys, Wyn Griffith, Idris Davies), on through the third, who were importantly influenced by the Welsh nationalism of Saunders Lewis (Emyr Humphries and R. S. Thomas). Glyn Jones stresses that there is indeed a connection between Anglo-Welsh and Welsh literature, mostly springing from the writers' mutual experience of their country, but sees (p. 41) no set of definable qualities which Anglo-Welsh writers hold in common. Jones sounds a familiar theme among Welsh critics by mocking the comments of foreign writers about Wales. Francis Scarfe's reference to the "hot-gospeling diabolical grimace of the Welsh Bethel" is laughable, considering the relatively restrained quality of Swansea Nonconformity (p. 185), as is Karl Shapiro's suggestion that remnants of Welsh fertility cults are still extant. Thomas's main inheritance from Wales, claims Jones, was probably his very sense of a *lack* of community with the Welsh tradition. In this Jones echoes the emphasis of many Welsh-speaking critics, who suggest that the self-destructive tendencies in the poet reflect the split in modern Welsh culture.

Raymond Garlick, the editor of Dock Leaves, represents the most "assimilationist" tendency among Welsh critics. In his editorial for the Thomas memorial number (1954, pp. 1–5), his underlying assumption is that the poet's "voice has a Welsh modulation,

the mind and heart were formed by the heart and mind of Wales."
While the sixteenth-century Welsh writer might still feel English
to be an alien tongue, he argues, the modern Anglo-Welsh poet
"speaks to his fellow Welshmen in the only language most of them
possess." More traditionalist critics insist that, unlike the situation in
Ireland, where Gaelic has almost vanished, in Wales nearly a third
of the population speaks Welsh (G. Jones, 1968, p. 47); Garlick defends the language of the majority, pointing to an Anglo-Welsh
literature stretching back to "the Welsh Dean Donne," George
Herbert, the "poor Welsh parson" Thomas Traherne, Henry
Vaughan, and of course Gerard Manley Hopkins. Thomas is "the
product, the epitome, the exposition, and the extension" of this tradition. English and American readers might be surprised to find
the great metaphysical poets thus lifted from the British literary
context, and question the rationale which assimilates them under the
rubric "Anglo-Welsh," but Garlick is certainly not alone in his
opinions. He further defends the idea that there is a long and rich
Anglo-Welsh poetic tradition, which he admits is a minority
opinion, in the *University of Wales Review* (1965, pp. 18–20).

Ackerman's book (1964) contains one of the fullest attempts to
characterize the Anglo-Welsh tradition with particular reference
to Thomas. He argues (p. 14) that the group of Anglo-Welsh
writers active after World War I—Caradoc Evans, Dylan Thomas,
Gwyn Jones, Watkins, Alun Lewis, R. S. Thomas, Gwyn Thomas,
and Glyn Jones—are not really part of the English literary tradition.
They share an enthusiasm and energy, a richness of metaphor, and a
sensuous imagination with a delight in fantasy. Their work usually
has a pervading sense of pathos. Poets among them tend to begin
from the *word* rather than the *idea;* their writing is marked by both
a sense of humor and an emphasis upon formal control. They are
subjective and introspective, turning to themes of childhood, death,
sexuality, and a sort of primitivism. Most share a theological bias
which leads them to celebrate all natural life, an almost Hebraic
sense of the holiness of all things. Most show the clear influence
of the seventeenth-century metaphysicals, particularly Donne,
Vaughan, and Traherne. Much of what Ackerman argues is true,
but at such a level of generality that it is difficult to judge its significance. Some of the judgments about the "tone" of a group of
writers are clearly very subjective; Geoffrey Moore, for instance
(Tedlock, 1960, p. 257) finds that the style and tone of W. H.
Davies and Alun Lewis differs markedly from that of Thomas because they "did not allow themselves to be artistically and emotionally responsive to the natural facts of the Welsh scene."

The debate over Welsh and Anglo-Welsh continues in the national periodicals, with Thomas defended or attacked depending upon the writer's position in the melee. He is discussed in the context of Anglo-Welsh writers by E. Glyn Lewis (1946) and by Aneirin Talfan Davies (1953), who treats the question more fully here than in his book on Thomas. Huw Menai (1958) discusses poetic effects typical of "the Bilingual Mind," while Anthony Conran's "The English Poet in Wales: II. Boys of Summer in their Ruin" (1960) ambitiously examines the peculiar predicament of the modern Anglo-Welsh writer. Numerous other articles treat Thomas as Welsh storywriter or compare him with Edward Thomas, Alun Lewis, Caradoc Evans, and so forth. A minor but persistent refrain is the odious comparison of the poet with another Welsh writer, as Harding (1957) does with Edward Thomas or Holbrook (1964) does with T. F. Powys. F. W. Bateson in Walford Davies's collection (1972, pp. 221–27) discusses "The Conversation of Prayer" as a typically Anglo-Welsh poem in structure and theme, which ironically counterpoints the argument of Aneirin Talfan Davies that the poem embodies a Catholic doctrine.

Hopkins and Welsh Prosody. Thomas himself wrote on Anglo-Welsh writers for his newspaper during his days as a cub reporter, and later discussed "Welsh Poets" in a broadcast talk included in *Quite Early One Morning.* Although he was unable to discover any "logical thread running through the centuries of traditional poetry in English which can be said to possess a particularly Welsh characteristic," he spoke briefly on Vaughan, Edward Thomas, W. H. Davies, Idris Davies, Glyn Jones, and Alun Lewis. A notable omission was Hopkins, who, he apologized, "cannot be included in even the broadest survey of this kind." Yet Hopkins's name, more than any other, recurs in discussions of Thomas's Welsh inheritance. Hopkins, a Roman Catholic priest who died in 1889, had been stationed in Wales for a time by the Jesuits. Though he published nothing in his lifetime, his friend Robert Bridges rather apologetically published a selection of his poems in 1918, which caused little stir. But with their second edition, in 1930, the generation of young poets who were to be headed by Auden, Spender, and Day Lewis reacted enthusiastically. Hopkins's metrical experiments and his unusual diction and syntax soon became evident in the work of these younger writers.

Aneirin Talfan Davies (1962), in a rather technical article tracing the influence of Welsh prosody on Thomas's work, explains that Hopkins probably learned about Welsh metrics from William

Barnes, an early nineteenth-century dialect poet who was also a friend of Hardy. Barnes had tried to duplicate the effect of the Welsh rhyming and alliterative system called "cynghanedd" in English. Inspired by this attempt, Hopkins tried his own hand at it in both English and Welsh. There are four main types of cynghanedd, Davies explains. In "Groes" the same consonants must be repeated, in order, in each line-half, with the exception of the final consonant, which must differ; vowels are not repeated. In "Draws" an unbalanced consonant is allowed in the second half-line. Cynghanedd "Sain," a more complex form, divides the line into three parts, the first two of which rhyme, while the second and third alliterate as in "Draws." In "Lusg," the line ends in a multisyllabic word whose penultimate syllable rhymes with the syllable preceding the caesura. Welsh metrics are equally complex and formalized. In "cywoydd," the most popular, a couplet of seven-syllable lines is written, each line in cynghanedd, and the end rhyme scheme juxtaposes an accented and an unaccented syllable (e.g., "bet" and "bucket"). Other forms involve an "outriding" syllable following the rhyming syllable, which may alliterate with some prescribed syllable of the couplet.

In many of his poems Hopkins attempts these effects, which are particularly noticeable in "The Wreck of the Deutschland." His favorite kind of cynghanedd seems to have been "sain," the easiest to mimic in English. He frequently used "sangiad," a prosodic device which allowed the poet to break up the syntax of a sentence in order to insert a parenthetical thought; sometimes Hopkins (and Thomas) will even break up a word this way, as in the line "Brim, in a flash, full." Davies claims that he himself frequently discussed cynghanedd with Thomas, and feels that the echoes of it in his work are mainly from Hopkins, "the one great and deciding influence on his work." This influence, Davies claims, becomes increasingly apparent with "Vision and Prayer" in 1945, when Thomas's religious theme began to approach that of Hopkins, though Thomas himself (*Letters to Vernon Watkins*, p. 123) denied the Jesuit's influence on the poem. But many other examples of something like Welsh prosody can be found in his poetry, such as the rhymed half-lines of "The Conversation of Prayer."

Davies claims that Wyn Griffith wrote an article on the Welsh influence upon Hopkins for *New Verse* in 1934. Thomas began to publish in that periodical five years later, and by 1947 the editor, Tambimuttu, was engaged in a heated controversy with Grigson over whether Thomas was using a modified form of cynghanedd. Tambimuttu waxed assertive as Grigson grew more violently cynical. Two years later, Treece's book on Thomas included a chapter on "The Debt to Hopkins" (1949, pp. 58–71) where he stressed the similarities in theme and tone between the poets. The alliterations, inversions, and the violence of his syntax were reflected in Thomas; so were the advanced metrical schemes, which allowed for "out-riding" syllables, or a highly irregular variant of the normal English meters, or even a variable number of unstressed syllables in his "sprung rhythm." Similarly, his use of half-rhyme antedated its usage by Wilfred Owen. Both are poets of tension and disorder, Hopkins calling out to God for resolution, while Thomas looks within. In both there is a sense of passionate inquiry and "a terror of fearful expectation." Treece suggests that much of Thomas's vocabulary, both the "clinical" anatomical words and the compound words, comes from Hopkins.

In the following chapters, Treece, evidently inspired by an article by Glyn Jones on Hopkins's prosodic borrowing from Welsh poetry, briefly discusses (pp. 81–84) the variants of cynghanedd in Thomas. He concludes that the influence of the form must have come to Thomas through Hopkins rather than directly. This whole discussion was dropped from the second edition (1956), probably at Jones's suggestion, according to Maud (1963, p. 159, n. 14). Nevertheless, the discussion continues; Ackerman (1964, pp. 7–10) devotes some space to the classical Welsh forms. Again, it seems that something more rigorous than impressionistic criticism is called for. Some of the Welsh forms may perfectly well occur by accident in a highly alliterative poetry which uses rhymes and half-rhymes; Glyn Jones (1954, p. 25) mentions seeing the line "Fifty Nifty Naughties" above a London music hall, an example of "cynghanedd sain." A substantial prosodic comparison of Thomas with a poet like Hart Crane, for instance, and of both with Hopkins, ought to establish whether there is a genuine subject for study. Meanwhile, critics range from Maud's position (1963, p. 5) that "if there are one or two lines in Thomas that fit the Welsh patterns it is purely accidental" to Geoffrey Moore's assertion (Tedlock, 1960, p. 256) that Thomas's patterns of rhyme and assonance form "a more wilful patterning than Hopkins allowed himself, and to this extent more Welsh." Probably Thomas's own comment on Glyn Jones's attempts to adapt Welsh bardic meters to English should be kept firmly in mind: "these effects in English have, in the hands of the few who have attempted to use them, succeeded only in warping, crabbing, and obscuring the natural genius of the English language" (QEOM, p. 71).

It seems likely that, while Thomas was undoubtedly aware of the

existence of Welsh poetic techniques, he never attempted to duplicate them in any sustained manner. He was a consistent enough pro-
sodist that, had he attempted a clear echo of cynghanedd, it would
be quite apparent in his work; his sophisticated rhyme and assonantal patterns and his syllabic metrics are apparent in numerous poems.
Tindall claims (*A Reader's Guide to Dylan Thomas*, 1962, p. 11)
that Thomas once told him "that he was content to hint the Welsh
techniques he lacked." And as for the " 'deep Celtic significance'
detected by critics in image and theme, Thomas cheerfully dis-
claimed it." Such a response, of course, depends on the phrasing of
the question, and Thomas may have been more Celtic than he knew.
But it does not sound as if he felt any special immersion in the culture of Wales to be a prerequisite to reading him.

For the reader who has not spent a great deal of time in Wales,
the discussion of Thomas's relationship to his native culture must
remain academic. His feelings for his country mingled love and
hate, often an effective recipe for a powerful literary response, as
Terence Hawkes (1965, p. 991) points out. Purists may deny the
Welshness of his work and the accuracy of his portrayals of Welsh
life in the prose, but at least in one respect they cannot deny his place
in the modern literature of Wales: he was, for a generation of writers younger than himself, a piece of twentieth-century Welsh
mythology. Gwyn Thomas (*A Welsh Eye*, 1964, p. 64) writes,

he was a sort of living revenge on all the restrictions and respectabili-
ties that have come near to choking the life out of the Welsh mind . . .
[He] represented for a mass of young Welsh people a dramatic moment in the restoration of joy to a people who for years had taken
their religious sanctions too grimly . . .

It is something approaching a literary law that when a writer has
the breadth, force, and personal vision to come into international
prominence, he will be accused of having betrayed his natural
inheritance. Thomas may or may not occupy a comfortable position
in the Welsh literary pantheon; he seems to fit there as uneasily as
he does in the British. Both contexts are relevant, but we can be sure
that neither will fully define or circumscribe his work.

References

Ackerman, John
  1964. *Dylan Thomas: His Life and Work.* London and New York:
  Oxford Univ. Pr.
Adams, Robert M.
  1958. "Crashaw and Dylan Thomas: Devotional Athletes." In

Strains of Discord: Studies in Literary Openness, pp. 128–45. Ithaca, N. Y.: Columbia Univ. Pr.

Bayley, John
1957. *The Romantic Survival: A Study in Poetic Evolution.* London: Constable.

Conran, Anthony
1960. "The English Poet in Wales: II. Boys of Summer in their Ruin," *Anglo-Welsh Review* pp. 11–21.

Cox, C. B.
1966. (editor) *Dylan Thomas: A Collection of Critical Essays.* Englewood Cliffs, N. J.: Prentice-Hall.

Davies, Aneirin Talfan
1953. "A Question of Language," *Yr Einion (The Welsh Anvil)* pp. 19–31.
1962. "William Barnes, G. M. Hopkins, Dylan Thomas. The Influence of Welsh Prosody on Modern English Poetry." In *Proceedings of the IIIrd Congress of the International Comparative Literature Association.* The Hague: Mouton, pp. 90–122.
1964. *Dylan: Druid of the Broken Body.* London: J. M. Dent.

Davies, Walford
1972. (editor) *Dylan Thomas: New Critical Essays.* London: J. M. Dent.
1972a. *Dylan Thomas* (Writers of Wales). N. p.: Univ. of Wales Pr.

De Bedts, Ruth
1957. "Dylan Thomas and the Eve of St. Agnes," *Florida Review* Fall, pp. 50–55.

FitzGibbon, Constantine
1965. *The Life of Dylan Thomas.* Boston: Little.

Garlick, Raymond
1954. "Editorial," *Dock Leaves* Spring, pp. 1–5.
1965. "An Anglo-Welsh Accidence," *University of Wales Review* Summer, pp. 18–20.

Harding, Joan
1957. "Dylan Thomas and Edward Thomas," *Contemporary Review* Sept., pp. 150–54.

Hawkes, Terence
1960. "Dylan Thomas's Welsh," *College English* March, pp. 345–47.
1965. "Playboys of the Western World," *Listener* Dec. 16, pp. 991–93.

Holbrook, David
1964. *Dylan Thomas and Poetic Dissociation.* Carbondale: Illinois Univ. Pr.

Jones, Bobi
1955. "Imitations in Death," *Yr Einion (The Welsh Anvil)* pp. 82–86.

Jones, Glyn
1954. "Dylan Thomas and Welsh," *Dock Leaves* Spring, pp. 24–25.
1968. *The Dragon Has Two Tongues.* London: J. M. Dent.

Jones, Gwyn
1954. "Welsh Dylan," *Adelphi* 1st. qtr., pp. 108–17.

1957. *The First Forty Years: Some Notes on Anglo-Welsh Literature.* Cardiff: Univ. of Wales Pr.

Jones, T. H.

1966. *Dylan Thomas.* New York: Barnes & Noble.

Kidder, Rushworth M.

1973. *Dylan Thomas: The Country of the Spirit.* Princeton: Princeton Univ. Pr.

Korg, Jacob

1965. *Dylan Thomas.* New York: Twayne.

1966. "Receptions of Dylan Thomas," *Antioch Review* Summer, pp. 281–88.

Lander, Clara

1958. "With Welsh and Reverent Rook," *Queen's Quarterly* Autumn, pp. 437–47.

Leitch, Vincent B.

1972. "Herbert's Influence in Dylan Thomas's 'I see the boys of summer'," *Notes and Queries* p. 341.

Lewis, E. Glyn

1946. "Some Aspects of Anglo-Welsh Literature," *Welsh Review* Autumn, pp. 176–86.

Lewis, Min

1967. *Laugharne and Dylan Thomas.* London: Dennis Dobson.

Mathias, Roland

1954. "A Merry Manshape (or Dylan Thomas at a distance)," *Dock Leaves* Spring, pp. 30–39.

Maud, Ralph N.

1963. *Entrances to Dylan Thomas's Poetry.* Pittsburgh: Univ. of Pittsburgh Pr.

1968. (editor) *Poet in the Making: The Notebooks of Dylan Thomas.* London: J. M. Dent.

1970. *Dylan Thomas in Print: A Bibliographical History.* Pittsburgh: Univ. of Pittsburgh Pr.

Melchiori, Giorgio

1956. *The Tightrope Walkers: Studies of Mannerism in Modern English Literature.* London: George Routledge & Sons.

Menai, Huw

1958. "The Bilingual Mind," *Wales* Oct., pp. 8–14.

Miller, James E., Jr.

1957. "Four Cosmic Poets," *University of Kansas City Review* June, pp. 312–20.

Miller, James E., Jr.; Karl Shapiro; Bernice Slote

1960. *Start with the Sun.* Lincoln: Univ. of Nebraska Pr.

Moynihan, William T.

1966. *The Craft and Art of Dylan Thomas.* Ithaca, N. Y.: Cornell Univ. Pr.; London: Oxford Univ. Pr.

Nowottny, Winifred

1962. "Symbolism and Obscurity." In *The Language Poets Use*, pp. 174–222. London: Athlone Pr.; New York: Oxford Univ. Pr.

Ochshorn, Myron

1954. "The Love Song of Dylan Thomas," *New Mexico Quarterly* Spring, pp. 46–65.

Olson, Elder
  1954. *The Poetry of Dylan Thomas*. Chicago: Univ. of Chicago Pr.
Press, John
  1955. *The Fire and the Fountain: An Essay on Poetry*. London:
  Methuen; New York: Barnes & Noble.
Rhys, Keidrych
  1946. "Contemporary Welsh Literature." In *British Annual of Literature*, pp. 17–22. London: British Authors' Pr.
Rosenfeld, Paul
  1940. "Decadence and Dylan Thomas," *Nation* March 23, pp. 399–
  400.
Sitwell, Edith
  1960. "Dylan the Impeccable," *Observer* Nov. 20, p. 24.
Spender, Stephen
  1952. "A Romantic in Revolt," *Spectator* Dec. 5, pp. 780–81.
Sweeney, John L.
  1946. "Introduction" to *Selected Writings of Dylan Thomas*, pp.
  vii–xxiii. New York: New Directions.
  1952. "Intimations of Mortality," *New Republic* March 17, pp. 18,
  22–23.
Taig, Thomas
  1968. "Swansea Between the Wars," *Anglo-Welsh Review* Summer, pp. 23–32.
Tedlock, E. W.
  1960. (editor) *Dylan Thomas: The Legend and the Poet*. London:
  Heineman.
Thomas, Gwyn
  1964. *A Welsh Eye*. London: Hutchinson; New York: Greene,
  1965.
Thomas, R. George
  1963. "Dylan Thomas: A Poet of Wales?" *English* Spring, pp.
  140–45.
Tindall, William York
  1962. *A Reader's Guide to Dylan Thomas*. New York: Noonday.
Treece, Henry
  1949. *Dylan Thomas: 'Dog Among the Fairies'*. London: Lindsay
  Drummond.
Wain, John
  1965. "Dylan Thomas Today," *New York Review of Books* Feb.
  25, pp. 14–15.
Williams, Harry
  1972. "Dylan Thomas's Poetry of Redemption: Its Blakean Beginnings," *Bucknell Review* Winter, pp. 107–20.
Wittreich, Joseph A., Jr.
  1969. "Dylan Thomas' Conception of Poetry: A Debt to Blake,"
  English Language Notes March, pp. 197–200.
Woodcock, George
  1954. "Dylan Thomas and the Welsh Environment," *Arizona Quarterly* Winter, pp. 293–305.
Yerbury, Grace D.
  1964. "Of a City Beside a River: Whitman, Eliot, Thomas, Miller,"
  Walt Whitman Review pp. 67–73.

Selected Additional Readings

Blissett, William F.

1956. "Dylan Thomas: A Reader in Search of a Poet," *Queen's Quarterly* Spring, pp. 45–54.

Davies, Pennar

1954. "Sober Reflections on Dylan Thomas," *Dock Leaves* Winter, pp. 13–17.

Griffith, Wyn

1950. *The Welsh.* Harmondsworth, England: Penguin.

Highet, Gilbert

1960. "Thomas: The Wild Welshman." In *Powers of Poetry*, pp. 151–57. New York: Oxford Univ. Pr.

Hughes, Richard

1951. "Wales Through the Looking-Glass," *Listener* May 24, pp. 838–39.

Jenkins, David Clay

1959. "Dylan Thomas and *Wales* Magazine," *Trace* Feb.-March, pp. 1–8.

Jones, Glyn

1953. "Three Anglo-Welsh Prose Writers," *Rann* April, pp. 1–5.

Jones, Richard

1961. "The Dylan Thomas Country," *Texas Quarterly* Winter, pp. 34–42.

Lander, Clara

1957. "The Macabre in Dylan Thomas," *Canadian Forum* March, pp. 274–75, 278.

Lewis, Saunders

1939. *Is There an Anglo-Welsh Literature?* Cardiff Branch, Guild of Graduates of University of Wales.

Maud, Ralph N.

1968. "Dylan Thomas in Welsh Periodicals," *National Library of Wales Journal* pp. 265–89.

McCormick, Jane

1970. "Sorry, Old Christian," *Anglo-Welsh Review* pp. 78–82. [On Thomas and Vernon Watkins]

Morgan, W. John

1956. "Evans, Thomas, and Lewis," *Twentieth Century* Oct., pp. 322–29.

Potts, Abbie Findlay

1967. *The Elegaic Mode: Poetic Form in Wordsworth and Other Elegists.* New York: Oxford Univ. Pr.

Pratt, Annis

1970. *Dylan Thomas's Early Prose: A Study in Creative Mythology.* Pittsburgh: Univ. of Pittsburgh Pr. [See chapter 4, "Blake and the Occult in the Early Prose."]

Raine, Kathleen

1953. "Dylan Thomas," *New Statesman* Nov. 14, p. 594.

1967. "Vernon Watkins and the Bardic Tradition." In *Defending Ancient Springs*, pp. 17–54. London and New York: Oxford Univ. Pr.

Rhys, Aneurin
    1948. "Dylan Thomas—A Further Estimate," *Poetry Review* April–
    May, pp. 214–16.
Rowlands, Sheilah
    1954. "The Literary Topography of Laugharne," *Dock Leaves*
    Winter, pp. 38–40.
Thomas, R. George
    1962. "Bard on a Raised Hearth: Dylan Thomas and His Craft,"
    Anglo-Welsh Review pp. 11–20.
Williams, Michael
    1947. "Welsh Voices in the Short Story," *Welsh Review* Winter,
    pp. 290–98.

CHAPTER 7

Poetics

In the past few chapters we have considered Thomas's poetry from some necessary distance, comparing it with the work of other writers in a search for relevant contexts. Now I shall focus more closely on the poetry itself. Under the general heading of "poetics" we can consider first Thomas's conception of poetry, its source and function. A discussion of the "obscurity" or "ambiguity" of his work follows, involving both Thomas's poetic "world" and his unusual methods of narration and rhetoric. Finally comes consideration of his poetic technique proper—his prosody, diction, imagery, auditory experiments, and so forth. In each section I shall place some emphasis upon the poet's development and the changing texture of his work.

Each of these areas, but particularly the latter two, is centered on the idea of technique. In criticism, unfortunately but unavoidably, we tend to separate technique from theme, form from content; and this is especially true in thinking about a poet as "mannered" as Thomas. The danger is that we may come to regard his technique as merely a sort of adornment or embellishment separable from the poetic statement itself. Such a view does a greater disservice to Thomas than it would to most other poets; both positive and negative critics have pointed out repeatedly that, stripped of its rhetoric and artifice, a poem by Thomas shrinks to the vanishing point. Paraphrase does him a far greater injustice than it does to Frost or Auden, for example. Throughout the following discussion, the point made by Thomas's most perceptive critics must be borne in mind: his mode of expression is inextricably bound to what he is expressing in his successful work, and where his technique does seem separable from the poem itself, that is a measure of the particular poem's weakness.

The Poetic Conception

Poetry was an obsession with Thomas, as with most important poets. Laconically but poetically, he called it "statements made on the way to the grave" (to Harvey Breit, in Brinnin, *A Casebook on Dylan Thomas*, 1960, p. 197). Although hardly a professional critic, he did at various times say a good deal about the art; in general, his earlier statements are more intricate and programmatic, his later ones more lyrical and ambiguous. The fullest expression of his views as a young man can be found in his replies to the *New Verse* "Enquiry" (in *Quite Early One Morning*, pp. 119–20). There he defines poetry as "the rhythmic, inevitably narrative, movement from an overclothed blindness to a naked vision . . ." and as "the record of my individual struggle from darkness toward some measure of light." Illumination of some kind and self-revelation seem to be central. Asked about the original impulse behind a poem, he stressed craftsmanship:

The writing of a poem is, to me, the physical and mental task of constructing a formally watertight compartment of words, preferably with a main moving column (i.e., narrative) to hold a little of the real causes and forces of the creative brain and body . . . the poetical "impulse" or "inspiration" is only the sudden, and generally physical, coming of energy to the constructional, craftsman ability.

As cited in chapter 5, he went on to bow toward Freud and "revolutionary bodies."

Such statements do not seem outwardly evasive, but on closer examination turn curiously opaque. Why and in what way is the compartment of words "formally watertight"? Is this simply a gesture toward the modernist notion of poetic autonomy, or a formalist assertion that a poem exists only in its own self-generated complexities? Is the "physical" inspiration behind a poem merely a subjectively experienced surge of energy, or does the poem begin in a "physical" image or in the "physical" world? We must remember that Thomas was twenty years old when he wrote this passage and, by all accounts, sensitive about his lack of academic training. And yet the "moving column" of words he describes does, however ambiguously, capture something of our experience of his early verse. The point is that Thomas's "explanations," here and throughout his prose writings, are really alternative metaphors for the thing explained. Practically nothing he writes has an ordinary or analytic "prose" value as explanation.

Perhaps the most famous explanation Thomas ever offered for his method of poetic creation is contained in a letter to Henry Treece. Treece (*Dylan Thomas: 'Dog Among the Fairies,'* 1949, p. 47) had criticized Thomas's poetry for its "diffuseness," its failure to move concentrically around a "central image" in a given poem. Thomas replied:

it is not my method to move concentrically round a central image . . . I make one image—though 'make' is not the word; I let, perhaps, an image be 'made' emotionally in me and then apply to it what intellectual and critical forces I possess—let it breed another, let that image contradict the first, make, of the third image bred out of the other two together, a fourth contradictory image, and let them all, within my imposed formal limits, conflict. Each image holds within it the seed of its own destruction, and my dialectical method, as I understand it, is a constant building up and breaking down of the images that come out of the central seed . . . Out of the inevitable conflict of images . . . I try to make that momentary peace which is a poem (Treece, 1949, pp. 47–48).

This complex and—for Thomas—rather analytical statement has attracted considerable comment from critics. Treece himself called it a "rationalization" of a process Thomas could only guess at, and asserted that "in actual fact, Thomas's poems seem to proceed by a simple associative mechanism." But in the first place, the method behind Thomas's poetry, whatever else it might be, is clearly not "simple"; in the second, the idea of association does not necessarily contradict the idea of "dialectical" creation of warring images, since opposites are closely associated even in strict Freudian "free association." Ralph Maud (*Entrances to Dylan Thomas' Poetry,* 1963, pp. 26–30) traces the "breeding and contradicting process" in "I see the boys of summer in their ruin" as a demonstration of the essential accuracy of Thomas's description. He finds a general opposition of negative images of sterility and decay to positive images of generation throughout the poem. The "momentary peace," the "reconciliation is in the unifying concept shared by all the images." Similarly in an important early essay, Marshall W. Stearns (Tedlock, *Dylan Thomas: The Legend and the Poet,* 1960, pp. 124–31) traces the "dialectical" progression of images through "Light breaks where no sun shines," justifying Thomas's statement through his explication.

Some other critics share Treece's cynicism, though with different reasons. Roland Mathias (1954, p. 37) sees Thomas as a "metaphysical" poet whose poetry is "philological," springing directly from words themselves. Citing the letter to Treece, he comments, "Apart from the fact that Dylan has been reading David Gascoyne little to the purpose emerges from this." William T. Moynihan (*The Craft and Art of Dylan Thomas*, 1966, pp. 100–4) interprets Thomas's statement so as to play down the element of conflicting images which, he claims, is no more prominent in Thomas's work than in that of many modern poets. More important, he feels, is the single "central seed" from which emerges a "mood," a "feeling," or an "idea" instead of a literal image. Where Treece had dismissed Thomas's comments because they seemed overly intellectual for someone he considered supremely unintellectual, Moynihan tends to stress the intellectual unity in Thomas's successful poems and consequently subordinates the element of conflict. Even where he finds an "imagistic potpourri" (p. 111), Moynihan believes that the "generative idea," if strong enough, can redeem the poem and lend the images their effectiveness. He takes issue with C. Day Lewis who, in *The Poetic Image* (1947, pp. 124–25), tries to demonstrate the process Thomas describes in "After the funeral." Lewis finds two groups of images, centered about the "real living Ann and the dead mythical Ann," with the poem turning upon "an opposition between the natural earthly woman and the religious object she has become." On the contrary, Moynihan (1966, p. 118) sees the thematic identification of water and life as the poem's mainspring, while the contradictions are general and incidental to the poem.

Other critics prefer simply to modify or elaborate upon Thomas's explanation. Richard Morton (1962, p. 155) sees two different sorts of warring images as central: one sort is archetypal, images with obvious or traditional associations for the reader, while the other sort is "artificial," images whose meanings are imposed by the poet. The poetry in general changes from a reliance on archetypal images to a preponderance of artificial ones. In the early poetry, Thomas allowed a set of unrelated images to conflict; later, he developed them in series, letting the image-sequence and the poem's argument reinforce one another; in the last poems, he comes close to consistent allegory, the only time when the warring images are really united. On the other hand Kent Thompson (1965, pp. 84–85) finds the real basis of the poems in another term Thomas invoked both in the "Enquiry" reply and in the letter to Treece, i.e., "narrative." "Narrative," he asserted (*QEOM*, p. 119), "is essential . . . There must be a progressive line, or theme, of movement in every poem. The more subjective a poem, the clearer the narrative line." To Treece (1949, p. 48) he stated, "I believe in the simple thread of action through a poem, but that is an intellectual thing aimed at lucidity through narrative." Thompson (1965, p. 82) admits the obvious difficulty in applying these statements, in that "the early poems often do not seem to be narrative poems at all." But they are: unconventional, sometimes fantastic, the narrative line is always present. Thompson admits that the narrative line is not often the poem's primary source; he cites E. F. McInery, a schoolboy friend of the poet, who recalls Thomas admitting that he sometimes "received" whole lines of whose meaning he was completely ignorant. But given a set of contradictory phrases or images, the poem's "donnée," "these images were assembled in a way which was to allow the reader to receive their contradictory qualities in a recognizable and logical structure, i.e., in a narrative."

Thompson here raises the perennial problem of poetic composition. A poem may have its genesis in an image, a phrase (meaningful or not), an idea, or even a disembodied rhythm. Thomas apparently was "inspired" in many of these ways at different times, despite his assertion about conflicting images. Daniel Jones (Brinnin, 1960, pp. 279–82) stresses Thomas's fascination with words and word games, and many critics have noted the importance of verbal association in the construction of his poems. Alastair Reid (Tedlock, *Dylan Thomas: The Legend and the Poet*, 1960, p. 54) recalls his statement that "when I experience anything, I experience it as a thing and a word at the same time, both equally amazing." In his so-called "Poetic Manifesto" (FitzGibbon, 1965, pp. 323–28), Thomas says, "I wanted to write poetry in the beginning because I had fallen in love with words . . . What the words stood for, symbolised, or meant, was of very secondary importance: what mattered was the *sound* of them . . ." Similarly, Brinnin (*Dylan Thomas in America*, 1955, p. 126), who observed Thomas at work late in his life, says that "He began almost every poem merely with some phrase he had carried about in his head. If this phrase was right . . . it would suggest another phrase." Yet immediately afterward, he speaks of a poem's genesis in "the emotional experience, the instant of vision or insight, the source of radiance, the minute focal point of impulse and impression" which is later developed through "poetic logic." It is unclear here whether the epiphanic "experience" is to be identified with the germinal "phrase," or whether both have the same reference.

And indeed there is some question whether a poem's genesis is of any real relevance to the finished poem, except from a theoretical standpoint. Ralph Maud (1963, p. 163) claims that Thomas's friend A. E. Trick told him that "I see the boys of summer" was inspired when the poet saw a group of middle-aged men in business clothes wading along the seashore. Clearly, little or nothing of this original image survives in the poem. Cecil Price (Tedlock, 1960, p. 22) states, correctly, that "much of his work . . . owes its inspiration to particular places and people," yet it is equally true that those particular places and people often have vanished from the finished poem. In the course of Thomas's innumerable drafts and revisions he might easily eliminate or alter the "donnée"—a process familiar to most poets. Similarly, important elements of a poem may be added by what appears to be accident, or by "mechanical" means. David Holbrook (W. Davies, *Dylan Thomas: New Critical Essays*, 1972, pp. 182–94; cf. Holbrook, *Dylan Thomas: The Code of Night*, 1972) has attempted to demonstrate that important revisions in "Poem on his birthday" were "inspired" by a search through Roget's *Thesaurus*. While Holbrook seems to feel that this fact, if true, prejudices Thomas's "bardic" role, others might find nothing unusual in the process. As was pointed out in chapter 5, in the context of surrealism, Thomas was capable of utilizing more or less "random" elements in his work as well. Late in his life, when the element of landscape had become more obtrusive in his poetry, Thomas admitted to Brewster Ghiselin (Tedlock, 1960, p. 65) that the progress of a poem might be influenced by what he was looking at during the writing: "Yes, if I see a bird, I put it in whether it belongs or not." As for a poem's impetus, "Twenty years ago I would have said 'inspiration.' It's hard work. But sometimes the mood is enough . . . You can't always follow your original plan."

It seems that the most Thomas is willing to do, in speaking about the genesis and execution of his work, is to hint at attitudes and areas of concern; one receives the impression that he not so much would not as *could* not describe his working method in easily accessible terms. In this, of course, he is far from unique. His wife Caitlin once asked him how to write poetry (Thomas, *Leftover Life to Kill*, 1957, p. 69): "I only wanted the rules, like a piece of music, to follow, but he said that there weren't any, you made up your own rules; and it either was or wasn't a poem." Apparently Thomas had no idea at all what made a poem "work," in analytical terms: either it did or it didn't. In a broadcast discussion with James Stephens (Thomas, 1954, pp. 23–26; partly reprinted in *QEOM*, pp. 121–22) he defines poetry as "memorable words-in-cadence which move and excite me emotionally," and specifies that it always is improved by reading aloud; but, apart from A. E. Housman's hair-prickling test, he seems to have little notion of how one determines that a poem is good.

Nor is this an unreasonable or ignorant position—witness Housman himself, certainly an erudite writer. It is easy to forget that most critical writing about Thomas, including that which focuses on his concept of poetry, is necessarily biased by the very fact that it *is* criticism. A critic, such as Moynihan, is always tempted to stress the rational or the explicable thematic elements in the poet's work, and then, working backwards, to assume that those elements were also of prime importance to the poet. At least for much of Thomas's work, this is probably a misleading attitude. Critics, by and large, explicate, and thus tend to overvalue the explicable. Further, it is evident that much in Thomas *demands* explication, and rewards it as well. Much of the early work is perilously close to cypher: "I like difficulties," said Thomas in a *Sunday Referee* interview in 1934 (Maud, *Dylan Thomas in Print*, 1970, p. 98), "just as I like things that are difficult to write and difficult to understand." But at the same time, this difficulty need not be a disguised statement: "no poet ever understood everything he wrote himself." Eventually, in Thomas's mind, the heart of poetry always reduced to "the magic beyond definition" (Thomas, 1954, p. 25). And "the magic in a poem is always accidental. No poet would labour intensively upon the intricate craft of poetry unless he hoped that, suddenly, the accident of magic would occur."

Of course, all of this assumes that Thomas's idea of poetry did not change radically over the years. While this is probably true, his *emphasis* did change markedly. Most obvious is the trend toward clarity, implying a change in the poet's attitude toward the importance of his statement or narrative. One must never deliberately confuse the reader, he told Ghiselin in 1953 (Tedlock, 1960, pp. 61–62).

It is impossible for me to be too clear. I am trying for more clarity now. At first I thought it enough to leave an impression of sound and feeling and let the meaning seep in later, but since I've been giving these broadcasts and reading other men's poetry as well as my own, I find it better to have more meaning at first reading.

Thomas describes the empirical situation accurately enough when he speaks of the later poetry having "more meaning at first reading." But in the same conversation, he asserts that his style has not really changed, in that he is "still after the same things."

It is just this problem, the dilemma of continuity and development, that plagues most critics whose orientation is thematic. If Thomas is "saying" the same things in the later poems as in the earlier, then it would seem that he could have said them more simply in the beginning; and occasionally Thomas does admit that, in places, the earlier work is needlessly obscure and ornate. On the other hand, critics sympathetic to the early work assert that the poet is attempting to put into language a vision which transcends language's ordinary resources. Further, the "domain" of the later poetry's vision seems quite different from the earlier; some critics, indeed, feel that the later work is a rhetorical and somewhat inauthentically simplified embodiment of the poetic vision. But those problems, it should be stressed again, are paramount only from a thematic perspective. When Thomas asserts that there has been no fundamental change in his work, he may be implying that the question of obscurity versus clarity is not of fundamental concern to him, since the "heart" of the poetry lies elsewhere. In speaking of "vision" rather than "meaning" we can play down the thematic orientation or perhaps confuse it, but we do not abandon it. Perhaps it would be best to return to the beginnings of Thomas's conception of poetry and look more closely at how he came to write the sort of poems he did.

This is Ralph Maud's procedure in his introduction to Thomas's *Notebooks* (1968). These notebooks, which span the period from Thomas's clearly juvenile productions on through poems which appear essentially unaltered in *18 Poems* and *Twenty-five Poems*, provide clues to the development of techniques and themes the poet later exploited. Maud's central thesis (p. 10) is that his edition "confounds previous assumptions about the poet's later development by showing . . . how much of the poetry printed up to his twenty-sixth year was really a reworking of earlier poems." The clear implication is that Thomas arrived at his essential idea of poetry relatively early in his career—according to Maud, around 1933. The notebooks, then, show phases through which he passed en route to his characteristic mature style.

Maud quotes Thomas's coeditor of the *Swansea Grammar School Magazine* to the effect that Thomas was known to be writing two different sorts of poems in his youth—the "delightful light verse" which he published in the school magazine and a more private and experimental sort of poetry which he kept in his notebooks. Maud suggests (p. 12) that a group of earlier notebooks, now lost, probably contained a great deal of derivative verse; the 1930 notebook, like the 1930–32 notebook, contains the heading "Mainly Free Verse Poems," marking a new and experimental departure. As Maud points out, this new style also owed much to Richard Aldington and Sacheverell Sitwell in its reliance on the "obscure, unglossed image." Further, Thomas's later revisions of early poems which were to form part of his major work usually involve the "imagification" of what had been exposition in the earlier version. Clearly Maud here has textual evidence for his validation of Thomas's statement to Treece.

A second major stage in the early development Maud finds in the middle of the 1930–32 notebook, around mid-1931. Some of these poems look like automatic writing; they introduce a new morbidity and an obsession with corruption and vileness. Maud relates this new turning to the fact that Thomas, at nineteen, had just entered the "outside world" and had begun work as a reporter. There follows a seven-month gap in the notebooks; the last two, from early 1933 to early 1934, have a steady development toward his own style and subject matter. Attitudes of disgust and a phase of satirical world-weariness are gradually outgrown in the movement toward an inner vision, an "antithetical" development of the poem, and the realization of the continuing process of death and germination of which his own body is microcosm. Finally, Maud finds (p. 24) in a July 1933 poem, an early version of "Find meat on bones," the first complete expression of Thomas's mystical vision. He quotes a letter to Trevor Hughes written in January 1934 (*Selected Letters of Dylan Thomas*, pp. 86–92) in which Thomas dismisses "public" poetry and asserts,

I become a greater introvert day by day, though day by day again, I am conscious of more external wonders in the world. It is my aim as an artist . . . to bring the wonders into myself, to prove beyond doubt to myself that the flesh that covers me is the flesh that covers the sun, that the blood in my lungs is the blood that goes up and down in a tree. It is the simplicity of religion.

Here is the Thomas of *18P* and *25P*, as clearly as in the letter to Glyn Jones of March 1934 (*SL*, pp. 95–98), where he describes his own symbolism as derived from "the cosmic significance of the human anatomy."

Maud expands on the implications of his study of the notebooks in his *Entrances to Dylan Thomas's Poetry* (1963), particularly in the appended "Chronology of Composition." Here he makes the point (p. 22) that about half of the poems in *25P* and *The Map of Love* were actually begun between 1932 and 1934, relatively early in his youthful writing, and these are just the poems which are usually cited as indicating a trend toward clarity in mid-career. In general, he argues, the simpler poems of the first three books tend to be those Thomas had written earlier and revised for later publication. He suggests (p. 147) that the actual trend toward clarity, when it occurred, probably resulted from Thomas's revisions of relatively

minor poems, like "The spire cranes," and led to a real change in
approach in "major and unobscure" poems such as "Twenty-four
years," written in 1938. Thus the general trend of his writing was
from relatively clear "juvenile" poems to increasing obscurity in the
mid-thirties, and then to a new conscious clarity beginning in the
late thirties.

A great wealth of Thomas's rather ambiguous statements about
his (and others') poetry is in *SL*. His attitudes are much too complex
and variable to summarize briefly. Further, Thomas's emphasis and
area of interest in each letter tends to vary with the recipient, an
example of the personal traits which allowed him to appear in different ways to different people. Thus he stresses sincerity and the
expressive aspects of poetry when writing to Trevor Hughes, implying that poetry can be a means of therapeutic self-discovery,
while he confines himself almost exclusively to technique when
writing to Vernon Watkins, discussing "pure" phrases and lines
with a writer whose ear is as exacting as his own. When writing to
Pamela Hansford Johnson, he naturally enough emphasizes the
personal element in his work, its reflection of his own moods and
situations.

William Moynihan's *The Craft and Art of Dylan Thomas*
(1966) is the first major study to incorporate a thorough knowledge
of Thomas's notebooks and correspondence; unfortunately, for
copyright reasons, Moynihan was forced to resort to paraphrase
of these sources. The entire first half of the study, expanding upon
Moynihan's earlier articles (1959; 1964), deals with the poet's approach and techniques. He cites Thomas's various characterizations
of his "craft or sullen art"; and gleans from the early correspondence
a few key terms which recur in his references to poetry (pp. 47–
48): *freshness, intensity, concentration,* and *magic.*

Thomas's poems, he felt, would be 'fresh' if they contained frequent
and actual accounts of physical life . . . For Thomas's mind, in fact,
freshness and truth were synonymous . . . Thomas stressed that all
ideas and actions begin in the body. As a result, he insisted, the best
way to render a thought or action, however abstract, was to express it
in as physical a way as possible . . . He saw it as his particular task to
find and express all the equations between the body and world, between body and idea.

Moynihan follows Tindall's lead in stressing the importance of
the Word in Thomas's ideas about life and poetry. One aspect of
poetic "freshness" is of course revitalizing language, but this is not
merely a matter of technique for Thomas (pp. 54–55): "One of

the most interesting creations in his poetry is, in fact, that of a world which is entirely verbal and entirely capable of replacing the ordinary material world." Words are tangible to Thomas, things to be "hewn" and "shaped," which gives them a peculiar autonomy. Further, following the evangelical gospel, Thomas identifies the vivifying Word with light; light equals life equals language. Yet language (particularly obscure or idiosyncratic language, like Thomas's own) can be a restriction and a barrier; man is sometimes imprisoned in his "tower of words." The poet (p. 57) is the man who abolishes the distinction between word and reality and so becomes prophetic and Christlike.

Moynihan's argument here is related to standard modernist doctrine; much the same can be said of Joyce or of Mallarmé. But Thomas seems less at home in this autotelic word world than does, say, the later Joyce. To turn Thomas into what used to be called a "pure" poet, whose language turns endlessly upon itself, seems to deny the physical, experiential basis of most of the poems. Certainly words had a definite, even a transcendent "reality" for Thomas, but few critics indeed would say that they *were* reality for him. Here, as throughout the book, there is a curious unsubstantiality to Moynihan's arguments. Many of his insights are valuable, but it is difficult for the reader to fuse them into a coherent view of the poet. After extensive discussion, Moynihan leaves us unsure of whether the poetry "begins" in a concept, an experience of the narrative sort, a feeling, or a word. Probably much of this confusion, though, reflects the poetry's own ambiguities and alternatives; in some poems the world does seem word, in others sensation, in others event or idea. Even the early poetry is more various than it initially appears.

Moynihan and Maud have only scratched the surface of the notebooks, which are among the most interesting evidence we have of the early development of a major poet. Aside from showing early, in-process versions most of the poems from *18P* and *25P*, and even a few from *Deaths and Entrances*, they also enable us to see Thomas's mind at work in the revision process, much as do the later worksheets. Even Maud's interpretation of Thomas's early development and his dating of the individual poems is not final. Other critics might put less emphasis on the early years, during which so many of the poems originated, and stress the considerable differences between the final, published version of poems in *25P* and their first drafts. Finally, as FitzGibbon (*The Life of Dylan Thomas*, 1965, p. 247) points out, Thomas's decision to sell the notebooks in the spring of 1941 can only be seen as crucial; no critic has exhaustively discussed the implications of this abandonment of the poet's reservoir of inspiration at the age of twenty-six. What he feared, Thomas claimed, was not a "cessation or drying up," but "an ingrowing, the impulse growing like a toenail into the artifice" (*Letters to Vernon Watkins*, p. 27). Surely his sale of the notebooks was an effort to avoid this fate, a premeditated fresh start.

Meanwhile *SL* and the criticism of Thomas's work, reprinted in Walford Davies's *Dylan Thomas: Early Prose Writings* (1971) invites reinterpretation of the poet's general stance and of individual poems as well. Nearly all of the general studies of Thomas and his work were written before this material became easily available. Even if Thomas's opinions hold relatively few surprises, the early letters particularly permit the critic a kind of scrupulous study of the poet's changing orientation which we find only in the most recently published essays.

Obscurity and Ambiguity

Even within the context of modern poetry, including the work of Eliot and Pound, the first thing to strike most readers of Thomas's poems was their obscurity—what sympathetic critics call their "difficulty" or "complexity." The distinction in terms is important, and often overlooked: to call a poem "difficult" implies a possible resolution, whereas obscurity may be permanent, whether willed or unconscious. Technically, bad poetry is never difficult, merely impenetrable. Until fairly recently, few of Thomas's critics could discuss this problem objectively. His early defenders tended to speak of his work's emotional power and evocativeness, avoiding any discussion of the paraphrasable "meaning" of particular poems. For them, the poem was an irreducible whole, and talk about its meaning violated the integrity of the poem's incommunicable experience. Similarly his attackers usually dismissed his work as totally incomprehensible rant, at best citing several lines, out of context, as evidence. Little dialogue was possible between the two camps. John Press, (*The Chequer'd Shade*, 1958, pp. 1–2) tells the story of the presentation of an award to John Betjeman in 1955. Lord Samuels, who made the presentation, took the opportunity to denounce poetic obscurity, reading several lines from "A grief ago" in a mocking tone. Stephen Spender walked out.

In retrospect, this was an untenable situation. Henry Treece, in one chapter of his early study (1949, pp. 85–94), discusses Thomas as "straight poet," in reference to poems like "The hand that signed the paper," "Twenty-four years," and "The Hunchback in the

Park" which at least in the modern context are neither obscure nor difficult. Treece mentions the fact that such poems become increasingly frequent in the later work but were present from the beginning; they tend to occur when the poet is discussing other problems than his own. Treece, of course, saw Thomas's more obscure work as the spearhead of a new poetic movement, and is inclined to discount the simpler work: "Naturally, no one who values rightly Dylan Thomas's main contribution to the poetry of his time will call these poems great," he asserts rather apodictically. But whatever Treece's attitude, there were many who valued Thomas chiefly for these commonly anthologized pieces, and read the remainder of his work on faith. His less responsible detractors, meanwhile, were annoyed that the man they had regarded as a crypto-surrealist could produce clear, controlled, and undeniably admirable verse. Others, like Day Lewis, revised their evaluations.

The first major dialogue on Thomas's obscurity, ironically enough, was between his admirer Edith Sitwell and Thomas himself (reprinted as Appendix I in Treece, 1949). Sitwell, who wished to acclaim the appearance of *25P* in the Sunday *Times*, ventured a loose explication of parts of "A grief ago" and "Altarwise by owl-light." Thomas replied that her reading of the latter poem's first two lines, as an evocation of the "sensation-loving, horror-loving craze of modern life," ignores what he calls "the literal meaning," that "a world-devouring ghost creature bit out the horror of tomorrow from a gentleman's loins." He describes the poem as "a particular incident in a particular adventure" rather than a general impression of life. This interchange has fascinated later commentators, chiefly because it implies that Thomas did have a particular "literal" meaning in mind even for his most obscure lines. The idea has galvanized hosts of explicators. Only recently have the more subtle aspects of the interchange drawn attention: what does Thomas mean by "literal meaning," and what does he mean by "a particular incident?"

Keeping such questions in abeyance for the moment, let us move to the next famous dialogue on a poem by Thomas. Robert Graves in a public lecture (Brinnin, 1960, pp. 164–65) offered a prize of one pound to anyone who could satisfactorily explicate the first five lines of "If my head hurt a hair's foot." The challenge was part of an attack Graves mounted against modern poetic "idols." Thomas, he claimed, "was drunk with melody, and what the words were he cared not." His point is not that the poems are uncontrolled; on the contrary, "the poems show every sign of an alert and sober intelligence." Unfortunately, in Graves's view, the intelligence was never applied to a poem's narrative or argument, which usually emerged as "nonsense" or double-talk. A Mr. M. J. C. Hodgart of Cambridge soon proposed what is now the accepted "explanation" of the poem, that it is a dialogue between unborn child and mother, turning upon the pain and necessity of childbirth (Moynihan, 1966, p. 72). Graves, needless to say, was not satisfied, and put forth specific objections to Hodgart's comments, some of which have been countered by later explicators, but some of which seem mere nitpicking to Thomas's interpreters. Again, the argument opens a perspective onto Thomas's whole approach. In the terms Graves sets forth, in which a poem must "make prose sense as well as poetic sense on one or more levels," the poem may well fail—though not necessarily nor obviously. But even if it does fail in this way, many modern critics would argue, it does so because it is attempting (and succeeding in) a kind of "narrative" which is more complex than that of earlier poetry. Speakers, situations, and tenses may change without warning, while it is often difficult to tell what is metaphor and what is "literal" event, in Thomas's special sense. "Poetic license" takes on a new dimension in his poetry, and there are readers who reject the rules by which he plays the game.

The argument over Thomas actually serves as focus for a larger argument over poetic clarity which has continued through the present century. Pound's and Eliot's erudite allusiveness, Yeats's references to his private occult symbology, Stevens's and Empson's intellectual difficulty all are involved. The first problem is to establish the nature of Thomas's obscurity. The easiest and most popular explanation among the poet's early critics is that proposed by Stephen Spender (1952, pp. 781), among many others: Spender sees Thomas as an alternative to the "classicism" of Auden and Eliot, both of whom saw poetry as the "intensely imagined portrayal of ideas." In contrast, Thomas chooses words not for their classical precision, but for their "feel." "He suppresses the intellectual links between a chain of images because they are non-sensuous," says Spender. While it is clear from his other comments that Spender is much in favor of Thomas's writing, at this level of generality the same assessment could be intended either positively or negatively. A critic who is fairly representative of the argument against Thomas is Julian Symons (1940, pp. 61–71). Symons attempts to distinguish between two "levels" of obscurity common in modern poetry, that which is caused by difficult thought being represented in "relevantly obscure language" and that caused by a simple thought being expressed in language whose obscurity is irrelevant to the thought expressed. Among poets whose matter and manner are both obscure, Symons feels, one could point to Donne as a poet whose language is relevant to the difficulty of the thought, Meredith as a poet whose language is not. Swinburne, on the other hand, disguises a rather simple subject matter with an obscure manner. Thomas, he feels, falls into Swinburne's category.

This is a weighty theoretical framework for a rather simple attack on Thomas. The problem with a poem like "Altarwise by owl-light," he feels, is that it has "too many meanings," or too many *possible* meanings: such poems are "rhetorical intellectual fakes of the highest class" (Treece, 1949, in rebuttal addresses the question, "Is Dylan a Fake?"). Other poems, like "Why east wind chills," in Symon's view have "no story, no continuity," and are "not about very much"; the obscurity of such poems is purely one of manner and is "*imposed* from *outside*," half-consciously, "to conceal real, simple subjects." Although he admits Thomas's enormous technical skill, he concludes, "what is said in Mr. Thomas's poems is that the seasons change; that we decrease in vigor as we grow older; that life has no obvious meaning; that love dies. They mean too little."

Perhaps this is true, but as Thomas's defenders, beginning with Treece (1949, p. 133), have pointed out in reply, poets such as Shakespeare and Keats seldom "mean" more than this when reduced to prose generalities. Marshall Stearns (Tedlock, 1960, p. 187) calls Symons's procedure one which "paraphrases the poem and then criticises the paraphrase" (cf. Berryman, 1951, p. 256) while David Aivaz (Tedlock, 1960, p. 187) accuses Symons of the "opposite error" to that of Edith Sitwell, who asks, "if you heard a tree speak to you in its own language, its own voice, would not that, too, appear strange to you?" Sitwell, dismissing the conceptual dimension, and Symons, subordinating all else to it, are equally far removed from the mainstream of Thomas criticism.

John Press in his book on obscurity in modern poetry touches on the problem (1958). He notes that Shelley, Keats, Wordsworth, and Tennyson were all accused of obscurity by their early readers, and alludes to C. S. Lewis's contention that the obscurity of modern verse is different in kind from this. Press's main attempt is to distinguish among differing sorts of modern obscurity: for example, he notes that Auden's syntax is much trickier than Thomas's, but in the latter poet "the profusion of heady images blurs the clarity and the coherence of the poetic argument" (p. 170). (Interestingly, William Carlos Williams [1954, p. 327] asserts the opposite: "the clarity of his thought is not obscured by his images, but rather emphasized.") Press apparently gives tacit consent to Thomas's description of his image-breeding process, noting only that a "logic of images" is harder to achieve than the argumentative logic of a poet like Auden. Durrell (*A Key to Modern British Poetry*, 1952, p. 198) makes essentially the same distinction in a comparison with Empson: Empson's obscurity is only apparent, a product of "syntax working overtime," whereas Thomas's obscurity is—in some sense—real.

Modern critics thus are faced with a choice in attempting to explain a poem by Thomas. They can choose to treat it as difficult in the classical sense, and thus explicable through a process of tracking down allusions, unravelling syntax, and expounding upon Empsonian ambiguities, or they can approach it as a new *kind* of poem, amenable only to a kind of analysis based upon Thomas's own conception of poetry. In practice, of course, most explications combine these two methodologies in an informal compromise; but that does not negate the distinction. Probably the "purest" form of standard analysis is that of Empson himself (1947). A. J. Smith (1962, p. 68) has pointed out the irony in this situation: Thomas, who is so often held up as the major figure in an anti-Empsonian, anti-intellectual strain of modern poets, finds his work susceptible to a characteristically brilliant analysis by Empson. A variant of the standard approach would be Olson's famous analysis of the sonnets (*The Poetry of Dylan Thomas*, 1954), which relies upon identifying what Olson claims is a semi-private symbology based upon the constellations. The implications of Olson's analysis are discussed thoroughly by Beardsley and Hynes (1960) and in chapter 4 above.

The second approach, a sort of "explication" which deemphasizes theme while still paying close attention to the internal workings of the poem itself, was probably initiated by David Aivaz's seminal essay in the Autumn 1950 *Kenyon Review* (Tedlock, 1960, pp. 186–210). Aivaz pointed out that most of the early poems are both a celebration and an embodiment of "Process"—the process of decay and germination which continues its endless round within and without the poet's body. Since Thomas ignores the usual subject-object, self-world oppositions of Western philosophy, his poems are not really amenable to academic dissection and cannot be reduced to paraphrase without grave injury. John Bayley—and, in less sophisticated fashion, Treece—are major apologists for this approach, while phenomenological discussions (Miller, 1965; Dodsworth in W. Davies, 1972) have strong affinities with it. Jacob Korg (*Dylan Thomas*, 1965) articulates another variant of the antianalytical approach, with his thesis that Thomas's early poems conform to Cassirer's description of primitive thought process. In general, Moynihan more closely resembles the former, Empsonian approach; Maud, with his deeper immersion in the process of the poem itself, is closer to the latter. The reader who is primarily interested in the problem of Thomas's obscurity should, of course, consult the "Index of Explications" below, with an eye to the explicators' tacit assumptions about what sort of a poem he is tackling.

This preliminary discussion of critical approaches still leaves unanswered our earlier question: why Thomas chose to write obscurely—if, indeed, he had a choice. Thomas's claim that he liked difficulties may be sufficient for readers who enjoy the ludic aspects of literature, but readers who become annoyed when a poem resembles a puzzle will demand a more substantial justification for wrestling with its difficulties. A. J. Smith (1962, pp. 73–74), writing in the Empsonian tradition, calls Thomas's ambiguity a

calculated indirection, obtained by the omission of almost all clues to the actual drift; by the clotting of fairly simple notions by odd but dynamic images; by a conscious confusing of syntax, to give an impression of strangeness and pregnancy.

This "atmospheric" explanation is, of course, only one aspect of the wealth of justifications for difficulty evolved by Empson and the American New Critics; the problem is that most of these critical apologia for ambiguity, irony, paradox, and the other rhetorical mechanisms of the modern poem hang upon the assumption that a peculiarly complex sort of statement is being made, whereas in Thomas this does not necessarily seem to be the case. Indeed, as Martin Dodsworth has recognized (W. Davies, 1972, p. 108), the effect of an early Thomas poem, once it has been digested, is of "a perversely obscure redundancy of expression" through frequent appositions, echoes, and repetitions, rather than a fecund complexity of the sort found in Stevens or Empson.

Olson (1954) studies the problem at some length in a characteristically neo–Aristotelian search for categories and justifications. Since he is assuming that the poems with which he deals are both difficult and explicable, he speaks in terms of "complexity." He finds three varieties (p. 37): complexity of argument and statement, of emotional process, and of subconscious process (these latter two being somewhat difficult to separate). These complexities crop up, often simultaneously, because Thomas's poems deal with internal moral processes, frequently in pseudo-dramatic form. Ambiguities abound, but the most sweeping (p. 45) is what Olson terms "circumstantial ambiguity"; although most of the poems seem to be narratives of a sort, it is very hard to tell who does what, where. Thomas's avoidance of titles in the majority of his poems, of course, fosters this ambiguity. Although he admits that the circumstantial ambiguity is sometimes just silly, Olson stresses that it is a *device*, essentially (p. 49) a device to intensify our feelings as the poem unfolds: "emotions are particularly heightened by suspense and the unexpected."

Dodsworth (W. Davies, 1972, p. 108) criticizes Olson's justification, pointing out that the obscurity often drives us not toward a cathartic illumination but into incomprehension; many readers simply fail to feel growing suspense as they read a given poem. Although Dodsworth does not make this point, it seems clear that Olson's concept of suspense is linked to his assumption that (in the sonnets at least) there is a single major "key" which provides the illumination and consequent release of tension. A similar though less schematic assumption is made by W. E. Yeomans (1966, p. 104), who quotes Thomas's statement that his obscurity is caused by a symbolism derived from the cosmic significance of the human anatomy (*SL*, p. 97) and attempts to apply it literally to several poems. The list could be expanded indefinitely to include all interpreters who rely on a single insight or key. Freudian and Jungian analysts, of course, have the advantage of being able to identify complex symbologies which need not be consciously manipulated by the poet, while they can justify his obscurity by reference to repression and other avoidance mechanisms. Most psychologically oriented critics find Thomas's obscurity a psychological necessity for him, which avoids the esthetic problem.

The argument of critics in the tradition of Aivaz and Bayley has a psychological dimension as well, but relates more directly to the esthetic problem. Basically, their assertion is that the "vision" or "world" which Thomas's poems attempt to articulate is one which ordinary language and normal modes of expression cannot convey. The poetry does not describe, it *embodies*. Korg (1965, pp. 26–53), for example, discusses the "rhetoric of mysticism" in Thomas's verse. Thomas's innovative language, he claims, is intended to jar the reader out of his everyday understanding of words, in a radical way: "his rhetorical innovations observe neither limits nor consistency." Similarly, "rational analysis cannot satisfactorily explain Thomas's images." Since the poet's "mystical vision" is one in which opposites fuse, the body and the world are conjoined, and words and things fuse together, we will look in vain for the distinctions and discriminations of more intellectual poetry. The rhetoric adapts to the vision, the vision shapes the rhetoric.

While Korg does attempt some analysis, identifying recurrent images and so forth, most of his book attempts to describe Thomas's world "from the inside" as it were. In this respect, his approach is somewhat self-limiting. Similarly, Bayley (*The Romantic Survival*, 1957, p. 217), in a radical variant of the approach, finds nothing to be explained in Thomas: "there is no gap—no intellectually sensible gap that is—between our grasping of the words and our deduction of what they are supposed to stand for." "Meaning," in Thomas, is by definition "a concealed significance." Later, Bayley (W. Davies, 1972, pp. 56–72) elaborates a distinction between the more normal poems of Thomas, where an experience is described, and those more characteristic early ones which "embody" experience, wherein for the first time a modern poet was able to "make his poetry the feeling of his being."

This line of apologia for obscurity is difficult to attack. Thomas himself complained to Pamela Hansford Johnson that his words "are not the words that express what I want to express; they are the only words I can find that come near to expressing a half" (*SL*, p. 122). The main problem with critics who take this position is that they frequently fail to help us with the individual poem. Perhaps the critic who is most helpful in unravelling individual poems while still remaining within Thomas's own frame of reference is Ralph Maud. Maud has an uncanny ability to discuss poems both from the "outside" and the "inside," to give a perspective on the work without appearing to stand very far from it. His own explanation of Thomas's obscurity (1963, pp. 83–87), as a method of "distancing" the event from the poem and the poem's meaning from the reader, is convincing. "Distancing is achieved . . . by using syntax as though it were a lock-gate, allowing meaning to come slowly through regulated compartments." Note the echo of Thomas's own imagery in describing his composition. The "delay in completing the sense," he asserts, is "important in dealing with intimate things; it avoids the danger of flippancy." Thomas's subjects, which include masturbation, sexual union, and other easily mishandled topics, are insulated by his rhetorical strategies from superficial or false reactions on the part of the reader. Maud notes that though Thomas's syntax is confusing, it is nearly always grammatically correct. Thomas's special variety of metaphor, he continues (p. 87), also serves to "distance": the erotic is distanced through a variety of penetration metaphors, the religious through a nonsacramental context. Dodsworth (W. Davies, 1972, p. 110) comments that while Maud's explanation works for many poems, Thomas is often obscure whether the subject needs distancing or not.

Moynihan (1966, p. 69), more of an Empsonian analyst than Maud, suggests that Thomas's obscurity is the result of his habitual "imaginative leap" in progressing from one image or metaphor to the next. Moynihan feels his idea is akin to Maud's concept of distancing the intimate, but puts more emphasis on the poet's imagination, which he feels is in perpetual need of restraint, constantly threatening to render the poem unintelligible to others. Perhaps another factor is what Moynihan terms (p. 64) "enthusiasm," Thomas's trait of "projecting onto ordinary events great cosmic, terrestrial, spiritual, or physiological significance." Note that what Moynihan here seems to regard as a separable, perhaps even regrettable, tendency of the poet is in the view of a critic such as Korg an integral part of the poetry. Moynihan argues that Thomas's confusing verbal devices "also enabled him to sustain states of emotion in his reader by demanding attention and concentration;" Dodsworth (W. Davies, 1972, p. 109) reasonably questions whether such effort does indeed tend to sustain an emotion in the reader, and suggests two alternative justifications for the obscurity (p. 117): in the first place, it follows necessarily from Thomas's attempt to resolve the duality of mind and body along Blakean lines, and in the second, it serves "as a means of combatting the 'ratio' in English poetry in his own day." The urge to resolve traditional philosophical dualities (p. 132) "tends to break down the distinction between tenor and vehicle in the use of metaphoric language," while Thomas's distrust of pure intellect leads him to produce poetry not accessible to the intellect alone.

Narrative and Syntactic Devices

The immediate cause of the difficulty of many of Thomas's poems is his peculiar idea of narrative, coupled with his use of practically every verbal device known in the poetic art. Asked about his technique (FitzGibbon, 1965, p. 327), Thomas admitted to using "puns, portmanteau-words, paradox, allusion, paranomasia, paragram, catachresis, slang . . . ," to which Moynihan (1966, p. 78) adds "dialectal words, clichés, words based on hidden metaphors, common words with uncommon meanings, grammatical shifts, and wrenched syntax." Moynihan gives illustrations and expands upon each of these categories. The reader can discover them for himself with little trouble, and there is no need to recapitulate Moynihan's analysis here. But these devices do interact with the central "narrative" Thomas felt to be essential in a poem—sometimes, apparently, distracting the reader from it—and the implications of this deserve discussion. "Narrative," in Thomas's sense, does not characterize a *kind* of poem, which might be opposed to "lyric," since all of his verse is lyric, but merely the means by which the lyric statement is made. Thomas's verbal gymnastics are seen by some critics as interruptions or embellishments of the narrative line, by others as an integral part of it.

The immediate question is whether Thomas's devices do indeed "work" in the poems. Kenneth Rexroth (1957, p. 31), in an amazing comparison of the art of Thomas and that of the saxophonist Charlie Parker, claims that in the poet "the special syntactical effects of a Rimbaud or an Edith Sitwell—actually ornaments—become the main concern . . . Thomas's ellipses and ambiguities are ends in themselves." Rexroth apparently does not see this as a fault in Thomas; Donald Davie, who is more conservative, does. In his study of syntax in English poetry entitled *Articulate Energy* (1955, p. 126) he states that Thomas uses what he terms "pseudo-syntax"— a syntax which is formally correct, but wherein the verbs do not really drive the sentence forward in time. Thus, "what appears to be narrative . . . is in fact an endless series of copulas." Some critics accept Davie's analysis but fail to see why this "pseudo-syntax" should be, as he claims, "radically vicious." Yet if in fact the analysis is correct, it would seem to vitiate the idea of narrative and destroy Thomas's assertion that his poems may describe particular incidents in particular adventures. Certainly there is a sense in which a poem like "The force that through the green fuse drives the flower" seems to "go nowhere"—it ends with the same assertion with which it began. This is simply a more general description of the case Davie describes for individual sentences. Yet we do not feel that the poem really fails because of this lack of development. It would seem that Thomas's syntax is doing something other than, or in addition to, moving the sentence forward in time.

One aspect of the syntax—the "interruptive" or "distractive" aspect—has already been touched upon in the discussion of obscurity above. Many of Thomas's devices, such as repetition and redundancy, parallelisms and internal echoes, are intended to give the poem a "timelessness," a sense of incantation rather than exposition. In an early essay, Maud (1954, p. 411) noted that "the basic unit of Dylan Thomas's poetry is the short rhetorically coherent phrase," a unit which gradually lengthens to include several lines in poems following "A Refusal to Mourn." As the worksheets demonstrate, Thomas worked at these phrases almost as a sculptor might; or to shift the metaphor, he arranged them in mosaic fashion, with particular attention to the tonal "hues" of the unit in its context. It would appear that this approach to the poem, concentrating as it does on units shorter than the sentence, would tend to threaten both

syntactic coherence and the movement from sentence to sentence—
in short, conventionally "narrative" values. Yet, as Maud frequently
points out, Thomas usually makes his tortured syntax work for him.
The parenthetical statements, qualifications, appositives, and other
tactics which delay completion of the sentence sense function as
they do *because* of their position. Richard Ohmann (1966) has
shown the relationship between Thomas's vision of the world as
process and his syntax by analyzing a representative sentence, using
the formal techniques of generative grammar, while Margaret
Schlauch (*Modern English and American Poetry*, 1956, pp. 43, 56,
67) discusses Thomas's successful use of interruptions, inversions,
and so forth briefly but in the context of general poetic practice.

Meanwhile, Davie's attack has been answered by several critics,
notably A. D. S. Fowler and Ralph Maud. Fowler (1958, p. 83)
takes issue with Davie's unsupported assertion that the syntax of
Thomas's poetry "cannot mime, as it offers to do, a movement of
the mind." That is in fact just what it does, he suggests, and prof-
fers examples. Maud (1963, p. 26) describes Thomas's narrative
as a series of imaged actions which follow their own logic, basically
through association of ideas. He makes the point (pp. 47–48) that
Thomas's syntax actually offers little problem when we take him,
as he asks, "literally." The line Davie finds nonsensical, "Time tracks
the sound of shape on man and cloud," Maud reads as a real, if peculiar event: "Time (personified) tracks sound (like a sound track),
sound which is really the expression of shape or form." "The particular adventure in this line may not be very comfortable to con-
template," Maud admits, "but Davie will not have it as an event
at all."

This seems to me to be the crux of the problem of narrative in
Thomas. The "literal" events his poetry portrays are not events of
the sort we are used to confronting, and we blame this on his syntax. But then neither are the "events" of a medieval allegory. Maud
(p. 49) suggests two lines of approach to a poem by Thomas: first,
"each image is looked upon as isolated, having its own internal logic
and only superficial associations with adjacent imagery on the narrative level"—an allowance for the poet's "image-breeding" dialectic which respects the aspect of "literal event" in the line; and secondly, the full significance of the poem is found "in the literary
narrative plus the central concept inherent in the symbolic power of
the wording." I think that what Maud is somewhat awkwardly pro-
posing here is really two different sorts of "explication": one which
remains closely tied to Thomas's own terms of expression, and
thus may retain some degree of obscurity itself, and one which

generalizes or "translates" the poem's narrative into a more standard
sort of poetic statement. The former would lay bare what Kent
Thompson (1965, p. 83) calls the "fantastic" narrative of much of
the early poetry, as Tindall (1962) usually does; the latter leads
to a statement about the human condition, of the kind Moynihan
(1966) pursues.

Probably because they are the most keenly interested in the
"translation" of Thomas's narratives, Olson and Moynihan both
give alternative ways of looking at them. Olson (1954, pp. 43–44)
identifies a "pseudo-dramatic dialogue" in poems such as "I see the
boys of summer" (the boys versus their critics) and "Find meat
on bones" (father versus son); he finds a "pseudo-dramatic mono-
logue" in "Before I knocked" (where the poet's "mask" is Jesus).
He reserves the term "pseudo-narrative" for poems like the sonnets, "A Winter's Tale," and other late poems where the narrative
line is more explicit and there is more emphasis on "events." In
those, as in the former categories, the "characters" are masks for
differing aspects of the underlying lyric character. Using a less scrupulous terminology than Olson's, we might describe all of the above
as narratives of different kinds. Moynihan (1966, pp. 94–95) feels
that what Thomas calls "narrative" in the early work is not so much
a story as a "thread" or "leit motif." He finds two main "voices" in
the poems: that of the Poet in his avatars as singer, bard, prophet,
or Thomas himself; and that of Everyman, a sort of "concrete universal" who "shifts character and point of view as the poem demands."

One of the major elements that distract the reader from the
poem's narrative line—if we are to accept that designation—is the
metaphor, which Thomas employs frequently and often bafflingly.
Olson (1954, p. 56) identifies three kinds of confusing metaphor in
Thomas: the farfetched, the paradoxical, and the mixed. He finds
metaphors which seem self-contradictory because a crucial element
of the metaphor occurs later or earlier in the poem or sequence,
and metaphors which deceive the reader as to what is being compared to what. Thomas uses "composite metaphors" which are involved in a larger assumption he is making in the poem, often by
means of compound words; he also uses implied metaphors as well as
metaphors which look like literal statement, that is, part of the narrative. Perhaps the most important kind for the reader to recognize
is what Korg (1965, p. 39) calls the "submerged" metaphor, which
Thompson (1965, pp. 86–87) discusses more fully under the designation "half-metaphor." Here only one half of the metaphoric comparison is explicit, leaving the other half to the reader's inference.

Thompson's example is the phrase "this four-winded spinning," which refers to the earth with its four winds and four seasons spinning in time. A more complex example, really a "doubly-implied metaphor," would be "your calm and cuddled is a scythe of hairs," wherein a "child-like beloved" one is identified with a strength-stealing Delilah-figure. Thomas's adjectives further disrupt the line. The "transposed epithet," a species of paradox, is a particularly upsetting technique noted by many critics, where Thomas exchanges the expected modifiers of two substantives. Where we expect "spectacled eyes" and "enamelled claws" he speaks of "sharp enamelled eyes and spectacled claws." Similarly, as Moynihan (1966, p. 92) notes, Thomas enlists echoes of common phrases or twisted clichés to play off of our expectations: "boy of common thread," "common clay clothes," "you with a bad coin in your socket," or the famous "happy as the heart was long" from "Fern Hill." Although Thomas has been attacked for his use of the "refurbished cliché," which may appear to be a trivial verbal mannerism, Moynihan astutely defends his use of it. In fact, Moynihan's discussion of Thomas's multiple verbal ambiguities (pp. 77–92) is excellent throughout. Stanford (1964, p. 151) rather surprisingly defends Thomas's use of the "cliché turned" as a part of his "adaption of colloquialisms to a lyrical end and purpose." Whereas Eliot had interspersed colloquialisms in serious poetry, it was always by way of direct or indirect quotation; with Thomas, Stanford suggests, colloquial language was made a part of the essential lyric line. Stanford's point is questionable on at least two grounds: first, it seems likely that Auden and his group had already adapted colloquial language to the lyric and second, it is debatable whether Thomas's influence pointed in this direction. Nevertheless, when we examine contemporary verse in England and America we do typically find a large dose of colloquialisms, often subtly twisted in syntax or diction, within a lyrical context. Williams comes first to mind as an antecedent, but perhaps the greater "richness" of contemporary poetry does point to a delayed legacy from Thomas.

Thomas's tactics may be defended or attacked one by one, either as general practice or in the context of a single poem, but the basic question remains their effect *en masse*. Perverted colloquialisms and clichés, metaphors and half-metaphors, puns, compounds, neologisms, and archaisms all join with more strictly syntactic ploys—inversion, ambiguous reference, extended appositives, and parenthetical clauses—to produce Thomas's distinctive sort of sentence. Their cumulative effect is to distract us from the progressive movement we expect of a narrative. Davie implies that Thomas is playing a sort of trick on the reader, mimicking ordinary English syntax just far enough to let him believe he is going somewhere in the poem when in actuality he is standing still. This is a sophisticated version of the "empty rhetoric" accusation. In the most general terms, the reply of Thomas's defenders to this sort of criticism is that he is in fact not interested in "going somewhere" in the poem, or that his direction is at ninety degrees to our expectations. Because of the nature of his vision, Thomas must end where he began. It is the journey which matters, not the destination, and this is mirrored even on the syntactic level:

> In the final direction of the elementary town
> I advance for as long as forever is.

Poetic Technique: Diction and Imagery

The most basic narrative element is of course a poet's diction and associated imagery. Rather dubiously, Treece (1949, p. 41) argued that Thomas's originality does not lie in his other poetic techniques and forms, which he finds conventional, but in his vocabulary. Shapiro (Tedlock, 1960, pp. 273–74) agrees that Thomas's technique is conventional, yet recognizes that Thomas "captured the young poets" through "the personal idiom, the twists of language, the bending of the iron of English."

Even when we examine the texture of his language we fail to find anything original. But at the same time, we find something completely distinctive. It is hard to locate the distinctiveness of Thomas's idiom. There are a few tricks of word order, a way of using a sentence, a characteristic vocabulary . . . But no system, no poetic, no practice that adds up to anything you can hold on to.

Later research has tended to contradict Treece's and Shapiro's assertions about Thomas's lack of technical innovation, which was probably the result of their failure to appreciate the subtlety and systematization of his various partial rhymes and his syllabic line. But their attention to his diction has been seconded by contemporary critics. Indeed, this was the first aspect of his verse most readers noticed. Conrad Aiken (1944, p. 26) remarked that he had initiated a "New Euphuism" in poetry which, for decoration, favored words with English roots rather than Latin; Robert Lowell (1947, p. 494), while he paid tribute to Thomas's metrical technique, noted that his work was really characterized by a group of typical words

—*locks, keys, sun, grains, fire,* and *death.* He itemized Thomas's
faults: repetition and redundancy in its various forms, and "over-
loading," which might involve the insertion of words which disrupt
the context or of symbols unsupported by the context, or might be
the result of his omitting "numb" or "supporting" lines. All of these
criticisms, it should be noted, follow from Thomas's stress on diction over syntax and his avowed dislike for what he termed "weak"
lines (*LVW*, p. 29).

John Berryman (1951, p. 255), another American poet influenced by Thomas, agreed that the "unmistakable signature of Dylan
Thomas's poetry . . . , is certainly its diction." He gives a list of the
poet's favorite words and mentions his predilection for unusual
epithets, compounds, archaic, new, coined and colloquial words, as
well as the operations "halving" and "doubling." Thomas's use of
compound words has been thoroughly discussed by Treece and
others since, usually in connection with Hopkins's influence (see
chapter 6), but probably the first essay to deal at length with his
verbal inventions was that of Francis Scarfe (Tedlock, 1960).
Scarfe argues (pp. 97–98) that his "basic device," borrowed from
Joyce, is the invention of words. His fresh use of words in combi-
nation emphasizes for the reader the idea of poetry as a process of
discovery, and was necessitated by his attempt to put into language
"half-perceived, incoherent sensations and ideas." Scarfe finds compound words which involve puns and those which involve distor-
tion and suggestion ("minstrel angel" and "ship-racked gospel").
Thomas's use of "false epithet" may be expressive ("dead nui-
sance") or, Scarfe feels, merely annoyingly obscure, as in "colic
season" or "cadaverous gravel." Scarfe claims that the poet approaches real surrealism in his attributive phrases, such as "man of
leaves" or "tree of nettles," and sometimes in his "inaccurate use of
verbs," but "most of those verbal tricks are from time to time completely successful and justified."

Thomas's diction can be approached from numerous angles.
Probably Thomas used a given word for different reasons at different times. Sometimes a word may be used merely for its "sound
and exotic unfamiliarity" rather than its denotation—what Bayley
(1957, p. 193) calls a "stock romantic usage." Moynihan (1966, p.
122) says that most critics underrate the importance of sound for
Thomas; often, it takes precedence over sense. Thomas himself admits that some obscure words like "parhelion" in the early poems
were "thrown into the poem in a kind of adolescent showing-off"
(FitzGibbon, 1965, p. 326). Sometimes the auditory qualities of a
word predominate, sometimes its sensuous connotations, sometimes

(as in "six-gunned Gabriel") the context it suggests. Bayley has remarked that Thomas appears to show several different attitudes toward language even within a single poem. But probably the most interesting aspect of his diction is the tantalizing way in which certain "key words" keep popping up, words which seem to have a symbolic value of their own for Thomas. Brewster Ghiselin (1954, p. 248) has called for an investigation of Thomas's special use of words like "marrow" and "wax"; Roland Mathias (1954, p. 34) who notes that "death's feather" is used five times in the first sixty-four pages of *Collected Poems 1934–1952*, insists that this and other obsessively repeated words—*weather, shape, father, muscle, worm, screws, oils, forks, maggot*—must hold symbolic import. Applying this idea literally, Olson (1954) includes in "Appendix B" of his book a "Glossary" of terms from Thomas. Some of these entries, such as "Mnetha," are necessary identifications of allusions in themselves symbolic; others, such as "fork," fall into Mathias's category; still others, such as "Gentleman" (in the sonnets, the "sun" and "time"), identify elements of the constellation symbology Olson hypothesizes.

According to Korg (1965, p. 36), Thomas kept a personal "dictionary" of words with interesting multiple meanings, associations, or possibilities. Korg suggests that the presence among these of words with antithetical meanings shows Thomas's peculiar, almost childlike sense of language, and cites Freud's essay "The Antithetical Sense of Primal Words." Another conclusion that might be drawn is that Thomas was more interested in words for what they could *do* in a poem than for what they *meant*: words such as "fork," which function both as noun and as adjective, and have multiple meanings as both (including the archaic one of "groin"), heighten the difficulty of many lines but enrich their possibilities of meaning. More importantly, if this is true of much of Thomas's characteristic vocabulary, it would suggest that a hunt for fixed symbolic meanings will prove fruitless. Indeed, Olson himself admits that the meaning of a word like "fork" varies greatly from poem to poem, depending upon its context.

Maud, who has explored Thomas's use of "Obsolete and Dialect Words as Serious Puns" (1960), asserts with considerable authority (1963, p. 62) that Thomas's words and images "rarely have exactly the same meaning twice." Yet the idea of "key" words is certainly not irrelevant. In a sort of compromise (pp. 59–61) Maud suggests that there is, in the poems before 1939, a "process vocabulary" of words which characterize "process poems." Here he is adopting, with modifications, David Aivaz's idea that the core of the early work is a vision of the process of decay and germination within the poet's body and in the world about him, all presided over by time. Maud lists the words—*process, tides, eye, flesh, ghost, bone, blood, fork, bud, force, womb, vein, root, oil, wax, matter, skin, dry, damp,* and *weather(s)*—and gives the frequency with which they occur in *18P* and later books. He contends that a high frequency of such words in itself serves to identify a "process poem"—unlike Aivaz, he stresses that Thomas has other themes—and thus gives us a strong hint at its meaning. The particular words may vary in meaning from poem to poem, but their collective presence signals an area of meaning for the poem.

If individual words and their frequency of occurrence seem this important in the poetry, then obviously a rigorous statistical investigation should be useful. The first such study was Josephine Miles's pioneering survey *The Primary Language of Poetry in the 1940's* (1951), part of a series of statistical surveys of poetic vocabulary since the 1540s. Miles's procedure was to select twenty important poets of the decade and, choosing a recent volume from each, analyze the vocabulary of the first one thousand lines or so. While she displays the resultant data in a series of tables, her sensitive discussion of its implications and the groupings of poets she derives from the data have been most interesting to literary historians. Her first concern is to distinguish among poets on the basis of the balance of adjectives, nouns, and verbs, which leads her to detect four groupings: the older "major poets" (pp. 415–17)—Stevens, Eliot, Yeats, and Pound—show a moderate balance in qualification and predication, that is, write a relatively abstract sort of verse; Warren, Auden, Lowell, Millay, and Frost (p. 424), who write narrative or argumentative verse, represent a "predicative extreme"; Williams, Cummings, and H. D. (p. 439), apparently even more extremely predicative, are treated separately because of their radical alterations in line length and revision of the traditional language structure; and finally, the most "substantival poets" (p. 445) are Crane, Sitwell, Thomas, Jeffries, and Shapiro. These poets stress the powers of noun and adjective and characteristically invoke colors such as green and white; the sea, the sky, and many natural references appear, while their verbs are ones of living, loving, and seeming, rather than thinking, acting, and speaking. Miles characterizes this last, youngest group as "sensuous and receptive" and notes that, for the decade, they are the most typical of the whole current of English poetry in the luxury of their verse.

In a series of later tables, Miles investigates the "majority" and "minority" words of the group—those used ten or more times within one thousand lines by, respectively, ten poets or more and four poets or more. She concludes (p. 456) that Crane, Sitwell, Thomas, and (surprisingly) the Eliot of *Four Quartets*, her highly substantival group, write a ritualized, poised, quiet, and masterful verse which is less active, lively, or colloquial than that of the other poets she examines. Their work is dominated by the adjectives *old*, *new*, *green*, and *white*, and the nouns *day*, *night*, *light*, *time*, *love*, *air*, and *water*; verbs involve *coming*, *going*, *lying*, and *seeming*. There is relatively little use of the words *goodness*, *greatness*, *thought*, or *speech*; their lines are the longest, their cadence the richest, their vowels the roundest, and consonants the most liquid, while their sentences are most invocative, accumulative, and exclamatory. Most importantly from the point of view of literary history, she asserts that "toward this status most of the poetry in the decade seems in some degree to be moving."

Miles's later study *Style and Proportion: The Language of Prose and Poetry* (1967) more easily allows study of Thomas's individual characteristics. The tables of "first major use" credit Thomas with the words *boy* and *hold* (p. 87), while a tabulation of the diction of fifty major poets from the sixteenth century onward reveals some interesting peculiarities of his language. Thomas uses a group of major prepositions, particularly *on*, *of*, *from*, *by*, *in* and *to*, 94 times in the same representative sample of lines, a number exceeded only by Sitwell with 95 and rivalled by Swinburne with 93 (p. 91). Auden, for example, uses these 52 times. Yet Thomas's total number of connectives is average: the explanation is his radical poverty in relative conjunctions and prepositional conjunctives. Although Miles fails to make this point, Thomas, we might conclude, thinks in simple, broad relationships rather than complex ones. A reorganized list of major words (p. 150) shows that of the first 7,960 words of *Selected Writings*, Thomas uses 1,020 adjectives, favoring *black*, *dead*, *golden*, *green*, *red*, and *white*. Most common among his 2,300 nouns are *man*, *love*, *sea*, *time*, *blood*, *death*, *eye*, *hand*, *heart*, *sun*, and *wind*, followed by *bell*, *bird*, *bone*, *boy*, *child*, *day*, *face*, *grave*, *head*, *heaven*, *house*, *land*, *light*, *moon*, *mouth*, *night*, *sky*, *sleep*, *stone*, *summer*, *tongue*, *tower*, *tree*, *voice*, *water*, *weather*, *word*, and *world*. Of 790 verbs, most common is *make*, followed by *break*, *drive*, *fall*, *hold*, *lie*, and *turn*, all of which are kinesthetic. On casual examination it seems that he is rivalled only by Swinburne in the frequency with which he uses his favored nouns and in their number.

Miles's special methodology has undeniable advantages but, particularly for the study of a single poet, undeniable limitations. Our subjective experience of a poet's diction gives emphasis to words and phrases which he uses with some frequency (for example, "death's feather") but which we do not find in his contemporaries. Maud (1963, pp. 163–65) points out that the first one thousand lines of *Selected Writings* are simply not representative of Thomas's work as a whole, nor do they characterize any specific period. A complete count of *CP* necessitates rather drastic emendations: of the adjectives, *golden* and *red* drop out, while *long, black, old, last,* and *still* are added; of nouns, *bell, tower, word, land, month, voice, weather, boy,* and *face* drop out, while *wind, dark, ghost, fire, flesh, hill, bed, cloud, star,* and *wound* are added; of verbs, *drive* and *drop* disappear, but *sing, see, cry, hear, die,* and *come* become prominent. Maud points out that this places Thomas's vocabulary much more in line with that of his contemporaries. A tabulation volume-by-volume, which Maud includes, suggests something about Thomas's preoccupations at the time of each, but not enough. Maud concludes that such a study has very limited validity; "only when certain words are found to be repeated to the same effect in the same group of poems can a count begin to confirm one's judgment about the type and quality of the vocabulary." Neither Maud nor anyone else has paid much attention to the implications of Thomas's use of connectives, nor explored the philosophical implications of what can be learned about his syntax from such word counts and groupings.

Robert Williams's *Concordance to the Collected Poems* (1967) should make further studies in this area a good deal easier. So far, few critics have made use of the *Concordance,* but James Ayer (1968), who had access to it before publication, comes to some interesting conclusions. His main interest is in the contention of various critics, including Roy Campbell (1954) and A. T. Davies (1954) that Thomas's experience reading his poetry aloud for the BBC produced a noticeable change in style. He notes (p. 7) that after 1938 there is a sharp reduction in the use of possessives, "fused words," and compound words, none of which can be distinguished orally. But really, this is little more than a footnote to the obvious fact that Thomas's work after World War II becomes clearer, less "clotted" with word and image, and more obviously narrative.

One of the few essays which approach Thomas's use of language at a fundamental level in order to explore a particular poem is found in Winifred Nowottny's *The Language Poets Use* (1965; excerpted in Cox, *Dylan Thomas: A Collection of Critical Essays,* 1966). Nowottny's aim (p. 187) is "to show how the peculiarity of the language compels us to set about constructing a meaning for

it, and how it is that the poem contrives to direct us towards the
particular kind of meaning that must be apprehended in order to
make sense of the language of the poem." The poem she chooses to
examine is "There was a Saviour." Considerably more than an explication, her discussion bears upon the problem of Thomas's syntax
as well as his diction. Since it is embedded in a chapter entitled
"Symbolism and Obscurity," it is relevant to this problem as well.
Her argument is too complex to reproduce here, but she makes the
point (pp. 188–91) that the gradual shift in tense through the
poem, from past to a prophetic present, demonstrates that the poem
involves "continuous identities with an changing outlook," and that
the wide contrasts in diction all hang upon "the process expressed
by the changing pronouns ['I,' 'we,' 'you'] and tenses." The lines
beginning with the word "Now" each mark a "turning" in the
poem, a change of attitude within it. Like Korg, she argues that
Thomas's reference to the "literal" meaning of his lines really implies a sort of linguistic innocence; he uses language idiosyncratically,
as a child does. His diction, she notes (p. 219), is "polyvalent" because it is "bare." The relatively simple words are nonrestrictive as
to their possible areas of significance. A given word may be symbolic, allusive, or "direct," and only a study of the poem itself can
reveal which of these aspects is predominant. The work of Thomas
demonstrates in acute form a problem presented by poetic language
since Blake, that is, the reader's difficulty in distinguishing between
literal and figurative language. The very simplicity of his diction
exacerbates the problem.

Probably the most important point Nowottny makes about
Thomas's diction is the one hinted by Maud (1954, p. 416): "we
rarely find uncommon words; yet all the words seem tantalizingly
unfamiliar, pressed by the poet into strange image-combinations."
It is hard to decide how we are supposed to feel about "keyless
smiles," "safe unrest" and the other oxymoronic expressions. Irony
is hard to recognize. Nowottny starts with the fundamental patterns
of diction and syntax to discover what words are emotively associated or opposed, then moves outward—to Blake and Freud, in this
case—for further help in interpreting them. Essentially her procedure is like that of Maud (1963, pp. 17–40) reading "I see the
boys of summer." From either essay we learn how to identify words
which have symbolic import within the poem, ways of narrowing
their possible areas of meaning, and means of proceeding from this
to the poem's statement.

Words with special value in Thomas are nearly always images as
well, usually either pseudo-Freudian objects or basic elements of

nature, although particularly in the early poems there is an admix-
ture of the mechanical. Yet to talk about these words as "images"
almost assumes too much, for the early poetry is seldom clearly
pictorial, auditory, or tactile. It is sensual, but obliquely or ambiguously so. Early reviewers were inclined to indulge in unfortunate phrases reflecting their confused apprehension of the poems;
Thomas was once applauded for his "astonishing gift for evoking
images which follow one another with the colourful swiftness of a
Walt Disney Symphony" (Botterill, 1946, p. 93). He reminded reviewers of Sitwell's rapid barrage of images, if of any literary antecedent.

The problem in speaking about Thomas's imagery grows naturally from his sculptural approach to words, his varying attitudes
towards language, and his doctrine of "warring images." He continually juxtaposes words which we have never before seen linked
and cannot apprehend as a sensual unity—"green age," "a scythe of
hairs," "a serpent caul." Synesthesia runs rampant. Some of the
words we are expected to experience sensually, some for their associations, some for their sound. To read a poem by Thomas is to
be presented with a rapid series of intellectual, sensual, and emotional alternatives. Rushworth M. Kidder's distinction among "referential," "allusive," and "referential imagery" (1973; see chapter
4 herein) is enlightening in this regard. Maud (1954, p. 417) rather
optimistically crystallizes the dilemma:

The effort of the imagination involved in abstracting the concept
symbolized by the particular image or metaphor at the same time as
we try to grasp the image as a concrete representation of the concept
is perhaps the most rewarding experience in reading these poems.

Giorgio Melchiori (*The Tightrope Walkers*, 1956, pp. 219–29),
who discusses Thomas as a mannerist artist, insists that his use of
pictorial imagery is quite limited, except in the last poems. Color,
he feels, is generally emblematic; the inspiration, as with Joyce, is
fundamentally verbal rather than visual. Unlike Hopkins, Thomas
in his imagery appeals "not to what we see, but to what we know."
In this respect he is akin to Donne, as he is in his use of metaphors
taken from science or technology. Like Blake (p. 240), he is physical instead of pictorial. Comparisons are probably the best way of
demonstrating the peculiar quality of the imagery. Merely on the
basis of word counts, we might feel justified in calling Thomas a
"nature poet"; yet comparison of his work with that of Jeffers or
Frost or Lawrence shows the fundamental diffuseness and generality
of his references to nature. There are an abundance of leaves, trees,

and flowers, but a scarcity of elms, azaleas, or sycamores. If he is a nature poet, he is a thoroughly suburban one. By the same token, his frequent invocation of the body and viscera and his use of sexual themes and images should qualify him as an erotic poet; but, the BBC notwithstanding, few poets are less erotic than Thomas. Our senses are constantly involved, yet constantly thwarted; there is nothing for them to focus upon.

This lack of a sensual "narrative line" of course gives the early poems their characteristic quality of being either "clotted" or "packed," depending upon one's point of view. Davie (1955, p. 125) points out that in traditional poetry, syntax allows the poet to "space" his images; the moderns, particularly Pound and Eliot, substituted typographical breaks in order to keep the images suitably separate from one another. In Thomas, on the other hand, "the articulation and spacing of images is done by rhythm instead of syntax"; in his more successful poems the varying line lengths and stanza breaks provide additional "breathing space."

In the later work these problems all become less acute. Syntax performs more traditionally, and thus a clearer narrative emerges. Often, landscape becomes an organizing factor, lending a new visual emphasis and coherence to the imagery. Ackerman (1964, p. 61) suggests that "Wales, with its much-loved landscape and distinctive way of life, was the major factor in Thomas's movement towards clarity and control of emotion and image," and certainly in poems like "Fern Hill," "Over Sir John's hill," or "Poem on his birthday" the regular reference to a Welsh landscape provides the reader with a reassuring *point d'appui.* Moynihan (1966), in an attempt to catalogue the different sorts of image Thomas employs, notes the "Romantic pictorialism" of the later work, as opposed to the use of arbitrary associations, surrealist irrationality, violent juxtapositions for their own sake, "metaphysical" intellectual conjunctions, and purely verbal connections of the earlier imagery. The critical battle over "early Thomas" versus "late Thomas" rages over the field of imagery just as it does upon the more substantive field of statement.

John Bayley (1957, p. 213) has said that in Thomas's work, *seeing* and *being* are both perceived as a language: words become things and things become words in unending flux. Perhaps this terribly abstract formulation does point to the difficulties encountered in tackling the poet's syntax, diction, and imagery: our ordinary grammatical distinctions tend to lose their meaning when applied to a poetry perpetually in the process of inventing its own grammar. Again, this effect lies behind the effort of so many Welsh

critics to suggest that Thomas was really trying to approximate
Celtic modes of thought in a language unable to stand the strain.
Probably he was not, but equally probably he was pursuing a poetic
"logic" different from the logic of our language. The real question
about his work, Bayley suggests (p. 196),

arises from the fact that we still do not know whether language is capable of what he tried to do with it; or rather whether the consciousness of the receiver can adapt itself to such a variety of linguistic uses
and such a multiplicity of verbal stimuli.

"Probably," he adds with hope, "it can."

Sound, Rhythm, and Pattern

Emerging from the morass of philosophical and semiological problems surrounding the syntax and diction, we find reassuringly firm
ground for discussing the auditory qualities of the poetry. No one
claims that Thomas's poetic line is conventional enough in meter to
involve us in the subtleties of that field; and whereas there are some
theoretical difficulties in the analysis of his systems of rhyme, at
least the sounds themselves are there before us. For many of the
poems, recordings of the poet's own readings are available to settle
any questions regarding rhythm or enunciation. Further, we have
the poet's own testimony, reiterated from his earliest letters to his
latest interviews, that he considered the auditory qualities of poetry
to be of extreme importance. Each phrase was tested by reading it
aloud, and he would try endless alternatives for a word which did
not suit his ear. Perusing his letters to Vernon Watkins is sufficient
proof of his passion for the sound of a line, a passion Watkins
shared; indeed, at one point Thomas feels forced to protest that he
is also concerned with significance (*LVW*, p. 66).

Technical virtuosity evidently came easily to him, although he
labored over lines as strenuously as if he had a wooden ear. In his
youth, he claimed, "I wrote endless imitations, though I never
thought them to be imitations . . . I tried my callow hand at almost
every poetical form." (FitzGibbon, 1965, p. 325). "I am a painstaking, conscientious, involved and devious craftsman in words,"
he asserted toward the end of his life, "however unsuccessful the
result so often appears, and to whatever wrong uses I may apply
my technical paraphernalia" (p. 327). As evidence of his nearly
obsessive concern for pattern, most critics point to the "Author's
Prologue," whose hundred-and-second (and last) line rhymes with

the first, the hundred-and-first with the second, and so forth. The auditory dimension is scarcely involved here, nor is it in the famous hourglass- and diamond-shaped poems of "Vision and Prayer." Despite the fact that relatively few of the poems in *CP* adhere to any of the conventional poetic forms, his villanelle "Do not go gentle into that good night" has been almost universally praised for its craft; "I can think of no other villanelle in the language which seems so little contrived," writes Harvey Gross (*Sound and Form in Modern Poetry*, 1964, p. 269).

Although most modern poets have publicly paid tribute to Thomas's craftsmanship—the list includes Lowell, Berryman, Watkins, Spender, Roethke, Campbell, Merwin, and many others—the myth of the ranting bard which dogged his early career led most early critics to minimize this aspect of his work. Even Spender (1946, pp. 233–34) once asserted that the "principle of Thomas's poetry is completely free." The rhythms of the mid-war poetry, which are somewhat innovative, are a result of applying to it the rhythms of his prose, which in turn are based on those of ordinary speech. Most contemporary critics would agree with Spender's analysis of the rhythm (cf. Maud, 1954, p. 411), but would add that by this point Thomas was experimenting with a syllabic line and with complex assonantal patterns. Whatever Spender means by the "principle" of his poetry, Thomas certainly did not abandon technical restrictions. Howard Nemerov (1953, p. 82), usually a sensitive reader, complains that in some of the later poems, "the energy has nothing to hold it back, it is under no pressure from the theoretical pattern of the line." Brewster Ghiselin (1954) in reply points out some of the formal limitations which he feels Nemerov missed.

But by and large, from today's perspective, Thomas appears to be a poet deeply concerned with form. Much of the criticism which treats him as a Welsh poet or as heir to Hopkins's prosody (see chapter 6) elaborates upon this assumption. Thomas's early verse has a strong iambic beat; indeed, as Treece first pointed out (1949, p. 45), one of his "technical battles" after *25P* was to discover a substitute for the pentameter. Moynihan (1966, pp. 125–35), whose discussion of rhythmic and auditory technique is the best of the major critics, points out that the general movement in the poetry is from a strong metrical stress to a flowing cadence. He notes the implications of this development: the compressed imagery of the early poetry leads to a "one-dimensional" auditory stress, whereas in the later work the images are given more breathing room and the auditory elements attain greater range and variation. Most of the poetry, he maintains, is "accentual syllabic," with a generally iambic stress pattern. In the later poetry there is a much greater variety of weakly stressed or partially stressed syllables which, other critics have claimed, sometimes gives it an anapestic sound. The variation in stress is partly the result of a greater use of polysyllabic words in the later work, along with prepositional phrases, adverbial compounds, and even articles. The effect of this, of course, is a greater approximation of ordinary speech rhythms; indeed, a few critics complain (Gross, 1964, p. 271) that the last poems are written for declamation, and "Thomas's voice imposed similar rhythms on any poetry he read." Moynihan analyzes the prosody of several representative poems and refers us to Katherine Loesch's dissertation "Prosodic Patterns in the Poetry of Dylan Thomas" (1961; cf. Loesch, 1968). He mentions Thomas's growing concern for the syllable count, analyzing "Poem on his birthday" and noting that the "hewn" quality of such syllabic workmanship nicely counterpoints the flowing cadence of the rhythms. Maud (1963, pp. 6, 160–61) gives syllable counts for "Poem in October," "Into her Lying Down Head," and "Over Sir John's hill," revealing their impressive consistency. More surprisingly, he reveals that "I dreamed my genesis," from *18P*, is regularly syllabic, as is the "shaped" poem "Vision and Prayer."

By now, Thomas's technical virtuosity is sufficiently well established that the main question is whether he successfully wedded sound, shape, and rhythm to the matter of the poem. Mathias (1954, p. 31) suggests that his least successful poems are the "direct result of a vigorous technique fully capable of rushing on alone." Grigson (1964, p. 968) more cantankerously argues that a great many work sheets should not be confused with craft, and furthermore, Pope himself maintained that his best lines were ones he had written quickly. There is a real point behind this assumed critical naiveté. Many critics do feel a loss of spontaneity and freshness in the later poems, some of which were literally years in the writing. And indeed, contrivance is not craft. We may well wonder (as Thomas himself did) at the point of the mirror-image rhymes of the "Author's Prologue."

Moynihan (1966, pp. 135–41), in his discussion of what he calls "phonemic symbolism" in Thomas, suggests one reply to these questions. Thomas, he feels, wanted an "auditory correlative" to the literal sense of each poem and by the time of the later poems had developed a complete esthetic of sound. His argument is illustrated by convincing examples, the simplest of which is the movement backward in the mouth of the vowels in "Lament," mirroring the increasing gloom of the aging protagonist. Moynihan's discussion of "affinitive patterns" (pp. 141–55) employs some of Kenneth Burke's terminology ("cognate alliteration," "augmentation," "diminution") to describe Thomas's more sophisticated sound effects, including his rhyme schemes. Again he relates the sound to meaning, by way of a theory of Sir Richard Paget and Alexander Johannesson that many "gestural sounds" have specific cognitive associations. At least in the later poems, he concludes, the patterns of sound always augment the meaning.

Moynihan's conclusions are essentially duplicated by the most ambitious study of sound and prosody, Louise Baughan Murdy's *Sound and Sense in Dylan Thomas's Poetry* (1966). Apparently Murdy set out to use precise analysis of the extensive recordings of Thomas reading his own poems (she includes a discography) as a key to their form and meaning. In an appendix she shows charts measuring the "striking power," "tone," and "pitch" of his readings of several poems. Because of inadequate instruments, the original plan could not be carried out; it would have been a highly scientific, if dubiously fruitful, approach to the auditory dimension of poetry. Instead, she has analyzed a group of poems from each of Thomas's three "periods," 1933–39, 1939–45, and 1946–53. For each poem she analyzes the prosodic structure (syllabic, metrical, or both) and the auditory repetitions and links, especially in the arrangement of vowel and consonantal sounds.

This approach gives Murdy's book a certain resource value and reveals some interesting sidelights along the way, such as the fact that Thomas was apparently using syllabic patterning even in many of the earliest poems. But Murdy's discussion of sound is actually less sophisticated than Moynihan's, and sometimes lacks point. In a review, David Halliburton (1968, p. 104) complains that "the data lie alongside the interpretations (which are sometimes interesting and sometimes banal) with a minimum of cross-fertilization." Murdy finds less correlation of sound pattern with sense and more obvious auditory repetitions in the first period; the second period shows more metrical irregularity, while the last shows more complex auditory patterns and a flowing cadence. The type of sound characteristic of the poems changes from consonant clusters, particularly explosives—*p, t, k, b, d, g*—to vowels and consonants, especially *s, l, m,* and *r*. Like Moynihan, she sees a progression toward a "phonetic symbolism" where sound echoes sense.

By far the most sophisticated study of Thomas's auditory techniques is Russell Astley's "Stations of the Breath: End Rhyme in the Verse of Dylan Thomas" (1969). Astley's analysis is too complex to reproduce here, for several reasons. He finds it necessary to develop his own critical vocabulary to describe the sorts of "rhyme" found in Thomas; further, he ties his discussion to particular poems, which is illustrative and convincing but difficult to paraphrase. Astley notes (p. 1596) the influence of the consonantal end rhymes Yeats used after 1904, sometimes mixed with true rhyme. He points out Owen's more radical use of words with differing vowels and no terminal consonant; of "partial consonance," where consonant clusters are rhymed even though one or more members may be lacking ("shape" and "maps") and of "close consonance," which rhymes similar consonants, such as *s* and *z*. Thomas, he claims, elaborates this system with some further distinctions; more importantly, though (p. 1602), he uses a hierarchy of degrees of alliteration, assonance, and consonance within a stanzaic patterning which plays off among themselves the varying strengths of the different classes of "rhyme." This, Astley feels, is original with Thomas and something entirely new in English poetry. Despite the complexity and subtlety of the system Astley develops, he shows it demonstrated faithfully by a number of Thomas's poems; in passing, he emends the prosodic analyses of earlier critics. His main concern is not to show how Thomas's rhyme schemes abet the meaning of the poem, but merely to show their consistency. Nevertheless, it would not be difficult to connect these patterns of sound with the patterns of image and sense, as Moynihan does, and as Maud, Nowottny, and others do for the syntax and diction. Astley's analysis is synecdoche for the bulk of contemporary criticism of Thomas's technique: the more carefully we examine what he is doing in the poems, the more fully we are rewarded.

In the course of this chapter I have been forced to bypass numerous aspects of the poet's technique, usually because they are brought out properly only in the thorough examination of a single poem. "The Conversation of Prayer," for example, is a critic's paradise in its interplay of internal and end rhyme, rhythm, diction, syntax, image, metaphor, and shape; and, of course, it is in the interplay and integration of all of these with meaning that we find the real triumph of technique. For Thomas this is of fundamental importance, not so much because the message of his poems justifies his means as because his technique, in the broadest sense, embodies his meaning. Undeniably the body of his work includes failures—usually interesting failures—but there is surprisingly little critical unanimity as to just which poems these are. Some of his notable successes, like "Do not go gentle into that good night," are remarkably resistant to analysis through their very simplicity; like Thomas, we find ourselves invoking their "magic." But despite the limitations of the critical art it is likely that Thomas's poems will continue to attract imaginative minds and acute sensibilities. They demand reading in their own terms; if we must find new methods for unravelling them and a new vocabulary to hint at their workings, then that is one measure of their success. Not, of course, the final measure. Thomas, after all, did not exercise his craft for the critics who have so amply condemned and rewarded him,

> But for the lovers, their arms
> Round the griefs of the ages,
> Who pay no praise or wages
> Nor heed my craft or art.

References

Ackerman, John
  1964. *Dylan Thomas: His Life and Work*. London and New York: Oxford Univ. Pr.
Aiken, Conrad
  1944. "The New Euphuism," *New Republic* Jan. 3, pp. 26–27.
Astley, Russell
  1969. "Stations of the Breath: End Rhyme in the Verse of Dylan Thomas," *PMLA* Oct., pp. 1595–1605.
Ayer, James R.
  1968. "Dylan Thomas in the Aural Dimension," *Computer Studies in the Humanities and Verbal Behavior* Jan., pp. 6–9.
Bayley, John
  1957. *The Romantic Survival: A Study in Poetic Evolution*. London: Constable; New York: Oxford Univ. Pr.
Beardsley, Monroe C., and Sam Hynes
  1960. "Misunderstanding Poetry: Notes on Some Readings of Dylan Thomas," *College English* March, pp. 315–22.
Berryman, John
  1951. "The Loud Hill of Wales." In *The Kenyon Critics*, edited by John Crowe Ransom, pp. 255–59. Cleveland: World.
Botterill, Dennis
  1946. "Among the Younger Poets," *Life and Letters* Nov., pp. 93–94.
Brinnin, John Malcolm
  1955. *Dylan Thomas in America: An Intimate Journal*. Boston: Little.
  1960. (editor) *A Casebook on Dylan Thomas*. New York: Crowell.
Campbell, Roy
  1954. "Dylan Thomas—the War Years," *Shenandoah* Spring, 26–27.
Cox, C. B.
  1966. (editor) *Dylan Thomas: A Collection of Critical Essays*. Englewood Cliffs, New Jersey: Prentice-Hall.

Davie, Donald
  1955. *Articulate Energy: An Inquiry into the Syntax of English Poetry*. London: Routledge & Kegan Paul.
Davies, Aneirin Talfan
  1954. "The Golden Echo," *Dock Leaves* Spring, pp. 10–17.
Davies, Walford
  1971. (editor) *Dylan Thomas: Early Prose Writings*. New York: New Directions.
  1972. (editor) *Dylan Thomas: New Critical Essays*. London: J. M. Dent.
Durrell, Lawrence
  1952. *A Key to Modern British Poetry*. Norman: Univ. of Oklahoma Pr.
Empson, William
  1947. "To Understand a Modern Poem," *Strand* Mar., pp. 60–64.
FitzGibbon, Constantine
  1965. *The Life of Dylan Thomas*. Boston: Little.
Fowler, A. D. S.
  1958. [Review of Davie, 1955], *Essays in Criticism* Jan., pp. 79–87.
Ghiselin, Brewster
  1954. "The Extravagant Energy of Genius," *Western Review* Spring, pp. 245–49.
Grigson, Geoffrey
  1964. "Dylan and the Dragon," *New Statesman* Dec. 18, p. 968.
Gross, Harvey
  1964. *Sound and Form in Modern Poetry: A Study of Prosody from Thomas Hardy to Robert Lowell*. Ann Arbor: Univ. of Michigan Pr.; London: Cresset Pr.
Halliburton, David G.
  1968. [Review of Murdy, 1966], *Journal of Aesthetics and Art Criticism* Fall, pp. 104–5.
Holbrook, David
  1972. *Dylan Thomas: The Code of Night*. London: Athlone Pr.
Kidder, Rushworth M.
  1973. *Dylan Thomas: The Country of the Spirit*. Princeton: Princeton Univ. Pr.
Korg, Jacob
  1965. *Dylan Thomas*. New York: Twayne.
Lewis, C. Day
  1947. *The Poetic Image*. London: Cape; New York: Oxford Univ. Pr.
Loesch, Katherine Taylor
  1961. "Prosodic Patterns in the Poetry of Dylan Thomas." Ph.D. dissertation, Northwestern Univ.
  1968. "The Shape of Sound: Configurational Rime in the Poetry of Dylan Thomas," *Speech Monographs* pp. 407–24.
Lowell, Robert
  1947. "Thomas, Bishop, and Williams," *Sewanee Review* Summer, pp. 493–503.
Mathias, Roland
  1954. "A Merry Manshape (or Dylan Thomas at a distance)," *Dock Leaves* Spring, pp. 30–39.

Maud, Ralph N.
  1954. "Dylan Thomas' Poetry," *Essays in Criticism* pp. 411–20.
  1960. "Obsolete and Dialect Words as Serious Puns in Dylan Thomas," *English Studies* Feb., pp. 28–30.
  1963. *Entrances to Dylan Thomas' Poetry*. Pittsburgh: Univ. of Pittsburgh Pr.
  1968. (editor) *Poet in the Making: The Notebooks of Dylan Thomas*. London: Dent; also New York: New Directions, 1967, as *The Notebooks of Dylan Thomas*.
  1970. *Dylan Thomas in Print: A Bibliographical History*. Pittsburgh: Univ. of Pittsburgh Pr.
Melchiori, Giorgio
  1956. *The Tightrope Walkers: Studies of Mannerism in Modern English Literature*. London: Routledge & Sons.
Miles, Josephine
  1951. *The Primary Language of Poetry in the 1940's*. (Univ. of California Publications in English. Vol. XIX, No. 3.) Berkeley and Los Angeles: Univ. of California Pr., pp. 383–542.
  1967. *Style and Proportion: The Language of Prose and Poetry*. Boston: Little.
Miller, J. Hillis
  1965. "Dylan Thomas," pp. 190–216. In *Poets of Reality: Six Twentieth Century Writers*. Cambridge, Mass.: Harvard Univ. Pr.
Morton, Richard
  1962. "Notes on the Imagery of Dylan Thomas," *English Studies* June, pp. 155–64.
Moynihan, William T.
  1959. "Dylan Thomas' 'Hewn Voice,' " *Texas Studies in Language and Literature* Autumn, pp. 313–26.
  1964. "Dylan Thomas and the 'Biblical Rhythm'," *PMLA* Dec., pp. 631–47.
  1966. *The Craft and Art of Dylan Thomas*. Ithaca, New York: Cornell Univ. Pr.; London: Oxford Univ. Pr.
Murdy, Louise Baughan
  1966. *Sound and Sense in Dylan Thomas's Poetry*. The Hague: Mouton; New York: Humanities Pr., 1967.
Nemerov, Howard
  1953. "The Generation of Violence," *Kenyon Review* Summer, pp. 477–83.
Nowottny, Winifred
  1965. *The Language Poets Use*. Rev. ed. London: Athlone Pr.
Ohmann, Richard
  1966. "Literature as Sentences," *College English* Jan., pp. 261–67.
Olson, Elder
  1954. *The Poetry of Dylan Thomas*. Chicago: Univ. of Chicago Pr.
Press, John
  1958. *The Chequer'd Shade: Reflections on Obscurity in Poetry*. London: Oxford Univ. Pr.
Rexroth, Kenneth
  1957. "Disengagement: The Art of the Beat Generation," *New World Writing* no. 11, May, pp. 28–41.

Schlauch, Margaret
1956. *Modern English and American Poetry: Techniques and Ideologies*. London: Watts.
Smith, A. J.
1962. "Ambiguity as a Poetic Shift," *Critical Quarterly* Spring, pp. 68–74.
Spender, Stephen
1946. "Poetry for Poetry's Sake and Poetry Beyond Poetry," *Horizon* April, pp. 221–38.
1952. "A Romantic in Revolt," *Spectator* Dec. 5, pp. 780–81.
Stanford, Derek
1964. *Dylan Thomas: A Literary Study*. Rev. ed. New York: Citadel; London: Neville Spearman.
Symons, Julian
1940. "Obscurity and Dylan Thomas," *Kenyon Review* Winter, pp. 61–71.
Tedlock, Ernest Warnock
1960. (editor) *Dylan Thomas: The Legend and the Poet*. London: Heinemann.
Thomas, Caitlin
1957. *Leftover Life to Kill*. Boston: Little.
Thomas, Dylan, James Stephens, and Gerald Bullet
1954. "On Poetry: A Discussion," *Encounter* Nov., pp. 23–26.
Thompson, Kent
1965. "An Approach to the Early Poems of Dylan Thomas," *Anglo-Welsh Review* No. 34, pp. 81–89.
Tindall, William York
1962. *A Reader's Guide to Dylan Thomas*. New York: Noonday.
Treece, Henry
1949. *Dylan Thomas: 'Dog Among the Fairies'*. London: Lindsay Drummond. Rev. ed. New York: De Graff; London: Ernest Benn, 1956.
Williams, Robert Coleman
1967. *A Concordance to the Collected Poems of Dylan Thomas*. Lincoln: Univ. of Nebraska Pr.
Williams, William Carlos
1954. "Dylan Thomas." In *Selected Essays*, pp. 326–28. New York: Random.
Yeomans, W. E.
1966. "Dylan Thomas: The Literal Vision," *Bucknell Review* March, pp. 103–15.

Selected Additional Readings

Arnheim, Rudolf, et al.
1948. *Poets at Work*. New York: Harcourt.
Brooke–Rose, Christine
1958. *A Grammar of Metaphor*. London: Secker & Warburg.
Ciardi, John
1958. "The Real Thomas," *Saturday Review* March 1, pp. 18, 31.

Coblentz, Stanton A.
   1946. "What Are They, Poems or Puzzles?" *New York Times Magazine* Oct. 13, pp. 24, 50–51, 53.
Hornick, Lita R.
   1958. "The Intricate Image: A Study of Dylan Thomas," Ph.D. dissertation, Columbia Univ.
Kleinman, H. H.
   1963. *The Religious Sonnets of Dylan Thomas.* Berkeley: Univ. of California Pr.
McKay, Don
   1969. "Dot, Line and Circle: A Structural Approach to Dylan Thomas's Imagery," *Anglo-Welsh Review* No. 41, pp. 69–80.
Skelton, Robin
   1956. *The Poetic Pattern.* London: Routledge.
Thomas, R. George
   1962. "Bard on a Raised Hearth: Dylan Thomas and his Craft," *Anglo-Welsh Review* No. 30, pp. 11–20.
Williams, A. R.
   1952. "A Dictionary for Dylan Thomas," *Dock Leaves* Winter, pp. 30–36.
Wittreich, Joseph A., Jr.
   1969. "Dylan Thomas' Conception of Poetry: A Debt to Blake," *English Language Notes* March, pp. 197–200.

Basic Sources for Thomas

Bibliography

J. Alexander Rolph, *Dylan Thomas: A Bibliography* (London: J. M. Dent; New York: *New Directions*, 1956). Foreword by Dame Edith Sitwell.

This is the basic bibliographical reference for Thomas's published work; it excludes unpublished talks, filmscripts, juvenilia, and manuscript material. The book is divided into six sections, each arranged chronologically, as follow:

A Literary Biographies of Poems, 1933–56
B Books and Pamphlets
C Periodical Contributions
D Contributions to Books
E Translations of Thomas's Books
F Phonograph Recordings of and by Thomas

Rolph includes information on alterations in the poems in successive publications; he also includes a considerable amount of interesting information in the form of casual comments throughout the book. There are numerous photographs of books and manuscripts, for the benefit of bibliophiles, and the rather sprawling organization of the volume is held together by an index. Rolph is not invariably reliable: for example, in his introduction he claims that an attribution to *John O'London's Weekly* in *Twenty-five Poems* is erroneous, whereas Maud (1970, below) has discovered that, indeed, "Ears in the turrets hear" was first published there. But in general his careful scholarship can be depended upon.

Sister Lois Theisen, "Dylan Thomas: A Bibliography of Secondary Criticism," *Bulletin of Bibliography*, Vol. XXVI, No. 1 (Jan.-March, 1969), pp. 9–28, 32; Vol. XXVI, No. 2 (April-June, 1969), pp. 59–60.

I list this unfortunate attempt at bibliography mainly in order
to warn the reader against it; the listing is so riddled with errors
both of substance and of typography as to be nearly useless.
Even the article's organization is unclear, as several headings and
subheadings were apparently dropped somewhere between manuscript and publication. All this is particularly unfortunate, since
Sister Theisen attempts something different from—and, for some
purposes, more useful than—what Maud accomplished. She makes
an effort to list separately books and articles for general reference, those of biographical interest, those of literary interest, and
finally those discussing separate books, stories, and individual
poems by Thomas.

Ralph Maud, assisted by Albert Glover, *Dylan Thomas in Print:
A Bibliographical History* (Pittsburgh: University of Pittsburgh
Press, 1970).

Thomas scholars—myself included—are extremely lucky in
having had Ralph Maud to compile this exhaustive and accurate
bibliography both of Thomas's writings and of writing about
him. Maud aims to include "everything written about Thomas
that seemed to be of possible interest to the literary historian or
the curious general reader." Since Maud's organization does not
distinguish between genuine critical articles and bits of gossip, a
scholar using the volume must do his own selection on the
grounds of author and periodical; often, however, Maud gives
helpful notes summarizing the content of an ambiguously titled
article, identifying short reviews, and so forth. The book has
five sections, as follow:

    I   Books, Anthologies, Theses
    II Welsh Periodicals and Newspapers
    III British Periodicals and Newspapers
    IV U.S. and Canadian Periodicals and Newspapers
    V   Foreign-Language Publications

Each section is arranged semichronologically; that is, the first
section gives a year-by-year listing, while the other four list periodicals and newspapers in the order in which their first entry
relating to Thomas appeared. With the help of Maud's compendious index, this arrangement is less confusing than it might initially appear, and has obvious advantages for someone tracing the
growth of Thomas's reputation, for instance.

Maud often quotes relevant sections from sources which are
particularly difficult of access, and sometimes refers in notes to
other articles by a given writer or to alternate sources for the
article. The volume's coverage stops with 1968, after which the
reader should consult the annual bibliographies by the Modern

Language Association of America, the *Year's Work in English Studies*, and the Modern Humanities Research Association.

Shorter bibliographies of criticism may be found in John Malcolm Brinnin, ed., *A Casebook on Dylan Thomas* (New York: Crowell, 1960), pp. 295–310, or in Jacob Korg, *Dylan Thomas* (New York: Twayne, 1965), pp. 193–97.

Textual cruxes in the *Collected Poems* are analyzed by Ralph Maud in Appendix II of *Entrances to Dylan Thomas' Poetry* (Pittsburgh: Univ. of Pittsburgh Pr., 1963). Appendix I, "Chronology of Composition," is the best attempt to establish the dating of Thomas's verse and prose. It includes a list of specially written broadcasts and a general discussion of the problems in establishing dates of composition with Thomas.

Some bibliographical essays:
Ralph Maud: "Dylan Thomas' Manuscripts in the Houghton Library," *Audience*, Feb. 4, 1955, pp. 4–6; "Dylan Thomas's First Published Poem," *Modern Language Notes*, Feb., 1959, pp. 117–18; "Dylan Thomas's *Collected Poems:* Chronology of Composition," *PMLA*, June, 1961, pp. 292–97; "Dylan Thomas in Welsh Periodicals," *National Library of Wales Journal*, 1968 (Pt. 3), pp. 265–89. Much of this material is available in Maud's books as well.

William White: "Dylan Thomas and A. E. Housman," *Papers of the Bibliographical Society of America*, Fourth Qtr., 1958, pp. 309–10; "The Poet as Critic: Unpublished Letters of Dylan Thomas," *Orient/West*, Sept., 1962, pp. 63–73; "Dylan Thomas, Mr. Rolph, and John O'London's Weekly," *Papers of the Bibliographical Society of America*, Third Qtr., 1966, pp. 370–72; "Beware the Poet's Widow, or a Note on a Dylan Thomas Manuscript," *American Book Collector*, May, 1970, p. 32.

Works by Dylan Thomas

These are the major book publications of Dylan Thomas. The short form of the title which precedes several of the entries will be used throughout this volume. This selective list stresses American publications.

18P   *18 Poems*. London: Sunday Referee and Parton Bookshop, 1934. Contains the first eighteen poems of *CP*.

25P   *Twenty-five Poems*. London: J. M. Dent, 1936. Contains the next twenty-five poems of *CP*.

Map   *The Map of Love*. London: J. M. Dent, 1939. Contains "Because the pleasure-bird whistles" through "Twenty-four years" in *CP*, plus seven stories.

The World I Breathe. Norfolk, Conn.: New Directions, 1939. Contains selected poems from *18P*, *25P*, and *Map;* six stories from *Map* and five additional stories.

Portrait Portrait of the Artist as a Young Dog. London: J. M. Dent; Norfolk, Conn.: New Directions, 1940. Contains ten stories. Also New Directions Paperbook #51 (1955).

D&E Deaths and Entrances. London: J. M. Dent, 1946. Contains "Poem in October" through "Fern Hill" in *CP*, but in *CP* "Do not go gentle" is substituted for "Paper and Sticks" and "Once below a time" is added.

Selected Writings of Dylan Thomas. New York: New Directions, 1946. Introduction by John L. Sweeney. A selection of poems and stories, all from earlier books.

ICS In Country Sleep and Other Poems. New York: New Directions, 1952. Contains last five poems of *CP* plus "Do not go gentle."

CP Collected Poems 1934-1952. London: J. M. Dent, 1952; New York: New Directions, 1953. Editions after 1956 include "Elegy," reconstructed by Vernon Watkins. Includes most of Thomas's previously published poetry, in Thomas's own arrangement.

The Doctor and the Devils. London: J. M. Dent; New York: New Directions, 1953. Screenplay originally written in 1944. 1966 New Directions edition also includes *Twenty Years, A Dream of Winter,* and *The Londoner.*

UMW Under Milk Wood. London: J. M. Dent; New York: New Directions, 1954. Also New Directions Paperbook #73 (1957).

QEOM Quite Early One Morning. London: J. M. Dent; New York: New Directions, 1954. Mainly scripts of BBC talks, assembled by Aneirin Talfan Davies. The American edition is fuller, including several additional stories and essays.

A Prospect of the Sea and Other Stories and Prose Writings. Ed. Daniel Jones. London: J. M. Dent, 1955. Fifteen stories, many from previous volumes.

AST Adventures in the Skin Trade and Other Stories. New York: New Directions, 1955. "Adventures" (the draft of an incomplete novel) plus twenty stories. Also New Directions Paperbook #183 (1964), with an introduction by Vernon Watkins. Includes *A Prospect of the Sea and Other Stories.*

LVW Letters to Vernon Watkins. Edited with an introduction by Vernon Watkins. London: J. M. Dent and Faber; New York: New Directions, 1957. A collection from a much larger correspondence between the poets from 1936 to 1952, but es-

pecially rich during the late thirties and early forties. Thomas
discusses his poetic techniques and aims, occasionally comes
close to explication of several of his poems, and discusses Watkins's own work as well as his reaction to and suggestions for
Thomas's work in progress. Watkins provides explanatory
and interpretive notes. A selection from these letters is also
available in *SL*.

The Beach of Falesá. New York: Stein and Day, 1963; London:
Jonathan Cape, 1964. Filmscript based on the R. L. Stevenson
story. Also Ballantine paperback (1965).

Twenty Years A-Growing. London: J. M. Dent, 1964. Filmscript based on Maurice O'Sullivan's autobiographical story,
originally in Gaelic.

Rebecca's Daughters. London: Triton; Boston: Little, 1965.
Filmscript.

Me and My Bike. New York: McGraw-Hill; London: Triton,
1965. Filmscript.

SL *Selected Letters of Dylan Thomas.* Constantine FitzGibbon,
ed. London: J. M. Dent, 1966; New York: New Directions,
1967. A short, rather puzzling selection, discussed here in chapter 3.

The Notebooks of Dylan Thomas. Ralph Maud, ed. New
York: New Directions, 1967. Published by J. M. Dent in London as *Poet in the Making*, 1968. This is Maud's edition of the
famous Buffalo Notebooks, the four manuscript exercise books
in which Thomas copied drafts of about two hundred poems
between 1930 and 1934, and which he sold to the University
of Buffalo's Lockwood Library in 1941. Maud's detailed notes
reveal Thomas's alterations in the poems along with other relevant information. Since, as is discussed in chapter 7, Thomas
drew heavily upon these notebooks for *25P* and *Map* as well
as *18P*, they are crucial for an appreciation of the development
of the poet.

Maud includes in an appendix an additional sixteen poems
from the British Museum collection which are not duplicated
in the Notebooks. Nearly all of this material is now available
in Jones's edition of the *Poems* (1971), but without the benefit
of Maud's editorship. Maud's introduction intelligently discusses the poet's composition and use of the Notebook material. There is an index of titles and first lines.

The Poems of Dylan Thomas. Daniel Jones, ed. New York:
New Directions, 1971. This volume, which has the advantage
of reprinting nearly all of the extant poems by Thomas, has
considerable disadvantages as well. The editor, Daniel Jones,
was a childhood friend of Thomas, and in fact collaborated

with him on numerous early verses. He is an accomplished musician and a student of literature as well, but his rather idiosyncratic product in this edition may prove confusing to the casual reader and annoying to the scholar.

Jones has chosen to rearrange the poems into his best estimation of the chronological order in which they were written; thus, the poems in *CP* reappear here in an unfamiliar sequence. Although he nowhere states the fact, it can be deduced from his notes on individual poems that his sources are:

1. The text of CP
2. The Buffalo Notebooks and British Museum manuscripts (see Maud, 1967)
3. Six poems contained in letters to friends (see *SL*), mostly comic or satirical
4. Three poems ("Homage to William Empson," "Last Night I Dived My Beggar Arm," and "Your Breath Was Shed") Thomas published in magazines and declined to place in *CP*, which are not part of the Buffalo Notebooks
5. "Paper and Sticks," published in *D&E* and not collected by Thomas in *CP*
6. A late, unfinished poem from the Texas manuscript collection, apparently a draft for "In Country Heaven," which Jones has reconstructed
7. Seven juvenile poems from the *Swansea Grammar School Magazine*, some of which appeared anonymously
8. Six juvenile poems, apparently from the editor's own collection, written by Thomas for music by Jones.

The volume begins with a short introduction, in which Jones discusses, in general terms, his aims, problems of dating, and his indebtedness—most obviously that to Maud. Then follows Thomas's "Prologue," which is followed by the bulk of the poems. Jones has rather arbitrarily drawn a line at the date November, 1930: poems composed before that date are relegated to the second appendix, "Early Poems," along with the Swansea grammar school poems, even though they, like most of the poems which begin the volume proper, are from the Notebooks. The first appendix includes the two unfinished poems, "In Country Heaven" and "Elegy." Jones's notes give basic publishing or source data for each poem; occasionally he adds rather impressionistic substantive comments. He has added to the volume his short essay on "Verse-Patterns" in Thomas. The volume concludes with an index of titles and first lines.

Jones admits that his volume makes no claim to completeness, and dodges the question of his grounds for inclusion or exclusion. Reasonably, he has not included poetry from

UMW, but on what grounds does he exclude one of Thomas's first published poems, "That Sanity Be Kept"? Fuller editing would improve this potentially invaluable book.

Dylan Thomas: Early Prose Writings. Edited with an introduction by Walford Davies. New York: New Directions, 1971. Part I contains eight stories from *AST*, three juvenile stories from *Swansea Grammar School Magazine*, a Notebook story and a story reprinted from the *New English Weekly*; an edited version of "The Death of the King's Canary," which is a fragment of a satirical novel written in collaboration with John Davenport; and an excerpt from the filmscript "Betty London." Part II contains critical essays from *SGSM* and Welsh newspapers; selections from letters to P. H. Johnson omitted from *SL*; the well-known "Answers to an Enquiry" and "Poetic Manifesto," with an essay on "The Cost of Letters" and a broadcast on idioms; and nineteen book reviews selected from those Thomas wrote for various magazines during the thirties and fifties.

Apparatus

COLLECTIONS OF ESSAYS AND CRITICISM

John Malcolm Brinnin, ed. *A Casebook on Dylan Thomas* (New York: Crowell, 1960)

E. W. Tedlock, ed. *Dylan Thomas: The Legend and the Poet* (London: Heinemann, 1960)

C. B. Cox, ed. *Dylan Thomas: A Collection of Critical Essays* (Englewood Cliffs, N.J.: Prentice-Hall, 1966)

Walford Davies, ed. *Dylan Thomas: New Critical Essays* (London: J. M. Dent, 1972)

George Firmage and Oscar Williams, eds. *A Garland for Dylan Thomas* (New York: Clarke & Way, 1963; London: Vision Press, 1966) is a collection of verse tributes to Thomas by numerous poets.

READINGS

Louise B. Murdy, *Sound and Sense in Dylan Thomas's Poetry*. (The Hague: Mouton, 1966; New York: Humanities Pr., 1967) appends a list of Thomas's lectures and readings in America and a discography. Constantine FitzGibbon, *The Life of Dylan Thomas* (Boston: Little, 1965) reprints these from Murdy's dissertation and adds a list of his public broadcasts and filmscripts. Ralph Maud and Aneirin Talfan Davies, eds. *The Colour of Saying* (London: J. M. Dent, 1963; Aldine paperback No. 42, 1965) is an anthology of verse spoken by Dylan Thomas. A slightly different version was published as *Dylan Thomas' Choice* (New York: New Directions, 1964).

MANUSCRIPTS, TYPESCRIPTS, AND WORKSHEETS

The basic collection of Notebook material is in the Lockwood Library of the State University of New York at Buffalo. Others are found in the British Museum, the BBC archives, the University of Texas, Harvard, and MIT libraries, and in various private collections.

CONCORDANCE

Robert Coleman, *A Concordance to the Collected Poems of Dylan Thomas* (Lincoln, Neb.: Univ. of Nebraska Pr., 1967).

Chronology

1914   Oct. 22, Dylan Marlais Thomas born in Swansea, only son of D. J. Thomas and Florence (Williams) Thomas.

1925–31 Attends Swansea grammar school. Edits and publishes juvenilia in school magazine.

1931–32 Works as journalist for *South Wales Daily Post*. Lives at home until 1934. Acts with Swansea Little Theatre. Writes draft of a majority of the poems in *18P* and *25P*.

1933   May 18, publishes first poem ("And Death Shall Have No Dominion") in London periodical, *New English Weekly*. Sept. 3, first poem in *Sunday Referee's* "Poet's Corner." Begins correspondence with Pamela Hansford Johnson.

1934   March 15, publishes first story, "After the Fair," in *New English Weekly*. April, wins "Poet's Corner" prize for poetry (offer of book publication). Nov. 11, moves to Soho, London. Dec. 18, *18P* published.

1935   Summer, vacations in Donegal with Geoffrey Grigson.

1936   June 26, attends and participates in London Surrealist Exhibition. Sept. 10, *25P* published. Rave review by Edith Sitwell in Sunday *Times*.

1937   July 11, marries Caitlin MacNamara. Oct., moves to Ringwood, Hampshire.

1938   Aug., moves to Sea View, Laugharne. Henry Treece works on book about Thomas. Extreme poverty. Works on stories for *Portrait*. Some BBC work.

1939   Jan., son, Llewelyn, born. Aug. 24, *Map* published. Dec. 20, *World I Breathe* published in America.

1940   April 4, *Portrait* published. Thomas circulates antiwar petition. Spring, is rejected for military service because of weak lungs. Scriptwriting for BBC. Sept., is hired by Strand Films as filmscript writer. Commutes to London.

1941   Spring, sells early poetic notebooks.

1942   Family moves to London.

1943   Feb., *New Poems* published. March, daughter, Aeronwy, born. Little work on poetry during this period.

1945   Spring, moves to New Quay, Cardiganshire. Nov., moves to Chelsea. Christmas, visits A.J.P. and Margaret Taylor at Oxford.

1946   Feb. 7, *D&E* published. March, Thomas hospitalized for alcoholic gastritis and hypertension. Moves to Taylor's summerhouse. Writes, reads, and acts for BBC. Nov. 8, *Selected Writings* published.

1947   Spring, trip to Italy.

1948   Thomas owes considerable back income tax. Summer, goes to work for Gainsborough Films as feature-length scriptwriter.

1949   March, trip to writers' conference in Prague. May, moves to the Boat House, Laugharne. July, birth of son, Colm.

1950   Feb.–May, first American tour, sponsored by YMHA and managed by Brinnin. Great extravagance. Love affair.

1951   Jan., trip to Persia for film work. Thomas's marriage in peril. Summer, last period of real poetic activity.

1952   Jan.–May, second American tour, accompanied by Caitlin. Feb. 28, *ICS* published. Nov. 10, *CP* published. Dec., D. J. Thomas dies.

1953   April–June, third American tour. Meeting with Stravinsky, plans collaboration on an opera. Oct., leaves for fourth American tour. Performs in readings of *UMW* in New York. Nov. 9, dies in St. Vincent's Hospital. Nov. 24, buried in Laugharne.

Index of Explications

"I doubt that any modern poet, even Eliot, has been so fully explicated as Thomas," observes William Moynihan. Thomas has always fascinated explicators because his poems are not only obscure or difficult, but popular as well. His work communicates so strongly on an emotional level that it seems to hover on the tantalizing border of meaning, even in passages which baffle cold analysis. Further, each single major poem of his presupposes and in part restates his entire poetic vision; an introduction to such a poem must also be an introduction to Thomas's thought and art. Conversely, the best entrance into his poetry as a whole may be through scrupulous examination of a single poem; this is Ralph Maud's procedure in his *Entrances to Dylan Thomas' Poetry* (1963).

There is no single satisfactory guide to explications. The general indexes to explications of modern poems are laughably inadequate and inaccurate; Sister Lois Theisen's "Dylan Thomas: A Bibliography of Secondary Criticism" (discussed in appendix A above) is only slightly better. Tindall includes a brief list of references at the end of each poem's discussion in his *Reader's Guide to Dylan Thomas* (1962), but it is neither comprehensive nor particularly selective; besides, it is more than a decade out of date.

The reader interested in a given poem may be satisfied with the interpretation of a general guide, such as Tindall or Emery (see below), or he may wish to consult one or all of the additional articles and passages in books cited here. For a thorough study it would be useful to consult Ralph Maud's edition of the *Notebooks of Dylan Thomas* (New York: New Directions, 1967; also London: J. M. Dent, 1968, as *Poet in the Making*). Maud's index lists the poems from *CP* for which earlier versions are found in the Notebooks. Reference might also be made to appropriate sections of Constantine FitzGibbon's *Selected Letters of Dylan Thomas* (London: Dent, 1966; New York: New Directions, 1967) and his *Life of Dylan Thomas* (Boston: Little, 1965). Theses and dissertations are not included in the list below.

Books of Explication

TINDALL: William York Tindall, *A Reader's Guide to Dylan Thomas*
(New York: Noonday, 1962). The best poem-by-poem discussion of Thomas's work; poems are discussed in the order of
CP. Tindall's discussions are almost never overly restrictive,
though sometimes they approach the poems themselves in ambiguity, wit, and complexity.

EMERY: Clark Mixon Emery, *The World of Dylan Thomas* (Coral
Gables, Fla.: Univ. of Miami Pr., 1962). Emery rearranges the
poems to reflect his own thematic stresses.

NEUVILLE: H. Richmond Neuville, Jr., *The Poetry of Dylan Thomas*
(New York: Monarch Pr., 1965). Pedestrian but usually sound
readings of the poems, in the order of *CP*. Neuville's main fault
is oversimplifying.

Books with substantial numbers of explications

Although none of the following books is a collection of explications, each includes a number of extensive discussions of individual
poems, often as part of a larger argument. Bibliographical information for these books will be given here only; references to them under separate poems below will include only page numbers.

KIDDER: Rushworth M. Kidder, *Dylan Thomas: The Country of the
Spirit* (Princeton: Princeton Univ. Pr., 1973). Kidder discusses only the religious poems at length, but his analyses are
excellent, particularly with regard to Biblical allusion.

MAUD: Ralph N. Maud, *Entrances to Dylan Thomas' Poetry* (Pittsburgh: Univ. of Pittsburgh Pr., 1963). In some ways the best
of all the explicators, Maud only treats individual poems as
part of a larger argument on Thomas's technique and vision.

MOYNIHAN: William T. Moynihan, *The Craft and Art of Dylan
Thomas* (Ithaca, N.Y.: Cornell Univ. Pr.; London: Oxford
Univ. Pr., 1966). Especially good on analysis of sound-struc-
ture and metaphoric and imagistic technique. Moynihan lists
all the poems he discusses under "Thomas" in his index; only
the more substantial readings are listed below.

MURDY: Louise B. Murdy, *Sound and Sense in Dylan Thomas's
Poetry* (The Hague: Mouton, 1966; New York: Humanities
Pr., 1967). Mainly a treatment of sound, prosody, and struc-
ture.

STANFORD: Derek Stanford, *Dylan Thomas: A Literary Study,* rev.
ed. (New York: Citadel, 1964). Spotty, although sometimes
excellent. Stanford appends a list of all the poems he discusses,
with page references.

WATKINS: Vernon Watkins, ed. *Dylan Thomas: Letters to Vernon
Watkins* (New York: New Directions, 1957). Includes
Thomas's comments on some of his poems, often technical in
nature, and comments by Watkins.

Index of Explications

"After the funeral (In memory of Ann Jones)"
Brinnin, John Malcolm
Dylan Thomas in America (Boston: Little, 1955), pp. 236–41.
Daiches, David, and William Charvat, eds.
Poems in English 1530-1940 (New York: Ronald, 1950), pp.
744–45.
Davies, Aneirin Talfan
Dylan: Druid of the Broken Body (London: Dent, 1964), pp.
32–35.
Davies, Walford
Dylan Thomas (Writers of Wales series) (N.p.: Univ. of
Wales Pr., 1972), pp. 43–47.
Fuller, John
"The Cancered Aunt on Her Insanitary Farm," in Walford
Davies, ed. *Dylan Thomas: New Critical Essays* (London:
Dent, 1972), pp. 208–18.
KIDDER, pp. 148–54.
Lewis, C. Day
The Poetic Image (London: Cape; New York: Oxford Univ.
Pr., 1947), pp. 123–25.
MOYNIHAN, pp. 86–87, 115–18.
MURDY, pp. 40–42.
Phillips, Robert S.
"Death and Resurrection: Tradition in Thomas' 'After the
Funeral'," *MacNeice Review* (La.) (1964), pp. 3–10.
STANFORD, pp. 86–87.
Stearns, Marshall W.
"Dylan Thomas's 'After the Funeral (In Memory of Ann
Jones)'," *Explicator* (May, 1945), #52.
————
"After the Funeral (In Memory of Ann Jones)," in Paul
Engle and Warren Carrier, eds. *Reading Modern Poetry* (Chi-
cago: Scott, Foresman, 1955), pp. 313–14.

Thomas, R. George
"Bard on a Raised Hearth: Dylan Thomas and His Craft,"
Anglo-Welsh Review (1962), pp. 18–19.
WATKINS, pp. 39–40, 57–58.

"All all and all the dry worlds lever"
Korg, Jacob
"Imagery and Universe in Dylan Thomas' *Eighteen Poems*,"
Accent (Winter, 1957), pp. 3–15.
MOYNIHAN, pp. 149–50.
Scarfe, Francis
Auden and After: The Liberation of Poetry, 1940–41 (London: Routledge, 1942), pp. 106–10.

Altarwise Sonnets: Thomas's early sequence of ten sonnets, beginning with Sonnet I, "Altarwise by owl-light in the half-way house," has frequently been discussed and explicated as a unit. The references immediately following refer to the sequence as a whole; explications of individual poems in the sequence are then listed.
Adams, R. M.
Strains of Discord: Studies in Literary Openness (New York: Cornell Univ. Pr., 1958), pp. 139–43.
KIDDER, pp. 132–39.
Kleinman, H. H.
The Religious Sonnets of Dylan Thomas (Berkeley: Univ. of California Pr., 1963; New York: Cambridge Univ. Pr., 1964).
Kneiger, Bernard
"Dylan Thomas: The Christianity of the 'Altarwise by Owl-light' Sequence," *College English* (May, 1962), pp. 623–28.
MOYNIHAN, pp. 254–57.
Olson, Elder
The Poetry of Dylan Thomas (Chicago: Univ. of Chicago Pr., 1954), pp. 63–89.
Schlauch, Margaret
Modern English and American Poetry: Techniques and Ideologies (London: Watts, 1956), pp. 84–85.
STANFORD, pp. 61–62.
Tindall, William York
The Literary Symbol (New York: Columbia Univ. Pr., 1955), pp. 183–85.
Sonnet I ("Altarwise by owl-light in the half-way house")
Essig, Erhardt H.
"Thomas' Sonnet I," *Explicator* (June, 1958), #53.
Kleinman (see above), pp. 12–22.
Kneiger, Bernard
"Thomas' Sonnet I," *Explicator* (Dec., 1956), #18.

Maud, Ralph N.
   "Thomas' Sonnet I," *Explicator* (Dec., 1955), #16.
Olson (see above), pp. 68–69.
Treece, Henry
   Dylan Thomas: 'Dog Among the Fairies' (London: Lindsay
   Drummond, 1949). Appendix I reprints Edith Sitwell's Sun-
   day *Times* discussion of the poem; Appendix II reprints
   Thomas's reply.
Sonnet II ("Death is all metaphors, shape in one history")
   Kleinman (see above), pp. 23–31.
   Kneiger, Bernard
      "Thomas' Sonnet II," *Explicator* (Nov., 1959), #14.
   Olson (see above), pp. 69–70.
Sonnet III ("First there was the lamb on knocking knees")
   Kleinman (see above), pp. 32–43.
   Kneiger, Bernard
      "Thomas' Sonnet III," *Explicator* (Jan., 1960), #25.
   Olson (see above), pp. 70–72.
Sonnet IV ("What is the metre of the dictionary?")
   Kleinman (see above), pp. 44–53.
   Olson (see above), pp. 72–74.
Sonnet V ("And from the windy West came two-gunned Ga-
      briel")
   Kleinman (see above), pp. 54–73.
   Olson (see above), pp. 74–76.
Sonnet VI ("Cartoon of slashes on the tide-traced crater")
   Kleinman (see above), pp. 74–84.
   Olson (see above), pp. 76–77.
Sonnet VII ("Now stamp the Lord's Prayer on a grain of rice")
   Kleinman (see above), pp. 85–93.
   Olson (see above), pp. 77–78.
Sonnet VIII ("This was the crucifixion on the mountain")
   Kleinman (see above), pp. 94–103.
   Olson (see above), pp. 78–80.
   Scarfe, Francis
      Auden and After: The Liberation of Poetry, 1940-41 (Lon-
      don: Routledge, 1942), pp. 106–10.
   Stearns, Marshall W.
      "Unsex the Skeleton," in E. W. Tedlock, ed. *Dylan Thomas:
      The Legend and the Poet* (London: Heinemann, 1960), pp.
      120–23.
Sonnet IX ("From the oracular archives and the parchment")
   Kleinman (see above), pp. 102–18.
   Olson (see above), pp. 80–81.
Sonnet X ("Let the tale's sailor from a Christian voyage")
   Empson, William, in John Malcolm Brinnin, ed.

A Casebook on Dylan Thomas (New York: Crowell, 1960),
pp. 113–14.
Kleinman (see above), pp. 119–29.
Olson (see above), pp. 81–83.

"Among Those Killed in the Dawn Raid Was a Man Aged One
Hundred"
Bartlett, Phyllis
"Thomas' 'Among Those Killed in the Dawn Raid'," *Explica-
tor* (Dec., 1953), #21.
Brooks, Elmer L.
"Among Those Killed in the Dawn Raid," *Explicator* (June,
1954), #49.
WATKINS, pp. 108, 137.

"And death shall have no dominion"
Connolly, Thomas E.
"Thomas' 'And Death Shall Have No Dominion'," *Explicator*
(Feb., 1956), #33.
MURDY, pp. 35–38.
STANFORD, pp. 75–76.
WATKINS, p. 16.

"And from the windy West came two-gunned Gabriel"
See Altarwise Sonnets, Sonnet V.

"Author's Prologue"
[Bozman, E. F.]
Adam, 1953 (No. 238), pp. 27–28.
Davies, Aneirin Talfan
Dylan: Druid of the Broken Body (London: Dent, 1964),
pp. 70–75.
STANFORD, pp. 142–43.

"Ballad of the Long-legged Bait"
Arnheim, Rudolf, *et al.*
Poets at Work (New York: Harcourt, 1948), pp. 53–54,
178–79.
Burdette, Robert K.
The Saga of Prayer: The Poetry of Dylan Thomas (The
Hague: Mouton, 1972), pp. 139–47.
Cambon, Glauco
"Two Crazy Boats: Dylan Thomas and Rimbaud," *English
Miscellany* (1956), pp. 251–59.
Condon, Richard A.
"The Ballad of the Long-legged Bait," *Explicator* (March,
1958), #37.

Leach, Elsie
"Dylan Thomas' 'Ballad of the Long-legged Bait'," *Modern Language Notes* (Dec., 1961), pp. 724–28.
MOYNIHAN, pp. 257–62.
MURDY, pp. 54–58.
Neuville, Richard A.; also Lee J. Richmond
"Thomas' 'Ballad of the Long-legged Bait'," *Explicator* (Feb., 1965), #43.
Olson, Elder
The Poetry of Dylan Thomas (Chicago: Univ. of Chicago Pr., 1954), pp. 24–25, 50–52.
STANFORD, pp. 118–19.
Tindall, William York
The Literary Symbol (New York: Columbia Univ. Pr., 1955), pp. 155–56.
WATKINS, pp. 103–4.

"Because the pleasure-bird whistles"
KIDDER, pp. 146–48.
Morton, Richard
"Notes on the Imagery of Dylan Thomas," *English Studies* (June, 1962), pp. 162–63.
Olson, Elder
"The Poetry of Dylan Thomas," *Poetry* (Jan., 1954), p. 218.
Treece, Henry
Dylan Thomas: 'Dog Among the Fairies' (London: Lindsay Drummond, 1949), pp. 137–40.
WATKINS, pp. 49, 54, 55–56, 85–86.

"Before I knocked"
KIDDER, pp. 120–23.
STANFORD, pp. 47–49.
Stearns, Marshall W.
"Unsex the Skeleton," in E. W. Tedlock, ed. *Dylan Thomas: The Legend and the Poet* (London: Heinemann, 1960), pp. 117–18.

"Cartoon of slashes on the tide-traced crater"
See Altarwise Sonnets, Sonnet VI.

"Ceremony After a Fire Raid"
Davies, Aneirin Talfan
Dylan: Druid of the Broken Body (London: Dent, 1964), pp. 59–63.
KIDDER, pp. 60–61, 175–80.
MURDY, pp. 61–65.

Ochshorn, Myron
"The Love Song of Dylan Thomas," *New Mexico Quarterly Review* (Spring, 1954), pp. 60–64.
WATKINS, pp. 112–14.

"The Conversation of Prayer"
Bateson, F. W.
" 'The Conversation of Prayer': An Anglo-Welsh Poem," in Walford Davies, ed. *Dylan Thomas: New Critical Essays* (London: Dent, 1972), pp. 221–27.
Fraser, G. S.
Dylan Thomas (London: Longmans, Green, 1957), pp. 26–28.
Jones, Robert C.
"The Conversation of Prayer," *Explicator* (April, 1959), #49.
KIDDER, pp. 156–58.
Moore, Geoffrey, in E. W. Tedlock, ed.
Dylan Thomas: The Legend and the Poet (London: Heinemann, 1960), pp. 255–57.
Rickey, Mary Ellen
"The Conversation of Prayer," *Explicator* (Dec., 1957), #15.
STANFORD, pp. 92–93.
WATKINS, p. 126.

"Death is all metaphors"
See Altarwise Sonnets, Sonnet II.

"Deaths and Entrances"
Fraser, G. S.
Dylan Thomas (London: Longmans, Green, 1957), pp. 25–26.
WATKINS, p. 101.

"Do not go gentle into that good night"
Evans, Oliver
"The Making of a Poem: Dylan Thomas' 'Do Not Go Gentle Into That Good Night'," *English Miscellany* (1955), pp. 163–73.
KIDDER, pp. 187–90.
MURDY, pp. 96–97.
Murphy, Michael
"Thomas' 'Do Not Go Gentle Into That Good Night'," *Explicator* (Feb., 1970), #55.
STANFORD, pp. 116–18.
WATKINS, p. 126.

"Do you not father me"
KIDDER, pp. 218–19.

"Ears in the turrets hear"
STANFORD, pp. 80–81.
WATKINS, p. 123.

"Elegy"

"Especially when the October wind"
KIDDER, pp. 85–87.
MOYNIHAN, pp. 210–11.
MURDY, pp. 29–31.
Perrine, Laurence
"Thomas' 'Especially when the October wind'," *Explicator*
(Sept., 1962), #1.
STANFORD, pp. 51–55.

"Fern Hill"
Ackerman, John
Dylan Thomas: His Life and Work (New York: Oxford Univ.
Pr., 1964), pp. 121–30.
Blissett, William F.
"Dylan Thomas," *Queen's Quarterly* (Spring, 1956), pp.
52–54.
Brinnin, John Malcolm
Dylan Thomas in America (Boston: Little, 1955), pp. 125–27,
236.
Combrecher, Hans
"Interpretationen zu drei Gedichten von Dylan Thomas,"
Neueren Sprachen (March, 1962), pp. 130–42.
Cox, C. B.
"Dylan Thomas' 'Fern Hill'," *Critical Quarterly* (Summer,
1959), pp. 134–38.
Davidow, Mary C.
"Journey from Apple Orchard to Swallow Thronged Loft:
'Fern Hill'," *English Journal* (Jan., 1969), pp. 78–81.
Davies, Walford
Dylan Thomas (Writers of Wales series) (N.p.: Univ. of
Wales Pr., 1972), pp. 59–63.
Fowler, Alastair
"Adder's Tongue on Maiden Hair: Early Stages in Reading
'Fern Hill'," in Walford Davies, ed. *Dylan Thomas: New
Critical Essays* (London: Dent, 1972), pp. 228–61.
Jenkins, Jack L.
"How Green is Fern Hill?" *English Journal* (Dec., 1966),
pp. 1180–82.
Joselyn, Sister M., O. S. B.
"Green and Dying: The Drama of 'Fern Hill'," *Renascence*
(Summer, 1954), pp. 219–21.
Laurentia, Sister M., C. S. J.
"Thomas' 'Fern Hill'," *Explicator* (Oct., 1955), #1.
MURDY, pp. 75–80.

Ochshorn, Myron
"The Love Song of Dylan Thomas," *New Mexico Quarterly* (Spring, 1954), pp. 56–60.

"Find meat on bones"
STANFORD, pp. 67–68.

"First there was the lamb on knocking knees"
See Altarwise Sonnets, Sonnet III.

"The force that through the green fuse drives the flower"
Frankenberg, Lloyd
Pleasure Dome: On Reading Modern Poetry (Boston: Houghton Mifflin, 1949), pp. 318–19.
Giovannini, G.
"The force that through the green fuse," *Explicator* (June, 1950), #59.
Happel, Nikolaus
"The force that through the green fuse," *Die Neueren Sprachen* (Sept., 1968), pp. 433–38.
Johnson, S. F.
"Thomas' 'The force that through the green fuse'," *Explicator* (June, 1950), #60. Also (Feb., 1952), #26.
MAUD, pp. 65–72.
Merwin, W. S.
"The Religious Poet," in John Malcolm Brinnin, ed. *A Casebook on Dylan Thomas* (New York: Crowell, 1960), pp. 60–61.
Ochshorn, Myron
"The Love Song of Dylan Thomas," *New Mexico Quarterly Review* (Spring, 1954), pp. 51–53.
Parshall, Peter F.
"Thomas' 'The force that through the green fuse'," *Explicator* (April, 1971), #65.

"Foster the light"
KIDDER, pp. 127–29, 216.
Olson, Elder
The Poetry of Dylan Thomas (Chicago: Univ. of Chicago Pr., 1954), pp. 95–96.

"From love's first fever to her plague"
Dodsworth, Martin
"The Concept of Mind in the Poetry of Dylan Thomas," in Walford Davies, ed. *Dylan Thomas: New Critical Essays* (London: Dent, 1972), pp. 125–29.
Hynes, Sam
"Thomas' 'From love's first fever to her plague'," *Explicator* (Dec., 1950), #18.

MURDY, pp. 21–24.

"From the oracular archives and the parchment"
    See Altarwise Sonnets, Sonnet IX.

"A grief ago"
    MAUD, pp. 81–84, 86–88, 90–94.
    Sitwell, Edith
        "Four New Poets," *London Mercury* (Feb., 1936), pp. 383–90.
    WATKINS, pp. 15–16.

"Grief thief of time"

"The hand that signed the paper"
    Hyams, C. Barry, and Karl H. Reichert
        "A Test Lesson on Dylan Thomas' Poem 'The hand that signed the paper'," *Die Neueren Sprachen* (April, 1957), pp. 173–77.
    MURDY, pp. 31–33.
    STANFORD, pp. 81–82.

"Here in this spring"

"Hold hard, these ancient minutes in the cuckoo's month"
    Nemerov, Howard
        "The Generation of Violence," *Kenyon Review* (Summer, 1953), pp. 478–80.

"Holy Spring"
    KIDDER, pp. 47–51, 56–57, 162–63.
    WATKINS, p. 123.

"How shall my animal"
    Montague, Gene
        "Dylan Thomas and *Nightwood*," *Sewanee Review* (Summer, 1968), pp. 420–34.
    STANFORD, pp. 84–85.
    WATKINS, pp. 39–40.

"How soon the servant sun"
    Halperen, Max
        "Thomas' 'How soon the servant sun'," *Explicator* (April, 1965), #65.
    WATKINS, p. 16.

"The Hunchback in the Park"
    Deutsch, Babette
        Poetry in Our Time (New York: Holt, 1952), pp. 340–41.

Fraser, G. S.
  Dylan Thomas (London: Longmans, Green, 1957), pp. 29–30.
Johnson, S. F.
  "The Hunchback in the Park," *Explicator* (Feb., 1952), #27
KIDDER, pp. 171–73.
MURDY, pp. 58–61.
Murty, G. Sri Rama
  "Dylan Thomas's 'The Hunchback in the Park'," *Triveni* 38,
  iv, pp. 22–32.
Perrine, Lawrence
  "Thomas' 'The Hunchback in the Park'," *Explicator* (Jan.,
  1962), #45.
STANFORD, pp. 113–15.
Treece, Henry
  Dylan Thomas: 'Dog Among the Fairies' (London: Lindsay
  Drummond, 1949), pp. 114–15.
WATKINS, pp. 109, 134.

"I dreamed my genesis"
  KIDDER, pp. 71–72.

"I fellowed sleep"
  KIDDER, p. 216.
  MAUD, pp. 77–79.

"I have longed to move away"
  Fraser, G. S.
    Dylan Thomas (London: Longmans, Green, 1957), pp. 15–16.
  Lewis, E. Glyn, in E. W. Tedlock, ed.
    Dylan Thomas: The Legend and the Poet (London: Heine-
    mann, 1960), pp. 182–83.
  STANFORD, pp. 66–67.

"I, in my intricate image"
  Bayley, John
    The Romantic Survival (New York: Oxford Univ. Pr., 1957),
    pp. 206–8.
  Morton, Richard
    "Notes on the Imagery of Dylan Thomas," *English Studies*
    (June, 1962), pp. 160–62.
  MOYNIHAN, pp. 106–7.
  STANFORD, pp. 71–72.
  WATKINS, p. 15.

"I make this in a warring absence"
  MOYNIHAN, pp. 67–70.

"I see the boys of summer"
    Leitch, Vincent B.
        "Herbert's Influence in Dylan Thomas's 'I see the boys of sum-
        mer'," *Notes and Queries* (1972), p. 341.
        MAUD, pp. 19–40.
        STANFORD, pp. 40–44.

"If I were tickled by the rub of love"
    Halperen, Max, "Thomas' 'If I were tickled by the rub of love',"
        Explicator (Nov., 1962), #25.
    MURDY, pp. 27–29.
    Ochshorn, Myron
        "The Love Song of Dylan Thomas," *New Mexico Quarterly
        Review* (Spring, 1954), pp. 47–49.
    Olson, Elder
        The Poetry of Dylan Thomas (Chicago: Univ. of Chicago Pr.,
        1954), pp. 37–41, 98, 100–1.
    STANFORD, pp. 55–56.

"If my head hurt a hair's foot"
    Drew, Elizabeth, and John L. Sweeney
        Directions in Modern Poetry (New York: Norton, 1940), pp.
        111–12.
    Maud, Ralph
        "A Clark Lecture Revisited," *Essays in Criticism* (Jan., 1968),
        pp. 60–62.
    MOYNIHAN, pp. 72–76.
    MURDY, pp. 46–48.
    STANFORD, pp. 85–86.
    Thomas, Dylan
        "On Reading One's Own Poems," in *Quite Early One Morn-
        ing* (New York: New Directions, 1954), p. 108.
    WATKINS, pp. 58–60.

"In country sleep"
    Burdette, Robert K.
        The Saga of Prayer: The Poetry of Dylan Thomas (The
        Hague: Mouton, 1972), pp. 120–38.
    Davies, Walford
        "An Allusion to Hardy's 'A Broken Appointment' in Dylan
        Thomas' 'In Country Sleep'," *Notes and Queries* (Feb., 1968),
        pp. 61–62.
    KIDDER, pp. 99–108.
    MOYNIHAN, pp. 147–48, 274–75.
    MURDY, pp. 85–89.
    STANFORD, pp. 132–35.

Tindall, William York

"The Poetry of Dylan Thomas," *American Scholar* (Autumn, 1948), pp. 431–39.

"In my Craft or Sullen Art"

Aguirre, Raul Gustavo

"Visión de la Poesía en un Poema de Dylan Thomas," *Asomante* (Jan.–March, 1968), pp. 19–25.

Frankenberg, Lloyd, ed.

Invitation to Poetry (New York: Doubleday, 1956), pp. 99–101.

Howard, D. R.

"In my craft or sullen art," *Explicator* (Feb., 1954), #22.

MURDY, pp. 80–83.

Spacks, Patricia Meyer

"Thomas' 'In my craft or sullen art'," *Explicator* (Dec., 1959), #21.

STANFORD, pp. 115–16.

"In the beginning"

Jones, E. Glyn, in E. W. Tedlock, ed.

Dylan Thomas: The Legend and the Poet (London: Heinemann, 1960), pp. 174–75.

KIDDER, pp. 118–20.

Merwin, W. S.

"The Religious Poet," in John Malcolm Brinnin, ed. *A Casebook on Dylan Thomas* (New York: Crowell, 1960), pp. 61–62.

STANFORD, pp. 50–51.

"In the white giant's thigh"

Chambers, Marlene

"Thomas' 'In the White Giant's Thigh'," *Explicator* (Oct., 1960), #1; also (March, 1961), #39.

Davenport, John

[review of CP] *Twentieth Century* (Feb., 1953), pp. 142–46.

KIDDER, pp. 83–85.

Maud, Ralph

"Obsolete and Dialect Words as Serious Puns in Dylan Thomas," *English Studies* (Feb., 1960), pp. 28–30.

MOYNIHAN, pp. 277–79.

Moynihan, William T.

"In the White Giant's Thigh," *Explicator* (May, 1959), #59.

MURDY, pp. 92–95.

Oppel, Horst

"Dylan Thomas: 'In My Craft or Sullen Art'," in Horst Oppel,

ed. *Die moderne englische Lyrik: Interpretationen* (Berlin: E.
Schmidt-Verlag, 1967), pp. 244–51.
STANFORD, pp. 140–42.

"Incarnate devil"
KIDDER, pp. 217–18.

"Into her Lying Down Head"
MAUD, pp. 40–46.
MOYNIHAN, pp. 193–97.
WATKINS, pp. 92–95.

"It is the sinners' dust-tongued bell"
KIDDER, pp. 145–46.
MURDY, pp. 38–39.

"Lament"
Evans, Oliver
"The Making of a Poem (II): Dylan Thomas' 'Lament'," *English Miscellany* (1956), pp. 244–49.
KIDDER, pp. 187–88, 190–92.
MURDY, pp. 98–100.

"Lie Still, Sleep Becalmed"
KIDDER, pp. 166–67.
MOYNIHAN, pp. 146–47.
STANFORD, pp. 126–27.

"Light breaks where no sun shines"
Fuller, John
"The Cancered Aunt on her Insanitary Farm," in Walford
Davies, ed. *Dylan Thomas: New Critical Essays* (London:
Dent, 1972), pp. 203–6.
Kneiger, Bernard
"Light breaks where no sun shines," *Explicator* (Feb., 1957),
#32.
Morton, Richard
"Notes on the Imagery of Dylan Thomas," *English Studies*
(June, 1962), pp. 159–60.
Moynihan, William T.
"Light breaks where no sun shines," *Explicator* (Feb., 1958),
#28.
MOYNIHAN, pp. 126–28.
MURDY, pp. 24–27.
Stearns, Marshall W.
"Unsex the Skeleton," in E. W. Tedlock, ed. *Dylan Thomas:
The Legend and the Poet* (London: Heinemann, 1960), pp.
125–29.

"Love in the Asylum"
Kneiger, Bernard
"Thomas' 'Love in the Asylum'," *Explicator* (Oct., 1961), #13.
STANFORD, pp. 121–22.

"My hero bares his nerves"
KIDDER, pp. 117–18.
STANFORD, pp. 38, 56–57.

"My world is pyramid"

"Not from this anger"
WATKINS, pp. 39–40.

"Now"
Treece, Henry
Dylan Thomas: 'Dog Among the Fairies' (London: Lindsay Drummond, 1949), pp. 132–33.
WATKINS, p. 16.

"Now stamp the Lord's Prayer on a grain of rice"
See Altarwise Sonnets, Sonnet VII.

"O make me a mask"
Harvill, Olga DeHart
"O make me a mask," *Explicator* (Oct., 1967), #12.
WATKINS, pp. 39–40.

"On a Wedding Anniversary"

"On no work of words"

"On the Marriage of a Virgin"
Johnson, S. F.
"The Marriage of a Virgin," *Explicator* (Feb., 1952), #27.
Kneiger, Bernard
"Thomas' 'On the Marriage of a Virgin'," *Explicator* (May, 1961), #61.
MURDY, pp. 53–54.
Robinson, Theodore R.
"Dylan Thomas' 'On the Marriage of a Virgin'," *English Studies in Africa* (1965), pp. 157–65.
STANFORD, pp. 120–21.
WATKINS, pp. 105–7.

"Once below a time"
MOYNIHAN, pp. 180–81.
MURDY, pp. 49–51.

STANFORD, pp. 127–28.

Treece, Henry
> *Dylan Thomas: 'Dog Among the Fairies'* (London: Lindsay
> Drummond, 1949), pp. 112–13.

WATKINS, pp. 78–80.

"Once it was the colour of saying"

Fraser, G. S.
> *Dylan Thomas* (London: Longmans, Green, 1957), pp. 19–20.

WATKINS, pp. 21, 52, 53–54.

"Our eunuch dreams"

KIDDER, pp. 215–16.

MAUD, pp. 72–74.

Smith, A. J.
> "Ambiguity as a Poetic Shift," *Critical Quarterly* (Spring,
> 1962), pp. 68–74.

STANFORD, pp. 38, 57–59.

"Out of the sighs"

Bayley, John
> *The Romantic Survival* (New York: Oxford Univ. Pr., 1957),
> pp. 202–5.

"Over Sir John's hill"

Bremer, R.
> "An Analysis and Interpretation of 'Over Sir John's Hill',"
> *Neophilologus* (July, 1969), pp. 307–20.

KIDDER, pp. 195–97.

MAUD, pp. 103–17.

MURDY, pp. 89–92.

Ormerod, David
> "The Central Image in Dylan Thomas' 'Over Sir John's Hill',"
> *English Studies* (Oct., 1968), pp. 449–50.

STANFORD, pp. 135–36.

"Poem in October"

Ackerman, John
> *Dylan Thomas: His Life and Work* (New York: Oxford
> Univ. Pr., 1964), pp. 130–34.

Deutsch, Babette
> *Poetry in Our Time* (New York: Holt, 1952), pp. 332–33.

Friedman, Stanley
> "Whitman and Laugharne: Dylan Thomas' 'Poem in Octo-
> ber'," *Anglo-Welsh Review* (1969), pp. 81–82.

KIDDER, pp. 181–84.

MOYNIHAN, pp. 211–13.

MURDY, pp. 65–69.

Perrine, Laurence

"Thomas' 'Poem in October,' Stanza I," *Explicator* (Feb., 1969), #43.

"Poem on his birthday"

Burdette, Robert K.

The Saga of Prayer: The Poetry of Dylan Thomas (The Hague: Mouton, 1972), pp. 77–97.

Evans, Oliver

"Dylan Thomas' Birthday Poems," in R. B. Davis and J. L. Lievsay, eds. *Studies in Honor of John C. Hodges and Alwin Thaler* (Nashville: Univ. of Tennessee, 1961), pp. 131–39.

Holbrook, David

"The Code of Night: The 'Schizoid Diagnosis and Dylan Thomas," in Walford Davies, ed. *Dylan Thomas: New Critical Essays* (London: Dent, 1972), pp. 181–95.

KIDDER, pp. 197–203.

MOYNIHAN, pp. 129–31, 213–16.

MURDY, pp. 100–4.

STANFORD, pp. 136–38.

"A process in the weather of the heart"

"A Refusal to Mourn the Death, by Fire, of a Child in London"

Clair, John A.

"Thomas' 'A Refusal to Mourn the Death, by Fire, of a Child in London'," *Explicator* (Dec., 1958), #25.

Combecher, Hans

"Tod und Transzendenz in zwei Gedichten von Dylan Thomas," *Die Neueren Sprachen* (Dec., 1963), pp. 554–62.

Daiches, David

"The Poetry of Dylan Thomas," *College English* (Oct., 1954), pp. 3–5.

Davis, William Virgil

"Several Comments on 'A Refusal to Mourn the Death, by Fire, of a Child in London'," *Concerning Poetry* (Fall, 1969), pp. 45–49.

Deutsch, Babette

Poetry in Our Time (New York: Holt, 1952), pp. 335–37.

Empson, William

"To Understand a Modern Poem," *Strand* (March, 1947), pp. 60–64.

Gibson, Henry

"A Comment," *Critic* (Autumn, 1947), pp. 19–20. Also in E. W. Tedlock, ed. *Dylan Thomas: The Legend and the Poet* London: Heinemann, 1960), pp. 151–52.

Gingerich, Martin E.
"Rhetoric and Meaning in 'A Refusal to Mourn'," *Notes on Contemporary Literature* (1971), pp. 5–6.
KIDDER, pp. 173–76.
MAUD, pp. 50–53.
MURDY, pp. 69–72.
Oppel, Horst
"Dylan Thomas: 'A Refusal to Mourn the Death, by Fire, of a Child in London'," in *Die moderne englische Lyrik: Interpretationen* (Berlin: E. Schmidt–Verlag, 1967), pp. 252–61.
Sitwell, Edith
"Comment on Dylan Thomas," *Critic* (Autumn, 1947), pp. 17–18.

———

"Dylan Thomas," *Atlantic* (Feb., 1954), pp. 44–45.

———

"The Love of Man, the Praise of God," *New York Herald Tribune Book Review* (May 10, 1953), pp. 1, 14.
STANFORD, pp. 96–98.

"A saint about to fall"
KIDDER, pp. 143–44.
WATKINS, pp. 45, 47, 49.

"The seed-at-zero"
STANFORD, pp. 68–69.

"Shall gods be said to thump the clouds"

"Should lanterns shine"
Lewis, E. Glyn, in E. W. Tedlock, ed.
Dylan Thomas: The Legend and the Poet (London: Heinemann, 1960), pp. 181–82.
MURDY, pp. 33–35.
WATKINS, pp. 16–17.

"The spire cranes"
WATKINS, p. 31.

"Then was my neophyte"

"There was a Saviour"
KIDDER, pp. 167–69.
MOYNIHAN, pp. 178–79.
MURDY, pp. 51–53.
Nowottny, Winifred
The Language Poets Use (New York: Oxford Univ. Pr., 1962), pp. 174–222.
WATKINS, pp. 81–83.

This bread I break"
KIDDER, pp. 129–30.
Leech, Geoffrey
" 'This bread I break': Language and Interpretation," *Review of English Literature* (April, 1965), pp. 66–75.
Martin, Richard
"For the Love of Man and in Praise of God: An Evaluation of Dylan Thomas' Poem 'This Bread I Break'," *Die Neueren Sprachen* (March, 1964), pp. 133–36.
STANFORD, pp. 73–75.

"This Side of the Truth"
Lewis, E. Glyn, in E. W. Tedlock, ed.
Dylan Thomas: The Legend and the Poet (London: Heinemann, 1960), pp. 172–73.
WATKINS, p. 126.

"This was the crucifixion on the mountain"
See Altarwise Sonnets, Sonnet VIII.

"To Others than You"
WATKINS, p. 68.

"To-day, this insect"
Casey, Bill
"Thomas' 'To-day, this insect'," *Explicator* (March, 1959), #43.
KIDDER, pp. 126–27.
Montague, Gene
"Thomas' 'To-day, this insect'," *Explicator* (Dec., 1960), #15.
MOYNIHAN, pp. 247–48.

"The tombstone told when she died"
Hassan, Ihab H.
"Thomas' 'The tombstone told when she died'," *Explicator* (Nov., 1956), #1.
WATKINS, pp. 43–45.

"Twenty-four years"
Kneiger, Bernard
"Thomas' 'Twenty-four years'," *Explicator* (Sept., 1961), #4.
Ormerod, David
"Thomas' 'Twenty-four years'," *Explicator* (May, 1964), #71.
STANFORD, pp. 83, 88–89.
Wanning, Andrews
"Criticism and Principles: Poetry of the Quarter," *Southern Review* (Spring, 1941), pp. 806–9.

WATKINS, pp. 47–48.

"Unluckily for a Death"
STANFORD, pp. 122–23.
WATKINS, pp. 63–67.

"Vision and Prayer"
  Burdette, Robert K.
    The Saga of Prayer: The Poetry of Dylan Thomas (Mouton:
    The Hague, 1972), pp. 98–119.
  Daiches, David
    "The Poetry of Dylan Thomas," *College English* (Oct.,
    1954), pp. 6–7.
  Friar, Kimon and John Malcolm Brinnin, eds.
    Modern Poetry, American and British (New York: Appleton,
    1951), pp. 540–41.
  KIDDER, pp. 158–62.
  Mayhead, Robin
    [review of *CP*] *Scrutiny* (Winter, 1952–53), pp. 142-47.
  MOYNIHAN, pp. 265–67.
  STANFORD, pp. 94–96.
  Treece, Henry
    Dylan Thomas: 'Dog Among the Fairies' (London: Lindsay
    Drummond, 1949), pp. 117–18.
  WATKINS, pp. 114, 122–23.

"Was there a time"

"We lying by seasand"
  Gibson, Henry, in E. W. Tedlock, ed.
    Dylan Thomas: The Legend and the Poet (London: Heine-
    mann, 1960), pp. 152–54.
  MOYNIHAN, pp. 90–91.
  Stephens, Raymond
    "Self and World—The Earlier Poems," in Walford Davies, ed.
    Dylan Thomas: New Critical Essays (London: Dent, 1972),
    pp. 44–47.
  Sitwell, Edith
    "Dylan Thomas," *Atlantic* (Feb., 1954), pp. 44–45.

"What is the metre of the dictionary?"
  See Altarwise Sonnets, Sonnet IV.

"When all my five and country senses see"
  MURDY, pp. 42–43.
  WATKINS, p. 62.
  Zigerell, James
    "When all my five and country senses see," *Explicator* (Nov.,
    1960), #11.

"When I Woke"
  Treece, Henry
    Dylan Thomas: 'Dog Among the Fairies' (London: Lindsay
    Drummond, 1949), pp. 124–25.
  WATKINS, pp. 41–42.

"When, like a running grave"
  Olson, Elder
    The Poetry of Dylan Thomas (Chicago: Univ. of Chicago Pr.,
    1954), pp. 93–95.

"When once the twilight locks no longer"
  KIDDER, pp. 77–78.
  MAUD, pp. 74–76.
  STANFORD, pp. 44–46.

"Where once the waters of your face"
  MOYNIHAN, pp. 203–4.

"Why east wind chills"
  STANFORD, pp. 78–80.

"A Winter's Tale"
  Frankenberg, Lloyd
    Pleasure Dome: On Reading Modern Poetry (Boston: Hough-
    ton Mifflin, 1949), pp. 321–23.
  Greiff, Louis K.
    "Image and Theme in Dylan Thomas' 'A Winter's Tale',"
    Thoth (Winter, 1965), pp. 35–41.
  Mayhead, Robin
    "Dylan Thomas," *Scrutiny* (Winter, 1952–53), pp. 143–45.
  Merwin, W. S.
    "The Religious Poet," in John Malcolm Brinnin, ed. *A Case-
    book on Dylan Thomas* (New York: Crowell, 1960), pp.
    65–66.
  MOYNIHAN, pp. 144–46, 267–70.
  MURDY, pp. 72–75.
  STANFORD, pp. 99–105.
  Tritschler, Donald
    "The Metaphoric Stop of Time in 'A Winter's Tale'," *PMLA*
    (Sept., 1963), pp. 422–30.
  WATKINS, pp. 125–26.

Index

Names, books, and essays listed in the References at the conclusion of each chapter or in the Appendixes are not included in the Index.

ab Ithel, William: *Y Barddas*, 12, 88

Ackerman, John: *Dylan Thomas: His Life and Work*, 38–39, 70, 92–96, 175–78, 182, 185, 224

Adam, 38, 73

Adams, Robert M.: *Strains of Discord*, 72, 168–71

Adelphi, 138

Adix, Marjorie: "Dylan Thomas: Memories and Appreciations," in Brinnin 1960, 61

Aesthetes, 141

Agee, James: "A Dylan Thomas Screen Play," 14, 142

Aiken, Conrad: "The New Euphuism," 128, 216

Aivaz, David: "The Poetry of Dylan Thomas," in Tedlock 1960, 3, 4, 75, 96, 206, 207, 209, 218–19

Aldington, Richard, 110, 199

Aleixandre, Vincente, 146

Algren, Nelson: "An Intimate look at Dylan Thomas," in Maud 1970, 59–60

Allott, Kenneth, 123, 124, 134

Alyn, Marc. *See* Bokanowski, Hélène

Amis, Kingsley: 13, 119, 125, 127, 143; "An Evening with Dylan Thomas," 59; *Lucky Jim*, 59; "Thomas the Rhymer," 10, 41

Apocalypse, the New, 89, 113, 123, 124, 125, 140, 142, 147–50

Aragon, Louis, 144, 147

Archer, David, 112

Arlott, John: "Dylan Thomas and Radio," 15

Arnold, Matthew: 177–78; *Study of Celtic Literature*, 176

Arrowsmith, William: "The Wisdom of Poetry," in Brinnin 1960, 75; "Menander and Milk Wood," 17

Astley, Russell: "Stations of the Breath: End Rhyme in the Verse of Dylan Thomas," 228–29

Astre, Georges-Albert: "Victoire de la Poésie," 73, 142

Atkin, Rev. Leon, 69

Atkinson, Frank: [Comments], *Adam*, 24

Auden, W. H., 25, 26, 29, 40, 54, 55, 108, 111, 112, 115, 118–22, 123, 124, 125, 128, 129, 133–34, 137, 139–40, 148, 149, 157–59, 163, 168, 171, 174, 183, 192, 205, 206, 207, 215, 219, 220

Austen, Jane, 110

Austin, Richard: "Dylan Thomas: A Religious Poet," 83

Ayer, James: "Dylan Thomas in the Aural Dimension," 221

Bach, Johann Sebastian, 159

Baker, A. T.: "The Roistering Legend of Dylan Thomas," 29, 38

Barker, George: 113, 115, 119, 121, 123, 124, 125, 126, 128, 142, 148, 150; [Memoir], in Tedlock 1960, 30, 31

Barnes, Djuna: *Nightwood*, 114

Barnes, William, 115, 183–84

Bateson, F. W.: " 'The Conversation of Prayer': An Anglo-Welsh Poem," in Davies 1972, 183

Baudelaire, Charles, 32, 117, 140–41, 164

Bayley, John: 207, 209; "Chains and the Poet," in Davies 1972, 167, 171,

218; *The Romantic Survival*, 80, 150, 157–58, 210, 217, 224–25

B.B.C., 14, 15, 16, 24, 43, 115, 126, 179, 221, 224

Beardsley, Monroe C., and Sam Hynes: "Misunderstanding Poetry: Notes on Some Readings of Dylan Thomas," 80–81

Beckett, Samuel, 115

Beddoes, Thomas Lovell, 108, 110, 113, 128

Berdyaev, Nikolai Alexandrovich: *Freedom and Slavery*, 76

Berryman, John: "Lowell, Thomas, etc.," 128, 206, 217, 226

Betjeman, John, 25, 115, 125, 203

Bhartrihari, 116

Bierce, Ambrose, 14

Binswanger, Herbert, 52

Bishop, Elizabeth, 129

Blake, William: 12, 69, 74, 84, 108, 110, 115, 124, 136, 143, 150, 158–59, 160–61, 164, 222, 223; *Milton*, 160

Blakeston, Oswell, 114

Bloom, Edward A.: "Dylan Thomas's 'Naked Vision,' " 77, 83

Bloom, Edward A., and Lillian D.: "Dylan Thomas: His Intimations of Mortality," 76–77, 131

Bloom, Harold: 108; *Yeats*, 157

Blunden, Edmund C., 110, 122

Bogan, Louise: "The Later Dylan Thomas," 97, 146

Bokanowski, Hélène, and Marc Alyn: *Dylan Thomas*, 28, 30, 31, 142, 147

Bollier, E. P.: "Love, Death, and the Poet—Dylan Thomas," 137

Borges, Jorge Luis, 106

Botterill, Dennis: "Among the Younger Poets," 223

Boyle, Kay, 115

Breit, Harvey: "The Haunting Drama of Dylan Thomas," 28, 29, 31; "Talks with Dylan Thomas," in Brinnin 1960, 50, 193

Breton, André: 144, 147; *First Surrealist Manifesto*, 144

Bridges, Robert, 110, 125, 183

Brinnin, John Malcolm: 32, 45, 143; (ed). *A Casebook on Dylan Thomas*, 2, 25, 28, 29, 30, 31, 33, 38, 40, 41, 43, 47, 49, 50, 61, 69, 72, 73, 74–75, 91, 106, 108, 111, 112, 122, 128, 131, 132, 146, 149, 193, 204; *Dylan Thomas in America*, 7, 8, 16,

27, 36–37, 48, 55–56, 57, 60, 61, 67, 113, 115, 116, 196

British Annual of Literature, 126

British Journal of Medical Psychology, 48

Brooke, Rupert, 110, 163

Browne, Sir Thomas, 110

Browning, Robert, 115, 163, 166

Broy, Evelyn: "The Enigma of Dylan Thomas," 41, 57, 58, 97

Buber, Martin, 52

Bullough, Geoffrey: *The Trend of Modern Poetry*, 147, 149

Burdette, Robert K.: *Dylan Thomas: The Saga of Prayer*, 86–88, 92

Burke, Kenneth, 228

Burton, Philip: [Memoir], in Tedlock 1960, 8

Butler, Frank: "On the Beat Nature of Beat," 27

Byron, Lord, 28, 40, 158, 163, 166

Caldwell, Erskine, 115

Cambon, Glauco: "Two Crazy Boats: Dylan Thomas and Rimbaud," 143

Cameron, Norman, 60, 111, 113, 115, 142

Campbell, Joseph, 11, 12

Campbell, Roy: 26, 44, 57, 112, 115, 226; "Dylan Thomas: The War Years," 44, 56, 221; [Memoir], in Tedlock 1960, 15, 44

Camus, Albert, 77

Cane, Melville: "Are Poets Returning to Lyricism?" 130

Capote, Truman, 115

Carew, Thomas, 167

Carr, John Dickson, 109

Cassill, R. V.: "The Trial of Two Poets," 30, 37

Cassirer, Ernst, 85, 101, 207

Catholic World, 38

Caudwell, Christopher: *Illusion and Reality*, 134

Chaplin, Charlie, 33

Chatterton, Thomas, 28, 126

Chaucer, Geoffrey, 109, 163

Christensen, Naomi: "Dylan Thomas and the Doublecross of Death," 98

Christie, Agatha, 109

Chums, 110

Church, Richard: 12, 113, 145; "The Poet in Contemporary Society," 25

Churchill, R. C.: (ed.) *Concise Cambridge History of English Literature*, 126

Clare, John, 115, 128
Claudel, Paul, 83, 141
Clement of Alexandria, 86
Cleveland, John, 171
Cleverdon, Douglas: *The Growth of Milk Wood*, 16
Cohen, J. M.: *Poetry of This Age*, 146
Coleridge, Samuel Taylor: 128, 146, 150; "Kubla Khan," 150
College English, 81
Comfort, Alex, 124, 129, 149
Communist Party, 114, 131–33
Connolly, Cyril, 121
Conquest, Robert: 121; (ed.) *New Lines*, 119–21
Conran, Anthony: "The English Poet in Wales: II. Boys of Summer in Their Ruin," 175, 183
Contemporary Poetry and Prose, 113, 145
Corbière, Tristan, 141, 144
Corman, Cid: "A Note on Dylan Thomas," in Maud 1970, 61
Cowley, Abraham, 167
Cox, C. B.: (ed.) *Dylan Thomas: A Collection of Critical Essays*, 11, 16, 17, 72–75, 82, 91, 120, 168, 221
Crane, Hart, 28, 108, 115, 125, 129, 142, 143, 146, 150, 164, 185, 219, 220
Crashaw, Richard: 72–73, 76, 160, 167–71; "The Weeper," 170
Crews, Frederick: *The Pooh Perplex*, 81
Cummings, E. E., 125, 219

Daiches, David: 127; "Contemporary Poetry in Britain," 121; [Memoir], in Tedlock 1960, 31, 46; "The Poetry of Dylan Thomas," in Cox 1966, 82, 83, 91; *The Present Age in British Literature*, 124–25, 128, 130
Daily Mail (London), 25
Dali, Salvador, 10, 113, 144–45
Damon, S. Foster, 161
Dante Alighieri, 163, 165
Darley, George, 128
Davenport, John: 113; [Letter], in Sunday *Times*, 140; [Memoir], in Tedlock 1960, 43, 46, 143; "Patterns of Friendship," 44
Davie, Donald: 119; *Articulate Energy: An Inquiry into the Syntax of English Poetry*, 212–13, 215, 224; [Letter], *The London Magazine*, 27

Davies, Aneirin Talfan: 115; *Dylan: Druid of the Broken Body*, 45, 68, 83, 90–91, 92, 175; "The Golden Echo," 221; "William Barnes, G. M. Hopkins, Dylan Thomas. The Influence of Welsh Prosody on Modern English Poetry," 183–84.
Davies, Hugh Sykes, 145
Davies, Idris, 181, 183
Davies, W. H., 110, 115, 122, 181, 182, 183
Davies, Walford: *Dylan Thomas*, 56, 146, 161, 178–79; (ed.) *Dylan Thomas: Early Prose Writings*, 9, 113, 115, 203; (ed.) *Dylan Thomas: New Critical Essays*, 13, 18, 119, 143, 157, 158, 161, 162, 166, 171, 183, 197, 207, 208–9, 210, 211; "Imitation and Invention: The Use of Borrowed Material in Dylan Thomas's Prose," 14, 139; "The Wanton Starer," in Davies 1972, 163, 173–74
Davis, W. Eugene: "The Making of 'A Child's Christmas in Wales'," 15
Day Lewis, C.: 26, 118–22, 124, 133, 183, 204; *The Poetic Image*, 195
Daylight, 149
de Bedts, Ruth: "Dylan Thomas and the Eve of St. Agnes," 161
Decadents, 141
de la Mare, Walter, 108, 110, 115, 122, 128
Demetillo, Ricaredo: *The Authentic Voices of Poetry*, 83
de Nerval, Gerard, 164
Denney, Reuel, 127
de Quincey, Thomas, 110
Desnos, Robert, 147
Deutsch, Babette: *Poetry in Our Time*, 89, 142, 149
Devas, Nicolette: *Two Flamboyant Fathers*, 56, 57, 109
Dickens, Charles, 14, 17, 108, 110, 114
Dickinson, Emily, 117
Dickinson, Patric, 115
Dobson, Austin, 110
Dock Leaves, 27, 38, 180, 181
Dodsworth, Martin: "The Concept of Mind in Dylan Thomas's Poetry," in Davies 1972, 143, 161, 207, 208–9, 210, 211
Donne, John: 42, 76, 93, 107, 108, 125, 133, 150, 158, 160, 165, 167–71, 181, 182, 205, 223; "Third Satire," 168; "A Valediction: Forbidding

Mourning," 168; "We think that Paradise," 159

Doolittle, Hilda (H.D.), 122, 219

Dos Passos, John, 115

Dostoevski, Fyodor, 50, 110

Dowson, Ernest, 59, 117

Drew, Elizabeth, and John Sweeney: (eds.) *Directions in Modern Poetry*, 121

Dublin Magazine, 36

Durrell, Lawrence: 124; "Correspondence," *Poetry*, 43; *A Key to Modern British Poetry*, 125, 207; [Memoir], in Tedlock 1960, 58, 114, 127

Eberhart, Richard: 50; [Memoir], in Tedlock 1960, 30, 40, 50

Edwards, Colin, 49

Egyptian Book of the Dead, 91, 116

Einstein, Albert, 131

Eliot, T. S.: 17, 24, 25, 28, 29, 54, 67, 74, 83, 107, 108, 110, 111, 112, 116, 117–18, 119–22, 124–25, 126, 128, 129, 130, 139–40, 141, 143, 147, 148, 150, 159, 161, 163, 164, 168, 174, 203, 205, 215, 219, 224; *The Confidential Clerk*, 17; *Four Quartets*, 76, 124, 220; "The Hollow Men," 118; *The Waste Land*, 118, 165

Emery, Clark Mixon: *The World of Dylan Thomas*, 81, 88, 130; "Two-Gunned Gabriel in London," 37

Empson, William, 69, 90, 108, 114, 116, 118, 119, 121, 125, 126, 129, 147, 205, 207–8, 210

Enright, D. J.: *Conspirators and Poets*, 42; (ed.) *Poets of the 1950's*, 119

Esquire, 38

Evans, Caradoc: 12, 127, 173, 182, 183; *My People*, 181

Every, George: *Poetry and Personal Responsibility*, 129–30, 137

Explicator, 80, 89

Faulkner, William, 115

Fiedler, Leslie: "The Latest Dylan Thomas," 140, 147, 150

Fielding, Henry, 166

Firmage, George J.: (ed.) *A Garland for Dylan Thomas*, 38

Fitzgerald, F. Scott, 28, 57

Fitzgerald, Zelda, 57

FitzGibbon, Constantine: "Dylan Thomas: A Letter," 36; *The Life*

of *Dylan Thomas*, 7, 12, 14, 16, 25, 36–37, 39, 42, 45, 46, 47, 50, 55, 56, 57, 58, 59, 60, 68–69, 109, 110, 113, 114, 131, 132, 133, 134, 139, 145, 172, 173, 177, 178, 196, 202, 211, 217, 225; (ed.) *Dylan Thomas: Selected Letters*, 39

Fletcher, John Gould, 110

Ford, Boris: (ed.) *The Modern Age*, 127

Ford, Charles Henri, 146

Fowler, A. D. S.: [Review of Davie 1955], *Essays in Criticism*, 213

Fraser, G. S.: 89, 124; *Dylan Thomas*, 5, 8, 27, 37, 40; "Dylan Thomas," in Brinnin 1960, 91; "The Legend and the Puzzle," 59, 92; *The Modern Writer and His World*, 136, 148–49

Fremantle, Anne: "The Death of a Poet," 29

French, Warren: "Two Portraits of the Artist," 14, 139

Freud, Sigmund: 48–51, 81, 107, 114, 131, 134–38, 144, 146, 148, 149, 193, 194, 209, 222; "The Antithetical Sense of Primal Words," 218; *The Interpretation of Dreams*, 134, 137

Frost, Robert, 25, 125, 175, 192, 219, 223

Fry, Christopher, 17, 42, 130, 150, 180

Frye, Northrop, 2

Fuller, Roy, 119, 124, 134

Garlick, Raymond: "An Anglo-Welsh Accidence," 182; "Editorial," *Dock Leaves*, 170, 181–82

Garrigue, Jean: 142; "Dark is a Way and Light is a Place," 73

Gascoyne, David, 113, 119, 123, 129, 144, 146, 195

Gauguin, Paul, 43

Gautier, Théophile, 140

Georgian Poetry, 122

Ghiselin, Brewster: 197, 198; "The Extravagant Energy of Genius," 218, 226

Gide, André, 108

Gilson, Etienne, 66

Glick, Burton S.: "A Brief Analysis of a Short Story by Dylan Thomas," 11

Goethe, Johann Wolfgang von: 86; *Faust*, 17

Góngora y Argote, Don Luis de, 79

Goodfellow, Dorothy: *Lectures on Some Modern Poets*, 131

Graham, W. S., 115, 150
Graves, Robert: 12, 110, 111, 115, 119, 136, 142; *The Crowning Privilege*, 29; "These Be Your Gods, O Israel!" in Brinnin 1960, 204–5; *The White Goddess*, 136
Greene, Graham, 129
Gregory, Horace: "The Romantic Heritage of Dylan Thomas," in Brinnin 1960, 128–29, 149
Grierson, Herbert, 170–71
Griffith, Wyn, 181, 184
Griffiths, J. Gwyn: [Letter], *South Wales Evening Post*, in Maud 1970, 180
Grigson, Geoffrey: 121–23, 126, 131; "Dylan and the Dragon," 227; "How Much Me Now Your Acrobatics Amaze," in Tedlock 1960, 150; "Recollections of Dylan Thomas," in Brinnin 1960, 43, 47, 108, 111–12
Grimm, Jacob and Wilhelm, 110
Grindea, Miron: "Editorial," *Adam*, 24
Gross, Harvey: *Sound and Form in Modern Poetry*, 226, 227
Grubb, Frederick: *A Vision of Reality*, 31, 40, 73
Guarini, Giovanni: *Pastor Fido*, 18
Guntrip, Harry, 52

Halliburton, David: [Review of Murdy 1966], *Journal of Aesthetics and Art Criticism*, 228
Hammerton, H. J.: "Christian Love in Dylan Thomas," 88–89
Hancock, Tony, 59
Harding, Joan: "Dylan Thomas and Edward Thomas," 183
Hardwick, Elizabeth: "America and Dylan Thomas," in Brinnin 1960, 28
Hardy, Thomas, 44, 108, 111, 115, 117, 125, 184
Hawkes, Terence: "Dylan Thomas's Welsh," 174
Hawkins, Desmond: [Review of *18P*], *Time and Tide*, in Maud 1970, 163
Hays, H. R.: "The Surrealist Influence in Contemporary English and American Poetry," 146
Heath-Stubbs, John, 136
Hegel, Georg, 86, 131
Heisenberg, Werner, 131
Henderson, Wyn, 44

Hendry, J. F.: 89, 148–49; (ed.) *The Crown and the Sickle*, 148; (ed.) *The New Apocalypse*, 148; (co-ed.) *The White Horseman*, 148
Heppenstall, Rayner: 121; *Four Absentees*, 45, 56, 112, 113, 115, 132
Herald of Wales, 26
Herbert, George: 93, 108, 115, 160, 167, 168, 170, 181; "Easter Wings," 171; "The Sacrifice," 159; "The Search," 171
Highet, Gilbert: *Powers of Poetry*, 82
Hodgart, M. J. C., 205
Hoffman, Frederick: *Freudianism and the Literary Mind*, 138
Holbrook, David: 48, 111; "The Code of Night: The 'Schizoid Diagnosis' and Dylan Thomas," in Davies 1972, 197; *Dylan Thomas and Poetic Dissociation*, 28–29, 50–52, 134–35, 139–40, 171, 183; *Dylan Thomas: The Code of Night*, 52–54, 134–35, 197; *Llareggub Revisited: Dylan Thomas and the State of Modern Poetry*, 50–52; "Metaphor and Maturity: T. F. Powys and Dylan Thomas," in Ford 1961, 127; "'A Place of Love': Under Milk Wood," in Cox 1966, 17–18
Hölderlin, Friedrich, 143
Holroyd, Stuart: "Dylan Thomas and the Religion of the Instinctive Life," in Brinnin 1960, 75; *Emergence From Chaos*, 142
Hopkins, Gerard Manley: 72, 108, 110, 115, 117, 120, 123, 130, 142, 143, 150, 160, 169, 175, 182, 183–85, 217, 223, 226; "The Wreck of the Deutschland," 184
Horan, Robert: "In Defence of Dylan Thomas," in Tedlock 1960, 128
Horizon, 121
Hornick, Lita: "The Intricate Image: A Study of Dylan Thomas" [Ph.D. dissertation], 147
Housman, A. E., 27, 115, 125, 197–98
Hughes, Richard: 16, 17, 174; [Review of *UMW*], Sunday *Times*, 32
Hughes, Trevor, 110, 164, 200, 201
Hulme, T. E., 118, 121, 124, 161
Humanitas, 129
Humphries, Emyr, 181
Huysmans, Joris-Karl, 166
Hynes, Sam, and Monroe C. Beardsley: "Dylan Thomas: Everybody's

Adonais," 32, 40; "Misunderstanding Poetry: Notes on Some Readings of Dylan Thomas," 80–81, 207

Imagism, 118

Jammes, Francis, 143
Janes, Alfred, 110, 173
Jeffers, Robinson, 223
Johanesson, Alexander, 228
John, Augustus: "Dylan Thomas and Company," in Brinnin 1960, 69, 132; [Memoir], in Tedlock 1960, 44, 69, 132
Johnson, Pamela Hansford, 39, 43, 45, 111, 161, 201, 210
Johnson, Samuel, 59, 167
Jolas, Eugène, 137, 145
Jonas, Hans: The Gnostic Religion, 86
Jones, Bobi: "Imitations in Death," 180
Jones, Daniel: 111, 173; "Dylan Thomas: Memories and Appreciations," in Brinnin 1960, 196; [Memoir], in Tedlock 1960, 49, 110
Jones, David, 180
Jones, Glyn: 173, 180, 182, 183, 185, 200; The Dragon Has Two Tongues, 47, 181, 182
Jones, Gwyn: 182; The First Forty Years, 180, 181; "Welsh Dylan," 175
Jones, Noel: "Dylan Thomas as a Pattern," 126
Jones, Sister M. Roberta: "The Wellspring of Dylan," 89
Jones, T. H.: Dylan Thomas, 7, 8, 11, 17, 26, 37, 38, 41, 55, 56, 60, 82, 143, 174, 175, 177, 178
Jonson, Ben, 165
Jouve, Pierre Jean, 147
Joyce, James: 68, 108, 110, 111, 114, 127, 129, 137–40, 164, 173, 202, 217, 223; Dubliners, 13–14, 139; Finnegans Wake, 116, 128, 137; Portrait of the Artist as a Young Man, 13–14, 139; Ulysses, 17, 18, 139
Julian, Sister Mary: "Edith Sitwell and Dylan Thomas: Neo-Romantics," 123
Jung, Carl, 81, 114, 136, 209

Kafka, Franz, 115, 123, 160
Kaye, Danny, 59
Kazin, Alfred: "Posthumous Life of Dylan Thomas," 30, 31, 38, 73
Keats, John: 110, 128, 150, 159, 161, 163, 206; "The Eve of St. Agnes," 161
Kelly, Richard: "The Lost Vision of Dylan Thomas's 'One Warm Saturday'," 13
Kendon, Frank, 127
Kenyon Review, 126, 127, 207
Kerr, Walter: The Theater in Spite of Itself, 16
Keyes, Sidney, 129
Kidder, Rushworth M.: Dylan Thomas: The Country of the Spirit, 70, 99–101, 267, 223
Kierkegaard, Soren, 77
Kleinman, H. H.: The Religious Sonnets of Dylan Thomas, 70, 91–92, 93, 96
Kneiger, Bernard: "Dylan Thomas: The Christianity of the 'Altar-Wise by Owl Light' Sequence," 81, 89; [Sonnet I], Explicator, 80; [Sonnet II], Explicator, 90; [Sonnet III], Explicator, 90
Korg, Jacob: Dylan Thomas, 11, 12, 80, 85–86, 162, 207, 209, 211, 214, 218, 222; "Receptions of Dylan Thomas," 36, 58, 176; "The Short Stories of Dylan Thomas," 10, 11

Laforgue, Jules, 141, 143, 166
Laing, R. D.: 53; The Divided Self, 52
Lander, Clara: "With Welsh and Reverent Rook," 94, 178
Larkin, Philip, 119, 125
Lautréamont, Comte de, 144
Lawrence, D. H.: 71, 73, 110, 114, 115, 121, 135, 137, 138–39, 150, 164, 223; Apocalypse, 138
Leavis, F. R., 42, 111, 122
Lee, Laurie, 119
Lehmann, John: 15, 118, 119, 123, 149; (ed.) Poems for Spain, 121
Leitch, David: "Dylan Thomas is Big Business," 25
Leitch, Vincent: "Herbert's Influence in Dylan Thomas's 'I see the boys of summer'," 171
Lerner, Lawrence: "Sex in Arcadia," in Davies 1972, 18
Lewis, Alun, 115, 119, 180, 182, 183
Lewis, C. S., 206
Lewis, E. Glyn: "Dylan Thomas," in Tedlock 1960, 75–76, 183; "Some Aspects of Anglo-Welsh Literature," 183

Lewis, Min: *Laugharne and Dylan Thomas*, 174
Lewis, Saunders, 173, 181
Lewis, Wyndham, 114
Lindsay, Jack: 114; "Memories of Dylan Thomas," 58, 59, 69, 132-33
Lindsay, Philip, 132
Lindsay, Vachel, 164
Lipton, Lawrence: *The Holy Barbarians*, 26
Listener, 44
Llewellyn, Richard, *How Green Was My Valley*, 178
Loesch, Katherine: "Prosodic Patterns in the Poetry of Dylan Thomas" [Ph.D. dissertation], 227; "The Shape of Sound: Configurational Rime in the Poetry of Dylan Thomas," 227
Logan, John, 29
Longcore, Chris: "A Possible Echo of Jonathan Swift in Dylan Thomas," 116
Lorca, Federico García, 146
Lovejoy, Arthur O., 165
Lowell, Robert: 115, 128, 143, 164, 219, 226; "Thomas, Bishop, and Williams," 129, 216-17
Luzi, Mario, 27

Mabinogion, 116, 177
McCall's, 39
McCord, Howard L.: "Dylan Thomas and Bhartrihari," 116
McDonnell, T. P.: "The Emergence of Dylan Thomas," 30, 38, 89
Machen, Arthur, 12, 181
McInery, E. F., 196
McKenna, Rollie, 38
McKuen, Rod, 25
MacNeice, Louis: 26, 115, 118-22, 123, 129; *Autumn Journal*, 121; [Memoir], in Tedlock 1960, 15, 59, 106, 143; *Modern Poetry*, 146
MacPherson, James, 88
Madge, Charles, 124
Magnet, 110
Mallarmé, Stéphane, 117, 140-42, 144, 202
Manley, Frank: "The Text of Dylan Thomas's 'Under Milk Wood,'" 16
Marles, Gwilym. *See* Thomas, William
Marlowe, Christopher, 42, 110

Marriott, R. B., 45
Marsh, Ngaio, 109
Marshall, Percy: *Masters of English Poetry*, 26
Martin, J. H.: [Letter], *Times Literary Supplement*, 42, 113-14
Marvell, Andrew: 108, 167, 170, 171; "The Gallery," 171
Marx, Harpo, 48
Marx, Karl, 69, 107, 114, 131-34, 144
Masses and Mainstream, 132
Mathias, Roland: "A Merry Manshape (or Dylan Thomas at a distance)," 145, 168, 194, 218, 227
Maud, Ralph N.: "Dylan Thomas Astro-navigated," 81, 95; *Dylan Thomas in Print*, 162, 163, 180, 198; "Dylan Thomas's Poetry," 212-13, 223, 226; *Entrances to Dylan Thomas's Poetry*, 115, 134, 136, 143, 171, 185, 194, 196-97, 200-1, 207, 210, 211, 213, 218-19, 222, 227, 229; "Last Poems," in Cox 1966, 72; "Obsolete and Dialect Words as Serious Puns," 218-19; *Poet in the Making: The Notebooks of Dylan Thomas*, 45, 67, 110, 160, 199-200, 122, 202
Mayhead, Robin: "Dylan Thomas," 120
Maynard, Theodore: "The New Artificiality," 127
Melchiori, Giorgio: *The Tightrope Walkers*, 159-60, 166, 223
Melville, Herman, 108
Menai, Huw, 181, 183
Menninger, Karl, 51
Meredith, George, 206
Merleau-Ponty, Maurice, 52
Merwin, W. S.: 226; "The Religious Poet," in Brinnin 1960, 74
Meyerhoff, Hans: "The Violence of Dylan Thomas," 49
Michaels, Sidney: *Dylan*, 30
Miles, Josephine: *The Primary Language of Poetry in the 1940's*, 219-20; *Style and Proportion*, 220
Millay, Edna St. Vincent, 33, 219
Miller, Henry: 114, 149; *Tropic of Cancer*, 165
Miller, James E., Jr., Karl Shapiro and Bernice Slote: *Start with the Sun*, 150, 164-65
Miller, J. Hillis: *Poets of Reality*, 2, 3-4, 81, 82, 207

Mills, Ralph V.: "Dylan Thomas: Poetry in Process," in Scott 1965, 82

Milton, John: 165; "On the Morning of Christ's Nativity," 171

Mitchie, James: [Letter], *London Magazine,* 27

Mizener, Arthur: "Verse and Reality," 127–28

Moore, Geoffrey: "Dylan Thomas," in Tedlock 1960, 55, 126, 150, 172, 178, 182, 185

Moore, Henry, 126

Moore, Nicholas, 124, 149

Morning Post, 109, 111

Morton, Richard: "Notes on the Imagery of Dylan Thomas," 195

Mosher, Harold F.: "The Structure of Dylan Thomas's 'The Peaches'," 13

Moss, Howard: 143; "Dylan Thomas," in Brinnin 1960, 30, 61; "A Thin, Curly Little Person," 42, 49

Moss, Stanley: "Fallen Angel," 75

Movement, The, 119–21, 143

Moynihan, William T.: *The Craft and Art of Dylan Thomas,* 83–85, 86, 99, 125, 131, 138–39, 161, 163, 164, 172, 175, 195, 198, 201–2, 205, 207, 210–11, 214–15, 217, 224, 226–28, 229

Muecke, C. C.: "Come Back! Come Back!—A Theme in Dylan Thomas's Prose," 11

Muir, Edwin, 136

Murdy, Louise Baughan: *Sound and Sense in Dylan Thomas's Poetry,* 25, 228

Murphy, B. W.: "Creation and Destruction—Notes on Dylan Thomas," 48–51, 54

Nemerov, Howard: "The Generation of Violence," 226

Neuburg, Victor, 111

New Country, 118

New English Weekly, 13, 115

New Masses, 132

New Poetry, 149

New Road, 149

New Signatures, 118, 124

New Verse, 111, 121, 124, 131, 184, 193

New Writing, 123, 149

New York Times, 28

New Yorker, 49

Newbolt, Henry, 110

News Chronicle (London), 25

Newsweek, 25

Nicholson, Norman, 115, 119, 149

Nietzsche, Friedrich, 32, 69, 84, 131

Nin, Anaïs, 149

Nist, John: "No Reason for Mourning: A Reading of the Later Poems," 90

Nowottny, Winifred: *The Language Poets Use,* 140, 161, 221–22, 229

O'Brien, Conor Cruise: "The Dylan Cult," 28, 52

O'Brien, Flann, 115

Ochshorn, Myron: "The Love Song of Dylan Thomas," 162

Ohmann, Richard: "Literature as Sentences," 213

Olson, Elder: *The Poetry of Dylan Thomas,* 4–5, 6, 7, 52, 70, 77–81, 88, 91, 92, 96, 98, 125, 136, 163, 169, 170, 207, 208–9, 214, 218

Orczy, Baroness Emmuska, 110

Origen of Alexandria, 86

Orpheus, 149

O'Sullivan, Maurice: *Twenty Years A-Growing,* 14

Owen, Wilfred, 96, 108, 110, 115, 127, 185, 229

"Oxford Collective Poem," 132

Paget, Sir Richard, 228

Parker, Charlie, 27, 212

Parker, Dorothy, 115

Patchen, Kenneth, 127

Peele, George, 115

Penguin New Writing, 118

Peters, Robert L.: "The Uneasy Faith of Dylan Thomas," 97–98

Phelps, Robert: "In Country Dylan," 13

Pinto, Vivian De Sola: *Crisis in English Poetry,* 126

Pitter, Ruth, 115

Plath, Sylvia, 150

Poe, Edgar Allan, 28, 32, 110, 128, 142, 163

Poetry, 38, 124, 128, 149

Poetry (London), 121–22, 149

Poetry Quarterly, 119

Poggioli, Renato: "In Memoria di Dylan Thomas," 25, 86

Polemic, 122

Pope, Alexander, 125, 166, 227

Porteous, Hugh, 114, 118
Pound, Ezra, 25, 26, 29, 54, 108, 110, 117–18, 120, 125, 126, 128, 129, 140, 150, 159, 164, 203, 205, 219, 224
Powys, T. F., 12, 127, 129, 181, 183
Pratt, Annis: *Dylan Thomas's Early Prose*, 11, 12, 13, 88, 116, 136, 147
Praz, Mario: *Romantic Agony*, 164
Press, John: *The Checquer'd Shade*, 203, 206; *The Fire and the Fountain*, 159, 160
Price, Cecil: [Memoir], in Tedlock 1960, 197
Pritchett, V. S., 93
Prokosch, Frederic: 123; *Night of the Poor*, 132
Proust, Marcel, 110
Pryse-Jones, A. G.: "Death Shall Have No Dominion," 27, 44
Punch, 109

Rainbow, 109
Raine, Allen, 181
Raine, Kathleen: 124, 136; "Dylan Thomas," 30
Rann, 180
Ransom, John Crowe: 115; "The Poetry of 1900–1950," 125
Rawson, C. J.: "Randy-Dandy in the Cave of Spleen," in Davies 1972, 162, 166–67
Ray, Paul C.: *The Surrealist Movement in England*, 144–45, 147, 149
Read, Bill: *The Days of Dylan Thomas*, 38, 43–44, 50, 109, 111, 114, 115
Read, Sir Herbert: 49, 106, 112, 115, 119, 124, 144, 145, 148, 149; *The True Voice of Feeling*, 150
Reddington, Alphonsus M.: *Dylan Thomas: A Journey from Darkness to Light*, 71, 95–96
Reid, Alastair: [Memoir], in Tedlock 1960, 196
Rexroth, Kenneth: 31, 125; "Disengagement: The Art of the Beat Generation," 26, 212
Rhys, Ernest, 181
Rhys, Keidrich: 180, 181; "Contemporary Welsh Literature," 180, 181; (ed.) *Modern Welsh Poetry*, 180
Richards, Ceri, 173
Rickword, Edgell: 114; *Rimbaud: The Boy and the Poet*, 143
Ridler, Anne, 149
Rig Veda, 116

Rilke, Rainer Maria, 73, 123, 143, 164
Rimbaud, Arthur: 28, 32, 42, 43, 46, 48, 74, 83, 108, 110, 112, 113, 117, 140–44, 146, 212; "Le Bateau Ivre," 143; *Illuminations*, 9; "Les Premières Communions," 142; "Les Voyelles," 141, 142
Robinson, Edgar Arlington, 125
Rodgers, W. R., 115, 149, 150
Roditi, Edouard: "London Reunion," 55
Roethke, Theodore: 113, 115, 226; [Memoir], in Tedlock 1960, 39
Roget, P.M.: *Thesaurus*, 197
Rolph, J. Alexander: *Dylan Thomas: A Bibliography*, 44, 60
Rosenberg, Harold, 146
Rosenfeld, Paul: "Decadence and Dylan Thomas," 166
Rosenthal, M. L.: *The Modern Poets*, 125
Ross, Maclaren, 14
Rossetti, Dante Gabriel, 43, 108
Roughton, Roger, 113, 145
Roussilat, Suzanne: [Memoir], in Tedlock 1960, 39
Rukeyser, Muriel, 127

Samuels, Lord, 203
Sandburg, Carl, 164
Santayana, George: 97; *Animal Skepticism and Faith*, 97
Saroyan, William: "The Wild Boy," 41
Sartre, Jean-Paul, 77
Sassoon, Siegfried, 110
Saturday Review, 130
Saunders, Thomas: "Religious Elements in the Poetry of Dylan Thomas," 66, 83
Savage, D. S.: 124; "The Poetry of Dylan Thomas," in Tedlock 1960, 89, 171
Scarfe, Francis: *Auden and After*, 149–50, 181; "Dylan Thomas: A Pioneer," in Brinnin 1960, 40, 91; "Dylan Thomas: A Pioneer," in Tedlock 1960, 73–74, 137, 217
Schimanski, Stefan, 149
Schlauch, Margaret: *Modern English and American Poetry*, 213
Scott, Tom, 149
Scott, Winfield Townley: "The Death, and Some Dominions of It," in Brinnin 1960, 31
Scrutiny, 42, 122, 180

Sergeant, Howard: "The Religious Development of Dylan Thomas," 89
Service, Robert W., 110
Shakespeare, William: 108, 109, 110, 150, 163, 206; *King Lear*, 17
Shapiro, Karl: 128, 181, 219; "Dylan Thomas," in Brinnin 1960, 25, 29, 33, 41, 73; "Dylan Thomas," in Tedlock 1960, 92, 119–20, 141–42, 163–64, 216
Shelley, Percy Bysshe, 127, 128, 161, 163, 165, 171, 206
Sillen, Samuel: "Mr. Sillen Comments," 132
Sinclair, May, 137
Sitwell, Edith: 42, 80, 106, 110, 112, 114, 126, 128, 136, 146, 206, 212, 219, 220, 223; [Appendix] in Treece 1949, 83, 204; "Dylan the Impeccable," 165; "Lecture on Poetry Since 1920," 122–23; "The Young Dylan Thomas," in Rolph 1956, 44, 60
Sitwell, Osbert, 110
Sitwell, Sacheverell, 110, 122, 199
Skelton, John, 123
Smart, Christopher, 115
Smith, A. J.: "Ambiguity as a Poetic Shift," 207, 208
Smith, Harrison: "Whose is the Guilt?" 31
Sommerfield, John, 114
Soupault, Philippe, 144
South Wales Evening Post, 32
Southwest Review, 97
Spencer, Bernard, 111, 115
Spender, Stephen: 26, 43, 54, 108, 112, 118–24, 127, 133, 150, 183, 203, 226; "Dylan Thomas," 29, 120, 134; "Greatness of Aim," 40, 82; "Poetry for Poetry's Sake and Poetry Beyond Poetry," 226; *Poetry Since 1939*, 123–24; "A Romantic in Revolt," 161, 205; "Ultima Ratio Regnum," 112
Stanford, Derek: *Dylan Thomas: A Literary Study*, 11, 27, 45, 46, 59, 60, 70, 97, 121, 143, 215, 133; "Dylan Thomas's Animal Faith," 47
Stearns, Marshall W.: "Unsex the Skeleton," in Tedlock 1960, 76, 78, 91, 194, 206
Steiner, George: "The Retreat from Word," 143
Stephens, James, 197

Sterne, Lawrence, 166
Stevens, Wallace, 115, 125, 129, 141, 164, 205, 208, 219
Stevenson, Robert Louis, 15
Stoker, Bram: *Dracula*, 109
Stout, Rex, 109
Strachey, Lytton, 59
Stravinsky, Igor, 8, 59
Strong, L. A. G., 115
Sunday Referee, 54, 111, 198
Sunday *Times*, 25, 204
Supervielle, Jules, 146
Surrealism, 137, 140, 144–49, 150, 170, 197
Sutherland, Graham, 126
Swansea Grammar School Magazine, 199
Sweeney, John: "Intimations of Mortality," 162; (ed.) *Selected Writings of Dylan Thomas* and "Introduction," 82, 134, 135, 171
Swift, Jonathan, 116, 166
Swinburne, Algernon Charles, 108, 142, 158, 206, 220
Swingler, Randall, 114, 121
Symbolism, 117, 128–29, 140–44, 150, 163
Symons, Julian: 124; "Obscurity and Dylan Thomas," 123, 124, 205–6; "Of Crisis and Dismay: Writing in the Thirties," 123; *The Thirties: A Dream Revolved*, 118, 123
Sypher, Wylie, 160

Taig, Thomas: "Swansea Between the Wars," 54, 56, 173
Tambimuttu, M. J.: 121–22, 149, 184; (ed.) *Poetry in Wartime*, 121
Tasso, Torquato: *Aminta*, 18
Tate, Allen, 125
Taylor, A. J. P., 114
Taylor, Donald, 14, 43
Taylor, Margaret, 114
Tedlock, E. W.: (ed.) *Dylan Thomas: The Legend and the Poet*, 8, 15, 27, 30, 31, 38, 39, 40, 43, 44, 46, 49, 50, 55, 57, 58, 59, 61, 73, 75–76, 89, 91, 92, 106, 109, 110, 113, 114, 115, 119, 122, 126, 128, 132, 137, 141, 143, 150, 163, 171, 172, 178, 182, 185, 194, 196, 197, 198, 206, 207, 216, 217
Tennyson, Alfred Lord, 29, 108, 206
Texas Quarterly, 145
Thomas, Caitlin: 12, 24, 28, 36–37, 39,

43, 50, 55, 56, 57–58, 69, 172, 179; *Leftover Life to Kill,* 30, 38, 46, 55, 110, 197; *Not Quite Posthumous Letters to My Daughter,* 38

Thomas, D. J., 53, 109, 177

Thomas, Dylan:

BOOKS: POETRY AND PROSE

Adventures in the Skin Trade, 9, 10, 11, 12, 14, 15, 50, 147, 165

A Child's Christmas in Wales, 15

Collected Poems 1934–1952, 73, 81, 82, 218, 221, 226

Deaths and Entrances, 6, 7, 82, 94, 109, 133, 202

18 Poems, 6, 85, 123, 137, 199, 200, 202, 219, 227

In Country Sleep, 97, 146

Letters to Vernon Watkins (ed. Watkins), 111, 114, 184, 203, 217, 225

The Map of Love, 6, 7, 9, 11, 139, 200

Notebooks (ed. Maud), 45, 52, 67, 109, 110, 160, 199–200, 202–3

Portrait of the Artist as a Young Dog, 8, 11, 13, 14, 15, 19, 26, 41, 97, 139, 174, 180

A Prospect of the Sea, 9, 10

Quite Early One Morning, 7, 8, 14, 15, 26, 41, 46, 68, 113, 115, 183, 185, 193, 197

Selected Letters of Dylan Thomas (ed. FitzGibbon), 39, 52, 111, 113, 145, 148, 160, 161, 200, 201, 203, 209, 210

Selected Writings, 220–21

Twenty-Five Poems, 6, 82, 83, 94, 137, 199, 200, 202, 204, 226

Under Milk Wood, 8, 11, 16, 17, 18, 19, 37, 54, 133, 174

The World I Breathe, 9, 10

POEMS

"After the funeral (In memory of Ann Jones)," 1, 7, 51, 90, 139, 174, 195

"All all and all the dry worlds lever," 50, 133

"Altarwise by owl-light in the half-way house," 204, 206

Altarwise Sonnets (Sonnet sequence), 71, 72–73, 74, 76, 77–81, 91–92, 159, 207, 218

"And death shall have no dominion," 84

"Author's Prologue," 7, 225–26, 227

"Ballad of the Long-legged Bait," 7, 14, 58, 90, 96, 136, 143

"Before I knocked," 90, 214

"Ceremony After a Fire Raid," 6, 133

"The Conversation of Prayer," 91, 183, 184, 229

"Dawn Raid," 133

"Deaths and Entrances," 56, 133

"Do not go gentle into that good night," 62, 226, 229

"Ears in the turrets hear," 6, 95

"Especially when the October wind," 142

"Fern Hill," 2, 6, 13, 85, 94, 159, 162, 167, 178, 215, 224

"Find meat on bones," 200, 214

"The force that through the green fuse drives the flower," 1, 212

"A grief ago," 203, 204

"The hand that signed the paper," 6, 132, 203

"Holy Spring," 100

"The Hunchback in the Park," 6, 7, 203

"I dreamed my genesis," 227

"I fellowed sleep," 5

"I have longed to move away," 6, 71, 90, 94, 174

"I, in my intricate image," 136, 165

"I make this in a warring absence," 57, 179

"I see the boys of summer," 133, 171, 194, 196, 214, 222

"If my head hurt a hair's foot," 138, 174, 204–05

"In Country Heaven" (uncompleted sequence), 7

"In country sleep," 7, 68, 162

"In my Craft or Sullen Art," 6

"In the white giant's thigh," 7, 68

"Incarnate devil," 94, 161

"Into her Lying Down Head," 179, 227

"Lament," 7, 54, 94, 163, 227

"Light breaks where no sun shines," 194

"Love in the Asylum," 96

"Not from this anger," 179

"On the Marriage of a Virgin," 142, 171

"Once below a time," 7

"Our eunuch dreams," 5, 133
"Over Sir John's hill," 7, 68, 90, 95, 97–98, 162, 224, 227
"Poem in October," 85, 96, 162, 179, 227
"Poem on his birthday," 6, 94, 96, 97, 98, 159, 197, 224, 227
"A Refusal to Mourn the Death, by Fire, of a Child in London," 1, 51, 56, 90, 94, 133, 138, 165, 212
"The seed-at-zero," 2
Sonnet sequence. *See* Altarwise sonnets
"The spire cranes," 201
"There was a Saviour," 56, 140, 222
"This bread I break," 6, 82, 90
"The tombstone told when she died," 6
"Twenty-four years," 6, 85, 96, 201, 203
"Vision and Prayer," 6, 7, 14, 51, 72, 91, 96, 98, 170, 171, 184, 226, 227
"We lying by seasand," 130
"When all my five and country senses see," 161
"When, like a running grave," 74
"When once the twilight locks no longer," 5
"Why east wind chills," 206
"A Winter's Tale," 7, 74, 89, 96, 136, 161, 214

STORIES

"The Burning Baby," 9, 10
"The Dress," 9
"The Followers," 11
"The Lemon," 147
"One Warm Saturday," 13, 50
"The Peaches," 9, 13, 97, 163
"A Prospect of the Sea," 50
"The Tree," 10
"Prologue to an Adventure," 165
"The Visitor," 9, 10

PROSE

"The Death of the King's Canary," 113
"How To Be a Poet," 113
"Poetic Manifesto," 196
"Quite Early One Morning," 16
"Red Prose Notebook," 11
"Reminiscences of Childhood," 15

"The Town Was Mad" (uncompleted play), 16
"Welsh Poets," 183
"The Beach of Falesá," 15
"The Doctor and the Devils," 14
"A Dream of Winter," 14
"Is Your Ernie Really Necessary?" 14
"The Londoner," 14
"Me and My Bike," 15
"Our Country," 14, 133
"Rebecca's Daughters," 15
"These are the Men," 133
"Three Weird Sisters," 172

Thomas, Edward, 115, 126, 181, 183
Thomas, Florence (Mrs. D. J.), 49, 52–53
Thomas, Gwyn: 182; *A Welsh Eye*, 186
Thomas, R. S., 181, 182
Thomas, William (Gwilym Marles), 177
Thomas, Wynford Vaughan, 173
Thompson, Francis, 43, 108, 128, 164, 170
Thompson, Kent: "An Approach to the Early Poems of Dylan Thomas," 195–96, 214–15
Thomson, James, 43, 108
Thwaite, Anthony: "Contemporary English Poetry: An Introduction," 126
Tiger Tim, 109
Time, 25
Times Literary Supplement, 79, 113
Times (London), 25
Tindall, William York: "Burning and Crested Song," 6, 148; *Forces in Modern British Literature*, 137; *The Literary Symbol*, 71, 143; "The Poetry of Dylan Thomas," 95, 135, 137; *A Reader's Guide to Dylan Thomas*, 5, 8, 39–40, 48, 52, 53, 55, 56, 67, 70, 71, 72, 76, 78, 79, 81, 91, 92, 108, 109, 111, 116, 126, 133, 137, 138, 139, 142, 170–71, 174, 186, 201, 214
Todd, Ruthven, 46, 111, 113, 145, 161
Tolstoy, Leo, 110
Traherne, Thomas, 89, 93, 94, 108, 170, 182
Transformation, 149
transition, 136, 137, 145
Treece, Henry: 89, 113, 124, 128, 148,

180, 195, 207; "An Apocalyptic Writer and the Surrealists," 148–49; "Chalk-Sketch for a Genius," 8; *Dylan Thomas: 'Dog Among the Fairies,'* 6, 83, 107–8, 109, 111, 130, 132, 133–34, 142, 145–46, 162, 164, 170, 175, 185, 194, 195, 203–4, 206, 216, 226; *How I See Apocalypse,* 143, 149

Trick, Bert (A. E.): 54, 110, 196; "The New Poetry," in Maud 1970, 162; "The Young Dylan Thomas," 69

Tritschler, Donald: "The Stories in Dylan Thomas's Red Notebook," 11

Twentieth-Century Verse, 124

Tzara, Tristan, 144

University of Wales Review, 182

Valéry, Paul, 141

Vanson, Frederic: "The Parables of Sunlight: Dylan Thomas as a Religious Poet," 83

Vaughan, Henry, 89, 93, 94, 108, 115, 167, 168, 170–71, 181, 182, 183

Vendler, Helen: [Review of Fitz-Gibbon], *Yale Review,* 30

Verghese, C. Paul: "Religion in Dylan Thomas's Poetry," 79

Verlaine, Paul, 42, 59, 164

Villon, François, 28, 42

Voices, 149

Wade, Rosalind, 47–48

Wain, John: 121, 125, 127, 178; "Dylan Thomas: A Review of His Collected Poems," in Brinnin 1960, 73, 76, 106, 122, 146; "Dylan Thomas Today," 178; "English Poetry: The Immediate Situation," 118, 119, 123; [Review of Ackerman, Read, and Holbrook], *New York Review of Books,* 52

Wales, 180, 181

Walters, Evan, 173

Wanning, Andrews: "Criticisms and Principles: Poetry of the Quarter," 146

Warner, Rex, 129

Warren, Robert Penn, 219

Watkins, Vernon: 69, 93, 94, 110, 115, 124, 128, 142, 149, 173, 180, 181, 182, 226; "Behind the Fabulous

Curtain," 42; "Introduction" to Thomas, *AST,* 9, 10; (ed.) Thomas, *LVW,* 60, 68, 92, 111, 114, 145, 164, 201, 225

Webster, John, 160

Wells, H. G., 115

Welsh Review, 180

West, Anthony: "A Singer and a Spectre," 41

West, Paul: "Dylan Thomas: The Position in Calamity," 41, 52, 56

Western Humanities Review, 77

Western Mail, 173

Wheels, 122

Whitman, Walt: 107, 108, 142, 150, 159, 164–65, 166; "Crossing Brooklyn Ferry," 165; "When Lilacs Last in the Dooryard Bloomed," 165

Whittemore, Reed: "The 'Modern Idiom of Poetry,' and All That," 143

Wickham, Anna, 43, 114

Wilbur, Richard, 143

Wilde, Oscar, 59, 117

Wilder, Amos: *Modern Poetry and the Christian Tradition,* 76

Williams, Emlyn: *Boy Growing up,* 15

Williams, Harry: "Dylan Thomas's Poetry of Redemption: Its Blakean Beginnings," 160

Williams, Raymond: "Dylan Thomas's Play for Voices," in Cox 1966, 16, 17

Williams, Robert, *A Concordance to the Collected Poems of Dylan Thomas,* 221

Williams, William Carlos: 115, 129, 164, 215, 219; *Selected Essays,* 125, 206

Winnicott, D. W., 52

Wishart, Ralph, 109

Wittreich, Joseph: "Dylan Thomas's Conception of Poetry: A Debt to Blake," 160

Woodcock, George: *British Poetry Today,* 124; "Dylan Thomas and the Welsh Environment," 176, 179, 180

Woolf, Virginia, 59, 120

Wordsworth, William: 85, 108, 128, 150, 158, 163, 164, 175, 206; "Prelude," 162; "Ode on Intimations of Immortality," 162; "Tintern Abbey," 85, 162

Yale Literary Magazine, 38

Yeats, W. B., 2, 27, 29, 40, 41, 108, 110, 111, 115, 117, 121, 122, 125, 126, 128, 129, 148, 157–58, 159, 163–64, 176, 205, 219, 229

Yeomans, W. E.: "Dylan Thomas: The 'Literal Vision'," 209

Yerbury, Grace: "Of a City Beside a River: Whitman, Eliot, Thomas, Miller," 165

Yr Einion, 180

Zooism, 111

103928

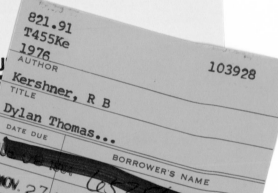